# UNDERSTANDING PKI

# UNDERSTANDING PKI

*Concepts, Standards, and Deployment Considerations*

**Second Edition**

Carlisle Adams
Steve Lloyd

**♦♦Addison-Wesley**

Boston • San Francisco • New York • Toronto • Montreal
London • Munich • Paris • Madrid
Capetown • Sydney • Tokyo • Singapore • Mexico City

Many of the designations used by manufacturers and sellers to distinguish their products are claimed as trademarks. Where those designations appear in this book, and Addison-Wesley was aware of a trademark claim, the designations have been printed with initial capital letters or in all capitals.

The authors and publisher have taken care in the preparation of this book, but make no expressed or implied warranty of any kind and assume no responsibility for errors or omissions. No liability is assumed for incidental or consequential damages in connection with or arising out of the use of the information or programs contained herein.

The publisher offers discounts on this book when ordered in quantity for bulk purchases and special sales. For more information, please contact:

U.S. Corporate and Government Sales
(800) 382-3419
corpsales@pearsontechgroup.com

For sales outside of the U.S., please contact:

International Sales
(317) 581-3793
international@pearsontechgroup.com

Visit Addison-Wesley on the Web: www.awprofessional.com

*Library of Congress Cataloging-in-Publication Data*

Adams, Carlisle, 1961–
    Understanding PKI : concepts, standards, and deployment considerations / Carlisle Adams, Steve Lloyd. — 2nd ed.
        p. cm.
    Revised ed. of: Understanding public-key infrastructure. 1999.
    Includes bibliographical references and index.
    ISBN 0-672-32391-5 (alk. paper)
    1. Public key infrastructure (Computer security)  2. Computer networks—Security measures.  3. Business enterprises—Computer networks—Security measures.  I. Lloyd, Steve.  II. Adams, Carlisle, 1961–. Understanding public-key infrastructure.  III. Title.

QA76.9.A25  A346  2002
005.8—dc21

                                                                2002074687

ISBN 0-672-32391-5
Text printed on recycled paper
12345678910—CRW—0605040302
First printing, October 2002

*To*
*Marion, Raphael, Gabrielle, Nathanael*
*and to*
*Brenda, Brandon, and Alex*
*with all our love and appreciation.*

# Contents

*Foreword*                                                          *xix*

*Preface*                                                           *xxi*

*About the Authors*                                                 *xxix*

**PART I  CONCEPTS**                                                1

*1  Introduction*                                                   3

*2  Public-Key Cryptography*                                        7

   *Symmetric versus Asymmetric Ciphers*             7

     Secret Key                            7

     New Directions: Public Key            11

   *Public/Private-Key Pair*                          12

   *Services of Public-Key Cryptography*              12

     Security between Strangers             12

     Encryption                            14

     Digital Signature                     14

     Data Integrity                        16

     Key Establishment                     16

     Other Services                        17

   *Algorithms*                                       17

     RSA                                   17

     DSA                                   17

     DH                                    18

     ECDSA and ECDH                        18

     SHA-1                                 18

     Ongoing Work                          19

   *Summary*                                          19

**3  The Concept of an Infrastructure**                                21

*Pervasive Substrate*                                                 21

*Application Enabler*                                                 22

Secure Sign-On                                                        23

End-User Transparency                                                 26

Comprehensive Security                                               26

*Business Drivers*                                                    27

*Public-Key Infrastructure Defined*                                  28

Certification Authority                                              28

Certificate Repository                                               29

Certificate Revocation                                              29

Key Backup and Recovery                                             30

Automatic Key Update                                                30

Key History                                                          31

Cross-Certification                                                 32

Support for Non-repudiation                                         32

Time Stamping                                                        33

Client Software                                                     33

*Summary*                                                            35

**4  Core PKI Services: Authentication, Integrity,**
**and Confidentiality**                                              37

*Definitions*                                                        37

Authentication                                                       37

Integrity                                                            42

Confidentiality                                                      43

*Mechanisms*                                                         43

Authentication                                                       43

Integrity                                                            44

Confidentiality                                                      45

*Operational Considerations*                                         45

Performance                                                          46

Online versus Offline Operation                                     46

Commonality of Underlying Algorithms                                47

Entity Naming                                                        47

*Summary*                                                            48

## 5  PKI-Enabled Services                                              49

*Secure Communication*                                                  49

*Secure Time Stamping*                                                  50

*Notarization*                                                          50

*Non-repudiation*                                                       51

   Connection with Other Services                        52

   Need for Secure Data Archive                           52

   Complexity of This Service                             53

   The Human Factor                                       53

*Privilege Management*                                                  53

   Authentication and Authorization                       54

   Authorization Authorities                              54

   Delegation                                             55

   Connection with the PKI                                55

*Privacy*                                                               56

*Mechanisms Required to Create PKI-Enabled Services*                    58

   Digital Signatures, Hashes, MACs, and Ciphers          58

   Trusted Time Sources                                   58

   Privilege Policy Creation Mechanism                    58

   Privilege Policy Processing Engines                    59

   Privilege Management Infrastructure Mechanisms         59

   Privacy Architecture                                   60

*Operational Considerations*                                           61

   Trusted Time Delivery Mechanism                        61

   Secure Protocols                                       61

   Server Redundancy                                      61

   Physically Secure Archive Facilities                   62

   Privacy Certificates and Identity Mapping              62

   Real Life                                              62

*Comprehensive PKI and Current Practice*                               63

*Summary*                                                              67

## 6  Certificates and Certification                                    69

*Certificates*                                                          70

   Digital Certificate                                    71

   Certificate Structure and Semantics                    72

Alternative Certificate Formats 78

*Certificate Policies* 82

Object Identifiers 83

Policy Authorities 85

*Certification Authority* 85

*Registration Authority* 86

*Summary* 87

**7 Key and Certificate Management** **89**

*Key/Certificate Life-Cycle Management* 90

Initialization Phase 91

Issued Phase 97

Cancellation Phase 100

*Summary* 104

**8 Certificate Revocation** **105**

*Periodic Publication Mechanisms* 107

Certificate Revocation Lists (CRLs) 107

Complete CRLs 114

Certification Authority Revocation Lists (CARLs) 114

End-Entity Public-Key Certification Revocation Lists (EPRLs) 115

CRL Distribution Points 115

Redirect CRLs 116

Delta and Indirect Delta CRLs 118

Indirect CRLs 119

Certificate Revocation Trees (CRTs) 120

Online Query Mechanisms 122

Online Certificate Status Protocol (OCSP) 122

Simple Certificate Validation Protocol (SCVP) 125

*Other Revocation Options* 126

*Performance, Scalability, and Timeliness* 126

*Summary* 129

**9 Trust Models** **131**

*Strict Hierarchy of Certification Authorities* 132

*Loose Hierarchy of Certification Authorities* 134

*Policy-Based Hierarchies*   135

*Distributed Trust Architecture*   135

    Mesh Configuration   137

    Hub-and-Spoke Configuration   138

*Four-Corner Trust Model*   138

*Web Model*   139

*User-Centric Trust*   142

*Cross-Certification*   143

*Entity Naming*   145

*Certificate Path Processing*   146

    Path Construction   147

    Path Validation   148

    Trust Anchor Considerations   148

*Summary*   149

**10 Multiple Certificates per Entity**   **151**

*Multiple Key Pairs*   151

*Key Pair Uses*   152

    Relationship between Key Pairs and Certificates   153

*Real-World Difficulties*   155

*Independent Certificate Management*   155

*Support for Non-repudiation*   156

*Summary*   157

**11 PKI Information Dissemination: Repositories and Other Techniques**   **159**

*Private Dissemination*   159

*Publication and Repositories*   160

    Locating Repositories   162

    Tradeoffs   163

*Interdomain Repository Issues and Options*   165

    Direct Access   166

    Border Repository   167

    Shared Repository   168

    Interdomain Replication   168

*In-band Protocol Exchange* 169

*Summary* 169

## 12 *PKI Operational Considerations* 171

*Client-Side Software* 171

*Off-line Operations* 173

*Physical Security* 174

*Hardware Components* 175

*User Key Compromise* 176

*Disaster Preparation and Recovery* 179

Relying Party Notification 179

Preparation 180

Recovery 181

Additional Observations 182

*Summary* 182

## 13 *Electronic Signature Legislation and Considerations* 183

*Electronic Signature Legislation* 183

E-Sign 183

Digital Signatures in Context 184

EU Electronic Signature Directive 186

The Significance of Electronic Signature Initiatives 187

*Legal Considerations for PKIs* 188

CA Requirements 188

Roles and Responsibilities 189

Private Enterprise PKIs 192

Other Contractual-Based Frameworks 193

*Confidentiality* 194

*Summary* 194

## 14 *PKI in Practice* 195

*What PKI Does* 196

*What PKI Does Not Do* 196

*The Value of PKI* 200

*When Certificates and People Meet* 203

An E-mail Scenario                                        203
A Web Scenario                                            205
*Summary*                                                  206

**15  *The Future of PKI***                               **207**
*What Happened?*                                           207
*How the World Is Changing*                               211
A Recognized Authoritative Body                            211
A Motivation                                               212
Users                                                      214
*Reasons for Cautious Optimism*                            215
*Summary*                                                  216

**16  *Conclusions and Further Reading***                 **217**
*Conclusions*                                              217
*Suggestions for Further Reading*                          218

**PART II  STANDARDS**                                    **219**

**17  *Introduction***                                    **221**

**18  *Major Standards Activities***                      **223**
*X.509*                                                    223
*PKIX*                                                     224
*X.500*                                                    225
*LDAP*                                                     226
*ISO TC68*                                                 226
*ANSI X9F*                                                 227
*S/MIME*                                                   227
*IPsec*                                                    228
*TLS*                                                      228
*SPKI*                                                     228
*OpenPGP*                                                  229
*EDIFACT*                                                  230

*IEEE*    230

*WAP*    230

*XML-Based Activities*    231

*Other Activities*    231

     U.S. FPKI    232

     MISPC    232

     GOC PKI    232

     SET    233

     SEMPER    233

     ECOM    234

     JCP    234

     ICE-CAR    234

*Summary*    235

**19 Standardization Status and Road Map**    **237**

*Current Standardization Status*    237

     X.509    237

     PKIX    238

     X.500    238

     LDAP    238

     S/MIME    238

     IPsec    239

     TLS    239

     Toolkit Requirements (APIs and Mechanisms)    240

     Others    240

*Ongoing Standardization Work*    240

*Summary*    242

**20 Standards: Necessary but Not Sufficient**    **243**

*The Role of Standards, Profiles, and Interoperability Testing*    243

     Profiles and Interoperability Testing    244

*Interoperability Initiatives*    245

     Automotive Network eXchange    245

     Bridge CA Demonstration    245

     Federal PKI    247

     Minimum Interoperability Specification    247

     National Automated Clearing House Association    248

PKI X.509                                                                   249
Securities Industry Root CA Proof of Concept                                250
EEMA PKI Challenge                                                          250
*Summary*                                                                   250

## 21  Conclusions and Further Reading                                      253
*Conclusions*                                                               253
*Suggestions for Further Reading*                                           253
Certificate/CRL Syntax and Life-Cycle Management Protocols                  253
Certificate/CRL Storage and Retrieval                                       254
XML-Based Initiatives                                                       256
Interoperability Initiatives                                                256
Standards Bodies' Web Sites                                                 257
Books                                                                       257

# PART III  DEPLOYMENT CONSIDERATIONS                                       259

## 22  Introduction                                                         261

## 23  Benefits and Costs of a PKI                                          263
*Business Case Considerations*                                              263
*Cost Considerations*                                                       265
*Deployment: Now or Later?*                                                 267
*Summary*                                                                   268

## 24  Deployment Issues and Decisions                                      269
*Trust Models: Hierarchical versus Distributed*                             270
*In-sourcing versus Out-sourcing*                                           271
*Build versus Buy*                                                          272
*Closed versus Open Environment*                                            272
*X.509 versus Alternative Certificate Formats*                              273
*Targeted Applications versus Comprehensive Solution*                       274
*Standard versus Proprietary Solutions*                                     274
*Interoperability Considerations*                                           274
Certificate and CRL Profiles                                               274
Multiple Industry-Accepted Standards                                        275

PKI-Enabled Applications 275

Policy/Business Control Issues 275

*On-line versus Off-line Operations* 276

*Peripheral Support* 276

*Facility Requirements* 277

*Personnel Requirements* 277

*Certificate Revocation* 277

*End-Entity Roaming* 278

*Key Recovery* 278

*Repository Issues* 279

*Disaster Planning and Recovery* 279

*Security Assurance* 279

*Mitigating Risk* 280

*Summary* 281

25 **Barriers to Deployment** **283**

*Repository Issues* 283

Lack of Industry-Accepted Standard 283

Multivendor Interoperability 284

Scalability and Performance 284

*Knowledgeable Personnel* 285

*PKI-Enabled Applications* 285

*Corporate-Level Acceptance* 286

*Summary* 286

26 **Typical Business Models** **287**

*Internal Communications Business Model* 287

*External Communications Business Model* 288

Business-to-Business Communication 289

Business-to-Consumer Communication 290

*Internal/External Business Model Hybrids* 290

*Business Model Influences* 291

*Government-Sponsored Initiatives* 291

*Interdomain Trust* 292

Identrus 292
Bridge CA 292
VeriSign Trust Network 293
GTE CyberTrust/Baltimore Technologies OmniRoot 293
Other Trust Networks 293
*Summary* 294

27 **Conclusions and Further Reading** **295**
*Conclusions* 295
*Suggestions for Further Reading* 296

*References* **297**

*Index* **311**

# *Foreword*

Public-Key Infrastructures (PKIs) are becoming a central part of enterprise security architectures. A PKI provides a focal point for many aspects of security management, as well as serving as an enabler for a growing number of standard and custom security applications. Most standard protocols for secure e-mail, Web access, virtual private networks, and single sign-on user authentication systems make use of public-key certificates and therefore require some form of PKI. Given the rapid evolution of PKIs in many enterprises, *Understanding PKI* is a very valuable book for any corporate IT manager, CIO, system security administration, or application protocol developer.

I have taught one- and two-day seminars on network security for almost two decades, for audiences around the world. At the end of each seminar, I am often asked what books I recommend for further study, additional topics, more details, and so on. It's an obvious question, but one for which I rarely have a good answer. Too many books on security devote page after page to discussion of cryptographic authentication protocols that are only of academic interest. Almost no books combine useful background information and motivation for security technology choices, along with a good exposition of technical details.

I am pleased to say that this is one of the very few books I can recommend to my students. Although PKIs are just a part of the overall security landscape, *Understanding PKI* does an outstanding job of covering all the bases, and it does so in a highly informative and user-friendly way. Carlisle and Steve have approached this complex topic in a very readable fashion. They don't waste the reader's time with topics that are of only narrow, academic interest. This book is well structured, with chapters that focus on well-bounded topics; it presents material in context, providing both the motivation and the technical details essential to developing a solid understanding of this complex topic. Most chapters are brief, making it easy to read this book incrementally, which is an important feature for all of us who have too much to read and not enough uninterrupted time.

I have had the pleasure of working with Carlisle, in my capacity as cochair of the IETF PKIX Working Group, on several IETF standards, including the Certificate Management Protocol [RFC2510] and the Certificate Request Message Format [RFC2511]. Carlisle Adams and Steve Lloyd are an ideal team to author this book. They have extensive experience in the PKI arena, including standards development and operational experiences with large-scale PKIs for the U.S. and Canadian governments. The result of this collaboration is an excellent guide to public-key infrastructure; one that will likely service as an oft-cited reference text.

Stephen Kent
Chief Scientist—Information Security
BBN Technologies

# *Preface*

Without doubt, the promise of *public-key infrastructure (PKI)* technology has attracted a significant amount of attention in the last few years. Hardly a week goes by without some facet of PKI being addressed in a newspaper, trade journal, or conference paper. We hear and read about the promise of authentication and non-repudiation services provided through the use of digital signature techniques and about confidentiality and key management services based on a combination of symmetric and asymmetric cryptography—all facilitated through the realization of a supporting technology referred to as PKI. In fact, many people consider the widespread deployment of PKI technology to be an important enabler of secure global electronic commerce.

Although the foundation for PKI was established over two decades ago with the invention of public-key cryptography, PKI technology has been offered as a commercially viable solution only within the last few years. But what started as a handful of technology vendors a few years ago has seen the birth of dozens, perhaps hundreds, of products that offer one form or another of PKI-related service. Further, the commercial demand for PKI-based services remains strong, and available evidence suggests that this will continue for the foreseeable future.

Still, as a technology, PKI is fairly new. And to many, PKI technology is shrouded in mystery to some extent. This situation appears to be exacerbated by the proliferation of conflicting documentation, standards, and vendor approaches. Furthermore, there are few comprehensive books devoted to PKI that provide a good introduction to its critical concepts and technology fundamentals.

Thus, the authors share a common motivation in writing this book: to provide a vendor-neutral source of information that can be used to establish a baseline for understanding PKI. In this book, we provide answers to many of the fundamental PKI-related questions, including

- What *exactly* is a PKI?

- What constitutes a digital signature?

## Vendor-Neutral Policy

We would like to emphasize that we have made every attempt to ensure that this book is as vendor neutral as possible. In fact, some of the original text has been modified at the request of one or more reviewers when (unintentionally) it even remotely appeared that we were advocating one approach over another. As authors, we are describing in this book our "vision" of what constitutes a *comprehensive PKI*. Although this viewpoint occasionally aligns more closely with some environments and certain specific vendor products than others, we hasten to point out that we are not aware of any one vendor that offers all the services that are described within this book.

We also recognize that some environments are necessarily more closely aligned with a subset of the components and services described herein (because of their specific requirements and target users), and we fully understand that these environments may never need to fully align with what we refer to as a comprehensive PKI. This is as it should be. This book is not about the "Internet PKI," nor is it meant to be limited to the "enterprise PKI"—although, arguably, the enterprise environment is closer today to our notion of the comprehensive PKI than many alternative deployment environments. This book attempts to describe all aspects of a PKI; specific environments will implement subsets as needed. We have provided a discussion of some of today's PKI variations at the end of Chapter 5 in order to clarify these concepts.

- What is a certificate?
- What is certificate revocation?
- What is a Certification Authority (CA)?
- What are the governing standards?
- What are the issues associated with large-scale PKI deployment within an enterprise?

These are just some of the questions we explore in this book.

# Motivations for PKI

It is important to recognize that PKI is not simply a "neat" technology without tangible benefits. When deployed judiciously, PKI offers certain fundamental advantages to an organization, including the potential for substantial cost savings. PKI can be used as the underlying technology to support authentication, integrity, confidentiality, and non-repudiation. This is accomplished through a combination of symmetric and asymmetric cryptographic techniques enabled through the use of a single, easily managed infrastructure rather than multiple security solutions. (See Chapter 2, Public-Key Cryptography; Chapter 3, The Concept of an Infrastructure; Chapter 4, Core PKI Services: Authentication, Integrity, and Confidentiality; and Chapter 5, PKI-Enabled Services.) PKI offers scalable key management in that the overhead associated with the distribution of keying material to communicating parties is reduced significantly when compared with solutions based solely on symmetric cryptography. (See Chapter 2 for a description of symmetric and asymmetric cryptographic techniques.) Ultimately, however, the primary motivations from a business standpoint are not technical but economic: How can PKI give a positive return on investment? To that end, judicious deployment of a single, unifying PKI technology can help, among other things

- Reduce administrative overhead (when compared with the deployment of multiple point solutions)

- Reduce the number of passwords required by end users (and, consequently, the administrative and help desk costs associated with managing them)

- Reduce paperwork and improve workflow efficiencies through more automated (and more secure) business processes

- Optimize work-force productivity (by ensuring that users spend less time contending with the security infrastructure and more time on the job at hand)

- Reduce requirements for end-user training related to the use of the security services (because there is one security solution rather than many)

Not only does PKI technology have the potential to realize cost savings, but in some cases it also might even be a source of revenue for an organization (through support for new services that might otherwise not be offered). Benefits and related business considerations associated with PKI technology are discussed further in Part III, Deployment Considerations.

## Changes in the Second Edition

The world, and PKI's place in the world, has evolved somewhat since the first edition of this book was written. Like many technologies, PKI has experienced the highs and lows of media attention and analyst focus: In three short years, the descriptions have covered the spectrum from "silver bullet" to "snake oil." There is still confusion regarding naming of entities and the use of PKI in real-world business applications such as e-mail. Occasionally, the long-term viability of PKI is questioned in journals or trade publications. In this second edition, two new chapters have been added to address precisely these areas:

- Chapter 14, PKI in Practice, looks at the use of this technology in the real world and tries to clarify where PKI can be beneficial and where it cannot.

- Chapter 15, The Future of PKI, is based upon an observation of how the world has been evolving and attempts to answer the question: Will this technology survive and, if so, why?

For the most part, however, the roller coaster of public opinion has now largely stabilized. There is general consensus that PKI is one viable option for a good, solid authentication technology with a number of appealing benefits compared with other technologies. In conjunction with this, PKI itself has matured and evolved to better meet the needs of the environments that might deploy it and rely on it for various services. In this edition, changes and additions have been made throughout the book to capture and explain this evolution. Some specific examples include the following:

- Chapter 5, PKI-Enabled Services, now includes a section on privacy as a service that may be enabled by a PKI.

- Chapters 6, Certificates and Certification, and 8, Certificate Revocation, have been updated to reflect new extensions and clarification text that were introduced in the X.509 (2000) standard.

- Chapter 9, Trust Models, now incorporates material on several additional trust models that may be appropriate in some environments.

- Chapter 13, Electronic Signature Legislation and Considerations, has been revised and updated to reflect the significant progress that has been made in that area since late 1999.

- The whole of Part II, Standards, has been updated to incorporate the latest achievements in that area, as well as the new initiatives that have been started, especially in the eXtensible Markup Language (XML) standards bodies. Numerous other, more minor, updates and revisions may be found throughout the book.

## Audience

The main purpose of this book is to provide a fairly comprehensive overview that will help the reader better understand the technical and operational considerations behind PKI technology. You will benefit from this book if you are responsible for the planning, deployment, and/or operation of an enterprise PKI. Those who are simply interested in the basic principles behind a PKI should also find this book useful.

We hope that this book will become an educational tool for many and a handy reference guide for others. This book is not intended to resolve extremely detailed implementation questions, although it can serve as a primer for someone who will eventually be more interested in the finer implementation details.

# Organization

The book is organized into three parts. Part I provides essential background information necessary to better understand the concepts and principles behind PKI.

Part II addresses standards and related activities (for example, industry-sponsored interoperability initiatives) related to PKI. There are two primary purposes for including this section in the book:

1. It provides an overview of the major standards bodies involved in the PKI arena and discusses the main focus of each group, giving a road map to some of these activities.

2. It demonstrates the relative maturity and stability of this area, highlighting the fact that a solid basis for implementation and interoperability has already been laid.

Part III discusses PKI deployment considerations, providing guidance for some of the initial and fundamental decisions that must be made prior to any PKI deployment.

## Part I: Concepts

Part I of this book deals with fundamental PKI concepts. This includes background information (for example, a primer on cryptography is included), as well as detailed information with respect to public-key certificates and certificate revocation schemes.

Chapter 1, Introduction, introduces Part I and provides a list of the contents of Part I on a chapter-by-chapter basis.

Chapter 2, Public-Key Cryptography, provides a brief, nonmathematical introduction to the concepts of public-key cryptography relevant to the material presented throughout the remainder of the book. It includes the distinction between symmetric and public-key ciphers, the concept of a key pair, the services of this technology, terminology, and sample algorithms.

Chapter 3, The Concept of an Infrastructure, discusses an infrastructure, highlighting its usefulness as an application enabler, its role in secure single sign-on, and its capability to provide end-user transparency and comprehensive security. This chapter also provides a working definition of PKI.

Chapter 4, Core PKI Services: Authentication, Integrity, and Confidentiality, and Chapter 5, PKI-Enabled Services, examine services that a PKI can provide. Chapter 4 discusses the core services of authentication, integrity, and confidentiality; Chapter 5 looks at PKI-enabled services such as digital time stamping, notarization, non-repudiation, and privilege management.

Chapter 6, Certificates and Certification, introduces the concept of a certificate and discusses the process of certification. Certificate contents and format are described, along with the role of a Certification Authority (CA) and a Registration Authority (RA).

Chapter 7, Key and Certificate Management, looks at the whole area of key/certificate life-cycle management, including generation, publication, update, termination, key history, key backup, and key recovery.

Chapter 8, Certificate Revocation, discusses common techniques for certificate revocation, including both periodic publication mechanisms and on-line query mechanisms.

Chapter 9, Trust Models, examines the concept of trust models. Strict hierarchies, loose hierarchies, policy-based hierarchies, distributed architectures, the four-corner model, the Web model, user-centric trust, and cross-certification are presented and compared. We also discuss certificate path processing in this chapter.

Chapter 10, Multiple Certificates per Entity, includes an examination of key pair uses, support for non-repudiation, and independent certificate management.

Chapter 11, PKI Information Dissemination: Repositories and Other Techniques, looks at the area of certificate dissemination and repositories. Options for sharing public-key-related information between two or more cooperating PKI domains are discussed.

Chapter 12, PKI Operational Considerations, discusses client-side software, on-line requirements, physical security, and disaster planning/recovery, along with tradeoffs between system security and ease of use.

Chapter 13, Electronic Signature Legislation and Considerations, discusses some of the recent legislation and directives that pertain to electronic signatures and clarifies some of the terminology associated with various forms of electronic signatures, including digital signatures. Some of the requirements and obligations that may apply to Certification Authorities (CAs), subscribers, and relying parties are briefly discussed.

Chapter 14, PKI in Practice, focuses on the use of PKI in the real world and tries to clarify some common misunderstandings and sources of confusion about what PKI can do and what it can't do (and was never intended to do).

Chapter 15, The Future of PKI, considers this oft-posed question: Why has PKI not "taken off" yet? This chapter offers an opinion about why PKI adoption has been slower than many people expected and discusses—with a view to emerging trends in the industry—the future of PKI.

Chapter 16, Conclusions and Further Reading, concludes Part I and suggests some sources to consult for further reading in this area.

## Part II: Standards

Part II of this book addresses standards activities and interoperability initiatives.

Chapter 17, Introduction, introduces Part II and provides a list of the contents of Part II on a chapter-by-chapter basis.

Chapter 18, Major Standards Activities, discusses some of the most prominent activities taking place within formal standards bodies, as well as related efforts being undertaken outside the standards bodies.

Chapter 19, Standardization Status and Road Map, provides the current and projected near-term standardization status of some of the most significant specifications.

Chapter 20, Standards: Necessary but Not Sufficient, considers the fact that the existence of a "standard," whether it is the product of a formal standards body or not, is necessary but not sufficient to guarantee that the products of different vendors will interoperate with one another. Some of the reasons for this are given, along with a discussion of the usefulness of profiling activities and interoperability pilots.

Finally, Chapter 21, Conclusions and Further Reading, provides concluding remarks and some suggestions for further reading.

## Part III: Deployment Considerations

Part III of this book addresses deployment. Not intended to be a deployment handbook, this part of the book primarily identifies many of the deployment questions that should be asked (and answered) when considering any large-scale enterprise PKI deployment.

Chapter 22, Introduction, introduces Part III and provides a list of the contents of Part III on a chapter-by-chapter basis.

Chapter 23, Benefits and Costs of a PKI, discusses the benefits realized through the deployment of a PKI. It also discusses cost considerations. This chapter helps identify sound business reasons for deploying a PKI in the enterprise environment.

Chapter 24, Deployment Issues and Decisions, discusses a number of issues that should be resolved before initial deployment occurs. Essentially, this chapter provides a basic foundation for product selection.

Chapter 25, Barriers to Deployment, addresses some of the more common hurdles to deployment, issues that one must consider in terms of long-term strategy.

Chapter 26, Typical Business Models, explains some of the more common business models one may want to implement. It also provides a brief discussion of some initiatives that can be used as a basis to establish interdomain trust.

Chapter 27, Conclusions and Further Reading, concludes Part III and offers suggestions for further reading.

# About the Authors

**Carlisle Adams** has been involved with the design, specification, and standardization of various aspects of Public-Key Infrastructures and Privilege Management Infrastructures (PMI) for many years and is recognized internationally for his contributions in these areas. He has participated actively in the IETF Public-Key Infrastructure—X.509 (PKIX) and Common Authentication Technology (CAT) working groups, among others, and he has authored or coauthored a number of standards-track and informational specifications, including RFCs 2025 (SPKM), 2144 (CAST-128), 2479 (IDUP-GSS-API), 2510 (CMP), 2511 (CRMF), 2560 (OCSP), 2612 (CAST-256), 2984 (CAST-128 for CMS), 3029 (DVCS), and 3161 (TSP). He has also contributed to several other PKI and PMI standardization efforts, including ISO/SC2, ISO/TC68, ANSI X9.F.1, and the US FPKI TWG. He currently participates in a number of XML-based security specification activities and is cochair of the OASIS eXtensible Access Control Markup Language (XACML) Technical Committee.

Dr. Adams holds B.S. and M.S. degrees in Computing and Information Science and a Ph.D. in Electrical Engineering. He is currently principal of advanced security and senior cryptographer at Entrust, Inc. His activities and research interests have included the structured design and analysis of symmetric block ciphers (including the CAST family of algorithms) and the design, analysis, and standardization of security protocols for the Internet.

**Steve Lloyd** has more than 20 years experience in data communications and distributed systems security. His areas of expertise include distributed message handling systems and directory services, TCP/IP, security protocols, security architectures, and large-scale PKI policy and technology. Steve has presented numerous seminars and tutorials in the areas of data communications and network security, and he has been a regularly invited speaker to a variety of technology conferences and symposiums. Steve was directly involved with the formation of the PKI Forum, and served as a member of the PKI Forum Executive Board and as executive sponsor to the PKI Forum Technical Workgroup. Steve is currently manager of IT security consulting at AEPOS Technologies Corporation, specializing in network security, PKI, and PMI.

# PART

# I

# Concepts

1  Introduction. . . . . . . . . . . . . . . . . . . . . . . . . 3

2  Public-Key Cryptography . . . . . . . . . . . . . . . . 7

3  The Concept of an Infrastructure . . . . . . . . . 21

4  Core PKI Services: Authentication,
   Integrity, and Confidentiality . . . . . . . . . . . . 37

5  PKI-Enabled Services . . . . . . . . . . . . . . . . . . 49

6  Certificates and Certification . . . . . . . . . . . . 69

7  Key and Certificate Management . . . . . . . . . 89

8  Certificate Revocation . . . . . . . . . . . . . . . . . 105

9  Trust Models . . . . . . . . . . . . . . . . . . . . . . . 131

10  Multiple Certificates per Entity . . . . . . . . . . 151

11  PKI Information Dissemination:
    Repositories and Other Techniques . . . . . . . 159

12  PKI Operational Considerations . . . . . . . . . . 171

13  Electronic Signature Legislation
    and Considerations . . . . . . . . . . . . . . . . . . 183

14  PKI in Practice . . . . . . . . . . . . . . . . . . . . . . 195

15  The Future of PKI . . . . . . . . . . . . . . . . . . . . 207

16  Conclusions and Further Reading. . . . . . . . . 217

# 1

# *Introduction*

This book is about understanding *Public-Key Infrastructure (PKI)*. The first step in understanding involves the *head:* knowing the concepts; becoming familiar with the terminology; and getting a sense for the parameters, the scope, and the limits of a topic. This helps us become conversant with others about the issues and allows us to read and follow the literature with a perceptive, critical eye.

The second step in understanding involves the *hands:* We learn by doing. We see what technical work others have done (and are doing) to enable concrete implementation of the concepts, and we set to work implementing the concepts for ourselves in our own environments. This, too, allows us to converse with others and to evaluate the literature fairly.

*Doing* leads to greater *knowing,* which in turn results in more successful *doing,* and so on. The end result is a fairly deep understanding of the topic under consideration.

The primary goal of this book is to be one of the tools in this process of understanding PKI. Given that some level of *knowing* must come first, Part I, Concepts, addresses this aspect of PKI understanding by discussing the underlying concepts and terminology, by explaining technical options wherever they arise, and by presenting the inherent strengths and limitations of this technology.

Part II, Standards, focuses on *doing* by describing the relevant work being undertaken within the standards bodies and related initiatives to enable PKI implementation and interoperability. Part III, Deployment Considerations, also focuses on *doing* by discussing many of the practical issues and decisions involved in deploying a PKI in the real world.

Part I consumes the majority of the book. Parts II and III are essentially guidelines to get readers started in their own PKI deployments.

The material presented in Part I is organized as follows:

- Chapter 2, Public-Key Cryptography, provides a brief, nonmathematical introduction to the concepts of public-key cryptography relevant to the material presented throughout the remainder of the book. Included is the distinction between symmetric and public-key ciphers, the concept of a key pair, the services of this technology, terminology, and sample algorithms.

- Chapter 3, The Concept of an Infrastructure, discusses the idea of an infrastructure, highlighting its usefulness as an application enabler, its role in secure single sign-on, and its capability to provide end-user transparency and comprehensive security. This chapter also gives a working definition of PKI.

- Chapter 4, Core PKI Services: Authentication, Integrity, and Confidentiality, and Chapter 5, PKI-Enabled Services, examine services that a PKI can provide. Chapter 4 discusses the core services of authentication, integrity, and confidentiality; Chapter 5 looks at PKI-enabled services such as digital time stamping, notarization, non-repudiation, and privilege management.

- Chapter 6, Certificates and Certification, introduces the concept of a certificate and discusses the process of certification. This chapter describes certificate contents and format, along with the role of a Certification Authority (CA) and a Registration Authority (RA).

- Chapter 7, Key and Certificate Management, looks at the whole area of key and certificate life-cycle management, including generation, publication, update, termination, key history, key backup, and key recovery.

- Chapter 8, Certificate Revocation, discusses common techniques for certificate revocation, both periodic publication mechanisms and on-line query mechanisms. This chapter discusses scalability issues, timeliness, and implementation considerations with respect to these techniques.

- Chapter 9, Trust Models, examines the concept of trust models. Strict hierarchies, loose hierarchies, policy-based hierarchies, distributed architectures, the four-corner model, the Web model, user-centric trust, and cross-certification are presented and compared. We also discuss certificate path processing in this chapter.

- Chapter 10, Multiple Certificates per Entity, discusses the concept of multiple certificates per entity and includes an examination of key pair uses, support for non-repudiation, and independent certificate management.

- Chapter 11, PKI Information Dissemination: Repositories and Other Techniques, looks at the area of certificate dissemination and repositories. Options for sharing public-key-related information between two or more cooperating PKI domains are discussed.

- Chapter 12, PKI Operational Considerations, examines PKI operational considerations and discusses client-side software, on-line requirements, physical security, and disaster planning/recovery, along with tradeoffs between system security and ease of use.

- Chapter 13, Electronic Signature Legislation and Considerations, discusses some of the recent legislation and directives that pertain to electronic signatures and clarifies some of the terminology associated with various forms of electronic signatures, including digital signatures. Some of the requirements and obligations that may apply to Certification Authorities (CAs), subscribers, and relying parties are briefly discussed.

- Chapter 14, PKI in Practice, focuses on the use of PKI in the real world and tries to clarify some common misunderstandings and sources of confusion about what PKI can do and what it can't do (and was never intended to do).

- Chapter 15, The Future of PKI, considers the oft-posed question: Why hasn't PKI "taken off" yet? This chapter offers an opinion about why the adoption of PKI has been slower than many people expected and discusses—with a view to emerging trends in the industry—the future of PKI.

- Chapter 16, Conclusions and Further Reading, concludes Part I and suggests some sources for further reading in this area.

We begin, then, with a brief introduction to public-key cryptography.

# Public-Key Cryptography

In this chapter, we introduce the main concepts of public-key cryptography. The treatment is intentionally high level and brief, touching only on aspects directly relevant to an understanding of the remainder of this book. For a broader and more thorough discussion, read the *Handbook of Applied Cryptography* [MvOV97], *Applied Cryptography: Protocols, Algorithms, and Source Code in C* [Schn96], *Cryptography and Network Security: Principles and Practice* [Stal99], or *Cryptography: Theory and Practice* [Stin95].

## Symmetric versus Asymmetric Ciphers

For as long as humans have communicated, there has been a desire to keep some communications confidential (that is, "hidden") from unintended recipients. Over thousands of years, countless methods for hiding data have been devised. One class of methods attempts to transform the words, letters, or bits to be communicated into something that looks like gibberish rather than a meaningful message. The intended recipient must be able to transform the gibberish back to its original form in order to read the sender's message, but any other recipient—such as an eavesdropper—should be able to recover nothing more meaningful than the transmitted gibberish.

Two categories of mechanisms exist for performing the transformation of text to gibberish and back. In the following section, we define and discuss symmetric (*secret key*) ciphers; asymmetric (*public key*) ciphers are the focus of the section New Directions: Public Key.

### Secret Key

Until the mid-1970s, only one mechanism was known in the open literature for the transformation to gibberish and back: The sender and the intended recipient shared some secret information specifying how the transformation was to be performed.

As one simple, well-known example of this, the shared secret information might specify that each letter in the original message be replaced with the letter 13 places ahead in the English alphabet. For example, *A* is replaced with *N*, *B* is replaced with *O*, and *Z* is replaced with *M* (13 places ahead after wrapping around to *A* again). In this case, the secret information to transform the transmitted gibberish back into a readable message is identical: The letter 13 places ahead of *N* is *A*; 13 places ahead of *O* is *B*; and 13 places ahead of *M* is *Z*.

The shared secret information specifying exactly how the transformation to and from gibberish is to be accomplished—for instance the value 13 in the preceding example—is called a *key*. The transformation to gibberish is *encryption*; the transformation back to the original text is *decryption*. The original message, called *plaintext*, is encrypted to gibberish, called *ciphertext*, which can then be decrypted by the intended recipient back to the corresponding plaintext. Figure 2.1 summarizes these processes. The entire confidentiality mechanism (that is, the encryption and decryption algorithms) is a *cipher*. More precisely, the confidentiality mechanism is a *symmetric cipher* when one of the following is true:

- The encryption key and the decryption key are identical (as earlier, where both have the value 13).

- One key is very easily derived from the other (as in a slight variation of the earlier example, where encryption is accomplished by rotating *ahead* five letters, and decryption is accomplished by rotating *back* five letters).

**Figure 2.1**    Symmetric cipher model.

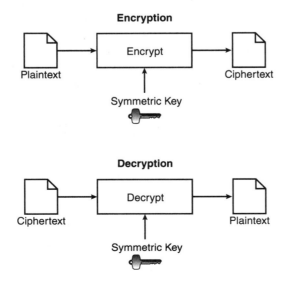

As noted earlier, symmetric ciphers, ranging from the very simple to the highly sophisticated, have existed for thousands of years, and new ones continue to be invented. The earlier example is commonly known as *ROT-13* or, more generally, a *simple substitution cipher.* More modern examples include DES [FIPS46], IDEA [Lai92], RC5 [Rive95], CAST-128 [Adams97; RFC2144], and the Advanced Encryption Standard [AES] (see Box 2.1).

Although symmetric ciphers can possess some very desirable characteristics (such as a small implementation size and encryption/decryption speeds that can reach tens of megabytes per second or more), they also suffer from some significant drawbacks in some environments. These drawbacks include the following:

- The need for secret key exchange

- Difficulties in initiating secure communication between previously unknown parties

- Difficulties of scale

The following sections briefly discuss these drawbacks.

### The Need for Secret Key Exchange

For their security, symmetric ciphers rely completely on the fact that the sender and the intended recipient alone share some secret information (a key) prior to the transmission of the message. Therefore, the conveyance of this key requires that a separate, out-of-band, secure communication must occur prior to the intended communication. This additional step, although feasible in some environments, can be extremely difficult or highly inconvenient in some circumstances.

## Box 2.1   Advanced Encryption Standard

The Advanced Encryption Standard is the outcome of a process organized by the National Institute of Standards and Technology (NIST) to select a symmetric cipher to officially replace the Data Encryption Standard (DES). Although done primarily for U.S. government use, it will likely find much broader application as well.

Selected in the summer of 2000 from an initial field of 15 candidates after 2 years of rigorous worldwide analysis, the AES cipher is expected to provide high cryptographic security for at least the next 20 to 30 years. Because of this long-term view, NIST requirements dictate that the AES must have a variable-length key size up to 256 bits, whereas many current ciphers have a key size up to 128 bits. Other important criteria in the selection of the AES cipher are its ease of implementation, small size, and operational efficiency in both hardware and software.

### Communications Difficulties between Unknown Entities

The need for a separate, out-of-band secret key exchange step can lead to tremendous difficulties when entities are unknown to each other (that is, when the entities have had no previous contact or relationship). For instance, Alice knows that there is a lawyer named Bob with whom she needs to have a confidential conversation. However, if she has not had any prior communication with Bob, how does she know with whom to share a secret key so that the confidential conversation can take place? That is, how can she be certain that she is sharing a key with Bob and not with David, who is posing as Bob to obtain Alice's confidential information?

Note that the need for an "introducer" between entities that have no previous relationship is not unique to symmetric technology. This fundamental problem also arises in asymmetric technology, just as it does in real life (where we use a common friend, or a government that issues a driver's license, to introduce people to each other). As you will see, however, the solutions to this problem are quite different in the two technologies. (Compare the following section, Symmetric Central Server Architectures, with the later section, Security between Strangers.)

### Difficulties of Scale

The secret key shared between Alice and Bob must be different from the secret key shared between Alice and Catherine; otherwise, the confidentiality of messages intended for Bob is compromised. In a community of 1,000 users, then, Alice could potentially have to maintain 999 secret keys (actually, 1,000 if she also wants to encrypt data just for herself). Because the same is true for each of the other users, this community could collectively hold something close to half a million unique secret keys! As the community grows, the storage and maintenance of such a large number of keys can quickly become unmanageable. A community of $n$ users may require up to $n^2/2$ unique secret keys, including the key each user holds for himself or herself. Manageability problems become even more pronounced because keys do not last forever but typically are replaced periodically with new ones to limit the amount of data encrypted under a single key.

### Symmetric Central Server Architectures

Some of the problems referred to earlier can be mitigated through the use of a symmetric-cipher-based central server architecture in which each entity in the community shares a secret key with the central server (usually called a *Key Distribution Center*, or *KDC*). In such an architecture, the number of secret keys that need to be stored and maintained in a community is essentially equal to the size of the community, and the central server can act as an "introducer" for entities that do not previously know each other. However, the security-critical central server must constantly be available on-line; when it is down, secure communication between unknown entities is not possible. (Entities that have previously established communications may still be able to communicate using cached keys, if this is allowed in a given environment.) So, the KDC represents a significant single point of failure and single point of attack for the entire community; it also can be a severe communication bottleneck in a large organization. Furthermore, interaction between the community associated with this server and any other external community can be difficult to manage.

## *New Directions: Public Key*

In the mid-1970s, two researchers—Whitfield Diffie and Martin Hellman—steered the public-domain field of cryptography into some interesting new directions. Pondering some of the difficulties with symmetric ciphers discussed earlier, Diffie and Hellman imagined a world in which ciphers were *asymmetric,* in which the key for encryption and the key for decryption were related but conspicuously different. These keys would be so different, in fact, that it would be possible to publicize one without danger of anyone being able to derive or compute the other (see the following section, Public/Private-Key Pair, for further discussion).

Such a concept was indeed new and interesting, but was it possible? Diffie and Hellman did not have a definitive answer; their paper, "New Directions in Cryptography" [DiHe76], did not contain a concrete example that provably met the requirements. What it did contain, however, was evidence that such a cipher *might be constructed.* It used, as a toy example, a cipher based on vector-matrix multiplication in which the sender and legitimate receiver only need to multiply a vector with a matrix to encrypt and decrypt. Any other unintended recipient, however, needs to perform the more difficult task of matrix inversion to recover the plaintext. Their suggestion, in general terms, was that "difficult" mathematical problems that had a simple solution if additional information was known might be an attractive underlying basis for asymmetric ciphers. Technically, such problems are known as *trapdoor functions with high computational complexity.* (See also Merkle's early and independent work in this field [Merk78, Merk79].)

It is impossible to overemphasize just how radical Diffie and Hellman's concept was when it appeared. The idea of having a key that can be revealed publicly without compromising communications security was unheard of in the open literature[1] and stimulated intensive research for a number of years. The search for concrete examples of asymmetric ciphers gave rise to a number of proposals (many of which were subsequently shown to be insecure). More fundamentally and perhaps more importantly, however, mathematicians, computer scientists, and engineers have been forced to explore the boundary between theoretical and practical com-

---

[1]Recently declassified documents show that, as early as the late 1960s, individuals in the British agency GCHQ knew of some of the concepts that Diffie and Hellman introduced. However, such information was unavailable publicly and was certainly unknown to Diffie and Hellman.

plexity and to try to understand the inherent difficulty of certain mathematical problems, such as factoring or finding discrete logarithms over finite fields. Much progress has been made since the 1976 publication of the now-classic Diffie–Hellman paper, but research into asymmetric ciphers and all related subjects continues at an ever-increasing pace.

# Public/Private-Key Pair

As discussed in the previous section, asymmetric ciphers make use of two related but different keys. In this *key pair,* the keys are sufficiently different that knowing one does not allow derivation or computation of the other, even for determined adversaries with a lot of computing power at their disposal. This means that one of the keys may be made publicly available (for example, stored in an open database, listed in a telephone book, or printed on a business card) without reducing security—provided that the other key remains private.[2] The idea that one of the keys in this pair can be revealed publicly was so radical and appealing that this whole method of protecting data quickly became known as *public-key cryptography.*

The keys in a key pair of a public-key cipher are different, but they are also related. This is necessarily true because, for example, one must decrypt what the other encrypts. The relationship is mathematical and may rely on information known only to the creator of the key pair, such as the factorization of a large integer. However, security in this technology is based on the fact that it is computationally infeasible for anyone other than the key pair creator to derive the private key from knowledge of the public key. Theoretically, of course, the private key can always be derived, but the amount of time, memory, or computing power necessary to do so in practice must be prohibitively high.

# Services of Public-Key Cryptography

The discovery of public-key cryptography has made a number of services available, some of which were either unknown or unachievable with symmetric ciphers. This section highlights some of the more important and more interesting of these services.

## Security between Strangers

One driving motivation behind public-key cryptography was the inherent difficulty of enabling secure communication between strangers in a symmetric cipher environment. In particular,

---

[2]The key that is not publicly revealed is generally referred to in the industry and the academic literature as a *private key,* rather than a *secret key.* This avoids confusion with the secret key of a symmetric cipher and derives from the idea that two people may share a secret, but a single person keeps something private.

given the difficulty of computing the private key even if all other details of the cipher are known, it is possible in such a system to take the public key and disseminate it widely. For example, this key can be stored in a public repository (at some level of abstraction, the electronic equivalent of a telephone book). Thus, even if Alice has had no previous communication with Bob, she can look up his public key and protect data for him. Figure 2.2 summarizes the process of asymmetric cryptography.

There is of course one caveat: Alice must feel fairly confident that the public key she retrieves really does belong to Bob. There are two general mechanisms for achieving this:

- *Alice trusts the repository.* The public repository may be trusted to return correct information. This is effectively the phone book scenario: When Alice looks up Bob's telephone number in the book, she assumes it is correct and does not do any independent verification of that number before using it to call Bob.

- *Alice finds a way to trust the information.* The public repository may be untrusted, but the information it returns can be independently verified for correctness.

In the paper world, a trusted public repository is achievable, at least to some degree. Alice does not worry that someone will break into her house and alter her phone book so that Bob's telephone number is replaced with another number. In the electronic world, however, such unau-

**Figure 2.2** Asymmetric cipher model.

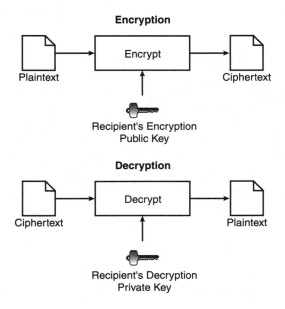

thorized data modification is a legitimate concern: Public repositories, in general, cannot be trusted to return correct information. Thus, the information itself must be independently verifiable. A common mechanism to achieve this is the *public-key certificate*. (See Chapter 6 for further discussion of this technology.)

As noted earlier, both symmetric and asymmetric technologies require an introducer. It may be argued, however, that the asymmetric introducer solution is preferable for a number of environments because an attacker must possess a much greater level of sophistication and skill to succeed in subverting the system. With the symmetric central server architecture, confidentiality is critical; simply being able to read the KDC data suffices to compromise the entire system. With the public repository (either itself trusted or holding independently verifiable data), confidentiality is unimportant: The attacker must be able to explicitly manipulate the contained data in a totally undetectable way. Such an active attack is generally harder to accomplish than the purely passive attack of trying to read data.

## Encryption

With some public-key algorithms, encrypting data with the public key is possible; then, the resulting ciphertext can be decrypted only with the corresponding private key. Generally, however, the computations involved in public-key cryptography are too slow, thus impractical for many environments. Typically what is done instead involves a two-step process, as follows:

1. The data is encrypted using a randomly generated symmetric key.

2. The symmetric key is then encrypted using the public key of the intended recipient of the data.

When the recipient receives the encrypted data, a similar two-step process takes place:

1. The recipient decrypts the symmetric key, using his or her private key.

2. The symmetric key is then used to decrypt the actual data.

Even when the total amount of data to be encrypted is very small, the two-step processes presented here are typically used rather than direct data encryption/decryption using the public/private-key pair. This serves to keep processing clear and simple so that there is never any confusion about whether the output of a private-key decryption operation is data or a symmetric key.

## Digital Signature

A service enabled by public-key cryptography that is not easily achievable with symmetric ciphers is the *digital signature*. This is analogous to a handwritten signature because a single entity can sign some data, but any number of entities can read the signature and verify its accuracy. However, it is much more secure because it is computationally infeasible for any other entity to create Alice's signature on some data. That is, forging is virtually impossible.

A digital signature fundamentally relies on the concept of a key pair. There must be a private key known only to Alice so that when she signs some data, the data is uniquely and explicitly tied to her. Furthermore, a public key must be available to a wider group of entities (potentially all entities) so that the signature can be verified and identified with Alice. With a symmetric cipher, Alice might encrypt or compute a Message Authentication Code (MAC) on some data, but the symmetric key used would have to be revealed to any entity wishing to verify this value. (For an explanation of MAC computation and verification, see [FIPS113].) However, after the key is revealed, the value can no longer be identified with Alice, because this verifier holds the secret information (that is, the key) necessary to have created this value as well. Thus, the computation that Alice performed cannot be considered to be a signature in any strict sense.

Conceptually, one can think of the digital signature operation (Figure 2.3) as a private-key operation on data in which the resulting value is the signature. If Alice is the only entity who knows this private key, she is clearly the only entity who could have signed this data. On the other hand, any entity (because it is able to retrieve a copy of Alice's corresponding public key) can verify the signature by doing a public-key operation on the signature and checking whether this result corresponds to the original data. (Note that this data must have known redundancy for the signature/verification process to be reliable. All digital signature mechanisms therefore specify particular padding conventions for the data, to be applied prior to the signature process itself and to be examined and then removed as part of the verification process.)

**Figure 2.3**    Generic digital signature process.

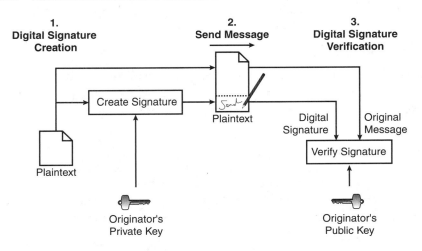

Data to be signed may be of any size (for example, a five-word e-mail message or a 10MB file), but a private-key operation takes a fixed-size input and computes a fixed-size output. To address this problem, a *cryptographic hash function* is used. (See [Pren93] and [PGV93] for an extensive discussion of this topic.) This function has the property that it maps an input of arbitrary size to a fixed-size output (suitable for the input of a private-key operation), and it is computationally infeasible to find two different hash inputs that produce the same hash output. Thus, the signing operation is a two-step process:

1. The signer hashes the data to a fixed-size value.

2. The signer then subjects this value to a private-key operation.

Verification is a similar two-step process:

1. The verifier hashes the data to a fixed-size value.

2. The verifier then examines this value, the transmitted signature, and the signing entity's public key. If the signature matches the key and the hash value, the signature verifies; otherwise, verification fails. (See Chapters 9 and 10 of [Stal99] for a more detailed discussion of hash functions and their use in digital signature creation and verification.)

### Data Integrity

A digital signature provides both data origin authentication (evidence about who originated the data) and data integrity (evidence that the data has not been altered in any way). Difficulty in finding two inputs that hash to the same output is an inherent property of a cryptographic hash function. Thus, any alteration to the data (with virtual certainty) will lead to a different hash value, which will cause a failure in signature verification. If the signature verification is successful, the recipient can feel confident that data integrity has been preserved.

### Key Establishment

Public-key cryptography can also be used to perform key establishment (sometimes called key exchange) between two entities; that is, a protocol can use public and private keys such that, at the conclusion of the protocol, the two entities share a secret symmetric key known by no other entity.

Key establishment can occur in two ways:

• In *key transfer,* one entity generates the symmetric key and sends it to the other entity. Public-key cryptography can be used to protect the confidentiality of this transfer. For example, Alice can encrypt the symmetric key, using Bob's public key.

- In *key agreement,* both entities jointly contribute to the generation of the symmetric key. Public-key cryptography makes such a procedure relatively simple (see, for example, the Diffie–Hellman key establishment protocol [DiHe76]), whereas this would be very difficult to achieve using purely symmetric technology.

## Other Services

The advent of public-key cryptography has enabled a number of other interesting services beyond those listed in the previous sections. These include the construction of provably secure pseudorandom number generators, protocols for playing games (such as poker) and flipping coins over networks in a provably fair way, mechanisms for conducting secure electronic elections, and techniques for Alice to prove to another entity that she knows a secret without ever having to reveal the secret to anyone (known as *zero-knowledge* or *minimum-knowledge* protocols).

If you're interested in these services, see the references listed in the first paragraph of this chapter or the annual proceedings of the major cryptography conferences over the past several years (particularly Crypto and Eurocrypt). (For example, see pages 667–698 in [MvOV97].)

# Algorithms

A number of public-key algorithms exist, and each is suitable for one or more of the services discussed in the previous section. The most well-known examples are mentioned briefly here; see [MvOV97] or [Schn96] for a much more complete explanation of the benefits and uses of the known algorithms.

## RSA

The algorithm proposed by Ron Rivest, Adi Shamir, and Len Adleman in 1978 [RSA78], known as *RSA,* is one of the earliest and most versatile of the public-key algorithms. It is suitable for encryption/decryption, for signing/verification (and, therefore, for data integrity), and for key establishment (specifically key transfer). It can be used as the basis for a secure pseudorandom number generator as well as for the security in some electronic games. Its security is based on the difficulty of factoring very large integers. The current state of factoring research suggests that RSA keys should be at least 1,024 bits long to provide adequate security for the next several years or more.

## DSA

The *Digital Signature Algorithm (DSA)* is a *Federal Information Processing Standard (FIPS)* publication of NIST of the U.S. Department of Commerce [FIPS186]. It is a variant of the

ElGamal signature mechanism [ElGa85]. The DSA was designed exclusively for signing/verification and therefore also for data integrity. Other algorithms in the ElGamal family can be used for encryption/decryption and therefore key transfer, if what is being encrypted and decrypted is a symmetric key. The security of these algorithms is based on the difficulty of computing logarithms in a finite field. The current state of research with respect to discrete logarithms suggests that DSA keys should be at least 1,024 bits long to provide adequate security for the next several years or more.

## DH

The algorithm that Diffie and Hellman proposed, known as *DH,* is a wonderful example of elegance and simplicity [DiHe76]. The earliest public-key algorithm, it is exclusively a key establishment, specifically key agreement, protocol. Each of two entities uses its own private key and the other entity's public key to create a symmetric key that no third entity can compute. The algorithm derives its security from the difficulty of computing logarithms in a finite field. As with DSA, the current state of research with respect to discrete logarithms suggests that DH keys should be at least 1,024 bits long to provide adequate security for the next several years or more.

## ECDSA and ECDH

The DSA and DH algorithms can also be computed over the group of points defined by the solution to an equation for an elliptic curve over a finite field [Kobl87; Mill86]. The resulting elliptic curve DSA (ECDSA) and elliptic curve DH (ECDH) algorithms have identical uses to their finite field counterparts earlier, but the security now rests on the difficulty of computing logarithms over the group of EC points. This different foundation leads to more complicated implementation and processing but has the benefit of significantly smaller key sizes for a similar level of security. The current state of research with respect to discrete logarithms over EC points suggests that ECDH and ECDSA keys should be at least 192 bits long to provide adequate security for the next several years or more.

Note that it is possible to do elliptic curve RSA as well; however, due to the different security basis (integer factorization as opposed to discrete logarithms), the key sizes are not significantly smaller than "ordinary" RSA. Thus, the added complication has no perceived benefit, and ECRSA appears not to be used anywhere.

## SHA-1

The *Secure Hash Algorithm SHA-1,* a slight revision of the original Secure Hash Algorithm SHA, is described in a NIST FIPS publication [FIPS180]. This hash algorithm was designed specifically for use with the DSA but can be used with RSA or other public-key signature algorithms as well. Its design principles are similar to those used in the MD2 [RFC1319], MD4 [RFC1320], and especially MD5 [RFC1321] hash functions proposed by Ron Rivest. Current computational capability suggests that the size of the SHA-1 hash value, 160 bits, provides adequate security for at least the next several years. Hash functions are not public-key algorithms but are included here because digital signature algorithms are always used in conjunction with hash algorithms to provide the services of signing/verification and data integrity. Thus, they are an essential component of the digital signature and integrity security services.

### *Ongoing Work*

The hash algorithm SHA-1 produces a message digest of 160 bits, providing no more than 80 bits of security against collision attacks. The AES offers three key sizes: 128, 192, and 256 bits. But hash algorithms are sometimes used in the generation of keys for symmetric ciphers (for example, a sufficiently long passphrase may be hashed to form a symmetric key that is then used to decrypt a file). Therefore, there is a need for companion hash algorithms that provide similar levels of enhanced security.

New hash algorithms SHA-256, SHA-384, and SHA-512 (informally referred to collectively as "SHA-2" in some circles) [SHA2] have been developed and are expected to be specified in a FIPS publication in the near future. SHA-256 is a 256-bit hash function that is intended to provide 128 bits of security against collision attacks, and SHA-512 is a 512-bit hash function that is intended to provide 256 bits of security. The 384-bit hash can be obtained by truncating the SHA-512 output.

A revised version of DSA that accommodates these larger hash functions is also being developed and is expected to be available as a FIPS publication within the next few years.

Work is also ongoing with respect to "modes of operation" for symmetric ciphers, including AES. See the NIST Special Publication SP 800–38A, "Recommendation for Block Cipher Modes of Operation" at `http://csrc.nist.gov/publication/nistpubs/index.html` for further details.

## Summary

Public-key cryptography is a critically important technology. It realizes the concept of a digital signature; provides a practical, elegant mechanism for symmetric key agreement; and enables secure communication. The idea of a key pair (one key kept private; the other made publicly available) also enables other services and protocols, including confidentiality, data integrity, secure pseudorandom number generation, electronic games, and zero-knowledge proofs of knowledge.

The underlying concepts of public-key cryptography, along with a number of the fundamental algorithms, have reached a stage of relative maturity. This is due to the intense scrutiny and research that has occurred in this area over the past two decades.

To bring the power of public-key technology to entities in a practical way, two related areas need to be explored:

- There needs to be a way to make this technology available to a wide variety of applications and environments in a uniform manner; this need for an infrastructure is discussed in Chapter 3, The Concept of an Infrastructure.

- There needs to be a way to ensure that a public key actually corresponds to the entity with whom Alice wishes to communicate; the concept of a certificate is discussed in Chapter 6.

CHAPTER 3

# The Concept of an Infrastructure

In this chapter, we introduce and discuss the idea of an infrastructure for security by considering the features and benefits of pervasive infrastructures with which we are currently familiar. This leads to a working definition of a *Public-Key Infrastructure (PKI)*, which forms the basis of understanding for all remaining chapters.

## Pervasive Substrate

A *pervasive substrate* is a foundation or underpinning for a large environment such as a corporate organization; an infrastructure may be considered a pervasive substrate. Two familiar infrastructures are the electronic communications infrastructure (that is, the network) and the electric power infrastructure. In the former, the *Local Area Network (LAN)* enables various machines to transfer data among themselves for a variety of purposes; in the latter, the power grid enables a plethora of electronic equipment to get the voltage and current needed for operation. Ultimately, however, the principle is identical: The infrastructure exists so that disparate entities can simply "tap into it" and use it on an as-needed basis.

An infrastructure for security purposes must recognize the same principle and offer the same fundamental benefits. A security infrastructure provides a security underpinning for the entire organization and must be accessible by all applications and objects in the organization that need security. The "entry points" into the security infrastructure must be convenient and uniform, like the TCP/IP stack or the power socket in the wall. Therefore, objects that want to make use of the infrastructure are not unduly hindered from doing so.

The pervasive security infrastructure is fundamentally the sensible architecture for many environments.[1] This architecture avoids piecemeal, point-to-point, ad hoc, non-interoperable solutions, thereby introducing the possibility of manageable, consistent security across multiple applications and computing platforms. It is not difficult to imagine the chaos that would result from every pair of communicants running their own communications lines or from individuals running their own power generators at arbitrarily chosen voltages and currents. Many facets of both ancient and modern society demonstrate that the uniformity and convenience offered by a well-designed, well-defined, pervasive infrastructure are worth the effort involved in the design and definition stages.

## Application Enabler

The primary goal of the security infrastructure is to function as an *application enabler*. The electric power infrastructure is an application enabler in the sense that it enables "applications," such as toasters and lamps, to operate correctly. Furthermore, the generality and utility of the electrical infrastructure is such that it can support "applications" (such as hair dryers, for example) that were unknown at the time it was designed.[2]

The security infrastructure enables applications to add security to their own data or resources and to add security to their interactions with other data or resources. The addition of security must be straightforward and quickly accomplished to be most useful. In particular, accessing the infrastructure is analogous to plugging an electrical device into a wall socket:

- There must be a known, easy-to-use interface.

- The result (that is, the service delivered by the infrastructure) must be predictable and useful.

- The way that the infrastructure achieves that result need not be known to the using device.

---

[1] The definition of a *security infrastructure* is fairly broad, encompassing many things, including consistent naming, authorization policies, policy enforcement, monitoring, auditing, asset management, device access control, and so on. The goal of this chapter is not to suggest that by itself a PKI is a security infrastructure. Rather, it suggests that a PKI can form the basis upon which many important aspects of a security infrastructure may be built and economically managed. (See Chapters 4 and 5 for further discussion.)

[2] The word *application* is used with respect to the security infrastructure in the sense of any module that uses the infrastructure for security purposes, such as a Web browser, an e-mail client, or an IPsec-enabled device.

In particular, it should make no difference to a toaster how electrical energy travels from a generating station to a house or to the various wall sockets within the house. However, when the toaster is plugged into any particular wall socket, the predictable "service" delivered (a given voltage and current) to this well-known interface should enable the toaster to draw the energy it needs to operate correctly.

The security infrastructure must similarly have well-known entry points that can deliver a security service to using devices. *How it does this* need not be known by those devices, but *that it does this* consistently and correctly is essential.

The following three sections discuss important aspects of the service delivered by the pervasive security infrastructure.

## Secure Sign-On

The concept of signing-on (often called logging-in) to an application is very familiar. Typically, the process involves the user entering (1) user identification (user ID or username) and (2) authenticating information (a password or other secret value). Under the assumption that no one other than the legitimate user knows that user's authenticating information, this process can be used to securely "introduce" the user to a specific application.

This process is familiar and commonly used; its associated problems are just as familiar. If the application requiring sign-on is remote from the user (that is, on a different piece of equipment, such as another computer), passwords traveling over unprotected networks are subject to interception and eavesdropping, and even encrypted passwords do not necessarily protect against replay attacks. Furthermore, users are notoriously bad at picking "good" passwords (ones with sufficient length and unpredictability), remembering them without writing them down, and changing them frequently when their local security policy encourages them to do so.

A security infrastructure can help address some of these problems. In particular, having security as a pervasive infrastructure implies that a sign-on event to the infrastructure happens locally (that is, at the device through which the user is physically interacting), and the successful result is securely extended to the remote application when required. Figure 3.1 illustrates this process. Thus, strong authentication mechanisms can be used for these remote sign-on events, and passwords need never travel over the network or be known outside the user's device.

The deployment of a security infrastructure may not eliminate the use of passwords altogether, because passwords may be the mechanism for user authentication to the infrastructure itself. However, it can eliminate a most serious problem commonly associated with the use of passwords: their conveyance over untrusted and insecure networks.

**Figure 3.1** Secure sign-on.

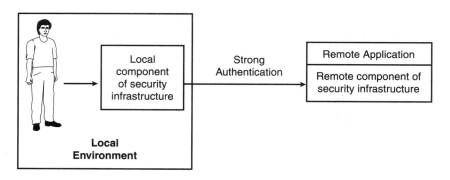

## Secure Single Sign-On

The sign-on problems cited in the preceding section are greatly exacerbated when a user needs to access multiple applications, all of which require an authenticated sign-on event. Using the same password for all applications reduces the overall security by providing multiple points of attack; using a different password for each application reduces overall ease of use. Users can be instructed in proper sign-on procedures, but if those procedures impede the user's work, the user will find ways around the procedures, and these ways will typically be less secure.

The use of a pervasive substrate for security can greatly improve this situation. As stated previously, the security infrastructure can enable the result of a successful sign-on event to be securely communicated to another device normally requiring sign-on, thus removing the need for a remote sign-on event. This feature can be extended so that a successful sign-on event can be communicated to *many* remote devices, thus removing the need for *multiple* sign-on events. Figure 3.2 illustrates a secure single sign-on event. Single sign-on (SSO) is an integral concept to a security infrastructure. Like any system or application requiring sign-on, the security infrastructure has some explicitly encoded sense of a user's "identity" so that it can compare an attempted sign-on with what it expects of the legitimate user. However, that "identity" is understood throughout the full extent of the infrastructure (which could conceivably be global), so it is available to every system and application that plugs into the infrastructure. (This approach to SSO has some disadvantages, such as reduced flexibility in naming entities throughout the infrastructure. However, from an administrative and manageability viewpoint, it may be more attractive than the alternative approach of allowing multiple "identities" for each entity and mapping from one to another "under the covers" as the entity moves among various systems and applications.)

One sign-on would therefore be sufficient to gain access to multiple devices, domains, servers, systems, applications, and so on. Note that these sign-on events may still be combined with

Figure 3.2     Secure single sign-on.

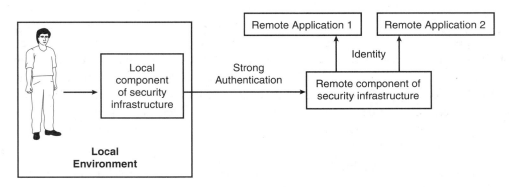

other access control (authorization) mechanisms (see Chapter 5 for further discussion). Thus, secure SSO is very desirable from a usability standpoint because the user has fewer passwords to remember and needs to know only a single procedure to access multiple systems.[3] It is also very desirable from a security standpoint because passwords travel less frequently over the network and because the possibility is higher that the single password chosen by the user will be a "good" one.

Secure SSO is a service that can be delivered by the security infrastructure to all using applications and devices. The infrastructure incorporates the mechanisms required to securely disseminate authentication information when and where it is needed; applications "tap into" the infrastructure to access this information when necessary. This infrastructural service frees the user from having to sign-on multiple times. An additional, important security benefit is that a well-designed infrastructure can ensure that the users sign-on only to the local machine at which they are working. Thus, at least in some cases, passwords do not travel over a vulnerable network, greatly reducing the risks associated with password sniffing/grabbing and password storage/replay attacks. (See pp. 14–15 of [Ande01.]) Furthermore, such a well-designed infrastructure eliminates some difficulties associated with other forms of an SSO solution, such as login state information that needs to be maintained centrally (which is vulnerable to attack and represents a single point of failure for the system).

---

[3]For environments that include a number of legacy applications, an actual SSO may be very difficult or impossible to achieve. In such situations, the discussion presented in this chapter is sometimes referred to as *reduced sign-on*. This may still represent a significant improvement in security, however, because each user has fewer passwords to remember and to manage.

## *End-User Transparency*

A vitally important yet often overlooked feature of a pervasive infrastructure is that it is almost totally transparent to users. The vast majority of users of the communications infrastructure do not need to know about IP headers or Ethernet packets; similarly, the vast majority of users of the electric power infrastructure do not need to know about voltage levels or current ratings. The services of an infrastructure can and should be delivered as a complete "black box" to the users of the infrastructure. A properly designed security infrastructure must have the same characteristic: Virtually all the security should be hidden from the user so that no extra manual intervention is needed, user awareness of keys and algorithms is not required, and user error that compromises security presents little danger.

The idea that users should not have to know the mechanics of how the infrastructure provides security can also be expressed in this way: Security should present no impediment to users in terms of hindering them from doing the tasks that need to be done. Security should require of users no special knowledge, should demand of users no special procedures, and should burden users with no special delays. Other than the initial sign-on event, the infrastructure should perform all security-related tasks in a way that is completely transparent to users.

There are, however, two exceptions to this rule. As with any infrastructure, users need to be made aware of the security infrastructure the first time they come into contact with it (that is, during some kind of initialization procedure) and when it cannot deliver its services. Just as users need to know when a remote machine is not accepting IP packets and need to know when the power is off in the house, they need to know when authentication has failed or when a secure communications channel cannot be established with a remote server. Simply put, the transparency provided by the infrastructure implies a level of trust on the part of users that the infrastructure is operating correctly and can deliver its services. Whenever this fails to be true, users must be notified immediately because the lack of security will typically necessitate a change in user behavior.

## *Comprehensive Security*

Arguably, the most important benefit of a pervasive security infrastructure is this: It ensures that a single, trusted, security technology, such as public-key technology, is available throughout the environment. Unlimited numbers of applications, devices, and servers can then work together seamlessly to secure (1) the transfer, storage, and retrieval of data, (2) transaction processing, and (3) server access, to name a few. E-mail applications, Web browsers, firewalls, remote access devices, application servers, file servers, databases, and more—all can understand and make use of the security infrastructure in a unified way. Such an environment greatly simplifies both the user's dealings with these various devices and applications and the complex job of administering these devices and applications, ensuring that they adhere to a particular level of security policy (which may be increased as needed for specific applications or devices).

One of the primary mechanisms that achieves this comprehensive security within the infrastructure is the ability to ensure that keys are used, understood, and processed in a consistent manner across the broad range of organizational entities and devices. Without a pervasive security infrastructure, it would be almost impossible to provide the same level of operational consistency.

# Business Drivers

*Business drivers* are actual (though not always quantifiable) or perceived benefits to an organization that will influence decision making in one direction or another. A comprehensive security infrastructure, as opposed to a collection of point-to-point solutions between specific applications or devices, offers a number of significant benefits to the organizational environment. These include the following:

- *Cost savings* Implementing a single security solution throughout a large organization will inevitably be less expensive than implementing several, more limited solutions because the incremental cost of adding new users or applications is very modest in the former situation. With multiple solutions, additional users or applications can be difficult or impossible to incorporate, and integration of a new solution with an existing collection of solutions can be a very complex and expensive activity. The cost of deploying, maintaining, and operating multiple point-to-point solutions is also likely to be high, compared with deploying, maintaining, and operating a single infrastructural solution.

- *Interoperability (intra-enterprise)* Multiple, point-to-point solutions can prohibit interoperability because these solutions are developed independently and have incompatible operating paradigms and underlying assumptions. An infrastructure, on the other hand, ensures interoperability because each application or device accesses and uses the infrastructure in an identical manner.

- *Interoperability (inter-enterprise)* Early adopters of any technology typically desire some confidence that their enterprise will be able to interoperate with other enterprises that will deploy solutions in the future. A recognized infrastructural technology based on open, international standards is more likely to instill this confidence than a proprietary, point-to-point technology that is not designed to handle the complexities of multiple domains.

- *Uniform solution* A security infrastructure provides a consistent, uniform solution to all using applications and devices. Such uniformity is much easier to install, manage, and maintain across an organization than a collection of incompatible solutions. Administration cost and complexity therefore strongly favors the infrastructure solution.

- *Possibility of actually achieving security* A security infrastructure offers the possibility that interactions between various applications and devices will actually be secure because all interactions are handled in a consistent manner. Furthermore, the operation and interactions of the infrastructure may have been validated for correctness, for example, by a professional, independent validation agency. Security between independent point-to-point solutions is much less likely, even if each solution has been rigorously validated, because the interaction between these solutions is largely untested.

- *Choice of provider* The provider of the infrastructure may be a particular group within the organization or may be selected from a list of external candidates. In either case, the choice of provider can be made based on expertise, price, functionality, reputation, longevity, and a number of other factors. With point-to-point solutions, the security functionality comes incorporated within the individual application or device. It is very difficult for an organization to make a purchasing decision based purely on the security offered because the application may be highly desirable for any of the other features it offers.

The business drivers for a pervasive security infrastructure are many and varied; the preceding list represents a handful of perhaps the most common arguments. However, the uniformity of the solution (which can lead to interoperability and significant cost savings in administration) and the security offered are probably the primary drivers for an infrastructural solution in many environments.

# Public-Key Infrastructure Defined

Having gained an understanding of public-key cryptography in the previous chapter and an understanding of an infrastructure in this chapter, we are now ready to contemplate the notion of a PKI. The seed idea is very simple:

> A *PKI* is the basis of a pervasive security infrastructure whose services are implemented and delivered using public-key concepts and techniques.

Exploring this rudimentary definition in terms of practical consequences leads to a slightly broader and more realistic definition, whose many parts we discuss briefly here and more fully in the following chapters.

## *Certification Authority*

The fundamental premise in the original formulation of public-key cryptography was that two strangers should be able to communicate securely. For example, when George wants to send a confidential message to Lisa, whom he has not met previously, he will somehow be able to associate a public key with Lisa so that he can encrypt the message for her. With a potential user population of hundreds of thousands or millions of entities, the most practical way to achieve this is to appoint a relatively small number of authorities. These authorities are trusted by a large segment of the population or, perhaps, the entire population to perform the function of binding a public key pair to a given identity. (Refer to Chapter 9 for a working definition of *trust* as it is used throughout this book and to Chapter 14 for a discussion of the concept of *identity*.) Such authorities are called *Certification Authorities (CAs)* in PKI terminology; they *certify* the key pair/identity binding by digitally signing a data structure that contains some representation of the identity and a corresponding public key. This data structure is called a *public-key certificate* (or, more simply, a *certificate*) and will be discussed in some detail in Chapter 6.

Although a CA is not an essential element of every conceivable PKI (especially those that are very limited in size or those that operate in relatively closed environments where users can effectively act as their own authorities), it is a critical component of many large-scale PKIs. The CA therefore forms a part of our expanded PKI definition.

## Certificate Repository

A CA solves only part of the problem mentioned in the previous section (that is, that George needs to associate a public key with Lisa in order to encrypt data for her). The certificate issued by the CA associates a public key with Lisa's identity; unless George is able to locate this certificate easily, however, he is effectively no further ahead than if the certificate had never been created.

Some sort of robust, scalable, on-line repository system must be in place for George to locate the certificates he needs to communicate securely. A *certificate repository* therefore forms a part of our expanded PKI definition; a large PKI would be useless without it. For a discussion regarding various repository technologies and choices (including X.500, LDAP, Web servers, FTP servers, DNS, corporate databases, and others), see Chapter 11.

## Certificate Revocation

The CA signs a certificate binding a public key pair to a user identity. In real-world environments, however, events will necessitate the breaking of that binding. Commonly cited examples include the changing of an identity, such as the transition from a maiden name to a married name or the discovery of a private key by a hacker. There must be a way of alerting the rest of the user population that it is no longer acceptable to use *this* public key for *that* identity. This alerting mechanism in a PKI is called *Certificate Revocation*.

An analogy for PKI Certificate Revocation may be drawn as follows. A driver's license is a form of certificate: a binding of an identity (name and picture) to a driver's license number (that is, a permission to drive) by a trusted authority. When a police officer pulls over a car, the officer does not simply check the expiration date on the license of the driver; he or she also calls an authority to see if the license has been revoked. A revocation check is necessary because sometimes circumstances dictate that the identity/permission binding present in the (unexpired) certificate should no longer be trusted.

Unless certificates have such a short lifetime that they are effectively for one-time use only, some form of revocation is required for those situations in which a certificate must be declared to be invalid. Single-use certificates are impractical in many PKI environments for a number of reasons, including the tremendous load this would place on the CA and the fact that the CA certificate, which holds the public key used to sign the end-user certificates, is necessarily not single use. Limited lifetime certificates (which may be used many times within a finite validity period) lessen the load on the CA but do not remove the need for revocation in all circumstances. Thus, we find that revocation also forms a part of our expanded PKI definition. (Certificate Revocation is discussed further in Chapter 8.)

## Key Backup and Recovery

In any given operational PKI environment, some percentage of users may be expected to lose the use of their private key each fixed time period (for example, each month or each year). This may be due to numerous situations, including the following:

- *Forgotten passwords* A given user's encrypted private key is still physically there but inaccessible.

- *Destruction of a medium* A hard disk crashes, or a smart card breaks, for example.

- *Replacement of a medium* An operating system is reloaded (effectively overwriting local credentials), or an older-model computer is traded for a newer model and the credentials are not transferred before the old disk is reformatted, for example.

For many environments (particularly corporate environments), the loss of data protected by the now-inaccessible key would be totally unacceptable. A business may have critical documents encrypted under a symmetric key that in turn is encrypted under a particular user's public key. If the corresponding private key is lost, those documents are rendered unrecoverable, which may severely hinder, or even halt, the functioning of the business.

One solution to this problem is to encrypt all data for multiple recipients, but this may not always be practical (for example, for highly sensitive data). A much more practical and commonly accepted solution is to implement backup and recovery of private decryption keys (but not private signing keys; see Chapter 2 for a discussion of different key types). The necessity of this approach for many environments means that key backup and recovery will form part of our expanded PKI definition. (See Chapter 7 for further discussion on this topic.)

## Automatic Key Update

A certificate has a finite lifetime. This may be for theoretical reasons, such as the current state of knowledge in cryptanalysis with respect to asymmetric algorithms and key lengths. Alternatively, it may be for reasons based on practical estimations, such as limiting the amount of data typically protected by a single key to a certain number of megabytes. Whatever the reason, however, in many PKI environments, a given certificate will need to "expire" and be replaced with a new certificate. This procedure is called a *key update* or a *certificate update*. (See Chapter 7 for the distinction.)

Most PKI users will find it cumbersome and annoying to go through a manual update procedure on a periodic basis for each of their certificates. Users will not typically remember the date on which their certificate is due to expire, and so they will find this out only when it is too late (that is, when the certificate fails to validate). Therefore, until they complete the update procedure, they will be out of service with respect to the PKI. Furthermore, when the user is in this state, the update procedure is slightly more complicated, requiring an out-of-band exchange with the CA, similar to the initialization process.

The solution is to implement the PKI in such a way that key or certificate update is handled in a totally automated way by the PKI itself, with no user intervention whatsoever. Whenever the user's certificate is about to be used for any purpose, its validity period is checked. When the expiration date is approaching, a renewal operation occurs, and a new certificate is generated. Then, the new certificate is used in place of the old, and the user-requested transaction continues.

Because automatic key update is so vital to an operational PKI in many environments, it will form part of our expanded definition of a PKI. (See Chapter 7 for further discussion on key update.)

## Key History

The concept of key update, whether manual or automatic, implies that, over the course of time, a given user will have multiple "old" certificates and at least one "current" certificate. This collection of certificates and corresponding private keys is known as the user's *key history* (perhaps more properly called *key and certificate history*, but typically the shorter name is used). Keeping track of this entire key history is very important because data that George encrypted for himself or that someone else encrypted for him five years ago cannot be decrypted with his current private decryption key. (Note that reencrypting all data whenever a key is updated is a completely impractical solution in most environments.) George needs his key history so that the correct decryption key can be found to decrypt the required data. Similarly, some of the certificates in this key history will be needed to verify George's five-year-old signatures.

Like key update, the management of key histories must be automatic and totally handled by the PKI. Users typically will not tolerate any system in which they need to somehow select the appropriate private key themselves or, worse, try each private key in turn until the data decrypts to something intelligible. The PKI must hold on to all the keys in the history, perform backup and recovery where appropriate, and find the appropriate key that corresponds to any protected data.

The importance of key history causes it to form a part of our expanded definition of a PKI. (See Chapter 7 for further discussion on key history.)

## Cross-Certification

The concept of a single, global PKI that every user in the world joins is unlikely to become a reality. Rather, what we see today is a model that seems likely to persist: multiple PKIs, independently implemented and operated, serving different environments and user communities.

Given this set of independently developed PKIs, however, it is inevitable that at least some of them will need to be interconnected over time. Changing business relationships or other reasons will necessitate secure communication between the user communities of some PKIs, even if secure communication was not previously a requirement.

The concept of *cross-certification* has arisen in the PKI environment to deal with precisely this need for forming trust relationships between formerly unrelated PKI installations. (See Chapter 9 for a discussion of trust models, trust relationships, and cross-certification.) In the absence of a single, global PKI, cross-certification (or a related concept, the Certificate Trust List; see Chapter 9) is an accepted mechanism for enabling users of one PKI community to validate the certificates of users in another PKI community. In a business setting, the need to interconnect PKIs can arise as a result of mergers, acquisitions, addition of new partners and suppliers, and so on. Without a mechanism for smooth, controlled PKI interconnection, radical and highly disruptive changes would have to occur in the environment, such as revoking all certificates in the acquired company and issuing new ones from the acquiring company. The importance of satisfying the business requirement for interconnected security means that some style of cross-certification will form a part of our expanded PKI definition.

## Support for Non-repudiation

Users of a PKI frequently perform actions intended to be irrevocably associated with their identity. For example, George digitally signs a document, thereby making the claim that the document came from him. For the smooth and uninterrupted flow of business, there is a requirement that users cannot arbitrarily break this association at any time in the future. Months after signing the document, George must not be able to deny that the signature really came from him by claiming that someone else had acquired his private signing key and used it on the document without his knowledge or approval.

Such a denial is referred to as *repudiation* of an action, so a PKI must provide support for avoiding or preventing repudiation—a property known as *non-repudiation*. A PKI cannot by itself provide true or full non-repudiation; typically, a human element is needed to apply discretion and judgment in weighing the evidence and to provide the final decision. However, the PKI must *support* this process by providing some of the technical evidence required, such as data origin authentication and a trusted attestation of the time the data was signed. Support for non-repudiation therefore forms part of our extended definition of a PKI. (Chapter 10 provides further discussion of this topic.)

## Time Stamping

One critical element in the support for non-repudiation services is the use of *secure time stamping* within the PKI. That is, the time source must be trusted, and the time value must be securely conveyed. There must be an authoritative source of time that a collection of PKI users will trust.[4] The authoritative source of time for the PKI (that is, the secure time-stamping server whose certificate is verifiable by the relevant community of PKI users) need not exist solely for the purposes of non-repudiation; many situations arise in which an authoritative time stamp on a document may be useful. However, support for non-repudiation services will perhaps be the primary driver for proper time stamping in many environments. In any case, time stamping forms part of our extended PKI definition. (See Chapter 5 for further discussion on PKI time-stamping services.)

## Client Software

A PKI may be viewed, at least at some level, as a collection of PKI servers that will "do things" for a user, such as the following:

- The CA will provide certification services.

- The repository will hold certificates and revocation information.

- The backup and recovery server will enable the proper management of key histories.

- The time-stamping server will associate authoritative time information with documents.

---

[4]Ironically, the actual time supplied by the authoritative source within the PKI need not be correct; it simply needs to be accepted by the collection of users as the reference time for their PKI-related transactions (for example, event B followed event A). There is no dispute, however, that the use of time that is as close as practicable to the world's official time sources would be preferable.

However, as anyone who understands client–server architecture knows, servers cannot typically do anything for the client unless the client asks for service (that is, makes a request). The same principle holds true for a PKI. The client on the user's local platform must request certification services. The client must ask for certificates and process relevant revocation information. The client must understand key histories and know when to ask for a key update or a key recovery operation. The client must know when it requires a time stamp on a document. On the receiving end of secure communications (where, from an application point of view, a "server" process may be executing), it is still PKI client software that will need to understand (1) policy, (2) if, when, and how revocation status is to be determined, and (3) certificate path processing, to name a few.

Client software is an essential component of a full-featured, fully operational PKI. Without it, the many services offered by the PKI are effectively impotent, because nothing is available to enable them or to make use of them. It is critical to note that this is *not* application software, not PKI-aware code that resides within an application such as a browser or an e-mail package. Such an architecture would fundamentally violate the concept of the PKI as a true *infrastructure*, providing security in a consistent manner across all applications and platforms. Rather, client software is code that exists outside every application and implements the required client end of the PKI services. Applications connect to this client software through standardized entry points, but the applications themselves do not interact with the various PKI servers. That is, applications *use* the infrastructure; they are not *part of* the infrastructure.

It is important to note that the necessity of client-side software implies nothing about the size or permanance of that software. In particular, the client-side component of the PKI may be big or little, ephemeral or long term; that is, it can be

- Quite large (the "fat client"), performing much of the PKI operational processing such as certificate path processing and validation (see Chapters 6 and 9 for discussion of these operations)

- Quite small (the "thin client"), simply calling out to external servers for these PKI functions

- A Java applet or similar mobile code, downloaded in real time on an as-needed basis and then erased when the calling application (such as a Web browser) is shut down

- A Dynamically Linked Library (DLL), or similar, that resides permanently on the client platform

There are many possibilities for how the client-side software is implemented and invoked, but it must be available as an independent component outside all PKI-using applications in order to provide the full benefits of the PKI to the client.

Our expanded definition of a PKI includes client software as an essential component. (See Chapter 12 for further discussion on this topic.)

## Summary

This chapter presented the concept and benefits of a pervasive infrastructure for security services. Like a communications infrastructure or an electric power infrastructure, the security infrastructure offers uniformity and consistency to all using applications and devices.

The benefits that flow from an infrastructural approach to security are varied and numerous. The infrastructure makes security readily available to individual applications, strengthens and simplifies the sign-on process, provides end-user transparency, and offers comprehensive security throughout the environment. Business drivers include cost savings, interoperability, simplified administration, the possibility of real security, and the opportunity to choose a provider with significant security experience and expertise.

A fully functional PKI, because it is the basis of a security infrastructure, encompasses a large number of components and services:

- Certification Authority
- Certificate repository
- Certificate Revocation
- Key backup and recovery
- Automatic key update
- Key history management
- Cross-certification
- Support for non-repudiation
- Time stamping
- Client software

This definition of a PKI, which is more comprehensive than simply *security infrastructure services implemented using public-key techniques,* describes the major areas of functionality required in an operational PKI.

It may be correctly argued that some specific environments do not need all this functionality to meet actual security requirements. For example, a PKI used to enable secure e-mail between friends over the Internet likely has little need of extensive support for non-repudiation. However, a true PKI—conceptually designed as an independent infrastructural entity—may conceivably be deployed in any environment. Thus, it makes sense to define the PKI as an infrastructure with all these components and features and build the PKI according to this definition. In any given deployment, any unnecessary services then can easily be turned off or not installed at all.

Given the concepts of a PKI conveyed in this chapter, two primary needs must be addressed to fill out the understanding of this technology:

- Comprehending in more detail the security services that a PKI can offer

- Discussing each aspect of the PKI definition in more depth

The first need is covered in Chapters 4 and 5; the second need is the focus of Chapters 6 through 12.

# Core PKI Services: Authentication, Integrity, and Confidentiality

In the previous chapter, we looked at the concept of a security infrastructure and gave a definition of a comprehensive PKI. Now, consider the services that a PKI offers an organization. In this chapter, we examine the fundamental, or core, security services associated with a PKI; in Chapter 5, we examine a number of additional services that a PKI can enable for various business purposes.

## Definitions

A PKI is generally considered to be associated with three primary services:

- *Authentication* is the assurance to one entity that another entity is who he, she, or it claims to be.

- *Integrity* is the assurance to an entity that data has not been altered (intentionally or unintentionally) between "there" and "here" or between "then" and "now."

- *Confidentiality* is the assurance to an entity that no one can read a particular piece of data except the receiver(s) explicitly intended.

The following sections explore these brief definitions in greater detail.

### Authentication

Authentication, the assurance that an entity is who he, she, or it claims to be, typically finds application in two primary contexts, entity identification and data origin identification.

*Entity identification*, by itself, serves simply to identify the specific entity involved, essentially in isolation from any other activity that the entity might want to perform. This is clearly of limited value (because the entity will typically want to perform other activities on the basis of its identity). Therefore, in practice, entity identification generally produces a concrete result that is then used to enable other activities or communications. For example, the process of entity identification may result in (or unlock) a symmetric key that can subsequently be used to decrypt a file for reading or modification or to establish a secure communications channel with another entity. The identity itself, once authenticated, may also be associated with a set of privileges on an Access Control List (ACL) for the purpose of making access control decisions.

The preceding remarks are not meant to downplay the importance of entity identification. Without a strong mechanism for this form of authentication, a secure system cannot exist. Authentication is a crucial and necessary first step to a secure system's operation, but it is only a first step, a means to an end. Authentication itself is not the ultimate goal.

*Data origin identification* identifies a specific entity as the source or origin of a given piece of data. This is not entity identification in isolation, nor is it entity identification for the explicit purpose of enabling some other activity. Rather, this is identification with the intent of statically and irrevocably binding the identified entity to some particular data, regardless of any subsequent activities in which the entity might engage. Such a process can provide support for a non-repudiation service. (See Chapter 5 for a discussion on non-repudiation.)

### Entity Identification: Local versus Remote

The area of authentication known as entity identification can be divided into two categories:

- Initial entity identification to the local environment—that is, to the entity's personal, physically proximate device with no communications to other devices on the network

- Entity identification to a remote device, entity, or environment

*Local authentication*—initial authentication of an entity to the local environment—almost always involves the user directly and explicitly (a password or PIN must be entered; a thumbprint scan must be taken). By contrast, *remote authentication*—authentication of an entity to some remote environment—may or may not involve the user directly. In fact, the more sophisticated remote authentication systems do not explicitly involve the user for two reasons:

1. It is hard to defend an authentication system that takes sensitive authenticating information, such as a password or thumbprint, and passes it over insecure lines (where it may be copied for later reuse by an unscrupulous party) to a remote location.

2. It is inconvenient for users to have to reenter authenticating information each time that they want to make a remote network connection.

Thus, a preferable solution is for the result, or the *effect,* of the local authentication process to be conveyed to the remote location without passing the actual authenticating value itself. For example, when the entity needs to access a remote environment, a secure communications session could be established between the two environments so that the local environment can essentially say, "Here is the identity; I have already ensured it is correct." Therefore, the password, PIN, or thumbprint does not need to be sent to the remote environment. Note that such a solution can also be used for *subsequent authentication* (that is, after a successful initial authentication) to other applications within the local environment to achieve secure single sign-on (SSO). (See Chapter 3.)

### Entity Identification: Single Factor versus Multifactor

There are many ways of proving an identity. These can be divided into four categories:

- Something you *have* (such as a smart card or a hardware token)

- Something you *know* (such as a password or a PIN)

- Something you *are* or something intrinsic to your body (such as a thumbprint or a retinal scan)

- Something you *do* (such as your typing characteristics or handwriting style)

The concept of *single-factor authentication* is that only a single method among the preceding options is used. *Multifactor authentication* uses more than one of the options simultaneously during the authentication process (two-factor uses two, three-factor uses three, and so on). A familiar example of two-factor authentication is the sign-on process at an ATM in which the user inserts a magnetic-stripe card ("something you have") and enters a PIN ("something you know") to gain access to his or her bank account. Clearly, multifactor systems are more burdensome for the user (more tasks need to be completed before the authentication process is finished). However, the security benefit is that impersonation attacks become much more difficult. (The would-be impersonator needs, for example, to know your password, imitate your typing style, and borrow your thumb without you knowing about it—all at the same time!)

### Authentication as a PKI Service

One reason to distinguish between local and remote authentication (and between initial and subsequent authentication) is to distinguish between where a PKI can be helpful and where it cannot. Specifically, a PKI would rarely, if ever (one might even say "never"), be used for initial authentication of a human entity to the local environment because a user is unlikely to *know* a private key (due to its length). Even if the key were known, it would be highly unlikely for the user to perform cryptographic calculations with it.

Also, nothing intrinsic to the user (such as a thumbprint or retinal scan) could be said to *be* the private key of a signing key pair. Similarly, nothing the user *does* (such as typing characteristics or handwriting style) is deterministic enough (in a strict sense) to be usable for generating a key pair. Finally, although the user may *have* something that contains a key pair and can do cryptographic calculations (such as a smart card), such devices are so easily lost or stolen that they are almost never allowed to function without the user entering a password or a PIN.

Thus, initial authentication to the local environment, whether single factor or multifactor, does not use the services of a PKI. Authentication to a remote environment (or subsequent authentication within the local environment), on the other hand, can. When remote authentication does not use a PKI, there are two possibilities:

1. The user must authenticate explicitly to the remote environment.

2. The proof of authentication from the local environment must somehow be conveyed to the remote environment.

In either case, the communication between the local and remote environments must be properly protected; otherwise, an eavesdropper can simply copy the relevant data and later replay it, thereby successfully masquerading as the original, legitimate entity. Properly protecting the communications may mean employing mechanisms that are difficult to administer or that do not scale well to large environments, such as preestablishing shared symmetric keys between the respective communicating processes. (See Chapter 6 for a discussion on scalability issues.)

For these reasons, the benefits in using a PKI for remote authentication can be attractive. The complexity of preestablishing shared keys between processes is eliminated, as is the security risk of transmitting sensitive authenticating information (such as a password or a thumbprint) over a network. Rather, public-key technology is used to achieve the authentication using sophisticated challenge-response protocols (see, for example, pages 397–405 of [MvOV97]) and signed messages.

The distinct advantage of public-key-based remote authentication over mechanisms that mimic authentication to the local environment is that sensitive authenticating information, such as a password, is never sent over the network. If server Alice holds a copy of client Bob's password or thumbprint, Bob must authenticate himself by proving that he knows or has this information; this is typically accomplished by Bob conveying this information to Alice upon sign-on. (See Figure 4.1.)

By contrast, if Alice holds a copy of Bob's verification public key, she can ask Bob to sign a one-time challenge message with the corresponding signing private key (which only Bob knows); if the signed response is returned, Bob has authenticated himself without having to reveal any sensitive information. (See Figure 4.2.) Nothing travels over the network that can be used by an eavesdropper to later impersonate Bob. Furthermore, Alice and Bob do not need to engage in a costly and inconvenient process to preestablish shared secret information

**Figure 4.1**   Bob authenticates to Alice, using an ID/password pair.

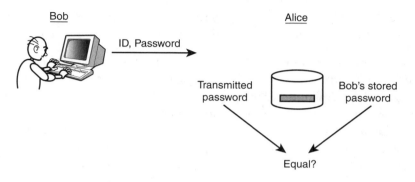

**Figure 4.2**   Bob authenticates to Alice, using public-key-based remote authentication.

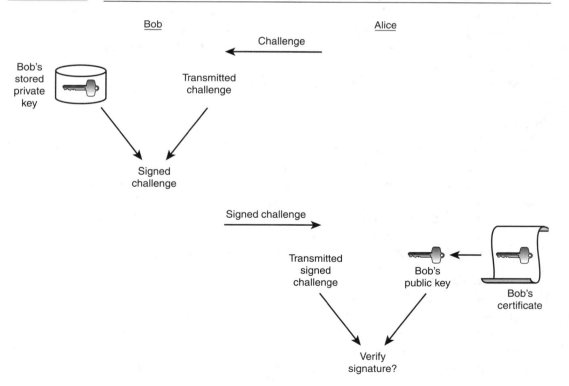

(for example, to preload Alice with a copy of Bob's password or thumbprint). Alice may simply retrieve a copy of Bob's public key from his verification certificate, which, for example, may be stored in a publicly known and publicly accessible repository or may have been sent directly to Alice from Bob. (See Chapter 6 for a discussion on certificates.)

One very appealing benefit of the authentication service associated with the PKI is the possibility of SSO to PKI-enabled devices (and perhaps, through gateway servers, to other types of devices as well). Specifically, a user may sign-on initially to the local environment (using single-factor or multifactor authentication, as appropriate). This process results in the user gaining local access to his or her private key(s). The signing private key can then be used to authenticate the user automatically and transparently to other servers and devices around the network whenever he or she wants to establish a connection with them. The user may freely roam both the local and remote environments without the need to enter a password or to place a thumb on the biometric print scanner again. (See Chapter 3 for a discussion on secure SSO.)

The PKI therefore offers an authentication service with a number of definite advantages over non-PKI–based authentication mechanisms. Entity identification is possible with PKI authentication, in which case the entity's signing private key is used to authenticate the entity to other entities in the local or remote environment. It also can be used for data origin authentication. In this case, the entity's signing private key is used to bind the entity to a particular piece of data (perhaps as non-repudiable evidence that can be used subsequently to prove to a third party that this entity did originate—or at least possess—this data).

## Integrity

*Data integrity* is the assurance of *nonalteration:* The data (either in transit or in storage) has not been undetectably altered. Clearly, such assurance is essential in any kind of business or electronic commerce environment, but it is desirable in many other environments as well. A level of data integrity can be achieved by mechanisms such as parity bits and *Cyclic Redundancy Codes (CRCs)*. Such techniques, however, are designed only to detect some proportion of accidental bit errors; they are powerless to thwart deliberate data manipulation by determined adversaries whose goals are to modify the content of the data for their own gain.

To protect data against this sort of attack, cryptographic techniques are required. Thus, appropriate algorithms and keys must be employed and commonly understood between the entity wanting to provide data integrity and the entity wanting to be assured of data integrity. The PKI service of integrity can be extremely useful in meeting the needs of both entities because it is the framework through which algorithm selection and key agreement can take place. Furthermore, such negotiations can occur in a way that is completely transparent to the entities involved so that integrity can be assumed in all PKI-related data transactions. (This situation changes only when integrity verification fails for some specific piece of data, in which case the user must be notified so that appropriate action can be taken.)

## Confidentiality

*Confidentiality* is the assurance of data privacy: No one may read the data except for the specific entity (or entities) intended. Confidentiality is a requirement when data is

- Stored on a medium (such as a computer hard drive) that can be read by an unauthorized individual

- Backed up onto a device (such as a tape) that can fall into the hands of an unauthorized individual

- Transmitted over unprotected networks

Furthermore, given the sophistication and power of determined adversaries today, cryptographic techniques for providing confidentiality must be employed for all sensitive data. As with integrity, this necessitates a common understanding between entities of appropriate algorithms and keys. The PKI confidentiality service is the framework through which such a common understanding can be reached in a way that is transparent to the actual entities involved. Other non-PKI–based confidentiality services require explicit entity interaction at some level and therefore are more error prone and more cumbersome to use.

# Mechanisms

This section gives a brief overview of the cryptographic mechanisms used to enable the PKI services of authenticity, integrity, and confidentiality. (See [MvOV97] for further discussion.)

## Authentication

The PKI service of authentication (as opposed to the non-PKI operation of initial authentication to the local environment, which may involve single-factor or multifactor authentication including passwords or biometric devices) employs the cryptographic technique of a digital signature. The signature may be computed over the hash of one of the following three values:

1. Some data to be authenticated

2. Some request that the user intends to send to a remote device

3. A random challenge issued by a remote device

The first issue supports the PKI service of data origin authentication; the latter two support the PKI service of entity authentication.[1]

A good cryptographic hash function is required to reduce the data or the request message to a size suitable for a single computation of the signature function. It is also helpful in preventing an attacker from getting the decryption of a random-looking value (in certain signature algorithms such as RSA [RSA78]), which may yield valuable information in some circumstances [KaRo95]. (Digital signatures and hash functions are introduced in Chapter 2.)

## *Integrity*

The PKI service of integrity may employ one of two techniques. First, a *digital signature*, although it serves the purpose of providing authenticity (that is, entity authentication), simultaneously provides integrity over the signed data. This is a consequence of a necessary property of cryptographic hash algorithms and signature algorithms; any change in the input data leads to a large, unpredictable change in the output with very high probability. In other words, if the data has changed (either by accident or by deliberate manipulation) between "there" and "here" or between "then" and "now," the signature will fail to verify, and the loss of integrity will be obvious to the recipient. If, on the other hand, the signature verifies, the recipient is very likely to be in possession of the original (that is, unaltered) data.

The second technique that can be employed for integrity is a *Message Authentication Code (MAC)*. This technique typically uses a symmetric block cipher (for example, DES-CBC-MAC [FIPS113]) or a cryptographic hash function (for example, HMAC-SHA-1 [RFC2104]). (See Chapter 2 for a discussion of ciphers and hash functions.)

Although these are both symmetric solutions (as opposed to public-key solutions), it is important to note that both are keyed mechanisms; in particular, they depend on a key that must be shared between both the sender and the "consumer" (for example, receiver) of the integrity-protected data. In some environments, the shared key can be derived using the key establishment functions of a PKI. (See IPsec [RFC2401, RFC2411], for example.)

The PKI service of integrity for this second technique, then, is that of putting in place the mechanisms to achieve this key sharing when necessary. If Alice wants to send to Bob some integrity-protected data and Bob has an encryption public key, Alice can employ the following sequence of steps:

---

[1]Whether entity authentication is done through a signature on a user request or through a signature on a random challenge depends on the operational characteristics and requirements of a particular environment. Typically, environments in which entities have access to a common, trusted source of time will use the first alternative; environments in which nonce values will be used (instead of time stamps) to provide replay protection will use the second alternative.

1. Generate a fresh symmetric key (that is, one that she has not used before).

2. Use the symmetric key to generate a MAC for the data.

3. Encrypt the symmetric key for Bob, using his encryption public key.

4. Send the data to Bob, along with the encrypted key.

Alternatively, if Bob has a key agreement public key (such as a Diffie–Hellman public key—see Chapter 2), Alice can instead use the following procedure:

1. Use Bob's key agreement public key in combination with her key agreement private key to generate a symmetric key.

2. MAC the data, using that symmetric key.

3. Send the data to Bob, along with her public-key certificate.

Bob can then regenerate the symmetric key, using Alice's public key and his own private key, to verify the integrity of the data.

Thus, digital signatures or MAC functions may be used in conjunction with a PKI to provide data integrity. (Digital signatures and MAC functions were introduced in Chapter 2.)

### *Confidentiality*

The PKI service of confidentiality uses a mechanism similar to one of the alternatives of the integrity service. That is,

1. Alice generates a symmetric key (perhaps by using her key agreement private key in combination with Bob's key agreement public key).

2. The symmetric key is used to encrypt the data (using a symmetric block cipher such as CAST-128 [RFC2144]).

3. The encrypted data is sent to Bob, either along with Alice's key agreement public key or with a copy of the symmetric key encrypted with Bob's encryption public key.

Chapter 2 introduces key agreement and key transfer mechanisms to establish a symmetric key between the entities, Alice and Bob.

## Operational Considerations

Operational considerations must be taken into account when a PKI is associated with its core services of authentication, integrity, and confidentiality. These include the following: performance, on-line versus off-line operation, commonality of underlying algorithms, and entity naming. Each is described further in the following sections.

## *Performance*

Public-key operations are significantly slower than symmetric key operations. Thus, although an encryption public key theoretically can be used to encrypt large quantities of data, in a practical system it is virtually never used for this purpose. Rather, the data is encrypted using a symmetric key, and that key is encrypted in a single operation using an encryption public key. Similarly, a symmetric-key-based MAC will typically be a preferred data integrity mechanism unless a digital signature is already required for the purpose of data origin authentication.

The PKI services of integrity and confidentiality therefore consist of the less-performance-intensive key-sharing (or key establishment) aspects, rather than the more-performance-intensive signature or data encryption aspects. This combination of public-key and symmetric key mechanisms provides the required services at a performance cost that is acceptable for many environments.

## *On-line versus Off-line Operation*

One significant advantage of a PKI over a purely symmetric key–based infrastructure is the possibility of off-line operation. That is, Alice can sign data, integrity-protect data, or encrypt data for Bob, or she can verify Bob's signature on data, verify Bob's integrity protection on data, or decrypt data from Bob, all while she is working off-line (for example, on her laptop, which is not connected to the network). Alice will not have access to the most current revocation status information (see Chapter 8) when she works in this mode; in some circumstances and for some types of communication, however, this may be acceptable.

The desire for off-line operation may determine the key establishment mechanisms available for use. For example, real-time, peer-to-peer key exchange using an algorithm such as *ephemeral–ephemeral Diffie–Hellman (DH)* would not be possible. (See Box 4.1.) However, non-real–time

## Box 4.1   DH Communication Configurations

In ephemeral–ephemeral DH, each party in the key establishment protocol generates an ephemeral key pair (that is, one that has never been used before and is never to be used again) solely for the purposes of this protocol. In ephemeral–static DH, one of the parties, Bob for example, generates an ephemeral key pair for this protocol, and the other party, Alice, uses a preexisting key pair. In particular, Alice's preexisting public key can be contained in a certificate that Bob can hold locally or obtain from a public repository prior to engaging in the protocol. In static–static DH, both Alice and Bob use preexisting key pairs.

key exchange using *ephemeral–static DH* or *static–static DH* is entirely possible, as well as key exchange using an algorithm such as *Rivest–Shamir–Adleman (RSA)*. Thus, although every mechanism choice may not be available, the core PKI services are available and operational during off-line mode.

## Commonality of Underlying Algorithms

A fundamental requirement for the PKI to operate is that a common understanding of algorithms can be achieved between PKI entities. This understanding may be limited and rigid in that a fixed, single algorithm for providing each PKI service is hard-coded into each entity upon start-up (that is, a digital signature algorithm, a hash algorithm, a key transfer algorithm, a key agreement algorithm, a MAC algorithm, and a symmetric cipher algorithm).

Much more often, however, this understanding is fluid and dynamic in that an entity, Alice, will "discover" the algorithm(s) acceptable to Bob at the time she needs to communicate with Bob. Alice will therefore use the algorithm appropriate for both the circumstances of the communication and the intended recipient(s) of the communication. Algorithm discovery can be accomplished through the use of certificates (that is, Bob's preferred algorithm is encoded within his public-key certificate; see Chapter 6 for a discussion on certificates), or through the "supported algorithms" attribute associated with Bob's directory entry (see example, Paragraph 11.2.7 of [X.509–00]).

Alternatively, algorithm discovery can be accomplished through the use of authenticated negotiation ("handshaking") protocols (such as Internet Key Exchange, or IKE [RFC2409], for example), out-of-band communications, or some other means. Whatever the mechanism, a commonality of underlying algorithms must be achieved so that communication between PKI entities and therefore the set of security services offered by the PKI can occur.

## Entity Naming

An assumption implicit in much of the preceding discussion is that entity Bob has an identity that is known to and understood by entity Alice. Alice somehow knows, prior to sending data to Bob, that this is the *particular* Bob to whom she wants to send this data. This problem is typically known as the entity-naming problem: How can names be assigned to entities in a way that is unique and meaningful to other relevant entities?

Many, varied techniques exist for solving this problem; they include the extreme suggestion that no solution exists and that the use of entity naming should be avoided entirely. This topic is discussed in more detail in Chapter 9; for the time being, note that Alice must have some way of knowing with whom she is communicating for that communication to be meaningful and relevant.

## Summary

Authentication (both entity authentication and data origin authentication), integrity, and confidentiality are the core security services provided by a PKI. These services enable entities to prove that they are who they claim to be, to be assured that important data has not been altered in any way, and to be convinced that data sent to another entity can be read only by that entity. Organizations can derive tremendous benefits from these services by using them to ensure, for example, that highly sensitive information gets into the hands of only those with an explicit "need-to-know."

Two needs must be addressed to make these core security services fully available to PKI entities:

- It must be possible for entity Alice to associate a public key unambiguously and correctly with Bob, the entity with whom she wants to communicate. This is the fundamental purpose for the concept of a certificate. (This topic is discussed in Chapter 6.)

- To deal with the relatively common situation in which Alice does not already have Bob's certificate, Alice must have the capability to retrieve that certificate from a public repository. In this way, she can communicate securely with him. (Recall that the underlying premise of public-key cryptography is that secure communication between strangers can be achieved precisely through the use of such public repository concepts. The description and use of public repositories for certificate information is the topic of Chapter 11.)

# 5

# PKI-Enabled Services

In the previous chapter, we discussed the core security services offered by a PKI: authenticity, integrity, and confidentiality. In this chapter, we look at security services that in some way can be *enabled* by a PKI. That is, these are not services inherent in or fundamental to any PKI; rather, they are services that can build on the core PKI services. Some PKIs may support these auxiliary services, and others may not.

## Secure Communication

*Secure communication* can be defined as the transmission of data from a sender to a receiver with one or more of the properties of authenticity, integrity, and confidentiality. This service clearly relies on the core PKI services, but it uses them in conjunction with traditional networking and communications protocols to create an expanded, PKI-enabled service. The following are just a few examples of secure communication:

- Secure e-mail (using, for example, a protocol such as Secure Multipurpose Internet Mail Extensions Version 2, S/MIMEv2, [RFC2311, RFC2312] or S/MIMEv3 [RFC2632, RFC2633])

- Secure Web server access (using, for example, a protocol such as Transport Layer Security, or TLS, [RFC2246])

- A secure Virtual Private Network, or VPN (using, for example, a protocol such as IPsec/ IKE [RFC2401, RFC2411])

Secure e-mail, for example, can be implemented as a PKI-enabled service simply by having the e-mail package access the core security services of the PKI to encrypt and sign messages and format the result using the S/MIME syntax. Messages can then be transported across an untrusted network without compromising their authenticity, integrity, or confidentiality.

## Secure Time Stamping

*Secure time stamping* involves a trusted time authority associating a time stamp with a particular piece of data with the properties of authenticity and integrity. What is important is not so much the actual time format itself but the security of the time/data association. In particular, for some applications the time stamp need not explicitly represent time at all; a simple sequence number demonstrating that this document was presented to the authority *before* document X and *after* document Y may be sufficient. However, interested parties must be able to verify that the time stamp associated with this document is authentic and has integrity.

The time-stamp authority is also not strictly required for this service. An alternative is to have secure (that is, trusted) time available at every entity's local environment; each entity can then securely associate a time stamp with its own data as needed. In practice, however, it is typically difficult to get secure time to every local environment (for example, every user desktop). Thus, the approach often taken is to get secure time to only a very small number of locations in the network (perhaps only one)—these then become the trusted time-stamp authorities—and to have entities request time stamps on data from these authorities when required.

The secure time-stamp service makes use of the core PKI services of authentication and integrity.[1] Specifically, the time stamp on a document involves a digital signature over the combination of some representation of time and a cryptographic hash of the document itself. (The signature of the authority provides both authenticity and data integrity.)

For this scheme to work, all relevant PKI entities need to know and trust the time-stamp authority verification public key so that the signature on the time stamp can be verified and trusted. If such a public key becomes untrusted (for example, through compromise of the time stamp authority's signing private key), the PKI entities need to be informed of this and then reinitialize with another trusted key for that authority, using some secure out-of-band process. All time stamps signed using that untrusted key would be recognized as invalid.

## Notarization

The term *notarization* (that is, the primary service of a notary) can be a source of confusion in some environments because it means different things in different legal frameworks. For the purposes of this book, the PKI-enabled service of notarization is defined to be synonymous

---

[1]Although secure time stamping can be implemented as a PKI-enabled service, it is entirely possible to implement a secure time stamping service without exclusive reliance on an underlying PKI. (See, for example, [HaSt91].)

with *data certification*. That is, the notary *certifies* that data is valid or correct, in which the meaning of *correct* necessarily depends on the type of data being certified. For example, if the data to be certified is a digital signature over some hashed value, the notary may certify that the signature is "valid" in the following sense:

- The signature verification computation with the appropriate public key is mathematically correct.

- The public key is still validly associated with the entity purporting to have signed the value.

- All other data required in the validation process (such as additional certificates to form a complete path; see Chapter 9 for details) is accessible and trustworthy.

The *PKI notary* is an entity trusted by some collection of other PKI entities to perform the notarization service properly. It certifies the correctness of data through the mechanism of a digital signature; the other PKI entities therefore need a trusted copy of the notary's verification public key so that the signed data certification structure can be verified and trusted.

The PKI-enabled service of notarization relies on the core PKI service of authentication. It will typically also rely on the PKI-enabled service of secure time stamping because the notary must include the time at which the notarization was done in the data certification structure.

# Non-repudiation

*Non-repudiation* is the term used for the service that ensures, to the extent technically possible, that entities remain honest about their actions. The most commonly discussed variants are *non-repudiation of origin* (in which a user cannot falsely deny having originated a message or document) and *non-repudiation of receipt* (in which a user cannot falsely deny having received a message or document). However, other variants have been defined, including *non-repudiation of creation, non-repudiation of delivery,* and *non-repudiation of approval.* The basic idea is that a user is cryptographically bound to a specific action in such a way that subsequent denial of that action, to some extent, constitutes an admission of malice or negligence.

As a particular example, if Bob sends a digitally signed receipt to Alice, claiming that he received a specific message from her, he cannot later deny having received the message without in effect admitting one of the following:

- He knowingly gave his signing private key to a third party to allow the possibility of repudiating the message receipt.

- His signing private key was compromised without his knowledge (and, he was therefore somewhat negligent in protecting it properly).

The "non-repudiation of receipt" service gives Alice some assurance that Bob will honestly stand by the digitally signed receipt that he sent.

### Connection with Other Services

Non-repudiation is necessarily a PKI-enabled service; it cannot be based on a symmetric infrastructure. This is because to communicate in a symmetric-key–based environment, Alice and Bob must share a symmetric key. Bob creates a receipt, protects it with the symmetric key, and sends it to Alice. However, Alice could instead have created the receipt to implicate Bob (since both Alice and Bob know the symmetric key). Bob can repudiate his actions simply by claiming that Alice created the incriminating evidence. As a PKI-enabled service, this avenue is closed to Bob because the incriminating evidence (the signed receipt) employs a key known to Bob alone; Alice cannot be blamed for the creation of the receipt unless Bob's private key has been compromised by some means.

Non-repudiation is not a stand-alone PKI-enabled service, however; it relies on the existence of other PKI-enabled services to function. In particular, non-repudiation requires the secure time-stamping service to provide evidence that a specific event occurred at a specific time or that a specific piece of data existed prior to a specific date. In addition, non-repudiation can benefit from the data certification (notarization) service as a convenient method for "packaging" evidence into structures suitable for storage. These services also necessarily rely on the core PKI services of authentication, integrity, and confidentiality.

### Need for a Secure Data Archive

Another service required for non-repudiation is *archival:* Evidence in the form of expired certificates, old Certification Revocation Lists (CRLs), time-stamp tokens, data certification structures, and other related data must be securely stored (archived) in preparation for a potential need when they may be required for dispute resolution.

It is important to note, however, that a "simple" archive service will not be sufficient in many environments. The stored evidence may need to be cryptographically protected for authenticity and integrity, using a digital signature (to allow easy public verification of the archive contents). Furthermore, as the signing key expires and is replaced by a new key (see Chapter 7 for a discussion of key/certificate life-cycle management), the associated evidence must be re-signed with the new key. This in effect produces an unbroken trail of keys leading back in time to the date at which the evidence was initially created. In practice, the unbroken trail of signing keys will be associated with the corresponding trail of verification certificates, as well as a statement attesting to the time of each successive signature.

### Complexity of This Service

In some ways, non-repudiation is the most difficult and complex of all the PKI-enabled services. Perhaps the biggest reason for this is that its primary purpose is to gather evidence attesting to the validity of an event that will be convincing to an unbiased, external third party. Clearly there are no hard and fast rules here. How much evidence is enough? What will a third party require at some indeterminate time in the future? How can it be proven that the evidence has never been manipulated or tampered with? How can a third party be assured that all due diligence was taken to gather as complete a set of evidence data as possible at the time of evidence creation?

These and other questions demonstrate the difficulties and intricacies involved in properly implementing a non-repudiation service.

### The Human Factor

Regardless of the best intentions of those involved in designing and implementing the technical aspects of the PKI-enabled non-repudiation service, there will almost always be a need for nonautomated (that is, human) judgment in the eventual dispute resolution. Yes, the receipt to Alice was signed with Bob's private key, but Bob makes a convincing case that it was only three days *after* the purported signing event that he discovered his key had been compromised two weeks *prior* to the signing event. The (human) judge will have to weigh all evidence (including this new noncryptographically protected claim) and rule in favor of either Bob or Alice.

For this reason, it is incorrect to say that a PKI can *provide* non-repudiation; this can never be done if humans must be involved in the dispute resolution phase. Rather, a PKI can be said to provide or implement a service that *supports* non-repudiation (in that it creates, maintains, and archives some of the evidence that will be needed when dispute resolution is performed).

## Privilege Management

*Privilege management* is a generic term for what is variously called authorization, access control, rights management, permissions management, capabilities management, and so on. Specifically, this topic addresses what an entity is allowed to see and do within a particular environment. This topic encompasses questions such as the following:

Is Alice allowed to read this record in the database?

Can Bob execute this application program?

Should Christine be granted remote access to this network?

Must David be prevented from seeing pages in this portion of the Web server?

Are purchase orders for over $10,000 from Erica to be accepted?

Policies (sometimes referred to as *rules*) must be defined for individual entities, particular groups of entities, or designated entity roles within an environment. These policies specify what these entities, groups, and roles are allowed to do and (either explicitly or implicitly) what they are not allowed to do. Privilege management is the creation and enforcement of these policies for the purpose of enabling day-to-day business while maintaining a desired level of security.

## Authentication and Authorization

Noting the distinction *and* the synergy between the concepts of authentication and authorization is important. *Authentication* is concerned with who an entity is; it is the association of an identity with an entity. *Authorization* is concerned with what that identity is allowed to see and do. Authorization does not prove that the entity requesting remote access to the network is Bob; it merely says that if it *is* Bob, he should be allowed in.

Authentication and authorization, then, must necessarily work together in many circumstances. Authentication without authorization is useful for some purposes (for example, for data origin identification, see Chapter 4). Conversely, authorization without authentication may be useful for some purposes (for example, to gain access to a Web site intended only for citizens of a particular country, being able to prove possession of the required citizenship without having to identify oneself as well may be desirable). However, authentication and authorization are often linked because the privileges of an identity, group, or role are of no help unless it can be determined that a specific entity has a particular identity or belongs to a particular group or role (and group/role membership is typically tied to an identity).

## Authorization Authorities

In the physical world, the concept of *authorization authorities* is widely recognized and well understood. When Bob is a child, his mother, father, baby-sitter, teacher, and others tell him what he can and cannot do. When he is an adult, he is still granted and denied specific privileges by his boss, his doctor, his financial institution, and his government.

In the electronic world, authorization authorities must still exist, though their presence may or may not be explicit. One or more entities will still have the authority to associate specific privileges with specific identities, groups, or roles within a given environment. Ideally, this association will be made using cryptographic techniques to prevent malicious tampering, but this may not be necessary in all environments (for example, where secure local storage of privilege information can be assumed for some particular entity locations).

Authorization authorities may be established in a centralized or distributed manner (that is, there may be a single authorization authority for all entities in the environment, or there may be a collection of authorities with varying needs for communication among them). The distributed scheme perhaps more closely models the physical world with which we are familiar, but both schemes have their utility.

## Delegation

The notion of privilege quickly leads to the notion of *delegation*. If Alice has a certain privilege, can she pass that privilege on to another entity, such as Bob (perhaps with some restrictions or limitations)? For example, if Alice has unrestricted access to a certain Web site in order to perform a specific job function, can she arrange that her colleague Bob have access to that site to do that job while she is out of the office next Tuesday? For a number of environments, such functionality can be very useful.

Delegation comes in two flavors: blinded and nonblinded. *Blinded delegation* occurs when Alice has delegated some privilege to Bob and the entity verifying Bob's authorization cannot determine that this delegation has occurred. That is, from the entity's point of view, Bob was granted this privilege directly by a trusted authorization authority, and Alice had no role whatsoever in this process. With *nonblinded delegation,* it is obvious to the entity that Alice originally had this privilege and has passed it on to Bob for some period of time. This is sometimes called *auditable delegation* (delegation with an audit trail), or power-of-attorney delegation, because the complete delegation path from authorization authority to final privilege holder is obvious to the verifying entity.

Both types of delegation may have their uses and benefits, but it can be argued that nonblinded delegation more closely suits the business requirements of corporate and financial environments (because, for example, there is more certainty with respect to liability in case of malicious use that causes financial loss).

## Connection with the PKI

As discussed earlier, privilege management generally requires authentication in order to be useful. In theory, any authentication mechanism can be used, although the benefits inherent in using the authentication service associated with a PKI can be very attractive in some environments. In particular, the strength of public-key-based authentication (compared with typically weak user passwords) and the convenience of secure single sign-on (SSO), coupled with the added features of a good authorization infrastructure, bring comprehensive security to an organization.

# Privacy

*Privacy* (an entity's ability to control how, when, and to what extent personal information about it is communicated to others; see Brands [Bran00], p. 20) is not commonly thought of or discussed as a possible PKI-enabled service, probably because PKI is often associated with certificates and certificates are generally assumed to contain some sort of (locally if not globally unique) identifying information. But privacy can be supported by a PKI if such "identifying information" is decoupled from the real-world identities of the human users. That is, certificates may be *anonymous* or *pseudonymous* to observers of a transaction. (See Box 5.1.)

---

**Box 5.1**   Anonymous and Pseudonymous Certificates

An anonymous certificate contains an *anonym* (no name, or a completely meaningless one-time name), and a pseudonymous certificate contains a *pseudonym* (false name). These contrast to the certificates generally associated with PKI, which are intentionally populated with the closest possible approximation to a *veronym* (true name), especially if non-repudiation services are desired.

These three types of "nyms" are distinguished by the amount of linkage that is possible across transactions. *Anonyms* are meaningless or null names for one-time use, and so no linkage can be made (1) to the actual human involved in the transaction and (2) between transactions; entering coins into a vending machine to purchase a candy bar is an anonymous transaction. *Pseudonyms* are either meaningless or apparently meaningful names for multiple uses that bear no relation to the true name. Thus, no linkage can be made to the actual human involved in the transaction, but it is clear that the same (unknown) entity is involved in different transactions; using a stolen credit card to purchase items from several Web sites is a set of pseudonymous transactions. *Veronyms* are, or very readily disclose, the real name of the user, and so linkage can be made both to the human involved and across different transactions. Each type of "nym" has its uses, and any of the three can be bound to a key pair through certification.

It should be noted that pseudonymity—enabling linkage of otherwise distinct transactions—can inadvertently allow an observer to derive the true identity (that is, the veronym) over time because of patterns or other characteristics in these transactions, thus compromising the whole intent of the pseudonymous activity.

Interestingly, though, PKI-enabled anonymity and pseudonymity have no effect on the availability and use of authentication. That is, the use of anonymous or pseudonymous certificates creates a separation between *authentication* and *identification*—Alice can strongly authenticate to Bob without revealing her identity. She does this in the usual PKI-based way (that is, in some sort of challenge-response protocol, by proving knowledge of the private key corresponding to the public key contained in her certificate); at the end of the authentication exchange, however, Bob is certain only that the "other entity" is the legitimate holder of the value of the subject field in the certificate, which is an anonymous or pseudonymous name. Privacy is preserved in that Bob has no way of knowing the identity (that is, "Alice") of this other entity.

The ability to do authentication without identification is valuable when privacy is required over multistep, multiparty transactions. In particular, consider the following scenario. Entity E authenticates to Web site $S_1$ pseudonomously. $S_1$ does not know the identity of E because E uses a pseudonym; however, $S_1$ knows that this is the same entity as on one or more previous visits and can assign a special status to E (for example, "E wants to see this type of information", or "E gets priority service"). To satisfy the current transaction, $S_1$ needs to redirect E to a second Web site, $S_2$. How can $S_1$ refer to E? That is, how can $S_1$ say to $S_2$, "*This* is the E with the special status"? (This is sometimes called the *indexical reference problem*.) There are three general categories of solutions to indexical referencing: bearer tokens, secret-based schemes, and public-key-based schemes. With bearer tokens, $S_1$ says to $S_2$, "Whoever presents this token (or perhaps a pointer to this token) to you is the entity I'm talking about." Simply holding the token (or pointer) and being able to present it to $S_2$ is the authentication mechanism for E. Clearly, if this token/pointer is stolen, then whoever steals it can successfully impersonate E at $S_2$. (Using Secure Sockets Layer, or SSL, over all connections can help alleviate this concern but cannot ensure that the token/pointer will be adequately protected against theft while residing at E's browser during the redirect, for example.)

With the second category, E and $S_1$ share some secret, such as a password or a symmetric key. $S_1$ says to $S_2$, "Whoever can tell you the following secret is the entity I'm talking about; the secret is oa8ue!^6." Proving knowledge of the secret to $S_2$ is the authentication mechanism for E. This solution suffers from the fact that the secret shared between E and $S_1$ must necessarily be revealed to $S_2$, who is then able to impersonate E to $S_1$ at a later time if it wishes. This problem is exacerbated if more sites are given the secret (in order to perform further steps in the transaction or for the purposes of SSO).

With the third category, E has a key pair and a certificate. $S_1$ says to $S_2$, "Whoever can authenticate with respect to this certificate is the entity I'm talking about." Proving knowledge of the private key corresponding to the public key in the (pseudonymous) certificate is the authentication mechanism for E. The multistep transaction can be strongly authenticated at every stage, without the possibility of impersonation (either from an observer to the communications or from the malicious behavior of $S_2$). This is still SSO from the point of view of the human entity E, who enters a password (or PIN, or biometric, or whatever) on the local system to unlock the key pair, but plays no part in the PKI-based authentication to $S_1$ or $S_2$ (or any subsequent sites).

The PKI-enabled service of privacy allows strong authentication—and therefore higher security than alternative mechanisms—in multistep, multiparty transactions. This is accomplished through the use of anonymous or pseudonymous certificates that do not expose identity to any of the relying parties in the transactions.

# Mechanisms Required to Create PKI-Enabled Services

A number of mechanisms are required to create the PKI-enabled services discussed in this chapter. Some of the most important mechanisms are discussed next.

## Digital Signatures, Hashes, MACs, and Ciphers

Secure communication, because it relies on the core PKI services, requires the mechanisms that make the core services possible. These include digital signatures, cryptographic hash functions, MAC algorithms, and symmetric block ciphers. (See Chapter 2 for a discussion of such mechanisms.)

## Trusted Time Sources

Secure time stamping can be implemented in such a way that it requires the presence of one or more trusted time sources for the environment. That is, a way may be needed to get a trusted representation of the current time (synchronous with the global clock, to some high level of accuracy) to one or more devices/entities in the local environment.

As discussed previously, getting trusted time to a small number of devices can be easier in practice than getting trusted time to every device in the network. However, getting trusted time to even a single device can be a nontrivial task. This can be one of the desirable features of the concept of a *Time Stamp Authority (TSA):* If every entity in the environment trusts the TSA's assertion of time, then (within this closed environment) it does not matter whether the TSA's time is accurate. However, to support non-repudiation (in which evidence may need to be brought to an external third party for arbitration), the TSA should have as accurate a value of time as possible.

## Privilege Policy Creation Mechanism

The PKI-enabled service of privilege management depends on the existence of policies that map identities, groups, or roles to specific privileges; a simple example of this is the well-known Access Control List (ACL), which lists access grant or deny decisions corresponding to entity names or roles.

In general, privilege policies can be complex Boolean expressions specifying precise conditions under which a claimant can invoke an object method under the control of a verifier. These expressions can include arbitrarily complicated time restrictions (for example, the second Tuesday of every fourth month from noon until 1 P.M.), as well as any other conditions on the validity of the privilege.

The potential for such complex expressions for privilege policy demands that a suitably general creation and editing mechanism exist. This is primarily a user-interface design issue, although a module for translating human-user-policy input into a precise, machine-readable privilege policy expression can require some delicate engineering as well.

## Privilege Policy Processing Engines

The privilege policy construct discussed in the preceding section does not simply need to be created and edited; it also needs to be processed and understood by some sort of verification engine (sometimes referred to as a Policy Decision Point, or PDP) at the time when an entity is requesting access to some resource. That is, the PDP uses the privilege policy as the law by which to decide whether to grant or deny a request by an entity to access a resource or service. The fact that this policy needs to be machine readable and yet flexible seems to necessitate a formal language for policy specification. (See, for example, eXtensible Access Control Markup Language, or XACML [XACML], or Annex D of X.509 [X509-00].) Mechanisms that can understand and act on encoded policies are an important requirement of general privilege management infrastructures.

## Privilege Management Infrastructure Mechanisms

A number of mechanisms exist to support the implementation of a *Privilege Management Infrastructure (PMI)*. They tend to fall broadly into three categories: .

- Mechanisms based on Kerberos [RFC1510], such as DCE [DCE, Lock94] and SESAME [AsVa99].

- Mechanisms based on the concept of a policy server (a central server that creates, maintains, and verifies privilege policy for identities, groups, and roles).

- Mechanisms based on *Attribute Certificates (AC)*, such as those specified in X.509 [X509-00] and *Security Assertion Markup Language (SAML)* [SAML]. An AC is similar in concept to a public-key certificate, but it need not contain a public key; it is an authenticity- and integrity-protected structure from an Attribute Authority binding some privilege or permission information to an identity (or perhaps to a bit string that corresponds to a specific authentication mechanism, such as a public-key certificate).

All three mechanisms have their proponents and their detractors because (not surprisingly) all have their advantages and disadvantages. Briefly, Kerberos schemes are symmetric-key-based, and so they have very attractive performance characteristics but somewhat unattractive key management and single-point-of-failure characteristics. Policy server schemes are highly centralized, and so they have attractive single-point-of-administration benefits but somewhat unattractive communications overhead. AC schemes can be fully distributed, and so they have attractive failure resistance but somewhat unattractive performance characteristics (especially if public-key operations are required for their verification).

Each PMI mechanism may be more suited to some environments than others. For example, a Kerberos-based technology may be the best choice for authorization in a high-volume, real-time transaction environment. A policy-server–based architecture may be most appropriate for geographically localized environments with strong central administrative control. Finally, an AC technology may be the ideal choice for interorganizational authorization activities that need to support a non-repudiation service. Note, however, that cooperation between mechanisms is sometimes possible, whereby one mechanism is used for some aspects in the PMI and another mechanism is used for other aspects.

Of the three PMI mechanisms listed here, the AC technology can make the most direct use of the PKI (because the AC may be digitally signed for authenticity and integrity and it may possibly contain attributes that are encrypted for confidentiality, all through the use of public-key technology). All three mechanisms can be implemented as PKI-enabled services, however, because authorization is generally tied to authentication and each technology can work with a PKI authentication service.

## Privacy Architecture

To implement the PKI-enabled service of privacy, a privacy architecture needs to be put in place. That is, at least one Certification Authority (CA) must understand how to issue anonymous or pseudonymous certificates, and relying parties must be able to accept and process such certificates in a useful way. Certificate-based architectures for privacy come in two flavors: (1) The CA knows the true identity but issues certificates that hide this identity from the rest of the world; (2) the CA does not know the true identity (this is known only to the entity) but can issue meaningful certificates anyway. An example of the former is the architecture described by the Trusted Computing Platform Alliance in their Main Specification (especially Section 9) [TCPA]. An example of the latter is the architecture described in some detail by Brands [Bran00].

# Operational Considerations

A number of operational considerations must be taken into account if some of the PKI-enabled services discussed in this chapter are to be offered in a given environment. Some of these are discussed in the following sections.

## Trusted Time Delivery Mechanism

For the secure time-stamping service (and consequently for the notarization and non-repudiation services that rely on it), there must be a way of delivering trusted time to (at least) the TSA (or TSAs) in the network.

Work has been done to transform the well-known Network Time Protocol, or NTP [RFC1305], to a Secure Network Time Protocol by cryptographically authenticating the identity of the sender and verifying the integrity of the data included in an NTP message. (See, for example, the efforts of the IETF STIME Working Group [STIME].) Such work may prove to be very valuable as more PKI deployments begin to implement the PKI-enabled service of secure time stamping.

## Secure Protocols

Many of the PKI-enabled services discussed in this chapter incorporate the concept of a server that will communicate with other PKI entities (for example, the TSA, the "notary" or data certification authority, and the authorization authority). Such communication relies on the existence of secure protocols; otherwise, tampering with the messages passed back and forth could invalidate the intended service provided.

The PKI must therefore incorporate secure client-server and peer-to-peer protocols wherever necessary (that is, employing authenticity, integrity, and confidentiality) to maintain the trustworthiness of the services being offered. Examples of on-line protocols that can be used for this purpose include TLS [RFC2246] and Simple Public Key GSS-API Mechanism (SPKM) [RFC2025].

## Server Redundancy

Servers are a critical architectural element in many of the PKI-enabled services discussed in this chapter. Therefore, the loss of a server (due to network segment outages or server crashes) can have a significant impact on the PKI entities in the environment.

For this reason, it may be required to have redundant servers available on warm- or hot-standby mode in the network. The TSA may be particularly critical in this regard, but for some environments, other authorities may provide a vital service that cannot be dysfunctional for any period of time as well.

### Physically Secure Archive Facilities

For the PKI-enabled service of non-repudiation, it is a requirement to have archival facilities (to hold old copies of CRLs at least, but perhaps to hold notarized documents and other data as well). See Chapter 8 for a discussion of CRLs.

Such archival facilities must be physically secure (for example, from damage due to fires, earthquakes, hurricanes, and other acts of nature; as well as from theft, bombs, and other acts of human nature). In many cases, it will be prudent to archive the data in physically redundant archive facilities as well.

### Privacy Certificates and Identity Mapping

There are two possible goals with respect to pseudonymous privacy: hiding identity information solely from observers of the transaction (for example, other Internet users) or hiding identity information from other participants in the transaction (for example, the server with whom the entity is communicating) and from observers. The first goal implies that some kind of mapping function (from the pseudonym to the veronym or other identifying information) takes place in the server backend. The second goal implies that this mapping takes place at a trusted third party (such as a TCPA-style "Privacy CA" [TCPA]) or that the mapping does not take place anywhere (such as a Brands-style CA [Bran00]). Thus, for the PKI-enabled service of privacy, typical operational considerations would be the backend real-time identity-mapping function at the server component or the running of an independent CA that issues anonymous or pseudonymous certificates.

### Real Life

Real life may be considered to be the most important operational consideration of all. Both the core services and the PKI-enabled services offered by the infrastructure will be subject to unpredictable behavior, incorrect operation, or unreliable results if the PKI has not been implemented properly or if users and administrators have not had some minimal level of security training.

For example, if PKI entities are not careful to keep their private keys hidden from other entities, the core service of authentication and the PKI-enabled service of non-repudiation are completely compromised. If the underlying S/MIME or IKE protocol is badly implemented, the PKI-enabled service of secure communications cannot be trusted.

In real life, humans occasionally make mistakes. Such errors can find their way into PKI implementation, deployment, and use; when this occurs, the errors can lead to PKI vulnerabilities (or at least to operational uncertainties). Reputable software and hardware vendors, rigorous testing, continuous monitoring, and user training can all help and should be used to deal with the problems that real life may introduce.

## Comprehensive PKI and Current Practice

Chapters 3 and 4, along with this chapter, have described an architecture for what may be called the *comprehensive PKI*. (See Figure 5.1.) That is, components, functions, and services have been defined for a PKI that would, in some abstract sense, be "perfect" because it would satisfy the requirements of virtually every environment. Specific environments would "turn off" (or not install) the pieces they did not need in order to tailor this generic solution to their particular problems of interest.

The comprehensive PKI is a vision of what the future may hold; it does not describe current practice (in particular, at the time of writing, no known PKI product implements every aspect of the PKI as described in Chapters 3–5). PKIs today are often implemented or deployed to solve only a particular problem or set of problems. However, these specific architectures may be viewed simply as proper subsets of the comprehensive architecture.

**Figure 5.1**    Comprehensive PKI.

| | | |
|---|---|---|
| Certification Authority | Certificate Repository | Certificate Revocation |
| Key Backup | Key Recovery | Automatic Key Update |
| Key History Management | Cross-Certification | Client Software |
| Authentication | Integrity | Confidentiality |
| Secure Time Stamping | Notarization | Non-Repudiation Support |
| Secure Data Archive | Privilege/Policy Creation | Privilege/Policy Verification |

Consider, for instance, four example PKI-usage scenarios that may be found in real-world environments today. In Figure 5.2, the *Internet PKI* encompasses such activities as casual e-mail between friends and Web browsing using SSL server authentication. In such usage, a CA is needed to issue the required public-key certificates, and the core services of authentication, integrity, and confidentiality may be used. However, there is no repository (certificates are sent via the communications protocol itself), revocation status of the e-mail recipient (or even of the server certificate) is not checked, key/certificate life-cycle management is unavailable, cross-certification is unnecessary (browser and server have at least one root key in common), client software (as a separate module called by the browser) does not exist, and none of the PKI-enabled services are required.

In Figure 5.3, the *extranet security* still uses a browser as the access mechanism but employs SSL client authentication for greater control over who may enter the corporate network. In such usage, Certificate Revocation checking is likely to be employed, as is some level of privilege and policy creation/verification (perhaps in the form of an ACL). Due to current browser limitations, life-cycle management, cross-certification, and other PKI-enabled services are not available.

In Figure 5.4, the enterprise uses a standard mail package and secures the messages using a PKI. Because this is a single-enterprise environment, key/certificate life-cycle management may be required, but cross-certification may still be unnecessary. Client software will likely be

**Figure 5.2**     Internet PKI.

| Certification Authority | Certificate Repository | Certificate Revocation |
|---|---|---|
| Key Backup | Key Recovery | Automatic Key Update |
| Key History Management | Cross-Certification | Client Software |
| **Authentication** | **Integrity** | **Confidentiality** |
| Secure Time Stamping | Notarization | Non-Repudiation Support |
| Secure Data Archive | Privilege/Policy Creation | Privilege/Policy Verification |

**Figure 5.3** Extranet security (via SSL client authentication).

| Certification Authority | Certificate Repository | Certificate Revocation |
|---|---|---|
| **Key Backup** | Key Recovery | Automatic Key Update |
| Key History Management | Cross-Certification | Client Software |
| **Authentication** | **Integrity** | **Confidentiality** |
| Secure Time Stamping | Notarization | Non-Repudiation Support |
| Secure Data Archive | **Privilege/Policy Creation** | **Privilege/Policy Verification** |

**Figure 5.4** Enterprise secure e-mail.

| Certification Authority | Certificate Repository | Certificate Revocation |
|---|---|---|
| **Key Backup** | **Key Recovery** | **Automatic Key Update** |
| **Key History Management** | Cross-Certification | **Client Software** |
| **Authentication** | **Integrity** | **Confidentiality** |
| Secure Time Stamping | Notarization | Non-Repudiation Support |
| Secure Data Archive | Privilege/Policy Creation | Privilege/Policy Verification |

employed (as a plug-in) because the standard e-mail package may not natively support PKI-based security. PKI-enabled services are not available because they are typically unnecessary for e-mail.

Finally, in Figure 5.5, inter-enterprise–signed transactions may require much of the functionality of the comprehensive PKI. In particular, the care that must be taken to ensure proper authentication and authorization necessitates proper revocation checking, privilege and policy creation/verification, and so on. Cross-certification is likely to be required if the different enterprises have independently deployed PKIs. Some aspects of non-repudiation support may be required (particularly, support for multiple key pairs, levels of commitment with respect to signed documents, and signed receipts), but for this usage scenario, time stamping, notarization, and data archiving may not be implemented.

It should be apparent from Figures 5.2 through 5.5 that current PKI-usage scenarios are often subsets of the comprehensive PKI architecture. This suggests that understanding the principles and concepts of the comprehensive architecture is helpful in understanding the more specific architectures available today.

More than this, however, it also suggests that as this field continues to mature, many PKI vendors will begin to implement comprehensive PKI products rather than single-use PKI products. It may prove to be simpler and more cost effective to tailor a comprehensive product to

**Figure 5.5**    Inter-enterprise signed transactions.

| Certification Authority | Certificate Repository | Certificate Revocation |
|---|---|---|
| Key Backup | Key Recovery | Automatic Key Update |
| Key History Management | Cross-Certification | Client Software |
| Authentication | Integrity | Confidentiality |
| Secure Time Stamping | Notarization | Non-Repudiation Support |
| Secure Data Archive | Privilege/Policy Creation | Privilege/Policy Verification |

a specific problem than to build and maintain several separate products, each solving only one or two specific problems.

Finally, it may be argued that in many environments PKIs will make the inevitable transition from a *particular tool to solve a particular problem to a pervasive substrate that solves security-related problems for a wide variety of applications.* Only the comprehensive PKI has the generality and capability to meet the demanding requirements of a true infrastructure.

This book espouses and discusses the comprehensive PKI architecture for all the reasons given earlier. Therefore, other architectures, being subsets of the comprehensive architecture, are implicitly (if not explicitly) included in the discussion, as appropriate.

## Summary

PKI-enabled security services build on the core PKI services to add more useful, business-oriented functionality to an environment. Secure communication, secure time stamping, notarization, non-repudiation support, privilege management, and others provide important benefits to an organization and greatly enhance the overall value of the PKI.

Together, the components, core services, and PKI-enabled services described in this and the previous two chapters define a *comprehensive PKI*. Many currently deployed PKIs and "single-use" PKIs may be seen to be subsets of this comprehensive architecture.

Two needs must be addressed to fully realize the PKI-enabled services discussed in this chapter:

- There must be a good understanding of the breadth of PKI concepts and terminology. This is the purpose of most of the remaining chapters in this part of the book: Chapters 6 through 12 discuss the important concepts of PKI, from the idea of a certificate to PKI operational considerations.

- An understanding of the legal framework for PKI operation is important, especially with respect to responsibilities and mitigation of risk. This discussion is the topic of Chapter 13.

# 6

# Certificates and Certification

As we discussed in Chapter 2, *public-key cryptography* involves the use of public/private-key pairs to facilitate digital signature and key management services. The fundamental principle that enables public-key technology to scale is the fact that the public component of the public/private-key pair may be distributed freely among the entities that need the public component to use the underlying security services. (See Chapters 4 and 5 for more information regarding security services enabled through the use of a PKI.)

However, distribution of the public component without some form of integrity protection would defeat the very foundation for these security services. Thus, the public-key component must be protected in such a way that it will not impact the overall scalability that public-key cryptography techniques offer. Further, we need to bind certain attributes with the public key.

Thus, a data integrity mechanism is required to ensure that the public key (and any other information associated with that public key) is not modified without detection. However, a data integrity mechanism alone is not sufficient to guarantee that the public key belongs to the claimed owner. A mechanism that binds the public key to the claimed owner in a trustworthy manner is also required. In the end, the goal is to provide a single mechanism by which a relying party (that is, the "user" of the key and associated data, as defined in [RFC2527]) is assured that

- The integrity of the public key (and any other associated information) is sound.

- The public key (and any other associated information) has been bound to the claimed owner in a trusted manner.

Our purpose in this chapter is to explain how the use of public-key certificates accomplishes these goals. In particular, we will focus on the syntax and semantics of the X.509 Version 3 public-key certificate, and we will explain how the integrity of these certificates is established and maintained.

# Certificates

Kohnfelder first introduced the concept of using a signed data structure or certificate to convey the public key to a relying party in his 1978 bachelor's thesis entitled "Towards a Practical Public-Key Cryptosystem" [Kohn78]. Thus, over two decades ago, it was recognized that a scalable and secure method (from an integrity perspective) would be required to convey the public keys to the parties that needed them. Simply stated, public-key certificates are used to bind an entity's name (and possibly additional attributes associated with that entity) with the corresponding public key.

When discussing the concept of a "certificate," it is important to recognize that a number of different types of certificates exist, including

- X.509 public-key certificates

- Simple Public Key Infrastructure (SPKI) certificates

- Pretty Good Privacy (PGP) certificates

- Attribute certificates

The certificate types listed here have separate and distinct formats. In some cases, one type of certificate may be defined in several different versions, and a single version may be instantiated in a number of different ways. For example, there are three versions of an X.509 public-key certificate. Version 1 is a subset of Version 2, and Version 2 is a subset of Version 3. Because a Version 3 public-key certificate includes numerous optional extensions (as discussed later), it can be instantiated in a number of application-specific ways; for example, Secure Electronic Transaction (SET) certificates are X.509 Version 3 public-key certificates with specific extensions defined solely for SET exchanges.

To complicate matters further, multiple terms commonly denote the same thing. For example, in many environments the terms *certificate* and *digital certificate* are synonymous with an X.509 public-key certificate.

For the purposes of this book, a *certificate* is synonymous only with a *Version 3 public-key certificate* as defined in the X.509 Recommendation [X509–00]. (See Box 6.1.) Any other type of certificate will be further qualified to avoid any confusion with this usage. In this chapter, we discuss the structure and content of a certificate. As we describe the structure of a certificate in the next section, you will notice that certificates can be issued to Certification Authorities

**Box 6.1**   Versions 1–3 of X.509

Three versions of an X.509 public-key certificate are defined. The original Version 1 public-key certificate, defined in the 1988 X.509 Recommendation, suffers from inherent inflexibility because this version cannot be extended to support additional attributes. The Version 2 public-key certificate did little to correct this shortcoming because it simply augments Version 1 with the addition of two optional fields. Because the demand for these fields was (and continues to be) negligible and the same inability to support extensions also applies, the Version 2 public-key certificate has failed to gain widespread acceptance.

Not surprisingly, Version 3 public-key certificates, as specified in the 1997 X.509 Recommendation [X509–97], were introduced to correct the deficiencies associated with the Version 1 and Version 2 definitions. Specifically, Version 3 offers significant improvements over Version 1 and Version 2 through the addition of optional extensions.

More recently (circa June 2000), the 2000 X.509 Recommendation [X509–00] was completed. The 2000 version includes numerous changes from the previous version, including the definition of two additional extensions to the Version 3 public-key certificate.

In the enterprise domain, it is fair to say that Version 3 public-key certificates are the preferred choice as they are the most flexible, and many of the extensions are required to fully support the requirements of the enterprise.

(CAs) and to end entities (for example, end users or devices). These are referred to as CA certificates and end-entity certificates, respectively.

## Digital Certificate

The term *digital certificate* is sometimes used to denote a certificate in electronic form. However, this term can be somewhat confusing in some circumstances because a number of quite different certificates (for example, an X.509 public-key certificate, an attribute certificate, a PGP certificate, and so on) are "digital." For that matter, a digitized birth certificate might be considered to be a "digital certificate." Thus, unless the term is either explicitly defined or further qualified, it is not precise enough to convey any intended meaning.

The use of this term has also introduced confusion when describing the relationship between *digital certificates* and *digital signatures*. In particular, a common mistake is to assume that Alice can authenticate herself by simply supplying a "digital certificate" without the corresponding "digital signature." Further, although a digital signature is meaningful in itself (that is, a digital signature is distinguished from a handwritten or a generic electronic signature), digital certificate does not offer the same connotation—especially when referring solely to a public-key certificate.

To be perfectly precise, any reference to a *certificate* should be fully qualified to avoid unnecessary confusion. However, in accordance with common practice in the PKI industry, we will simply use the term *certificate* as a shorthand notation for an X.509 Version 3 public-key certificate. We will explicitly identify all other types of certificates where appropriate—even the generic use of *certificate* will be qualified wherever any doubt may arise.

## Certificate Structure and Semantics

Although X.509 defines certain requirements associated with the standard fields and extensions of a certificate, other issues still must be further refined in specific profiles to fully address interoperability considerations. The Internet Engineering Task Force (IETF) Public Key Infrastructure X.509 (PKIX) Working Group introduced such a profile in January 1999 with the publication of RFC2459. In April 2002, RFC2459 was replaced with RFC3280. Although RFC3280 is targeted for the Internet community, a number of its recommendations could equally apply in the enterprise environment, and consistency should be maintained wherever possible. Therefore, we will provide references to some of the recommendations made in RFC3280 where appropriate.

Figure 6.1 shows the generic structure of a Version 3 certificate. The following list defines the fields represented in Figure 6.1:

**Figure 6.1**     Version 3 certificate structure.

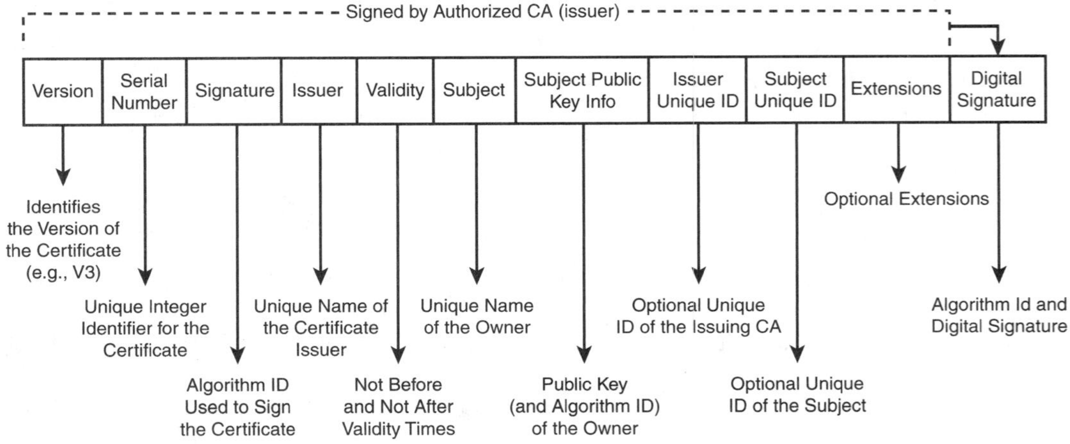

- *Version* indicates the version of the certificate (either 1, 2, or 3).

- *Serial Number* is the unique identifier for this certificate relative to the certificate issuer.

- *Signature* indicates the algorithm identifier (that is, the Object Identifier, or OID, plus any associated parameters) of the algorithm used to calculate the digital signature on the certificate.[1] For example, the OID for SHA-1 with RSA might be present, indicating that the digital signature is an SHA-1 hash encrypted using RSA.

- *Issuer* is the *Distinguished Name (DN)* of the CA that issued the certificate and must always be present.[2]

- *Validity* indicates the window of time that this certificate should be considered valid unless otherwise revoked (refer to Chapter 8 for more information on revocation). This field is composed of *Not Valid Before* and *Not Valid After* dates/times that may be represented in UTC Time or in Generalized Time (however, RFC3280 has specific rules associated with the use of these time representations).

- *Subject* indicates the DN of the certificate owner and must be non-null unless an alternate name form is used (refer to the Extensions field later).

- *Subject Public Key Info* is the public key (and algorithm identifier) associated with the subject and must always be present.

- *Issuer Unique ID* is an optional unique identifier of the certificate issuer present in Version 2 and Version 3 only; this field is rarely used in implementation practice, and it is not recommended for use by RFC3280.

---

[1]An OID is simply a unique representation for a given object. When expressed verbally or in writing among human beings, an OID is represented as a sequence of integers that are separated by decimal points or dots (much the same as an Internet Protocol (IP) address is expressed in the familiar dotted decimal notation). OIDs are hierarchical in nature, and they are registered with international, national, or organizational registration authorities in order to ensure that the allocated OID for a given object is unique. As an example, the OID for SHA-1 with RSA (which might be present in the Signature field of a certificate) is 1.2.840.113549.1.1.5.

[2]A DN is a hierarchical naming convention defined in the X.500 Recommendations. DNs are designed to help ensure entity names are unique. Without getting into too much detail regarding Directories and Directory Information Trees, DNs are expressed as a concatenation of Relative Distinguished Names (RDNs) from the top- or root-level node down to the last node of the DN. For example, "C = CA, O = ADGA, OU = AEPOS Technologies, CN = Steve Lloyd" is an example of a DN. Note that each RDN (C = CA is an RDN, O = ADGA is an RDN, and so on) must be unique at each level, otherwise the uniqueness of the DN as a whole would not be guaranteed.

- *Subject Unique ID* is an optional unique identifier of the certificate owner present in Version 2 and Version 3 only; this field is rarely used in implementation practice, and it is not recommended for use by RFC3280.

Each certificate extension described next is associated with a criticality flag. In general, extensions can be marked critical or noncritical, although the standards often recommend or even mandate the criticality associated with certain extensions.

An extension that has been marked critical must be processed and understood, or the certificate is not to be used. A noncritical extension is to be processed if possible, but it may be gracefully ignored if it is not recognized.

Extensions are optional standard and private extensions (present in Version 3 only) and include the following:

- *Authority Key Identifier* is a unique identifier of the key that should be used to verify the digital signature calculated over the certificate; it distinguishes between multiple keys that apply to the same certificate issuer. RFC3280 mandates the inclusion of this field for all but self-signed certificates. (Chapter 9 discusses self-signed certificates.)

- *Subject Key Identifier* is a unique identifier associated with the public key contained in this certificate; it distinguishes between multiple keys that apply to the same certificate owner. RFC3280 mandates this field for CA certificates, and it is recommended for end-entity certificates.

- *Key Usage* is a bit string used to identify (or restrict) the functions or services that can be supported by using the public key in this certificate; it can be used to indicate support for digital signature, non-repudiation, key encipherment, data encipherment, key agreement, certificate signature, Certification Revocation List (CRL) signature, encipher only, and decipher only. A profile typically specifies allowable combinations (for example, the U.S. Federal PKI (FPKI) profile [FPKIpro] explicitly identifies permitted key usage combinations).

- *Extended Key Usage* is a sequence of one or more OIDs that identify specific usage of the public key in the certificate. Although X.509 does not explicitly define identifiers for this purpose, RFC3280 identifies several OIDs associated with this extension, including Transport Layer Security (TLS) server authentication, TLS client authentication, code signing, e-mail protection, time stamping, and Online Certificate Status Protocol (OCSP) signing. (OCSP is discussed in more detail in Chapter 8.) The list of OIDs will likely be augmented over time as needs dictate, so this should not be considered an exhaustive list. RFC3280 also points out that this extension is typically used with end-entity certificates.

- *CRL Distribution Point* indicates the location of the CRL partition where revocation information associated with this certificate resides. (Refer to Chapter 8 for more information regarding revocation techniques and CRL Distribution Points.) RFC3280 provides additional guidance with respect to which attributes within the CRL Distribution Point extension should be populated and what it means when multiple distribution points are present.

- *Private Key Usage Period* indicates the time window that the private key associated with the public key in this certificate can be used; it is intended for use with digital signature keys/certificates. Like the certificate validity period, this window is specified in terms of *Not Valid Before* and *Not Valid After* dates/times (although only Generalized Time is permitted here). Judicious use of this extension can establish a buffer between the time the signing private key expires and the time the corresponding public key used to verify the digital signatures created with that private key expires. This should help eliminate many instances where perfectly valid digital signatures needlessly come into question because the key lifetimes of both the private and public key were too close together (or even identical).

  Note that when this extension is absent, the validity periods of the public key and the private key are identical. As Chapter 7 discusses, a new key pair should be issued before the private key expires in order to avoid any unnecessary downtime. It is interesting to note that RFC3280 recommends against the use of this extension. One reason for this is that the interpretation of this field is not universally agreed upon, which could give rise to inconsistent implementations.

- *Certificate Policies* indicates a sequence of one or more policy OIDs and optional qualifiers associated with the issuance and subsequent use of the certificate. If this extension is marked critical, the processing application must adhere to at least one of the policies indicated, or the certificate is not to be used. Although RFC3280 recommends that policy qualifiers should not be used (in order to promote interoperability), it does define two possible qualifiers: the Certification Practice Statement (CPS) qualifier and the User Notice qualifier. The CPS qualifier is a Uniform Resource Identifier (URI) at which one can find the CPS that applies to this certificate. A notice reference, an explicit notice (up to 200 characters), or both, can comprise the User Notice qualifier.

- *Policy Mappings* indicates one or more policy OID equivalencies between two CA domains and are present only in CA certificates. The Certificate Policies section in this chapter provides additional information related to policy mappings.

- *Subject Alternative Name* indicates alternative name forms associated with the owner of the certificate (for example, e-mail address, IP address, URI, and so on). Alternative name forms are to be considered just as binding as the subject DN, if present. RFC3280 further specifies that if the subject DN is null, one or more alternative name forms must be present, and this extension must be marked critical.

- *Issuer Alternative Name* indicates alternative name forms associated with the issuer of the certificate (for example, e-mail address, IP address, URI, and so on). RFC3280 specifies the same processing rules as specified under the Subject Alternate Name extension with the exception that the issuer's DN must always be present in the Issuer field. One reason for this requirement is to maintain compatibility with the S/MIME specification.

- *Subject Directory Attributes* indicates a sequence of attributes associated with the owner of the certificate. Although this extension is not currently in widespread use, several known applications exist where this extension conveys access control information. However, we recommend exercising caution when using a certificate to convey privilege-related information, because any change in those privileges would force the revocation of the existing certificate and a new certificate would have to be issued. (See Box 6.2.)

- *Basic Constraints* indicates whether this is a CA certificate. Typically, this field is absent in end-entity certificates. If it is present in an end-entity certificate, the value of the CA attribute in the Basic Constraints field must be *false*. For CA certificates, the Basic Constraints field should always be present, and the CA attribute in the Basic Constraints field must be set to a value of *true*. Note that X.509 [X509–00] recommends (but doesn't mandate) that this extension be marked critical. RFC3280 mandates that this extension be present and marked critical if the associated public key is to be used to verify digital signatures on certificates. However, RFC3280 makes a distinction between public keys used to verify digital signatures on certificates and those that might be used to verify digital signatures on CRLs only or those that are used in conjunction with certificate management protocols. In these cases, the extension may be marked critical or noncritical.

  For CA certificates, the Basic Constraints extension can also include a Path Length Constraint. In accordance with X.509 [X509–00], the Path Length Constraint indicates "the maximum number of CA certificates that may follow this certificate in a certification path." (Chapter 9 describes certification paths and certification path processing.) A value of zero indicates that the CA can issue only end-entity certificates. The absence of the

## Box 6.2 Certificate Perishability

Any change to the information contained within a given certificate before it naturally expires necessarily means that the existing certificate must be revoked and a new certificate must be issued. Therefore, exercise care to ensure that the attributes placed within the certificate are fairly static in order to avoid wasteful certificate revocation and (re)issuance. Attributes associated with an end entity that will tend to be fairly dynamic in nature should be conveyed through some other means (for example, via attribute certificates, which are briefly discussed later in this chapter and in Chapter 5).

Path Length Constraint in a CA certificate indicates that no restriction is placed on the length of the certification path (that is, the length of the certification path is unbounded). Note that the Path Length Constraint should not be present in an end-entity certificate and is meaningless therein; it should be ignored if it is present.

- *Name Constraints,* an extension present only in CA certificates, indicates required and/or excluded subtree names through the use of the *Permitted Subtrees* and/or *Excluded Subtrees* attributes, respectively. The specified names can take the form of a DN, a URI, an e-mail address, or any other name form that lends itself to a hierarchical structure. The idea is to qualify the name space that applies to the subject names that follow the CA certificate in which the restrictions took effect. If present, this extension should be marked critical [X509–00]. RFC3280 mandates that this extension be marked critical and points out that Name Constraints should not be applied to certificates where the Issuer and Subject fields are the same unless the certificate is the last one in the certification path. (Chapter 9 provides additional information regarding Name Constraints in relation to certification path validation.)

- *Policy Constraints,* an extension present only in CA certificates, indicates required policy identifiers and/or prohibited policy mappings through the use of the *Require Explicit Policy* and/or *Inhibit Policy Mapping* attributes, respectively. It is important to note that if the Require Explicit Policy comes into effect anywhere in a given certification path, it applies to the entire certification path. This is not the case with the Inhibit Policy Mapping attribute that applies only to subsequent certificates in the certification path. A value of zero for either attribute indicates that the restrictions apply immediately. A nonzero value for either attribute indicates where the restrictions might apply; that is, the value is an offset in the certification path, and the nominated CA certificate may or may not be encountered. If present, this extension should be marked critical [X509–00]. RFC3280 states that this extension may be critical or noncritical.

- *Inhibit Any Policy,* an extension present only in CA certificates, indicates that the any-policy identifier (OID value 2.5.29.32.0) should not be considered a legitimate match for other policy identifiers. A value of zero indicates that this restriction applies from this point forward. A nonzero value indicates where the restriction might apply; that is, the value is an offset in the certification path, and the nominated CA certificate may or may not be encountered. This extension was first standardized in the 2000 version of X.509 [X509–00]. In accordance with X.509, this extension may be marked critical or noncritical, but it is recommended that it be marked critical. RFC3280 states that this extension must be marked critical.

- *Freshest CRL Pointer,* an extension present in end-entity and CA certificates, provides a pointer to the "freshest" CRL information. In practice, this is likely to be a pointer to a Delta CRL. (Refer to Chapter 8 for more information on Delta CRLs.) The syntax is the same as is used with CRL Distribution Points. This extension was first standardized in the 2000 version of X.509 [X509–00]. The extension may be marked critical or noncritical, but if it is marked critical, the relying party must retrieve and use this information. RFC3280 states that this extension should be marked noncritical.

Private extensions can also be defined in accordance with X.509. Private extensions are typically defined for domain-specific use. For example, RFC3280 defines two private extensions for Internet use as follows:

- *Authority Information Access,* a private extension present in end-entity and CA certificates, indicates how information or services offered by the issuer of the certificate can be obtained. The type of information and services include on-line validation services and policy information but do not include CRL location information. (The CRL Distribution Point discussed earlier is used for that purpose.) The extension syntax is composed of a sequence of an access method OID that describes the type and format of the service/information and the associated location of the service/information in the form of a General Name (for example, a URI, Directory Name, or RFC822 Name). Two access method OIDs have been defined. One access method, referred to as "CA Issuers," retrieves information about CAs that are superior to the issuer of the certificate. This information can be used to help build certification paths. The other defined access method is for on-line validation services based on OCSP. (Refer to Chapter 8 for more information on OCSP.) Other access methods may be defined in the future. RFC3280 states that this extension must be marked noncritical.

- *Subject Information Access,* a private extension present in end-entity and CA certificates, indicates how information and services offered by the subject in the certificate can be obtained. Like the Authority Information Access private extension, the extension syntax is composed of a sequence of an access method OID and the associated location of the service/information in the form of a General Name. One access method OID has been defined for CAs (CA Repository), and one access method OID has been defined for end entities (time stamping). The CA Repository access method identifies the location of the repository where the CA publishes certificate and CRL information. The Time-Stamping access method indicates that the subject identified in the certificate offers a time stamping service. Other access methods may be defined in the future. RFC3280 states that this extension must be marked noncritical.

## *Alternative Certificate Formats*

As discussed previously in this chapter, certificate types other than the X.509 Version 3 public-key certificate are available. We discuss these further in the next few pages.

**SPKI**

In contrast to the IETF PKIX Working Group that focused on X.509 issues for the Internet (see Chapter 18), a separate IETF working group was formed to address a (potentially) simpler public-key infrastructure, referred to as the Simple Public Key Infrastructure (SPKI), for the Internet. Specifically, the charter of the IETF SPKI Working Group[3] was to

> develop Internet standards for an IETF sponsored public-key certificate format, associated signature and other formats, and key acquisition protocols. The key certificate format and associated protocols are to be simple to understand, implement, and use.

The IETF SPKI Working Group produced a number of technical and informational documents, including

- SPKI certificate format

- SPKI certificate theory

- SPKI requirements

- SPKI examples

You can retrieve the relevant SPKI documents from `http://www.ietf.org/html._charters/spki-charter.html`. Because the focus of the SPKI work was on authorization rather than on identity, the SPKI certificate is referred to as an *authorization certificate*. The primary purpose of the SPKI authorization certificate is to convey permissions. It also includes the ability to delegate permissions to others.

Although the SPKI authorization certificate has some things in common with an X.509 public-key certificate (for example, Issuer and Validity), the syntax and, in many cases, the semantics of these fields are not the same. Further, a number of fields are defined for one type of certificate that does not correspond to an equivalent mapping in the other. In addition, the naming conventions (and assumptions) are completely different because the SPKI work adopted the naming conventions as defined in SDSI.

The IETF work on SPKI has concluded. However, the extent to which this work will be used in practice still remains to be seen. There is currently very little demand for SPKI-based certificates, and in the absence of market demand, CA and PKI vendors are not likely to implement a completely different certificate syntax in addition to X.509 Version 3 public-key certificates.

---

[3]See `http://www.ietf.org/html.characters/spki-charter.html`.

Chapter 18 provides additional information regarding the role and status of the SPKI work.

## PGP

Essentially, *Pretty Good Privacy (PGP)* is a method for encrypting and digitally signing e-mail messages and files. Phil Zimmermann introduced the first version of PGP in the early 1990s [Zimm95]. Version 2.x of PGP was published a number of years later as an IETF standards-track specification entitled PGP Message Exchange Formats [RFC1991]. The latest version of PGP, referred to as *OpenPGP*, has been published as an IETF standards-track specification entitled OpenPGP Message Format [RFC2440]. A document on the Internet standards track also incorporates MIME with PGP and is entitled MIME Security with Pretty Good Privacy [RFC2015].

PGP specifies packet formats that convey messages and files from one entity to another. PGP also includes packet formats that convey *PGP keys* (sometimes referred to as *PGP certificates*) from one entity to another.

Significant differences exist between PGP keys (or certificates) and X.509 Version 3 public-key certificates, and the trust models they embody are also completely different. (Chapter 9 discusses the PGP trust model further.) The significant differences between PGP keys and the X.509 Version 3 public-key certificate have created interoperability barriers between the PGP-user community and other communities that base their certificate formats on X.509 (for example, the S/MIME-user community). This is much more than a protocol incompatibility issue because the very foundation for the underlying public-key-enabled security services is different and incompatible. One possible solution is for PGP (or OpenPGP) to adopt X.509 Version 3 public-key certificates in addition to (or perhaps in lieu of) the PGP certificate. In fact, Version 6.5 of OpenPGP has pursued this direction and is now capable of supporting X.509 certificates. Although allowing OpenPGP users to tap into X.509-based PKIs, this still does not solve the basic protocol incompatibilities between OpenPGP and S/MIME. Another possibility might be for PKI vendors to offer products that support both PGP and X.509 Version 3 public-key certificates, but this can lead to other difficulties due to the significant differences in the trust models. (For example, it would introduce significant administrative and control issues.)

Although PGP enjoys a significant amount of use over the Internet, it does not make a good candidate for the corporate intranet (that is, the enterprise domain) because all trust decisions rest with individuals rather than with the enterprise. Because many CA and PKI vendors seem to have concentrated their product development efforts on the enterprise domain, it is unclear that they have any motivation to offer PGP-compatible (or OpenPGP-compatible) products.

Chapter 18 provides additional information regarding the role and status of the PGP/Open-PGP work.

**SET**

The *Secure Electronic Transaction (SET)* specifications [SET1; SET2; SET3] define a standard to support credit card payment transactions over distributed communications networks such as the Internet. Essentially, SET defines a standard payment protocol and specifies requirements that the supporting PKI is expected to meet.

SET adopts the X.509 Version 3 public-key certificate format, and it defines specific private extensions that have meaning only in a SET context. SET also levies certain profile requirements on the standard extensions. Figure 6.2 illustrates a SET certificate. Note that Figure 6.2 does not represent all the possible extensions. (For example, it does not represent the Hashed Root Key extension present in a SET root CA certificate.)

Because non-SET applications will not understand the private extensions SET defines, one cannot expect a non-SET application (for example, S/MIME-based e-mail) to accept a SET certificate for use. This is true even though the SET certificate format is compliant with an X.509 Version 3 public-key certificate. Although one might suggest that a non-SET application could ignore the SET extensions, the *Certificate Type* extension is critical; therefore, by definition a non-SET application must reject a SET certificate. Note that it is accepted practice to intentionally mark certain extensions critical so that a particular type of certificate can be used only in the context of a specific application to minimize liability concerns.

**Figure 6.2** SET certificate structure.

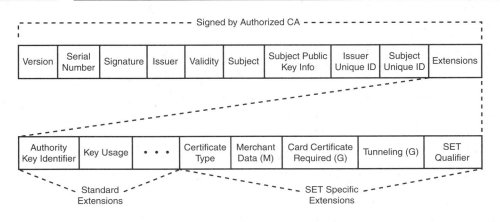

(G) - Payment Gateway Only
(M) - Merchant Only

Although it is not necessarily the case that end users will require a separate certificate for each application, this example helps illustrate that multiple certificates per end entity will be required. (Chapter 10 provides additional discussion regarding the requirements for multiple certificates.)

### Attribute Certificates

Attribute certificates were first standardized in the 1997 version of X.509 when the basic ASN.1 constructs for an attribute certificate were defined. The 2000 version of X.509 expands on the definition and use of attribute certificates significantly and even describes an attribute certificate framework that can be used as a foundation for building Privilege Management Infrastructures (PMIs). The subject of PMI is rather extensive and could very well be the topic of another book. For the purpose of this book, it is sufficient to say that—although attribute certificates are defined in the X.509 Recommendation—attribute certificates are *not* public-key certificates. Attribute certificates are designed to convey (potentially short-lived) attributes about a given subject to facilitate flexible and scalable privilege management. The attribute certificate may point to a public-key certificate that can be used to authenticate the identity of the attribute certificate holder. (Chapter 5 provides additional information regarding privilege management.)

# Certificate Policies

As indicated earlier, a number of policy-related extensions may be present in a given certificate. The policy-related extensions are extremely important in the sense that they help govern the acceptable use of the certificate in terms of policy compliance, potentially across multiple PKI domains.

The policy-related extensions refer either directly or indirectly to a certificate policy. The X.509 Recommendation [X.509–00] defines a *Certificate Policy* as

> a named set of rules that indicates the applicability of a certificate to a particular community and/or class of application with common security requirements. For example, a particular certificate policy might indicate applicability of a type of certificate to the authentication of electronic data interchange transactions for the trading of goods within a given price range.

The Internet X.509 Public Key Infrastructure Certificate Policy and Certification Practices Framework [RFC2527] also adopts this definition.

This can be contrasted with the definition of a Certification Practice Statement (CPS):

> a statement of the practices which a certification authority employs in issuing certificates [ABA].

In general, it is agreed that (1) a Certificate Policy is a high-level statement of requirements and restrictions associated with the intended use of the certificates issued under that policy and (2) a CPS is an extremely detailed (and potentially extremely sensitive) document that describes the internal operating procedures of the CA and/or PKI that issues those certificates. What is not universally accepted is the role that these documents have with respect to end-user notice and multidomain cross-certification arrangements.

Interesting sources of information related to Certificate Policies and CPSs include the following:

- "The Internet X.509 Public Key Infrastructure: Certificate Policy and Certification Practices Framework" [RFC2527]

- CARAT Guidelines [CARAT] sponsored by the National Automated Clearing House Association (NACHA)

- The American Bar Association (ABA), Digital Signature Guidelines: Legal Infrastructure for Certification Authorities and Electronic Commerce [ABA]

- The Automotive Network eXchange (ANX) Certificate Policy [ANX]

- The Government of Canada Certificate Policy [GOCCP]

- The U.S. Federal PKI "Model Certificate Policy" [MCP]

From a high-level perspective, most of this documentation reflects the common theme noted earlier. In particular, a Certificate Policy is expected to be a higher-level document than a CPS, and it is typically concerned with *what* will be supported rather than *how* it will be supported. (See Box 6.3.) Conversely, a CPS is expected to be a fairly detailed and comprehensive technical and procedural document regarding the operation of the supporting infrastructure. For example RFC2527 points out that CPSs

> may be quite comprehensive, robust documents providing a description of the precise service offerings, detailed procedures of the life-cycle management of certificates, and more— a level of detail which weds the CPS to a particular (proprietary) implementation of a service offering.

## *Object Identifiers*

To easily distinguish one Certificate Policy from another, each Certificate Policy is assigned a globally unique OID. One or more OIDs can be specified in the Certificate Policies certificate extension, which can be further qualified as appropriate. For example, RFC3280 defines two optional Certificate Policy qualifiers: a User Notice and a pointer to a CPS. Certificate Policies can be placed in end-entity certificates as well as CA certificates. Cross-certificates (as described in Chapter 9) may also contain the Policy Mappings extension, which permits a policy OID in

## Box 6.3 The Role of Certificate Policies and CPSs

The role that Certificate Policies and CPSs may have is not universally agreed upon and, to a large extent, depends on the type of PKI domain in question.

For example, the model we see in the Web environment demonstrates that suppliers of Web server and end-user certificates (such as Verisign) publish their CPS on their Web site, and the certificates that they issue point to their on-line CPS. The CPS contains a great deal of information, including warranties and obligations meant to be conveyed to the end user. Thus, the CPS is a public-domain document, subject to the scrutiny of many. On the other hand, an enterprise PKI domain typically considers the CPS to be extremely sensitive, usually reserved for internal audit purposes. The CPS is rarely a public-domain document in these cases, nor is it used to convey information to the end users in the enterprise domain.

The role these documents have in forging cross-certification arrangements (cross-certification is described in Chapter 9) can also vary. One school of thought suggests that the CPS of one domain should be scrutinized against the CPS of another. On the other hand, the CPS may not form a suitable basis for establishing cross-certification (or more generally, interoperability arrangements) for a number of reasons. First, as noted earlier, the CPS tends to be an extremely detailed and voluminous document, which would make CPS comparisons tedious and labor intensive (barring standardized markup languages and automated tools, of course). Second, terminology variations from one CPS to another that make equivalency comparisons problematic may be present [PAG]. Third, a given organization may consider their CPS to be too sensitive to be released externally, even for the purposes of establishing a cross-certification agreement with another enterprise. It can therefore be argued that Certificate Policies form a much more suitable basis for establishing cross-certification agreements. In the future, we may even see the use of PKI Disclosure Statements for establishing interoperability agreements between enterprise domains. See http://www.verisign.com/repository/disclosure.html for an example of a PKI Disclosure Statement.

Given the above, some would suggest that only a CPS is required for a CA service provider and only a Certificate Policy is required for an organization. However, it has been our experience that a CPS is typically used in an enterprise context to document the internal operating procedures of the organization's PKI and that the CPS is often used for internal audit purposes. It is also possible for an organization to adopt the CPS of a third-party service provider when that third party supplies some or all of that organization's PKI services.

one domain to be designated equivalent to a policy OID in another domain. Thus, if two PKI domains have each defined a Certificate Policy for the exchange of their own internal e-mail and the two policies are deemed to be equivalent by each domain, defining yet a third policy OID to allow e-mail exchanges between the two domains is not needed.

### Policy Authorities

*Policy authorities* (sometimes referred to as *policy management authorities*) establish Certificate Policies. The policy authority itself may vary from one organization to another. For example, each organization may establish its own policies under the authority of the internal Information Technology Security (ITS) department or equivalent. Alternatively, this authority may emanate from a policy advisory board made up of members from each major department in an organization. In concert with the internal authority (or perhaps in lieu of such an authority), an external policy authority may establish the Certificate Policies for a number of PKI domains that belong to the same community of interest. In any event, the applicable policy authority is responsible for registering Certificate Policies with the appropriate registration authority (for example, a national registration authority) so that the Certificate Policy OIDs can be assigned appropriately.

## Certification Authority

In the context of a PKI, *certification* is the act of binding a subject name (and potentially other attributes) with a public key. As discussed previously in this chapter, this binding occurs in the form of a signed data structure referred to as a *public-key certificate*. A *Certification Authority (CA)* is responsible for issuing these public-key certificates. (See Box 6.4.) These certificates are digitally signed with the private key of the issuing CA.

---

### Box 6.4 Certificate Authority versus Certification Authority

A CA is sometimes referred to as a *certificate authority* rather than a *Certification Authority* in much of today's literature. Although it may be too late to stop the growing use of this term, we would like to point out that using this term to denote a CA is technically (and logically) incorrect. There is no such thing as a "certificate authority" in X.509, and the implication that a CA is an authority on certificates is somewhat misleading. Specifically, a policy authority (or policy management authority) is the authority on certificates; the CA is simply an instrument that issues certificates in accordance with the Certificate Policy dictated by the policy authority. The term *Certification Authority* is used throughout this book because a CA is an authority on the process of certification.

Because the issuing CA digitally signs certificates, they are self-protected from an integrity perspective. Thus, the certificates can be freely disseminated, assuming that they do not contain any sensitive information. (In Chapter 11, we discuss the difficulties associated with the dissemination of certificates that might be considered sensitive in nature.)

The CA can take on a number of different representations, depending on the trust model embodied by that CA. For example, in an enterprise domain, one can expect one or more CAs to be responsible for issuing certificates to the employees of the enterprise. The employees essentially place their "trust" in the enterprise CA(s).[4] A completely different architecture is reflected in the PGP "web of trust" model where individuals can act as their own CA, and all trust decisions lie with the individual rather than a remote CA. (Chapter 9 provides a more detailed discussion regarding trust models and the role a CA plays in relation to those trust models.)

# Registration Authority

Although the registration function can be implemented directly with the CA component, it sometimes makes sense to off-load the registration function to a separate component referred to as a *Registration Authority (RA)*. For example, as the number of end entities in a given PKI domain increases and/or the end entities are widely dispersed geographically, the notion of centralized registration becomes problematic. Judicious deployment of multiple RAs (sometimes referred to as *Local Registration Authorities,* or *LRAs*) helps solve this problem. The primary purpose of the RA is to off-load certain functions from the CA to enhance scalability and decrease operational costs.

Although the functions implemented by the RA may vary, it can be designed to support one or more of the following:

- Establish and confirm the identity of an individual as part of the initialization process. (For example, the RA might verify the identify of an individual through a combination of physical presence and associated identification such as a driver's license, employee badge with picture, or a passport.)

- Distribute shared secrets to end users for subsequent authentication during an on-line initialization process.

- Initiate the certification process with a CA on behalf of individual end-users (including the registration of certain attributes to be associated with the end user).

---

[4]We recognize that the interpretation of the word *trust* is often the subject of lively debate. Chapter 9 provides the definition of *trust* as it applies in the context of this book.

- Generate keying material on behalf of an end user.

- Perform certain key/certificate life-cycle management functions, such as to initiate a revocation request or a key recovery operation on behalf of an end entity.

Regardless of the set of functions implemented in the RA, it should be noted that a RA is *never* allowed to issue certificates or CRLs. These functions rest solely with the CA.

End-entity registration requirements may vary significantly from one domain to another, between distinct applications in a given domain, or between distinct contexts in a given application in a given domain. (Chapter 7 discusses specific registration issues and procedures further.)[5]

## Summary

The primary focus of this chapter has been the structure and semantics of the X.509 Version 3 public-key certificate and the need for certification in order to maintain the integrity and trustworthiness of the certificate itself. The Version 3 X.509 public-key certificate is by far the preferred choice for the enterprise domain, and it is quickly becoming widely accepted in other environments such as the Internet. This chapter also introduced a number of other certificate types (which may or may not be encountered in wide-scale implementation practice).

We also addressed the importance and role of the CA and RA components. A CA is responsible for issuing certificates in accordance with one or more Certificate Policies. The CA may also be responsible for end-entity registration, although one or more RAs can implement this function separately. Deploying one or more RAs reduces cost and enhances the overall scalability of a large-scale PKI.

A full understanding of certificates and certification requires familiarity with two related topics: the details regarding key/certificate life-cycle management (see Chapter 7) and the concepts associated with trust models and certification path processing. (See Chapter 9.)

---

[5]Chapter 7 presents in detail all aspects associated with key/certificate life-cycle management (for example, registration and initialization, revocation, key recovery, and so on).

# CHAPTER 7

# *Key and Certificate Management*

As discussed in Chapter 2, asymmetric cryptography is based on the use of public/private-key pairs. A public key is typically distributed in the form of a certificate, whereas a private key is a separate and distinct data structure always protected from unauthorized disclosure in transit, use, and storage. The term *key/certificate life-cycle management* denotes the life-cycle management functions associated with the creation, issuance, and subsequent cancellation of public/private-key pairs and their associated certificates.

In this chapter, we discuss the various phases of key/certificate life-cycle management that must be offered as part of any comprehensive PKI. Where appropriate, we also discuss the relationship this has to the actual usage of the keying material.[1]

It is important to recognize that the discussion is based on a fundamental separation between the *identity* of the end entity (that is, an end user, process, or component) and the *keying material* associated with that end entity. In other words, the key/certificate life-cycle management process described herein is associated with the generation, issuance, and subsequent cancellation of the keying material, not with the identity of the individual, process, or component associated with that keying material.

---

[1]The key/certificate life-cycle management functions are considered separate from the actual *usage* of the public/private-keying material. As discussed in Chapter 2, *usage* is related to performing cryptographic operations. This includes applying the signing private key to generate a digital signature and applying the corresponding verification public key to perform digital signature verification. Similarly, *usage* includes applying the encryption public key to encrypt data and applying the corresponding decryption private key to decrypt the data.

**Figure 7.1** Key/certificate life-cycle management.

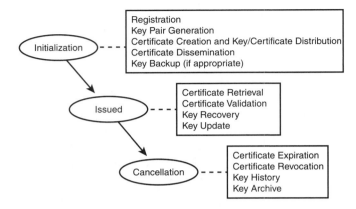

Underlying assumptions regarding a comprehensive key/certificate life-cycle management to keep in mind are as follows:

- End-entity management of key and certificate life cycle is not practical.

- The key/certificate life-cycle management must be automated as much as possible.

- The key/certificate life-cycle management must be as unobtrusive to the end entity as possible.

- Comprehensive key/certificate life-cycle management requires the secure operation and cooperation of trusted entities such as Registration Authorities (RAs) and Certification Authorities (CAs), as well as client-side software that interacts with these components when necessary.

## Key/Certificate Life-Cycle Management

Figure 7.1 illustrates the various phases of the key/certificate life-cycle management.[2] We note that some environments will not necessarily require every facet of the key/certificate life cycle shown here. Further, some environments may require certain aspects that are not required in others. To meet these varying demands, a comprehensive PKI must offer each of the services described in the sections that follow.

---

[2]A similar term, *key management* or *key exchange,* is often used to denote the method in which encryption/decryption keys are securely conveyed to the appropriate parties. This interpretation should not be confused with key/certificate life-cycle management as it is being used within this chapter.

## Initialization Phase

Before end entities can engage in services supported by the PKI, they must *initialize* into the PKI. Initialization is composed of the following: end-entity registration, key pair generation, certificate creation and key/certificate distribution, certificate dissemination, and key backup (if applicable).

The registration process can be achieved in a variety of ways. Figure 7.2 illustrates one possible scenario where end-entity initialization involves both an RA and a CA. (The RA and CA components are introduced in Chapter 6.) Note that other possible scenarios are also available. For example, all transactions could flow through the RA, or the RA component may not exist at all, and the transactions would flow directly between the end entity and the CA.

The aspects that comprise the initialization phase are discussed further in the sections that follow.

### End-Entity Registration

*End-entity registration* is the process in which the identity of an individual user or process is established and verified. The level of verification associated with assessing the identity of a given end entity depends on the Certificate Policy and/or Certification Practice Statement (CPS) that applies to that particular end entity's security domain. (Certificate Policies and CPSs are addressed in Chapter 6.)

In Figure 7.2, the end-entity registration is performed on-line, as illustrated by the exchange of the registration form. This on-line registration process should be authenticated and protected. The actual registration requirements will vary based on the environment as well as the associated privileges implied by the issuance of a given certificate.

| Figure 7.2 | End-entity initialization scenario. |

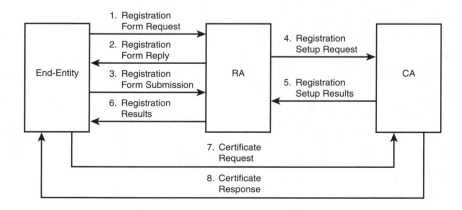

For example, one might expect the registration process for an end user authorized to approve multimillion dollar transactions to be rather rigid, including (1) physical presence at the appropriate RA or CA, (2) several forms of photographic identification such as a passport and employee identification badge, and (3) any requisite authorization forms. On the other hand, the registration procedures associated with credentials that will be used solely for noncommittal e-mail applications are expected to be much less stringent.

In any case, the registration process typically includes assigning one or more shared secrets to the end entity in order to authenticate that end entity to the CA later in the initialization process. The type(s) of shared secret(s) and the complexity of the authentication step(s) are likely to vary from one domain to another. For example, an RA or CA might assign a reference value and initial authentication key to the end entity through some trusted out-of-band mechanism [RFC2510]. Sometimes preexisting shared secrets can be exploited to facilitate the registration process. For example, a bank can make use of existing customer account information to verify the identity of the end user during the enrollment process.

### Key Pair Generation

*Key pair generation* consists of the generation of a public/private-key pair as described in Chapter 2. The keying material may be generated in advance of the end-entity registration process or in direct response to the end-entity registration process.

In the comprehensive PKI model, it is possible to generate the keying material within the end-entity's client system (for example, within a browser), within the RA, or within the CA. Alternatively, a trusted third-party key generation facility may be appropriate in some environments. The location of the key pair generation is an important consideration, and it is often the topic of some lively debate. Factors that may have an impact on this location include capability, performance, assurance, legal ramifications, and intended key usage.

Much of the controversy associated with the location of the key pair generation function centers around key usage. In particular, multiple key pairs per end entity can be used to support separate and distinct services. (Refer to Chapter 10 for more information regarding the use of multiple key pairs.) For example, one key pair might be used to support non-repudiation services while another key pair might be used to support confidentiality or key management functions.

Although it is not universally agreed upon, it can be argued that the location of the key generation must be within the client system if the keys are to be used for non-repudiation purposes. This is due to the assertion that possession of the signing private key by any other entity makes non-repudiation much more difficult to achieve. Alternatively, the view can be taken

## Box 7.1   Support for Non-Repudiation

Regardless of the level of trust that a given PKI entity places in the CA (and in those that operate the CA), true PKI support for non-repudiation requires the CA—or any other key backup facility that may be in place—to prove to the *satisfaction of a third party* that the private key could not possibly have been used by anyone other than the owner of the private key. In practice, this will often be very difficult to achieve. Therefore, for keys that may be used to authenticate transactions that are intended to have the property of non-repudiation, we recommend that the keying material should be generated by the "owner" of the public key and that private keys should never be revealed to anyone else (including a trusted third party).

that the CA should be the most trusted entity within the PKI, so knowledge of the signing private keys of individual users should not jeopardize the ability to support non-repudiation as long as that keying material is adequately protected by that CA. (See Boxes 7.1 and 7.2.)

Another factor that may have an impact on the location of the key generation is performance, although this may become less important as advancements in the underlying technology con-

## Box 7.2   Two-Key Pair Model

The notion of using distinct key pairs to separate non-repudiation services from confidentiality services is referred to as the *two-key pair model*. This orientation has existed since the earliest PKI systems were available, and it is now a widely recognized paradigm to be supported in any comprehensive PKI.

In the two-key pair orientation, the private key used to support digital signatures is referred to as the *signing private key,* and the corresponding certificate is referred to as the *verification certificate*. Similarly, the certificate used for encryption purposes is referred to as the *encryption certificate*, and the corresponding private key is referred to as the *decryption private key*.

More generally, the concept of three-key pairs has been introduced by the Swedish-based association Secured Electronic Information in Society (SEIS), which explicitly identifies an even finer degree of service separation between authentication and non-repudiation.

Chapter 10 provides additional details regarding multiple-key pairs.

tinue. For example, anyone who has requested a certificate using standard Web browser technology on an older (say, pre-Pentium) PC or laptop knows that the local key generation process is relatively slow. However, we have seen noticeable improvements with newer PCs and laptops, and this now appears to be less of an issue. Nonetheless, some would suggest that it might make more sense to relegate the key generation to the more powerful systems, such as a CA. This is especially true when the client systems are truly constrained devices such as cellular phones and the like. Alternatively, a counterargument can be made that centralized key generation will not scale because a single component (or limited number of components) will be required to perform CPU-intensive key generation for a large number of end entities. And as discussed previously, we recommend that key pairs used to support digital signature creation and verification should be generated by the client system whenever possible.

Another factor that may have an influence on the location of the key generation is related to assurance. It may be a requirement, for example, to have a trusted and independently evaluated cryptographic module generate the keying material. This would be in response to a requirement that the keying material must be generated in accordance with specific cryptographic guidelines. Specifically, the software or hardware module that is used to generate the keying material may be required to meet some minimum set of criteria to provide a sufficient level of assurance that the keying material is generated properly. The (U.S.) Federal Information Processing Standard (FIPS) 140–1 [FIPS140] is an example of evaluation criteria associated with cryptographic modules.

Yet another consideration would be based on legal and/or liability ramifications. For example, it may be a requirement to assert a certain amount of reliability in the key generation process. A PKI entity may not be capable of meeting the minimum criteria associated with this requirement, or it may not be willing to take responsibility for such a liability.

As you can see, a number of factors can have an impact on where the key pairs should be generated. It is therefore reasonable to conclude that each component (that is, the CA, RA, and client system) should be capable of generating the keying material, and protocols must be available to securely transfer the keys between these systems as necessary. This orientation is reflected in the more comprehensive certificate life-cycle management protocols that have been defined (as discussed later).

### Certificate Creation and Key/Certificate Distribution

The purpose and structure of a certificate is described in Chapter 6. Regardless of where key generation occurs, the responsibility for *certificate creation* lies solely with an authorized CA.

If the public key was generated by an entity other than the CA, that public key must be securely conveyed to the CA so that it can be placed within a certificate.

Once the keying material and related certificate have been generated, they must be distributed appropriately. The specific *key and certificate distribution* requirements depend on several factors, including where the keying material was generated, the intended use of the certificate, and any other considerations such as operational and/or policy constraints. For example, a given certificate may be distributed directly to the owner, to a remote repository, or both; this will depend on the intended key usage and operational considerations. Further, the distribution requirements associated with the private-keying material depends on where the keying material was generated and whether key backup is required.[3]

The requirement to request a certificate and to receive a certificate (and the associated private key, if applicable) back from a trusted entity (that is, the CA) requires the definition of a secure protocol mechanism. The IETF PKIX working group (see Chapter 18 for further details) has a pair of specifications on the standards track that addresses this requirement in both on-line and off-line modes as follows:

- The Internet X.509 Public Key Infrastructure Certificate Management Protocols (CMP) [RFC2510]

- The Internet X.509 Certificate Request Message Format (CRMF) [RFC2511]

(CMP Version 2 was in the works at the time of this writing.)

For some environments, other mechanisms, such as the Public Key Cryptography Standards (PKCS) 7 [RFC2315] and 10 [RFC2986], are a popular alternative. Other protocols—such as Certificate Management Messages over CMS (CMC [RFC2797]) and Cisco's Simple Certificate Enrollment Protocol—build on these basic PKCS 7/10 structures. CMP (in conjunction with CRMF) is the most comprehensive life-cycle management protocol compared to

---

[3]If the keying material was generated at the client system, the private key is already stored with the owner of the private key, and no further key distribution is required. (This does not apply to key backup, which is addressed in the section Key Backup.) However, if the keying material was generated elsewhere, the private key must be securely distributed to the owner of that key. Various mechanisms can be used to accomplish this, including RFC2510.

As a reminder, it is recommended that keying material intended for non-repudiation purposes should be generated at the client end. Therefore, the requirement to securely distribute private keys to their owner is typically associated with confidentiality keys (although these can be generated at the client's end as well).

these other alternatives, although CMC supports most of the life-cycle management functions as well.

### Certificate Dissemination

Once the private-key and corresponding public-key certificate have been distributed, one or more methods for conveying the certificate to other end entities must be available. Possible methods for disseminating this information include

- Out-of-band distribution (disseminating certificates to end entities using nonelectronic techniques such as physical delivery)

- Posting certificates in a public repository or database to facilitate on-demand and on-line retrieval

- In-band protocol distribution, for example, including the applicable verification certificate with a secure e-mail message (S/MIME)

Which of these alternatives is the most appropriate depends on a number of factors, including the key usage restrictions, privacy issues, scalability, and other operational considerations. Some of the more conventional methods are discussed later in this chapter in the section Certificate Retrieval.

The important point is that certificates must be readily available to fully realize the benefits of public-key cryptography. When a digital signature is verified, the verification certificate that corresponds to the signing private key used to create the digital signature must be available in order to verify the authenticity of that digital signature. Similarly, when a message originator is encrypting an e-mail message destined for one or more recipients, the encryption certificate for each recipient must be available so that the one-time symmetric key used to encrypt the e-mail message can be encrypted for each recipient.

In many cases, certificates used for digital signature verification purposes are automatically disseminated to the intended recipients. In other words, digitally signed documents such as an e-mail message usually include the certificate necessary to validate the digital signature. This saves recipients the trouble of retrieving the requisite verification certificate from a repository. On the other hand, certificates used for confidentiality purposes must be readily available to originators in order to facilitate scalable key management, and it is not the case that this information will always be available *a priori*. Thus, encryption certificates tend to be posted in some form of repository. Of course, variations of these practices are possible. For example, certificates used for digital signature purposes may be posted to a central repository in addition to or in lieu of distributing the certificate directly to the owner.

Certificate dissemination alternatives are discussed further in Chapter 11.

**Key Backup**

If the public/private-key pair is to be used for confidentiality, the initialization phase may also include key and certificate backup by a trusted third party.[4] Whether a trusted third party backs up a given key pair is determined by the governing policy for the environment under consideration. It should also be possible to indicate whether backup is desired during the initialization process [RFC2510].

The location of the backup facility may vary from one PKI domain to another. Factors that may have an impact on the specific choice include the dictates of the governing security policy and the liability model associated with each PKI component. In particular, the CA that issues the corresponding certificate might carry out the key backup function, or it might be supported by a separate key backup-and-recovery facility. (See Box 7.3.)

## Issued Phase

Once the private-key and the public-key certificate have been generated and appropriately distributed, the *issued* phase of the key/certificate life-cycle management begins. This phase includes the following:

- *Certificate retrieval* is the retrieval of a certificate from a remote repository (when required).

- *Certificate validation* is determining the validity of a certificate (including certificate path validation as described in Chapter 9).

- *Key recovery* is the retrieval of keying material from a CA or trusted third party when normal access to that material is no longer possible.

- *Key update* is the automatic generation of a new public/private-key pair and issuance of the corresponding certificate when a legitimate key pair is about to expire.

**Certificate Retrieval**

Certificate retrieval is concerned with the ability to readily access an end-entity certificate when and as required. As discussed earlier, the need to retrieve an end-entity certificate can be driven from two separate usage requirements:

---

[4]Again, it is our opinion that private keys designated for digital signature purposes in support of a non-repudiation service should *never* be backed up by a third party.

Also note that this section addresses trusted third-party backup, which is a completely separate issue from any backups that might be performed directly by the end entities. Although certain circumstances occur in which end entities should be capable of backing up their own keying material, this is not always possible nor something that is easily controlled at an organizational level. Backups performed by end entities simply cannot be relied on as a foolproof mechanism for recovering corporate data.

**Box 7.3**  Key Backup versus Key Escrow

The notion of *key backup* as discussed here should not be confused with *key escrow*. Key escrow is traditionally associated with the notion that keying material is somehow stored and made readily available to law enforcement and/or governmental agencies. Key escrow met with such widespread and visible resistance that it essentially forced the U.S. government to reverse its policy on mandatory key escrow in the late 1990s.

When we discuss the need for key backup, we are talking about responding to a legitimate business need to recover encrypted data that might otherwise be lost. Specifically, it is inevitable that a certain percentage of decryption keys will be rendered inaccessible to the owner of those keys. This could be the result of a forgotten password, a corrupted disk (where the keys are stored), a malfunctioning smart card (where the keys are stored), or an employee dismissal. A process for recovering decryption keys must be available under these circumstances, or recovering the encrypted data is impossible. The inability to recover this data could have severe financial and operational consequences, particularly in a corporate environment. Thus, the requirement for key backup in a comprehensive PKI is based on sound and practical business requirements.

1. The need to encrypt data destined for another end entity

2. The need to verify a digital signature received from another end entity

When encrypting data for one or more recipients, retrieving the encryption certificate of each recipient is necessary. The most common application of this requirement is to support key management between the originator of the protected data and the intended recipient(s). This allows for symmetric encryption of the data (for example, an e-mail message) using a newly generated secret key; this secret key can then be encrypted in the public key of each recipient (which is extracted from each recipient's encryption certificate). As a reminder, both symmetric and asymmetric cryptographic techniques are discussed in Chapter 2.

In the case of digital signature verification, the verification certificate of the originator is typically sent with the signed data as part of the protocol exchange. This avoids the need to look up the requisite verification certificate from a remote repository. However, it is also possible that retrieval of verification certificates from a remote repository might be preferred in some environments (for example, when the originator is forced to use an extremely low-bandwidth communication channel).

**Certificate Validation**

As discussed in Chapter 6, the integrity of public-key certificates can be verified because the certificate is digitally signed by the issuing CA. However, integrity is only one of several checks that need to be made before a certificate can be considered valid. The process of determining whether a given certificate can be used in a given context is referred to as certificate validation.

Certificate validation includes determining the following:

- The certificate has been issued by a recognized trust anchor. (Note that this may include certificate path processing. Trust anchors and certificate path processings are discussed in Chapter 9.)

- The certificate's integrity is sound (that is, the digital signature on the certificate is properly verified).

- The certificate is within its established validity period (as indicated by the Not Valid Before and Not Valid After parameters in the certificate).

- The certificate has not been revoked. (Refer to Chapter 8 for more information on certificate revocation.)

- The certificate is being used in a manner that is consistent with any name constraints, policy constraints, and/or intended usage restrictions (as indicated by client-side settings and specific certificate extensions such as the Certificate Policies, Name Constraints, Policy Constraints, and/or Key Usage extensions).

Certificate validation is performed before cryptographic operations based on its contained key are permitted. The order in which these operations should be performed is not universally agreed upon, but many implementations are designed to perform the more time-consuming operations after the less intensive operations have successfully completed.

## Key Recovery

As discussed earlier in this chapter, providing for an automated key backup-and-recovery facility in a comprehensive PKI is extremely important.[5] Inevitably, some number of end users will lose access to the private-keying material that is used for decryption purposes. Without a key backup-and-recovery capability, the result could be the permanent loss of enterprise-critical information. Thus, the key management life cycle includes the ability to recover private decryption keys from a remote backup facility such as a trusted key recovery center or a CA.

For reasons of scalability and to minimize the burden on both the PKI administrator and the end user, this process must be automated to the maximum extent possible. Any comprehensive life-cycle management protocol must include support for this capability [RFC2510].

---

[5]The discussion related to the key backup-and-recovery capability is reserved for encryption/decryption key pairs only. Signing private keys should not be backed up because this will inhibit the ability to provide non-repudiation. However, verification certificates should be archived, as discussed later in this chapter.

**Key Update**

Certificates are assigned a fixed lifetime (based on the applicable Certificate Policy and/or Certification Practice Statement, or CPS) when they are issued. When a certificate "nears" expiration, it is necessary to issue a new public/private key and the associated certificate. This is referred to as key update.

Although there is no universally agreed upon definition for what constitutes *near* in this context, it is suggested that key updates should occur automatically once 70% to 80% of the current key lifetime has been exhausted; the new keying material should then be used for all subsequent digital signature creation-and-encryption operations. (Note that appropriate verification certificates and decryption private keys may still be used when required.) This should allow a reasonable transition time for relying parties to acquire the new certificate so as to avoid service outages related to possession of the expired certificate.

As discussed in Chapter 6, private keys used for signing purposes may also have a specified lifetime that can be less than or equal to the corresponding verification certificate lifetime. If the private key expires before its companion certificate, the threshold established for the key update should be based on the private-key expiration rather than the verification certificate expiration so that the end entity is always in possession of a valid signing key.[6]

For reasons of scalability, this process must be automated, and any comprehensive life-cycle management protocol must include support for this capability [RFC2510]. In addition, this process should be totally transparent to the end user.

## Cancellation Phase

The key/certificate life-cycle management concludes with the *cancellation phase*. This phase includes the following:

- *Certificate expiration* is the natural expiration of a certificate.

- *Certificate revocation* is the assertion that an apparently legitimate certificate (and associated private key) is no longer valid.

---

[6]We emphasize the fact that key (and certificate) update should occur *before* the current certificate (or associated private key, if applicable) expires. This is to avoid any delays or gaps in the ability of the end entity to conduct business without any unnecessary interruption. Certificate update *after* the previously issued certificate expires essentially forces a reset to the initialization phase, which will involve direct user interaction that could have otherwise been avoided.

- *Key history* is the record maintenance of relevant keying material (typically with the end entity) so that data encrypted by keying material that has subsequently expired can be decrypted.

- *Key archive* is the secure third-party storage of keying material for key history recovery, audit, and dispute resolution purposes.

**Certificate Expiration**

As discussed in Chapter 6, certificates are assigned a fixed lifetime at the time of issuance (as indicated by the Not Valid After date/time within the certificate). Eventually, the established validity period of a given certificate will expire.

When a certificate expires, the following three events can occur with respect to the end entity associated with that certificate:

- *No action* occurs when the end entity is no longer enrolled in the PKI.

- *Certificate renewal* occurs when the same public key is placed into a new certificate with a new validity period.

- *Certificate update* occurs when a new public/private-key pair is generated and a new certificate is issued (although this step should take place before the certificate expires, as discussed earlier in this chapter).

(See Box 7.4 for an explanation of the difference between a certificate renewal and a certificate update.)

**Certificate Revocation**

As discussed in Chapter 8, certificate revocation is concerned with the timely cancellation of a given certificate before it might naturally expire. The requirement to revoke a certificate can stem from a number of factors, including suspected private-key compromise, a change in job status, or termination of employment. The specific reason codes are defined in the X.509 Recommendation [X509–00], and they are described further in Chapter 8.

Under certain circumstances, an end user may personally initiate the revocation of his or her own certificate (for example, due to suspected compromise of the corresponding private key). Such a request may be initiated on-line directly to an RA or a CA. Alternatively, the end user may need to contact the RA or CA through some other means (via telephone or through physical presence). For example, this would be necessary when the end user's laptop or smart

**Box 7.4** Certificate Renewal versus Certificate Update

The notion of *certificate renewal* is different from *certificate update*. The specific difference is that certificate renewal preserves the original public/private-key pair, whereas certificate update does not (that is, a new public/private-key pair is generated). Presumably, certificate renewal is used when (1) the circumstances associated with the issuance of the original certificate have not changed and (2) the cryptographic strength of the public/private-key pair is still thought to be sound.

However, it is dangerous to renew certificates unless certain precautions are taken. Specifically, you must be careful to ensure that digital signatures produced under the auspices of one set of certificate attributes can be distinguished from digital signatures produced under another set of certificate attributes. It has been suggested that one method for achieving this is to always (securely) couple the appropriate verification certificate with the digital signature.

card has been lost or stolen. In either case, the RA can be used to initiate the Certificate Revocation on the end user's behalf. (The functionality of an RA is not limited to registration.) Figure 7.3 illustrates these two scenarios. Of course, authorized administrators will also have the capability to revoke end-entity certificates when circumstances warrant.

**Figure 7.3** Certificate revocation sample scenarios.

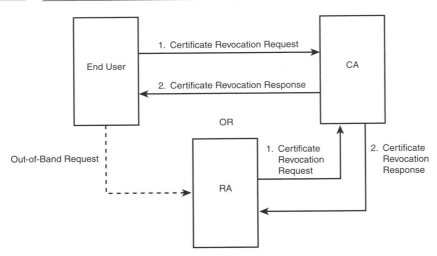

**Key History**

Since certificates are issued with fixed lifetimes, encryption keys eventually expire. However, this does not mean that all the data that was encrypted with that key should no longer be recoverable. It is therefore necessary to reliably and securely store keying material necessary for decryption even though the corresponding encryption certificate has expired. This is referred to as key history.

The requirement for this service is mainly for confidentiality keys. Specifically, private-keying material used for decryption must be stored so data that has been encrypted using the corresponding encryption public key can be recovered in the future. Some would argue that key history also applies to keys used for digital signature purposes, although this is more appropriately satisfied through key archive (as discussed in the next subsection).

Key history information is typically stored local to the owner for easy retrieval when necessary. However, it could also be stored with a CA or other trusted party, assuming that an automated mechanism is available to securely retrieve the necessary keying material when and as required.

## Box 7.5   Key History versus Key Archive

*Key history* is typically directly coupled with the end entity in order to provide easy access to that end entity's decryption keys when attempting to access data that has been encrypted in a key that has expired. *Key archive* is a service typically provided by a third party, and it involves the storage of keying material associated with many end entities. The services provided by the key archive may include (or be coupled with) notarization and time-stamping services, audit trails, and/or restoration of an end entity's key history. The latter service would be necessary when the local key history of an end entity is lost or destroyed. The key history of a given end entity can be restored by the key archive facility in response to a request from (1) the owner of the key history or (2) someone authorized to access that keying material in the absence of the end entity (for example, a corporate security officer).

Finally, a key archive facility may be necessary when attempting to verify a digital signature created by what is now expired keying material. Retrieval of the expired public-key certificate is required in this case (assuming that the public-key certificate is not available with the digitally signed data). This may also be coupled with a notarization service that could be used to prove that the signing private key was valid at the time the digital signature was created (even though that key has since expired).

**Key Archive**

Key archive is the long-term storage of keying material (including encryption and verification certificates) typically supported by a CA or other trusted party. Key archive differs from key history in the sense that archival can be used both for audit purposes and to help resolve disputes, especially when coupled with trusted time-stamping and notarization services. (These concepts are discussed further in Chapter 5; see Box 7.5 for an explanation of the difference between key history and key archive.)

## Summary

This chapter addressed the various phases that comprise the comprehensive key/certificate life-cycle management. Each phase was discussed in detail, and various issues associated with each phase were identified.

The importance of comprehensive key/certificate life-cycle management was addressed, and various pointers to additional information within this book were provided. In particular, the details regarding certificate revocation can be found in Chapter 8, the certificate dissemination mechanisms are described in Chapter 11, and the requirements associated with client-side software are discussed in Chapter 12.

# CHAPTER 8

# *Certificate Revocation*

As discussed in Chapter 6, certificates are used to bind a name with their corresponding public key. Normally, this binding is valid for the full lifetime of the issued certificate. However, circumstances arise when an issued certificate should no longer be considered valid, even when the certificate has not yet expired. Reasons for revocation vary, but they may involve anything from a change in job status to a suspected private-key compromise. Therefore, an efficient and reliable method must be provided to revoke a public-key certificate before it might naturally expire.

As we will discuss in Chapter 9, certificates must pass a well-established validation process before they can be used. Part of that validation process includes making sure that the certificate under evaluation has not been revoked. Essentially, Certification Authorities (CAs) are responsible for posting revocation information in some form or another. Relying parties (recall from Chapter 6 that a relying party is the *user* of a certificate for some express purpose) must have a mechanism to either retrieve the revocation information directly or rely on a trusted third party to resolve the question on their behalf. Figure 8.1 helps illustrate these concepts.

Certificate revocation can be implemented in a number of ways. One method is to use periodic publication mechanisms such as Certificate Revocation Lists (CRLs), which can be instantiated in a number of different forms or variations. (See Box 8.1.) There are also alternative on-line query mechanisms such as the Online Certificate Status Protocol (OCSP) [RFC2560]. The purpose of this chapter is to explore the various options that have been or are being defined. We will also explore circumstances in which the traditional notion of revocation information may not be required or desired.

This chapter does not address specific retrieval mechanisms or protocols unless they are explicit parts of the revocation method itself (as in the case of OCSP). In general, any number

**Figure 8.1** Certificate revocation model.

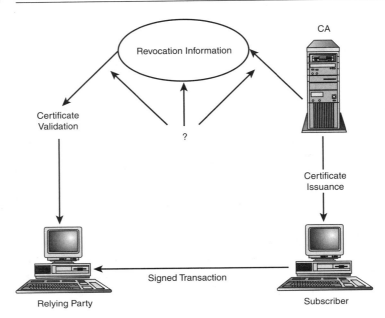

of protocols can be used to retrieve the revocation information described in this chapter, including the Lightweight Directory Access Protocol (LDAP), the File Transfer Protocol (FTP), and the Hypertext Transfer Protocol (HTTP). These retrieval mechanisms are addressed in Chapter 11.

## Box 8.1  Updating and Posting Revocation Information

The frequency with which revocation information is updated and posted is an extremely important consideration. The acceptable delay associated with knowing that a certificate should be revoked and actually disseminating this information to the relying parties who are processing that certificate must be established. In some environments, this delay may be relatively generous (say, on the order of hours or perhaps even days). In other environments, even minimal delay could be considered intolerable. The acceptable delay between discovering that the certificate should be revoked and actually posting the revocation information in a form that can be retrieved by a relying party should be specified as part of the governing Certificate Policy, and the revocation techniques used within a given domain must adhere to that policy.

# Periodic Publication Mechanisms

In this section, we describe the various periodic publication mechanisms available. The periodic publication mechanisms discussed within this section are complete CRLs, Certification Authority Revocation Lists (CARLs), End-entity Public-key Certificate Revocation Lists (EPRLs), CRL Distribution Points (also known as Partitioned CRLs), Delta and Indirect Delta CRLs, Indirect CRLs, Redirect CRLs, and Certificate Revocation Trees (CRTs). (See Box 8.2 for an explanation of new terminology.)

Generally, these periodic publication mechanisms can be considered "prepublication" techniques characterized by issuing the revocation information on a periodic basis in the form of a signed data structure. With the exception of Certificate Revocation Trees (CRTs), all these techniques are defined in the 2000 version of X.509, and they are based on the same basic ASN.1 data structure referred to as a Certificate Revocation List or, more commonly, a CRL. The basic CRL structure is discussed in the following section; the remaining sections address the periodic publication mechanisms listed above.

## Certificate Revocation Lists (CRLs)

Simply stated, CRLs are signed data structures that contain a list of revoked certificates. The digital signature appended to the CRL provides the integrity and authenticity of the CRL. The signer of the CRL is typically the same entity that signed the issued certificates that are listed in the CRL. However, the CRL may be signed by an entity other than the certificate issuer, as discussed later in this chapter.

CRLs can be cached to enhance performance. Caching CRLs also facilitates the ability to verify certificates while working off-line. Of course, the ability to cache CRLs and the reliance placed in a cached CRL must be in accordance with the applicable Certificate Policies.

## Box 8.2  New Terminology

The terminology used to describe CRL information associated with end entities and CAs has been updated in the 2000 version of X.509 [X509–00]. In particular, a CRL that contains end-entity information only is now referred to as an End-entity Public-key Certificate Revocation List (EPRL). These were referred to simply as CRLs in the 1997 and prior versions of X.509. A CRL that contains information about CAs only is referred to as a Certification Authority Revocation List (CARL). These were referred to simply as Authority Revocation Lists (ARLs) in the 1997 and prior versions of X.509. Note that we use terminology consistent with the latest version of X.509 [X509–00].

Currently two different versions of a CRL are defined. Version 1 was defined in the original X.509 specifications (circa 1988). Note that Version 1 CRLs are inherently flawed for several reasons:

- They have scalability concerns (that is, the size of a Version 1 CRL could easily grow beyond acceptable limits).

- They have functionality limitations specifically related to the inability to extend the CRL with additional features when needed.

- They are subject to CRL substitution attacks (that is, it is possible to maliciously substitute one CRL for another without detection).

Version 2 CRLs solve these problems by introducing the notion of extensions, much the same as the introduction of extensions with Version 3 X.509 public-key certificates (as discussed in Chapter 6). Certain extensions have been defined on a per-revoked-certificate-entry basis, and others are defined on a per-CRL basis, as described in the following sections. As with certificate extensions, these CRL extensions must be profiled for use in a given environment. (See Box 8.3.)

Note that extensions may be marked critical or noncritical. An extension marked critical should be processed and understood by the relying party, although X.509 does provide for some degree of flexibility that can be applied under certain circumstances [X509–00, Section

## Box 8.3  CRL Profiles

Although X.509 defines certain requirements associated with the standard fields and extensions of a certificate, specifying additional details is often necessary. As discussed in Chapter 20, this is because many standards tend to be general in nature, and additional levels of specificity are required to realize interoperability.

As noted in Chapter 6, the Internet Engineering Task Force (IETF) Public Key Infrastructure X.509 (PKIX) Working Group introduced a certificate and CRL profile for the Internet in January 1999 with the publication of RFC2459. This was replaced by RFC3280 in April 2002. RFC3280 reflects many of the enhancements that were introduced with the 2000 version of X.509.

Although RFC3280 is targeted for the Internet community, a number of its recommendations could equally apply in the enterprise environment, and we recommend that consistency should be maintained wherever possible. Therefore, references to some of the recommendations made within RFC3280 will be provided where appropriate.

7.3, Note 4]. At a minimum, the relying party is to assume that certificates on the list have been revoked, even if certain extensions are not understood. However, if a per-CRL extension is not understood, it cannot be assumed that the list of revoked certificates is complete. Non-critical extensions may be gracefully ignored if the relying party does not understand them (that is, the extension can be ignored without any further action on the part of the relying party).

The generic structure of a Version 2 CRL is represented in Figure 8.2. The fields represented within Figure 8.2 are defined as follows:

- *Version* indicates the version of the CRL (either the value is Version 2 or the field is not present, indicating that it is a Version 1 CRL; that is, this field was not defined as part of the Version 1 CRL syntax).

- *Signature* indicates the object identifier (OID) of the algorithm used to calculate the digital signature on the CRL. For example, the OID for Message Digest 5 (MD5) with RSA might be present, indicating that the digital signature is an MD5 hash encrypted using RSA.

- *Issuer* is the Distinguished Name (DN) of the CRL issuer (that is, the signer of the CRL) and must always be present and unique.

- *This Update* is the time that this CRL was issued, which may be represented in UTC Time or Generalized Time (however, RFC3280 has specific rules associated with the use of these time representations).

**Figure 8.2**    Version 2 CRL structure.

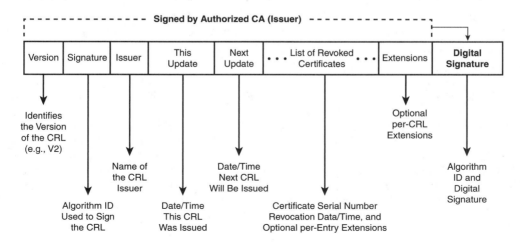

- *Next Update,* an optional field, is the time by which the next CRL will be issued. (Note that the same time representations for This Update also apply here and that RFC3280 actually mandates the use of this field even though it is designated as Optional in X.509.) Also note that a new CRL may be issued before the Next Update time specified.

- *Revoked Certificates* is the list of revoked certificates, in which a unique identifier references each certificate (that is, the list contains the unique serial numbers of the revoked certificates, not the actual certificates).[1] Each entry also includes the time that the certificate was no longer considered valid, and optionally, it may include per-entry extensions as discussed further in the following section.

- *Extensions* is the optional per-CRL extensions as discussed later in this chapter.

**Per-Entry Extensions**

The X.509 standard [X509–00] defines several extensions that can be used on a per-entry basis. This allows additional information to be conveyed with each individual revocation, which was not possible with Version 1 CRLs. The per-entry extensions are the following:

- *Reason Code* is the reason the certificate was revoked. Reason Code includes key compromise, CA compromise, affiliation change, superseded, cessation of operation, certificate hold, remove from CRL, privilege withdrawn, and unspecified. There is also an AA compromise revocation reason, but it applies only to attribute certificates.

- *Certificate Issuer* is the name of the certificate issuer, which is only required for indirect CRLs as described later in the chapter. If the Certificate Issuer extension is present, it must be marked critical in accordance with X.509.

- *Hold Instruction Code* is used to support the temporary suspension of a certificate. The suspended certificate can be subsequently reinstated or permanently revoked. The specific action to be taken when this extension is encountered is identified by an OID present in this extension.[2]

---

[1]Certificates are not actually recorded in the CRL; only a reference to the revoked certificate is included (for example, the unique serial number). Further, when the revoked certificate eventually expires (that is, when the not-valid-after date/time has been reached), it is no longer necessary to retain the serial number of that certificate on any subsequently issued CRLs. However, if a certificate is revoked, it should appear on at least one CRL (even if the certificate validity period has subsequently expired between the time revocation first occurred and the time the next CRL was issued). This is to ensure that evidence that a given certificate was revoked before it actually expired can be recorded and archived appropriately.

The information associated with that certificate (that is, when it was revoked, revocation reason, and so on) must be securely archived for future reference.

- *Invalidity Date* is the known (or suspected) time that the certificate was no longer considered valid.

**Per-CRL Extensions**

The 2000 version of X.509 [X509–00] has introduced significant enhancements when compared with the 1997 version of X.509 [X509–97]. Extensions that have been introduced in the 2000 version of X.509 are so designated. The standard CRL extensions are the following:

- *Authority Key Identifier* is the unique identifier of the key that should be used to verify the digital signature calculated over the CRL. The Authority Key Identifier distinguishes between multiple keys that apply to the same CRL issuer. Multiple (unexpired) keys may exist for the same CRL issuer for a number of reasons, including during overlapping periods of time to facilitate CA key rollover. This extension is always marked noncritical in accordance with X.509, but the inclusion of this field is mandated by RFC3280. RFC3280 also specifies that the key identifier method (as opposed to the use of issuer name/serial number) must be used.

- *Issuer Alternative Name* is one or more alternative name forms associated with the CRL issuer. The Issuer Alternative Name identifies the CRL issuer using something other than the DN designated in the Issuer Name field (for example, an IP address, DNS name, RFC-822 e-mail address, and so on). X.509 allows this extension to be marked noncritical or critical, but RFC3280 recommends that this should *not* be marked critical.

- *CRL Number* conveys a unique serial number for each CRL relative to the issuer of the CRL and the associated authority directory attribute or CRL Distribution Point. (Also see CRL Stream Identifier later.) It is a monotonically increasing integer that allows the detection of missing CRLs. This extension is always marked noncritical in accordance with X.509, but the inclusion of this field is mandated by RFC3280. RFC3280 suggests that the CRL Number should be unique relative to a given issuer and CRL scope. This can be used to detect when one CRL supercedes another, and it identifies complementary complete CRLs and Delta CRLs.

---

[2]The utility of the Hold Instruction Code has been the topic of some debate. Some have questioned the usefulness of temporarily suspending the use of a certificate, whereas others see legitimate business reasons for implementing this capability. RFC3280 defines several OIDs that can be used in the Internet environment. Specifically, three Hold Instruction Codes have been defined representing None, Call Issuer, and Reject. Note that RFC3280 points out that the use of None is semantically equivalent to the absence of the Hold Instruction Code and it has been "strongly deprecated for the Internet PKI."

- *CRL Scope,* formally standardized in the 2000 version of X.509 [X509–00], provides an extremely flexible method for partitioning CRL information. CRLs can be partitioned in a variety of ways, including by certificate type, certificate revocation reason codes, serial numbers, subject key identifiers, and name subtrees. In accordance with the 2000 version of X.509, this extension is always marked critical.

- *Status Referrals,* formally standardized in the 2000 version of X.509 [X509–00], this extension provides two primary functions. First, it provides for dynamic partitioning of revocation information. The Status Referrals extension includes CRL Scope (discussed earlier) within its syntax, so it can support dynamic partitioning in a variety of ways, including by certificate type, certificate revocation reason codes, serial numbers, subject key identifiers, and name subtrees. Additional information on this flexible partitioning mechanism is provided under the Redirect CRLs section later in this chapter. Second, it allows CAs to publish a list of current CRLs that can be used to ascertain whether a relying party already has the latest revocation information. This can help eliminate wasteful CRL downloads. It can also "advertise" new CRL information that may be published before the Next Update time of an older (but not yet expired) CRL. In accordance with the 2000 version of X.509, this extension is always marked critical.

- *CRL Stream Identifier,* formally standardized in the 2000 version of X.509 [X509–00], is used to "identify the context within which the CRL number is unique." For example, a unique stream identifier could be assigned to each CRL Distribution Point. Combining the stream identifier with the CRL number provides a unique identifier for each CRL issued by a given CA, regardless of the type of CRL. In accordance with the 2000 version of X.509, this extension is always marked noncritical.

- *Ordered List,* formally standardized in the 2000 version of X.509 [X509–00], indicates whether the list of revoked certificates is in ascending order based on serial number or revocation date. If this extension is absent, no specific ordering can be assumed unless dictated otherwise by local policy. In accordance with the 2000 version of X.509, this extension is always marked noncritical.

- *Delta Information,* formally standardized in the 2000 version of X.509 [X509–00], indicates that Delta CRLs corresponding to this CRL are available. This extension provides the location of the Delta CRL (specified as a General Name) and optionally the time when the next Delta CRL will be issued. In accordance with the 2000 version of X.509, this extension is always marked noncritical.

- *Issuing Distribution Point* indicates the name of the CRL Distribution Point (if any) and the types of certificates contained within the CRL (for example, end-user certificates only,

CA certificates only, and/or certificates revoked for a specific reason only). When applicable, it indicates that the CRL is an indirect CRL. (Additional information on indirect CRLs is provided later in the chapter.) Note that this extension, if present, must be marked critical in accordance with X.509. Even though this extension must be marked critical, RFC3280 does not require conforming implementations to support this extension.

- *Delta CRL Indicator* indicates that this CRL is a Delta CRL relative to the referenced "base CRL." The combination of the base CRL and the Delta CRL represents all revocation information known at the time when the Delta CRL was issued, relative to a given scope. The Delta CRL scope must be consistent with the base CRL scope. (Delta CRLs are discussed further later in this chapter.) This extension, if present, must be marked critical in accordance with X.509. RFC3280 provides additional implementation guidance surrounding the use of this extension.

- *Base Update,* formally standardized in the 2000 version of X.509 [X509–00], is used in Delta CRLs that contain the Delta CRL Indicator extension to indicate the date/time after which this Delta CRL provides revocation status updates. This extension is not necessary when the Delta CRL includes the CRL Scope extension. In accordance with the 2000 version of X.509, this extension is always marked noncritical.

- *Freshest CRL,* formally standardized in the 2000 version of X.509 [X509–00], points to the "freshest" CRL information available. In practice, this will typically be a pointer to a Delta CRL. RFC3280 points out that the scope of the Delta CRL must be the same as the scope of the CRL that contains this extension. In addition, Delta CRLs cannot use this extension (that is, it is not permitted for one Delta CRL to refer to another). In accordance with the 2000 version of X.509, this extension can be marked critical or noncritical. However, if it is marked critical, then the relying party has no choice but to check the freshest CRL information before using the certificate under evaluation.

**Private Extensions**

Private extensions can also be defined in accordance with X.509 on both a per-entry and per-CRL basis. Private extensions are typically defined for domain-specific use. As recommended in RFC3280, exercise care to avoid interoperability problems with other domains that do not recognize any privately defined extensions. Specifically, private extensions should not be marked critical unless it is absolutely essential to meet the operational requirements within a specific domain. This is of course true regarding any extension, standard or private. RFC3280 does not define any private CRL extensions.

## Complete CRLs

It is possible to create complete CRLs so that all revocation information associated with a particular CA domain is posted on a single CRL. Complete CRL postings may be appropriate for some CA domains, particularly those in which the number of end entities is relatively small.

However, there are two primary criticisms levied against the use of complete CRLs:

1. *The issue of scalability* Given that revocation information must survive throughout the life of an issued certificate, it is conceivable that full CRL postings can become quite voluminous in some domains. Although this is not a concern for relatively modest-sized communities, this can become an issue in the larger domains.

2. *The timeliness of the posted certificate revocation information* As the CRL size grows, it is reasonable to expect that the CRL validity period would be fairly generous, because continual downloading of new, voluminous CRLs every time a certificate is validated would represent unacceptable performance degradation with respect to network resources.

Although it is difficult to pinpoint the exact threshold at which complete CRL postings would become too voluminous for a given CA domain, identifying the primary factors likely to dictate this threshold is possible. Specifically, the number of end entities, the probability of revocation, the validity period of the issued certificates, and the certificate serial number size will all have an impact on the size of a given CRL.

Given that it is reasonable to think that this threshold will be exceeded in a significant number of environments, it is fair to conclude that complete CRL postings will not be a viable alternative in many instances. Fortunately, a number of standard alternatives can help alleviate this problem, as discussed throughout the remainder of this chapter.

## Certification Authority Revocation Lists (CARLs)

A CARL, as its name implies, is a CRL devoted exclusively to revocation information that is associated with CAs. Thus, by definition, CARLs do not contain end-user certificate revocation information. A CARL is identified using the Issuing Distribution Point and/or CRL Scope extension(s).

CARLs are used to revoke the public-key certificates of other CAs. The issuer of a CARL is typically either a superior CA (that is, it is responsible for revoking any subordinate CAs) or the issuing CA is revoking a cross-certificate issued by that CA. (The concepts associated with superior, subordinate, and cross-certified CAs are discussed further in Chapter 9.) Support for indirect CARLs is also possible. When validating a certificate path, a valid CARL must be available for each CA that has signed one or more certificates in that path. (This does not apply to self-signed CA certificates.) In general, revocation of CA certificates will be an exception rather than the rule.[3] Thus, the list of revoked certificates on a CARL will typically be absent or relatively small, making the overhead associated with retrieving CARLs minimal.

### End-entity Public-key Certificate Revocation Lists (EPRLs)

An EPRL, the converse to the CARL, is a CRL devoted exclusively to revocation information that is associated with end entities. Thus, by definition, EPRLs do not contain revocation information associated with CAs. An EPRL is identified using the Issuing Distribution Point and/or CRL Scope extension(s).

A single EPRL could contain all the end entity revocation information for a given PKI domain, or it could be partitioned in a variety of ways, as discussed further in the following pages.

### CRL Distribution Points

CRL Distribution Points (sometimes referred to as Partitioned CRLs) allow revocation information within a single CA domain to be posted in multiple CRLs. CRL Distribution Points have two significant benefits over complete CRLs:

1. The revocation information can be subdivided or partitioned into more manageable pieces to avoid the proliferation of voluminous CRLs.

2. The certificates can point to the location of the CRL Distribution Point, so the relying party doesn't need to have prior knowledge of where the revocation information for a particular certificate might reside.

Thus, the syntax of the CRL Distribution Point extension enables one to identify the specific location of the corresponding CRL partition. For example, a CRL Distribution Point can identify a specific server (for example, using a DNS name or IP address), as well as the specific location within that server where the CRL partition can be found (for example, a specific location within a Directory Information Tree [DIT] of a public repository or the name of a file resident on a Web server). Figure 8.3 illustrates the notion of a CRL Distribution Point.

---

[3]Revocation of CA certificates is expected to be quite rare. Generally, a CA certificate need only be revoked when it is decommissioned or when compromise of the CA's private key is known or suspected. Note also that in a strict rooted hierarchy, revocation of any given superior CA impacts all subordinate CAs and all end entities that fall under any of the affected CAs. The "higher" in the tree the revocation occurs, the more widespread the effect. Cross-certification has the distinct advantage that revocation of any given CA does not impact the internal operation of any other CA domain. These concepts are discussed further in Chapter 9.

**Figure 8.3**     CRL Distribution Point.

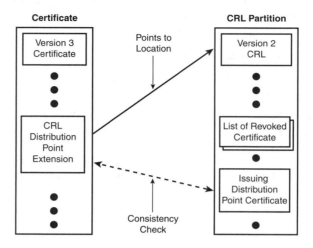

In summary, CRL Distribution Points offer a much more scalable alternative as compared with complete CRL postings. They can also be used to alleviate the performance issue when combined with proper partitioning and caching. However, one criticism levied against the use of CRL Distribution Points is that the CRL partitions are fixed or static. The notion of a more dynamic partitioning scheme is discussed next.

### Redirect CRLs

One drawback associated with the use of CRL Distribution Points is that once the associated certificate is issued, the CRL partition pointed to by the CRL Distribution Point is fixed for the life of that certificate. It also implies that the issuing CA has a prior knowledge regarding how the CRL information should be partitioned and that this partitioning cannot change over time. However, it may be desirable to make this more flexible, so the CRL partition sizes and storage locations may vary over time (for example, to optimize performance as the size and/or needs of the PKI community fluctuate).

Further, partitioning strategies could be based on a number of elements, including certificate serial number ranges, revocation reasons, certificate types, name subtrees, or any other range criteria that might apply to CRL information. It is therefore desirable to define new CRL extensions that would permit this more flexible and dynamic partitioning capability.

Members of the IETF PKIX working group developed the notion of dynamic partitioning, and these concepts were formally standardized in the 2000 version of X.509 [X509-00] through the definition of the CRL Scope and Status Referral extensions. The Status Referral extension provides a capability to "redirect" a relying party to the appropriate CRL. In other words, Status Referral can "point to" another location where the target CRL information actually resides. This intermediate CRL is referred to as a Redirect CRL.

As illustrated in Figure 8.4, the CRL Distribution Point certificate extension points to the Redirect CRL, and the Redirect CRL contains a Status Referral extension that points to the appropriate target CRL. Note that consistency checks are made along the way to prevent spoofing attempts such as CRL-substitution attacks. Also note that the Redirect CRL does not actually contain a list of revoked certificates. A Redirect CRL provides pointers only to target CRLs. This allows partitions to be changed over time without impacting the existing certificates. (Specifically, the CRL Distribution Point within the certificates need not change even if the CRL partitioning scheme happens to change.)

It is possible that this redirect process could be iterative, but this must be tempered with the additional performance overhead that would be incurred through multiple retrievals of the redirect information. In general, it is expected that one level of indirection will be sufficient.

The CRL Scope extension syntax is similar to the existing Issuing Distribution Point extension syntax, but it adds several new attributes such as the name of the CA (necessary if different from the issuer of the referral), specified ranges such as serial number range or subject public-key identifier range, and subtree name constraints. Given that the Issuing Distribution Point extension and the CRL Scope extension may contain overlapping fields (for example,

**Figure 8.4**    Redirect CRL orientation.

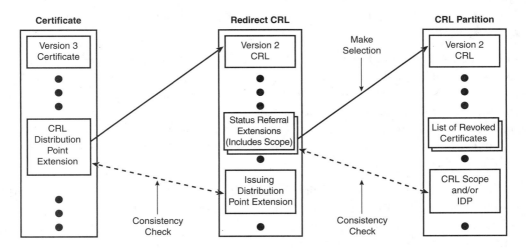

they both can identify the Distribution Point name, and they both can contain the Only Contains User Certs, Only Contains Authority Certs, and Only Some Reasons flags), it is possible that the two extensions can conflict with one another. As such, these two extensions are not meant to be used together. However, as this is not explicitly prohibited, care must be exercised to ensure consistency between them if they both are used.

## Delta and Indirect Delta CRLs

The idea behind Delta CRLs is to allow incremental postings of Certificate Revocation information. The revocation information can be relative to a base CRL or it can be relative to a particular point in time. If the Delta CRL references a base CRL, the combination of the base CRL and the Delta CRL constitutes all known revocation information, within the indicated scope, at the time the Delta CRL was issued. In this particular case, the Delta CRL Indicator extension is used to point to the base CRL Number. Alternatively, the Base Revocation Information component within the CRL Scope extension can be used to indicate that this is a Delta CRL. In this case, the Base Revocation Information references a particular point in time from which this Delta CRL provides updates. This may or may not reference a CRL that is complete for a given scope. (For example, it is possible to reference another Delta CRL.) Note that only one of these methods is permitted (that is, either the Delta CRL Indicator extension is used or the Base Revocation Information component of the CRL Scope extension is used).

Delta CRLs were included in the 1997 version of X.509 [X509–97], but they were not explained as clearly as they could have been. For example, it was implied that a full-base CRL posting must be published every time a Delta CRL was issued. This was clearly contrary to the intended purpose of Delta CRLs. Clarification surrounding the use of Delta CRLs has been added to the 2000 version of X.509 [X509–00]. In addition, support for Indirect Delta CRLs has been added. The main purpose of these CRLs is to enhance timeliness without significantly impacting performance.

To illustrate the power of Delta CRLs, let's take a closer look at the use of Delta CRLs relative to a complete base CRL for a particular scope. Delta CRLs are by definition based on some previously posted revocation information. This previous posting is referred to as a base CRL, and the Delta CRL contains revocation information that was not available when the base CRL was constructed. This allows for the publication of relatively small Delta CRLs that can be issued on a much more frequent basis than the base CRL, thus optimizing the often-competing goals of performance and timeliness.

It is possible to create and post multiple Delta CRLs against the same base CRL. Each subsequently issued Delta CRL contains the complete list of revoked certificates from the previously issued Delta CRL, plus any new certificates that have been revoked. Thus, it is only necessary to retrieve the latest Delta CRL; it is not necessary to accumulate previously issued Delta CRLs.

As an example, consider an enterprise domain that needs to restrict the issuance of complete CRL postings to once a week for performance reasons. However, the security policy within this domain dictates that revocation information must be disseminated within eight hours of the time a certificate is considered to be revoked (that is, the revocation delay can be no longer than eight hours). Obviously, the performance issue and the timeliness requirement associated with the dissemination of the revocation information are at odds with one another. The solution is to issue the base CRL once a week and issue Delta CRLs every eight hours. Thus, the more voluminous CRL posting only needs to be downloaded and cached once a week, and the relatively small Delta CRLs can be downloaded as required.

Delta CRLs can also be cached until the validity period associated with the Delta CRL expires. Alternatively, caching can be prohibited so that a Delta CRL would have to be retrieved every time a given certificate is validated; this may be a requirement in order to implement a near-zero latency policy with respect to the dissemination of timely revocation information.

A relying party can determine if Delta CRLs are implemented in a number of ways. For example, this can be determined through a published policy statement (which may be associated with a specific policy OID contained within a given certificate). It can also be accomplished through detecting the presence of the Freshest CRL certificate extension discussed earlier in this chapter. This certificate extension can be used to point directly to a Delta CRL, much the same as the CRL Distribution Point extension is used to point to a specific CRL partition.

When Delta CRLs are disseminated through the use of a directory service, they are typically expected to reside under the issuing CA's directory entry under the Delta CRL attribute as defined in X.509. However, as noted earlier, the Freshest CRL extension can be used as an alternative to point to a specific location where the Delta CRL resides.

The 2000 version of X.509 has also introduced the concept of Indirect Delta CRLs. Like Delta CRLs, Indirect CRLs are incremental postings based on some previously published or otherwise constructed CRL information. However, Indirect Delta CRLs can be used to update multiple CRLs issued by a single issuer (for example, a single Indirect Delta CRL can be used to provide updates to all CRL Distribution Points issued by a given CA). They can also be used to update multiple CRLs issued by multiple sources. The broader concept of Indirect CRLs is discussed in the following section.

## Indirect CRLs

Indirect CRLs enable revocation information normally supplied from multiple CAs to be issued within a single CRL. Indirect CRLs can be used to reduce the number of overall CRLs that need to be retrieved by relying parties when performing the certificate validation process. For example, a single PKI domain may have several CAs. Rather than force a relying party to retrieve multiple CRLs (one for each CA), the domain may decide to improve efficiency by combining all of that domain's certificate revocation information into one Indirect CRL. This may also prove useful in interdomain scenarios, to reduce traffic load and cost. There is also the possibility that trusted third-party service providers might offer this capability as a for-fee service. In all cases, the relying party must trust the Indirect CRL issuer to the same degree that they trust the CA issuing the certificate in question.

One way to determine if a CRL is an Indirect CRL is to examine the Indirect CRL component in the Issuing Distribution Point extension. If it is set to TRUE, then the CRL may contain revocation information from multiple sources. The Certificate Issuer component associated with each revocation entry is used to determine the associated issuer. For implementations that are compliant with the 2000 version of X.509, Indirect CRLs can also be supported through the presence of multiple Per Authority Scopes with different CA names specified in the Authority Name component.

The X.509 standard does not specify how revocation information is to be conveyed between the individual CAs and the CA issuing the Indirect CRL. However, it might be reasonable for the generator of the Indirect CRL to collate revocation information based on individual CRLs issued by each CA. This would allow an existing standard mechanism to be exploited, and it would still have the benefit of reducing the number of CRLs that each relying party must download. The reasonable assumption here is that the number of relying parties will far exceed the number of Indirect CRL issuers. However, the realized benefit is based on a number of factors, including assurance that the Indirect CRL does not become so large as to counter the performance benefit expected through combining revocation information from multiple sources.

### Certificate Revocation Trees (CRTs)

Certificate Revocation Trees (CRTs) is a revocation technology developed by a U.S.-based company named Valicert. Essentially, CRTs are based on Merkle hash trees, in which the tree itself represents all known certificate revocation information relevant to some known set of PKI communities. Although the information used to generate CRTs may be obtained from CRLs, the CRT technology is the only periodic publication mechanism discussed within this chapter that is not based on the CRL construct described in the section Certificate Revocation Lists (CRLs), earlier in this chapter.

To generate the hash tree, a sequence of expressions is generated for each participating CA. Each sequence represents a range in which the lower end point on the range represents the serial number of a revoked certificate for a given CA. For example, an expression might be "$CA_1 = CA_n$ and $1138 \leq X < 2001$," where $X$ is the serial number of the certificate issued by $CA_1$ that is currently under evaluation. This expression effectively indicates that (1) the certificate issued from $CA_1$ with serial number 1138 has been revoked and (2) certificates issued by $CA_1$ with serial numbers 1139 through 2000 (inclusive) have not been revoked. The expressions are ordered sequentially relative to a given CA, and the set of expressions for a given CA is also sequentially ordered relative to all the other known CAs. The entire set of mathematical expressions represents all that is known about the certificates that have been revoked for the universe of CAs currently known to the entity generating the hash tree.

A sample CRT is represented in Figure 8.5. The nodes on the extreme left represent the hashes of each mathematical expression known to the entity generating the tree. As illustrated by the arrows in the figure, each adjacent pair of nodes at a given level within the tree is then combined into one. If a pair exists, the two nodes are concatenated and hashed. The hash result is the value of the newly formed node to the right. If a pair does not exist (that is, there is an odd number of nodes at any given level), the single node is simply carried forward to the next level within the tree (as represented by nodes $N_{2,3}$ and $N_{3,1}$ in Figure 8.5). This process occurs repeatedly until a final "root" node is calculated, as represented by the rightmost node in Figure 8.5. This final node is signed for integrity and authenticity purposes.

To determine if the certificate has been revoked, the relying party checks to see if the certificate serial number is the lower end point on a range represented within the tree for a given CA. If it is, the certificate has been revoked; if not, it hasn't. This decision is based on comparing the certificate serial number being evaluated against the "nearest" equation to that value.

The integrity of this process must be verified, so the relying party must reconstruct the root node and compare it against the signed root node value. To accomplish this, the entity that

**Figure 8.5**   Sample CRT.

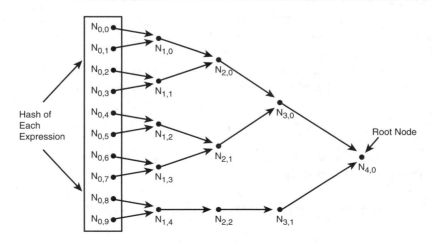

generated the tree supplies the nearest range to the serial number in question, all the necessary supporting nodes, and the signed (and time-stamped) root node. Again, this information is supplied by the entity that generated the tree, which is presumably a trusted third-party service or a service offered within a given enterprise domain. The necessary information can be supplied to the relying party so that it can perform the evaluation itself or it can rely on a trusted server to perform the evaluation on its behalf.

The main advantage associated with CRTs is that they can represent a large amount of certificate revocation information in a very efficient manner. In fact, the size of a CRT is on the order of $\log_2 N$, where $N$ is the number of revoked certificates.

### On-line Query Mechanisms

In this section, we discuss on-line query mechanisms for retrieving certificate revocation information. The on-line mechanisms differ from the periodic publication mechanisms in several respects—most notably because the on-line mechanisms typically require that the relying party be on-line whenever a question regarding the revocation status of a given certificate must be resolved. Periodic publication mechanisms are better suited for off-line operation because the revocation information can be cached. Of course, it is possible to allow information retrieved from on-line servers to be cached, but this must be tempered with any requirement to ensure that the freshest possible information is always made available to the relying party.

A significant amount of work has been devoted to developing on-line certificate status protocols within the IETF PKIX working group. The Online Certificate Status Protocol (OCSP) achieved RFC Proposed Standard status in June 1999. Because this was a first step in the direction of an on-line protocol to ask questions about a certificate of interest, OCSP was intentionally limited in terms of functionality. More recently, the PKIX group has explored the broader areas of Delegated Path Validation (DPV) and Delegated Path Discovery (DPD). An Informational RFC documenting the defined requirements for DPV and DPD has been issued and accompanying protocols satisfying those requirements (such as the Simple Certificate Validation Protocol, or SCVP, discussed later in this chapter) are being developed. See `http://www.ietf.org/html.charters/pkix-charter.html` for the latest status of this work.

### Online Certificate Status Protocol (OCSP)

Version 1 of the OCSP is documented in the Request for Comments (RFC) entitled "X.509 Internet Public Key Infrastructure Online Certificate Status Protocol—OCSP" [RFC2560]. OCSP is a relatively simple request–response protocol that offers a vehicle for obtaining on-line revocation information from a trusted entity referred to as an OCSP responder.

An OCSP request consists of the protocol version number (currently only Version 1 is defined), the service request type, and one or more certificate identifiers. The certificate identifier consists of the hash of the certificate issuer's DN, the hash of the issuer's public key, and the certificate serial number. Additional optional extensions may also be present.

Responses are also fairly straightforward, consisting of the certificate identifier, the certificate status (that is, "good," "revoked," or "unknown"), and the validity interval of the response associated with each certificate identifier specified within the original request. If the status of a given certificate is "revoked," the time that the revocation occurred is indicated; optionally, the reason for revocation may also be included.

The validity interval consists of This Update and, optionally, Next Update. However, whether the OCSP response can be cached locally will ultimately be a policy decision dictated by the governing domain. Their intended use is consistent with the same fields in a CRL as described earlier in the chapter. Like the request, the response may also contain optional extensions. OCSP also defines a small set of error codes that can be returned in the event that processing errors are encountered.

Figure 8.6 illustrates the interaction between a relying party and an OCSP responder. It also illustrates that numerous revocation strategies can be implemented behind the OCSP responder, as indicated by the dotted box labeled "Backend."

**Figure 8.6**     OCSP component interaction.

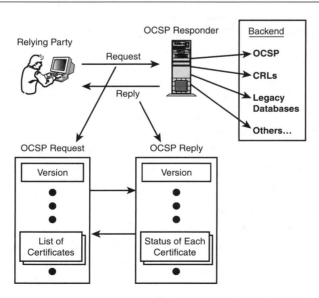

The OCSP responses must be digitally signed to provide assurance that the response is originating with a trusted entity and that it is not altered in transit. The signing key may belong to the same CA that issued the subject certificate, a trusted third party, or an entity that has been approved (through delegation) by the CA that signed the subject certificate. In any case, the relying party must be able to trust the response, which inherently implies that the relying party must trust the signer of the response. The relying party must therefore obtain a copy of the OCSP responder's public-key certificate, and that certificate must be signed by a trusted source. Requests may also be signed (useful, for example, if OCSP is operated as a "for-fee" service), but this is an optional feature within the protocol.

To help a relying party discover the appropriate OCSP responder(s), OCSP embraces the Authority Information Access private certificate extension as defined within RFC3280, Section 4.2.2.1. This allows the location(s) of the OCSP responder(s) applicable to a particular certificate to be conveyed as part of the certificate itself—much the same as the standard CRL Distribution Points extension is used to point to a CRL partition. Alternatively, the locations of one or more OCSP responders can be configured locally or via some other means.

### Understanding OCSP's Limitations

OCSP makes no claims whatsoever regarding the validity of the certificate other than its revocation status. In other words, OCSP is designed to indicate whether a given certificate has been revoked. OCSP does *not* verify that a certificate is within its validity period, nor does it ensure that the subject certificate is being used in the proper context as might be indicated through the Key Usage, Extended Key Usage, or any Policy Qualifier extensions that may be associated with the certificate. It is up to the relying party to perform all these checks via other means.

In addition, there seems to be some confusion regarding the utility of this protocol, especially in the sense of whether it can offer both real-time and up-to-date information regarding the revocation status of a given certificate. While the protocol itself offers a real-time response (assuming an appropriate OCSP responder is available on-line to service the requests), it does not necessarily mean that the reply from the OCSP responder will contain a zero latency response regarding the current revocation status of the certificate.

Stated another way, OCSP is nothing more than a protocol. It does not specify the backend infrastructure that might be used to collect the revocation information. Thus, it does not necessarily eliminate the need for CRLs or other methods for collecting certificate revocation information, and the "freshness" of the information supplied by the OCSP responder will be only as up-to-date as the latency involved in obtaining the revocation information from the responder's definitive source. This is not to say that it is impossible to implement a scheme based on OCSP that will be capable of offering near-zero latency revocation information—

especially if the source of the information (that is, the CA) is closely coupled with the OCSP service itself. However, it is inappropriate to simply assume that OCSP automatically offers fresh and up-to-date information, even if it is considered to be a "real-time" service.

In addition, the responses from an OCSP responder must be digitally signed in order to provide data integrity between the responder and the relying party, and this may result in a significant performance impact. This is not the case with CRL-based solutions since CRLs are signed on a strictly periodic basis, not in response to real-time requests. However, it also may be possible to preconstruct at least some subset of OCSP responses, which can be used to help alleviate some of the performance overhead. Also, issues associated with checking the revocation status of the OCSP responder's certificate should be reviewed [RFC2560, Section 4.2.2.2.1].

Section 5 of RFC2560 summarizes some of these concerns, as well as others (for example, concerns with denial of service due to flooding or by introducing false error responses).

### Simple Certificate Validation Protocol (SCVP)

SCVP is being developed within the PKIX Working Group to enable DPV and DPD in the Internet environment. DPV allows a relying party to off-load the certificate validation process to a trusted third party. It is expected that this will be extremely beneficial in certain environments in which local path validation is infeasible or undesirable. For example, consider a constrained device such as a cell phone. This device would be able to off-load the sometimes-intensive process of certification path validation. Another reason to off-load this process might be to enforce centralized validation policy within an environment without having to download that policy to every relying party device.

The second area addressed by SCVP is Delegated Path Discovery (DPD). DPD allows a relying party (such as a constrained device) to off-load the sometimes-intensive certification path construction process to a trusted third party. This can save the relying party from having to support a more extensive protocol such as LDAP in order to find and retrieve the certificates needed to build a path.

Some members of the PKIX group are also exploring alternative protocols for supporting DPV and DPD, including the definition of specific extensions to the basic OCSP request and response messages. This is not the first time that competing protocols have been proposed to accomplish the same objective. When this occurs, the IETF often lets the market decide which protocols will actually be implemented. It remains to be seen which and how many of the PKIX efforts in this area will survive in implementation practice. As always, the reader is advised to obtain the most recent status by consulting the IETF PKIX Working Group Web page.

## Other Revocation Options

Circumstances exist in which the direct dissemination of revocation information to the relying party is either unnecessary or undesirable. There are at least two cases of interest.

The first case involves the notion of short-lived certificates, in which the validity period of the certificates is shorter than the associated need to revoke them. For example, an enterprise may decide that it can accept a revocation window of up to eight hours. If the certificates they issue are valid for eight hours or less, there would not be a requirement to revoke those certificates. However, this orientation is only useful in relatively closed environments where performance issues associated with continual certificate renewal can be mitigated. It also assumes that any client software acting on behalf of a relying party recognizes that there is no need to retrieve certificate revocation information when validating certificates originating within this particular domain. This could be achieved through a policy OID contained within the short-lived certificates. (The concepts associated with Certificate Policies and the uses of OIDs are discussed in Chapter 6.)

The second case is where the approval of any given transaction is always rooted with the same entity. This orientation is prevalent in the banking industry where on-line transactions are always brokered through the consumer's bank. In this case, the bank uses backend databases to map the identity of the consumer to the specific accounts that the consumer is authorized to access. Because revocation information can be maintained along with the consumer account profile and all transactions are routed through the bank, there is no need to disseminate this information to the consumer's desktop. This orientation is also popular with a number of prominent banks when it comes to authorizing consumer debit or credit card transactions over the Web. Essentially, the current "brick-and-mortar" merchant orientation is favored such that the merchant must always go to its bank to have a financial transaction authorized by that bank. The authorization process would include verification that the consumer's certificate had not been revoked, which is achieved through direct interaction with the consumer's bank.

Note that in the second case the need to support a revocation capability has not been eliminated. It is simply that the method for facilitating the revocation need not be based on any of the methodologies described previously.

## Performance, Scalability, and Timeliness

Intuitively, one can make certain assumptions (or at least ask intelligent questions) regarding the performance, scalability, and timeliness characteristics of the various revocation information dissemination techniques described in this chapter. The key is to understand the principles behind these various techniques and to ask enough questions that will lead to solid engineering choices for a given PKI domain or set of interoperable PKI domains.

Unfortunately, little operational information with respect to performance in large-scale PKIs is available. However, several papers explore performance issues associated with some of the techniques described in this chapter. One such example is "A Model of Certificate Revocation" [Coop98]. Another paper that addresses general PKI performance issues is "Limits to the Scale of a Public Key Infrastructure" [Mose97].

In general, it is fair to assume that complete CRL postings will not scale in environments with a large number of end users. The threshold at which scalability becomes a concern depends on several factors, including the number of end users, the validity time of the issued certificates, and the frequency of revocation. CRL Distribution Points offer significant improvements in terms of performance and scalability, and Delta CRLs can be combined with CRL Distribution Points to achieve an efficient and timely revocation information distribution mechanism. (Implementation issues associated with the dissemination of this information are explored further in Chapter 12.)

On-line mechanisms such as OCSP may offer a viable service, but little is known with respect to the scalability and performance issues associated with the implementation of this type of model. For example, the number and physical distribution of OCSP responders that will be required to service a large, geographically distributed community of users requires further exploration. As well, the backend infrastructure is unspecified, and it may actually consist of a number of different revocation information distribution schemes.

It is important to note that OCSP responses must be digitally signed to guarantee the integrity of the response. Given that these digital signature operations are required on a per-transaction basis, this will likely have a non-negligible impact on performance. As the number of queries increases, this impact could become rather significant. Further, OCSP is by definition an on-line service. An appropriate OCSP responder must be available in order to respond to a given query. This orientation is clearly not well suited for off-line operation unless caching of responses is permitted.

In any case, timeliness is ultimately a function of policy, and it is up to the vendor community to respond to the specified requirement by selecting the appropriate revocation method(s).

Table 8.1 summarizes the various certificate revocation schemes and highlights specifics regarding each.

**Table 8.1** Certificate Revocation Scheme Summary

| Scheme | General Description | Remarks |
|---|---|---|
| CRLs (full postings) | Signed data structure containing a list of revoked certificates; defined in X.509. | Criticized from a performance, scalability, and timeliness perspective. However, X.509 standards-based alternatives exist to enhance performance, ensure scalability, and improve on timeliness. |
| CARLs | A type of CRL devoted solely to revocation information about CAs; defined in X.509. | Separation of end-entity and CA certificate revocation information is commonly found in implementation practice. |
| EPRLs | A type of CRL devoted solely to revocation information about end entities; defined in X.509. | Separation of end-entity and CA certificate revocation information is commonly found in implementation practice. |
| CRL Distribution Points | Used to point to CRL partitions; defined in X.509. | Allows certificate revocation information to be partitioned into more manageable pieces; however, partitions are static once established. |
| Delta and Indirect CRLs | Used to disseminate smaller, incremental postings; defined in X.509. | Can be used to greatly enhance performance and support timeliness requirements. Used in conjunction with other forms of CRLs (for example, CRL Distribution Points). |
| Indirect CRLs | Used to post revocation information originating from multiple CAs on a single CRL; defined in X.509. | Can be used to enhance performance under circumstances when concatenating revocation information from multiple sources is more advantageous than retrieving the information from each individual source. |
| OCSP | On-line capability used to return the revocation status of one or more certificates; defined in RFC2560. | Although designed to offer real-time responses, the "freshness" of the supplied information depends on the definitive source of the information. |
| Redirect CRLs | Used to support dynamic partitioning of revocation information; defined in X.509. | Relatively new concept that improves upon original Distribution Point techniques. |

| Table 8.1 | *Continued* | |
| --- | --- | --- |
| **Scheme** | **General Description** | **Remarks** |
| CRTs | Allows certificate revocation information to be expressed in low-volume binary hash trees; proprietary technique defined by Valicert. | May become one of several alternatives used by third-party service providers for representing revocation information. |
| None of the above | Either revocation information is not required or it is implemented in a manner other than those described within this chapter. (For example, it might be tied into a backend database.) | Alternate forms may be appropriate when transactions are authorized through a common point (for example, when a bank approves all transactions on behalf of the relying parties). |

## Summary

In this chapter, we have identified a number of certificate revocation schemes and discussed some of the pros and cons of each.

It seems clear that some techniques are well suited for certain environments but not for others. It is therefore reasonable to assume that PKI vendors will be required to offer a number of choices with their product range to offer the best possible revocation strategy (or collection of strategies) for any given PKI domain. Therefore, hybrids of these revocation techniques will likely be available in the future.

In order to understand revocation issues more fully, you are encouraged to review two related areas as follows: certificate revocation dissemination options, as discussed in Chapter 11, and client-side software requirements, as discussed in Chapter 12.

CHAPTER 9

# *Trust Models*

In this chapter, we discuss the concept of *trust models* in a PKI. It addresses questions such as the following:

- How is it determined which certificates an entity can trust?

- How can such trust be established?

- Under what circumstances can this trust be limited or controlled in a given environment?

An understanding of the prevalent PKI trust models is important because the trust models that might be implicitly assumed by someone new to this topic (that is, a PKI that parallels an organizational chart or an existing authorization schema in a company) are rarely used in practice.

We will consider several trust models (strict hierarchy of CAs, loose hierarchy of CAs, policy-based hierarchies, distributed trust architecture, four-corner model, Web model, and user-centric trust), along with a mechanism (cross-certification) that can, for some environments, serve an important role in extending and managing trust. This chapter also includes a brief examination of the sometimes-controversial issue of entity naming and a discussion of the difficulties and complexities that can arise during certificate path processing.

Before looking at trust models, however, it is important to clarify what is meant by *trust* in this context because different people can have quite different understandings of the word *trust;* this has led to (sometimes heated) debates in public meetings and on mailing lists. We have no intention of trying to resolve these disparate views or of trying to propose a new definition that will please everyone. Rather, we will simply state that the definition that the ITU-T Recommendation X.509 specification [X509–00, Section 3.3.54] gives is suitable for our purposes:

> Generally, an entity can be said to "trust" a second entity when it (the first entity) makes the assumption that the second entity will behave exactly as the first entity expects.

Therefore, trust deals with assumptions, expectations, and behavior. This clearly implies that trust cannot be measured quantitatively, that there is risk associated with trust, and that the establishment of trust cannot always be fully automated (for example, when the entities in the preceding definition are human users). However, the concept of a trust model is useful because it shows where and how trust is initiated in the PKI, which can allow more detailed reasoning about the security of the underlying architecture as well as any limitations imposed by the architecture. In particular, in the context of a PKI, the preceding definition can be applied as follows: An end entity trusts a Certification Authority (CA) when the end entity assumes that the CA will establish and maintain an accurate binding of attributes to a public key (for example, will accurately represent the identity of an entity to whom it issues a certificate).

The word *trust* is frequently used in another way that is useful to us as well: PKI literature often refers to a so-called trusted public key. This phrase (which we adopt during certificate path processing discussions within this chapter) does not describe assumptions and expectations about behavior. Rather, a public key is said to be "trusted" by Alice when Alice is convinced that the public key corresponds to a private key that legitimately and validly belongs only to a specific named entity. Typically, this name or identifying information will appear along with the public key in a certificate, but Alice may instead know the name by other means. (For example, it may be the identity of the root CA with which she is initialized into the PKI.)

This chapter uses *trust* in both of the ways mentioned earlier. The intended meaning of the word *trust* at any given point within this chapter (that is, trusted entity versus trusted public key) should be clear from the context.

## Strict Hierarchy of Certification Authorities

The strict hierarchy of CAs is typically shown pictorially as an inverted tree with the root at the top, the branches extending downward, and the leaves at the bottom. In this inverted tree, the root represents a particular CA, commonly known as the root CA, which acts as a root of trust, or "trust anchor," for the entire domain of PKI entities under it. Below the root CA are zero or more layers of intermediate CAs (also known as subordinate CAs because they are subordinate to the root), represented by the intermediate nodes, from which further branches spring forth. The leaves correspond to non-CA PKI entities, often called *end entities* or simply *end users*. (See Figure 9.1.)

The term *root*—although conveniently conjuring up the image given previously as the starting point for a large tree configuration with numerous branches and leaves—actually portrays something more fundamental. The root is not simply a starting point for a network, communications, or subordination architecture; it is a starting point for trust. All entities in this community (end entities as well as any intermediate CAs) hold this public key as their trust anchor,

Figure 9.1    Strict hierarchy of CAs trust model.

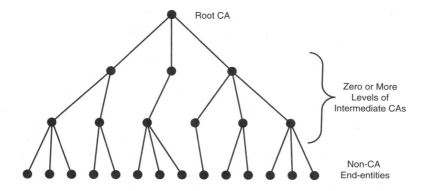

their starting or ending point of trust for all certificate verification decisions. Thus, it is appropriate to refer to this key as a *root* even if the configuration has no intermediate CAs (looking more like a bush than a tree) or if the configuration is drawn in any other manner.[1]

In this model, all entities in the hierarchy trust the single root CA. The hierarchy is established as follows:

1. A root CA is established, and a self-issued (or self-signed) root certificate is established as a basis of trust for all entities that belong to the strict hierarchy.

2. The root CA certifies (that is, creates and signs the certificates for) zero or more CAs immediately below it.

3. Each of those CAs certifies zero or more CAs immediately below it.

4. At the second-to-last level, the CAs certify end entities.

Each entity in the hierarchy (both intermediate CA and non-CA leaf) must be supplied with a copy of the root CA's public key. This public-key installation process is the foundation for certificate processing for all subsequent communication in this model; therefore, it must be accomplished in a secure, out-of-band fashion. For example, an entity may acquire this key via

---

[1]In some hierarchies an upper-level CA may certify end entities as well as other CAs. Although the standards do not preclude this, discussion of hierarchies in the literature typically tends to assume that a given CA will certify *either* end entities *or* other CAs (but not both). We will follow that convention in the text, but this is not meant to be restrictive.

a physical channel such as (paper) mail or via a telephone call. Alternatively, the key may be acquired electronically and then simply confirmed via the out-of-band mechanism. (For example, the SHA-1 hash of the key—sometimes called the "fingerprint" of the key—may be sent in a letter by mail, printed in a newspaper, or read out over the telephone.)

Note that in a multilevel strict hierarchy, end entities are certified (that is, issued certificates by) the CA immediately above them, but their trust anchor is a different CA (the root). For shallow hierarchies in which there are no subordinate CAs, the root and the certificate issuer are identical for all end entities. Such hierarchies are referred to as *trusted-issuer hierarchies*.[2]

An end entity, Alice, holding a trusted copy of the root CA public key, can verify the certificate of another end entity, Bob, in the following way. Suppose Bob's certificate is signed by $CA_2$, whose certificate is signed by $CA_1$, whose certificate is signed by the root CA. Alice (with the root's public key $k_R$) can verify the certificate of $CA_1$ and therefore extract a trusted copy of $CA_1$'s public key $k_1$. Then, this key can be used to verify the certificate of $CA_2$, which similarly leads to a trusted copy of $CA_2$'s public key $k_2$. Key $k_2$ can be used to verify Bob's certificate, leading to a trusted copy of Bob's public key $k_B$. Alice can now use the desired key $k_B$, depending on its type (see Chapter 2), to encrypt messages for Bob or to verify digital signatures that Bob purportedly created. That is, by following a procedure such as the one outlined above, secure communications between Alice and Bob can be enabled.[3]

## Loose Hierarchy of Certification Authorities

Although not commonly discussed in today's literature, the rigid notion of a strict hierarchy (that is, all trust emanates from the root under all circumstances) is not necessarily appropriate for all PKI domains, even though that PKI domain may deploy what otherwise appears to be a hierarchical trust model. The notion of a "loose hierarchy" would permit relying parties that

---

[2]We have seen examples in literature where a distinction is made between a strict hierarchy of CAs and a trust model in which one and only one CA exists. We recognize that this is the simplest form of a hierarchical PKI trust model and that certification path processing and business control logic are reduced to their most basic form. However, we do not single this out as a different trust model here. We treat it simply as a hierarchical trust model without any subordinate CAs.

[3]It is interesting to note that the strict hierarchy of CAs trust model (along with interesting enhancements, such as "policy CAs" and name subordination) is the one that the failed Privacy Enhanced Mail (PEM) specifications [RFC1422, RFC1424] adopted. However, PEM failed not because a strict hierarchy is a fundamentally flawed model, but because the strict hierarchy is not appropriate for every environment (particularly the Internet). For some environments such a model may be entirely suitable both in theory and in practice.

have been certified by the same CA to resolve a trusted path without involving any of the superior CAs, including the root CA. Although this may seem to stray from the traditional notion of hierarchies, ultimately this is a policy decision that might make sense in certain environments. This means that local policy could permit relying parties to implicitly trust their local CA directly. However, if a relying party were evaluating a certificate that had been issued by a CA other than the CA that issued their own certificate(s), this would revert back to the strict hierarchy in terms of certification path processing.

For example, if Bob's certificate is issued by $CA_2$ and Alice's certificate is also issued by $CA_2$, then Bob and Alice could validate each other's certificates without having to construct a certification path back to the root CA. Essentially, this is as though Bob and Alice belonged to their own trusted-issuer hierarchy. However, if a CA other than $CA_2$ has issued Carol's certificate, then Alice and Bob must process the complete certification path through the root CA before trusting Carol's certificate.

## Policy-Based Hierarchies

The traditional notion of a strict hierarchy is that each subordinate CA within the hierarchy has one and only one superior. Logically, this implies that the CAs within a given hierarchy embody a single Certificate Policy. However, we believe that it should be possible for a given CA to adhere to multiple policies that by definition would imply that a given CA might belong to more than one hierarchy. This in turn implies that a CA could be subordinate to more than one root CA. Note that we are talking about a logical separation here (that is, a single physical root CA may embody multiple policies). Also, in this case, the CA would have multiple verification certificates—one for each policy. Whether separate key pairs are employed is a local policy decision, but in general we recommend that different key pairs be used. This will minimize the amount of damage if a given signing private key is compromised, and it promotes the notion that different key lengths and/or algorithms might be used for different policies.

We do not know of a case where this trust model has been deployed, but we nonetheless believe that it is a viable trust model that may be seen in the future.

## Distributed Trust Architecture

The *distributed trust architecture* distributes trust between two or more (perhaps many) CAs. That is, Alice may hold a copy of the public key of $CA_1$ as her trust anchor, and Bob may hold a copy of the public key of $CA_2$ as his trust anchor. Because these CA keys serve as trust anchors, it follows that each corresponding CA is the root CA for a strict hierarchy involving some subset of the total PKI community. ($CA_1$ is the root for a hierarchy that includes Alice, and $CA_2$ is the root for a hierarchy that includes Bob.)

If each of these hierarchies is a shallow, trusted-issuer hierarchy, then the resulting configuration may be referred to as a fully peered architecture because all CAs are effectively independent peers. (There are no subordinate CAs in the architecture.) On the other hand, if each hierarchy is a multilevel hierarchy, the result may be called a full-treed architecture. (Note that the root CAs are peers with each other, but each root acts as a superior for one or more subordinate CAs.) The hybrid architecture is also possible (with one or more trusted-issuer hierarchies and one or more multilevel trees); this configuration is illustrated in Figure 9.2.

Typically (although not always), the fully peered architecture is a planned deployment configuration within a single organizational domain (for example, within a single company), whereas the fully treed and hybrid architectures arise as a result of interconnecting independent, pre-existing PKIs from different organizational domains.

The point is that many enterprise domains deploy their own PKIs, and these PKIs do not necessarily emanate from a common root CA. The isolated PKI domains may be configured in a variety of ways, including a strict hierarchy, a fully peered architecture, or any other trust model as discussed within this chapter. Interoperability between any combination of these trust models must be supported.

The process of interconnecting the peer root CAs is commonly known as cross-certification, although the term *PKI networking* is growing in use (particularly for the fully treed and hybrid architectures). This topic, along with the related issue of certificate path processing in

| Figure 9.2 | Distributed trust architecture model. |

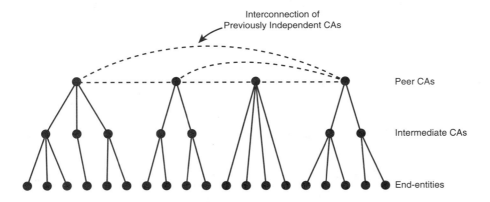

such an environment, is discussed later in this chapter. Note, however, that two different kinds of configuration are commonly employed for cross-certification: mesh and hub-and-spoke.

It is also worth noting that other methods for establishing trust relationships between PKI domains are being explored or are already available. A brief description of these methods is provided in a white paper, available from the PKI Forum Web site, entitled "CA-CA Interoperability" [CA-CA]. These alternatives include the following:

- *Cross-recognition* is a concept under consideration by the Asia Pacific Economic Cooperation (APEC) Telecommunications Working Group that would allow CAs to be recognized across multiple PKI domains by virtue of being accredited by a mutually recognized accreditation authority or trusted third party. As currently defined, cross-recognition is procedural in nature and is largely independent of technology (that is, how recognition is conveyed to relying parties across multiple domains is not yet specified and could be accommodated in a number of ways).

- *Certificate Trust List (CTL),* as defined by Microsoft, is a "signed list of root certification authority certificates that an administrator considers reputable for designated purposes, such as client authentication or secure e-mail." For additional information on CTLs, go to `http://www.microsoft.com/windows2000/` and search on "CTL."

- *Accreditation Certificate* is a concept developed under the Australian Government Gatekeeper project in which a well-known and trusted CA vouches for other CAs when certain criteria are met. This is somewhat analogous to unilateral cross-certification (that is, the accreditation CA issues an Accreditation Certificate for each CA that meets the requirements for accreditation), but no hierarchy is implied and the accredited CAs can be completely autonomous entities. This might also be considered a technology-specific mechanism that can be used to implement the notion of cross-recognition as described earlier.

## Mesh Configuration

In the *mesh configuration,* all root CAs are potentially cross-certified with each other. In particular, two root CAs will cross-certify whenever their respective communities need to communicate securely. In the fully connected case (sometimes called a full mesh), this requires roughly $n^2$ cross-certification agreements to be established when there are $n$ root CAs, although in practice implementations would be expected to be somewhat less than fully connected (a partial mesh). Figure 9.2 illustrates a partial mesh hybrid distributed trust architecture. (It is not a full mesh because no direct cross-certification agreement is in place between the first and third CAs.)

### *Hub-and-Spoke Configuration*

In the *hub-and-spoke configuration*, each root CA cross-certifies with a single central CA whose job is to facilitate such interconnection. This central CA is sometimes referred to as a hub CA with spokes out to the various root CAs (hence, the name of this configuration) and is sometimes referred to as a bridge CA, bridging communication gaps between pairs of roots. The attraction of this configuration is that the fully connected case requires only *n* cross-certification agreements for *n* root CAs (because each root CA cross-certifies only with the hub).

The hub CA should not be viewed as a root for all the systems that cross-certify with it; the hub-and-spoke configuration does *not* create a hierarchy. The fundamental difference between these two trust models lies in which keys end entities hold. In a strict hierarchy, all entities hold a trusted copy of the root CA key as an anchor (that is, a starting or ending point for certificate path processing). In the hub-and-spoke configuration, no end entity holds a hub CA key as an anchor. Instead, each end entity holds a trusted copy of the key of a CA in its own domain and, through certificate path processing, obtains the key of the hub CA, and then a CA in another domain, and eventually the key of the target end entity in that domain.

The U.S. government has devoted a significant amount of research in the area of bridge CAs. This work is discussed further in Chapter 20.

## Four-Corner Trust Model

The foundation for the *four-corner trust model* was originally tested during the National Automated Clearing House Association (NACHA) CA Interoperability Pilot project; we are aware of at least one application in which this trust model is employed (namely, Identrus; see www.identrus.com). Figure 9.3 illustrates the four-corner trust model. As shown, the four corners of this trust model are made up of the subscriber, the relying party, the subscriber's CA, and the relying party's CA. In the specific case of Identrus, both the subscriber's CA and relying party's CA are financial institutions that are subordinate to the Identrus root CA (not depicted in Figure 9.3).

At first glance this model may not seem all that different than the more traditional Web model involving a subscriber, relying party, and the subscriber's CA. However, the fundamental distinction with the four-corner model is that the relying party always depends on its issuing authority to resolve any question regarding a given transaction.

Let's take a look a simple example similar to that demonstrated as part of the NACHA CA Interoperability pilot initiative. (Note that Identrus offers a great deal more than might be implied with this example. We are simply describing the four-corner trust model from a generic perspective.) Picture a consumer "surfing" to a Web site for the purpose of buying a

Figure 9.3    Four-corner trust model.

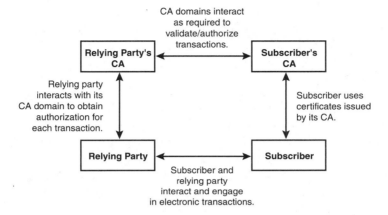

pair of shoes. Once the consumer makes the decision to buy, a digitally signed on-line purchase request is constructed and sent to the merchant Web site. The merchant Web site then forwards the purchase request to its bank for approval. Any certificate validation, revocation status checking, credit approval, and so on would be performed behind the scenes by the merchant's bank, not the merchant. This is an example in which revocation information need not be disseminated to the relying party because all transactions will be reviewed by the issuing authority. (Recall that this possibility was discussed in Chapter 8.) This model could apply to other forms of electronic transactions as well.

## Web Model

The *Web model* derives its name from its birth over the World Wide Web and its dependence on popular Web browsers such as Netscape Navigator and Microsoft Internet Explorer. In this model, a number of CA public keys are preinstalled in a standard, off-the-shelf browser. These keys define the set of CAs that the browser user will initially "trust" to act as roots for certificate verification. Note that although this set of root keys may be modified (for example, reduced or augmented) by the user, it is generally recognized that few browser users will be sophisticated enough, with respect to PKI and security issues, to understand or modify this aspect of browser behavior.

This model, similar on a cursory examination to the distributed trust architecture model, is fundamentally more similar to the strict hierarchy of CAs model. Rather than expanding the available subject community for a particular relying party, Alice, by interconnecting with the relevant domains, the Web model instantaneously makes Alice a relying party of all domains represented in the browser. For all practical purposes, each browser vendor has its own root, and it certifies the "root" CAs that are embedded in the browser. The only real difference is that the root CAs, rather than being certified by the browser vendor's root, are physically embedded in software releases as a means of effecting the secure binding between a CA name and its key. In essence, this is a strict hierarchy with an implied root (that is, the browser vendor is the virtual root CA and the first level down in the hierarchy is all the embedded CA keys). (See Figure 9.4.)

The Web model has clear advantages in terms of convenience and simple interoperability. However, a number of security implications with this model should be taken into consideration when making deployment decisions for an environment. For example, because browser users automatically trust the full set of preinstalled public keys, security may be completely compromised if even one of those root CAs is "bad" (for example, fails to exercise any due diligence whatsoever in certifying entities). Therefore, Alice will believe that what purports to be Bob's certificate is a legitimate certificate for Bob, even if it is really Eve's public key together with Bob's name, signed by $CA_{bad}$, whose public key is embedded in the browser. Alice, therefore, may unintentionally divulge confidential information to Eve or accept Eve's bogus digital signature. The reason such an impersonation can succeed is that Alice is typically unaware of which root key in the browser verified a given incoming certificate. Of the numerous root keys embedded in her browser (for example, some versions of the more popular browsers have on the order of 100 root certificates), Alice may recognize only a handful of the CAs represented; the rest may be completely unknown to her. Yet, in this model, her software trusts all of them equally and implicitly so that a certificate signed by any of them will be accepted without question.

Note that a similar situation can occur in some of the other trust models as well. For example, in the distributed trust architecture, Alice may not recognize a particular CA, but her software

**Figure 9.4**      Web model.

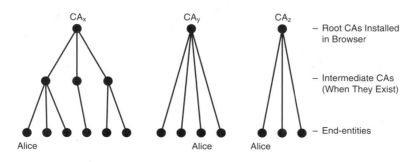

will trust its key if the relevant cross-certificate is valid. The Web model is arguably worse, however. In the distributed trust architecture, Alice explicitly agrees to trust her local CA to "do the right things" with respect to PKI security (including cross-certifying with "appropriate" CAs). In the Web model, Alice may acquire a particular browser for a variety of reasons, none of which has anything to do with security. She therefore has no reason to assume that the browser will hold "appropriate" CA keys (from her security perspective).

If Alice is somewhat sophisticated with respect to PKI issues (and if her particular browser supports this), she may have the understanding and the diligence to check which root key verified a given incoming certificate. She can then decide, if she wishes, not to rely on a certificate signed by a CA she does not recognize. However, even this may not produce the desired result. For example, Alice may recognize and trust the root key associated with "CA Company, Inc."; but if $CA_{bad}$ calls itself "CA Company, Ltd.," it is very unlikely that Alice will readily be able to distinguish between certificates that may be relied on and those that may not. Even if Alice's particular browser vendor was careful not to embed keys for two different CAs with such similar names, it may certainly happen that Alice trusts the CA named "Foo" and the company named "Bar," but not the CA named "Fred" who might issue a certificate to a rogue company calling itself "Bar." Again, without due diligence, Alice may simply see a certificate for "Bar" and think that all is well.

Another potential security consideration associated with the Web model is that no practical mechanism can revoke any of the root keys embedded in the browser. If it is discovered that one of the CAs is "bad" (as discussed earlier) or if the private key corresponding to any of the root (public) keys is compromised, it is effectively impossible to discontinue the use of that key in the millions upon millions of browsers around the world. This is partly because of the practical difficulty of getting an appropriate message to each site and partly because the browser software itself is not written to understand such a message. Removal of the bad key from the browser therefore requires an explicit action on the part of each user in the world. This action would need to be taken immediately around the world; otherwise, some users would be safe while others would remain at risk. It may be asserted with a fairly high degree of confidence that such a worldwide, instantaneous user action will never occur.

Finally, for some contexts it is important to note that in the Web model there is essentially no opportunity for any kind of legal agreement or contract to be put in place between a user (relying party) and the CAs represented in the browser. The browser may be freely downloaded from a variety of Web sites, or perhaps it comes preinstalled in the operating system; a CA does not know (and has no way of determining) who its relying parties are, and users cannot in general be expected to be aware enough of the potential issues to contact the CAs directly. Thus, all liability, regardless of circumstances, is likely to rest with the relying party and cannot be transferred to the CA or to any other party.

# User-Centric Trust

In the model typically referred to as *user-centric trust,* each user is directly and totally responsible for deciding which certificates to rely on and which to reject. This decision may be influenced by a number of factors, although the initial set of trusted keys often includes those of friends, family, or colleagues a given user knows personally. (See Figure 9.5.)

User-centric trust is probably best illustrated by the well-known security software program Pretty Good Privacy (PGP) [Zimm95, Garf95], particularly in its more recent incarnations (Version 5.0 and later). In PGP, a user builds (or effectively joins) the so-called web of trust by acting as a CA (signing the public keys of other entities) and by having his or her own public keys certified by others. When Alice later receives a certificate purportedly belonging to Bob, she will see that this certificate is signed by David, whom she does not know, but that David's certificate is signed by Catherine, whom she does know and trust (for example, Catherine may have a certificate signed by Alice herself). Alice may then decide to trust Bob's key (by trusting the chain of keys from Catherine to David to Bob), or she may decide to reject Bob's key (judging that the "unknown" Bob is too many links away from the "known" Catherine).

Because of its reliance on user actions and decisions, the user-centric model may be workable in a highly technical and highly interested community, but it is unrealistic for a general community (one in which many users have little or no knowledge of security or PKI concepts). Furthermore, such a model is generally inappropriate for corporate, financial, or governmental environments because these typically want or need to exercise some control over user trust; that is, such environments may want to enable or disable trust in a particular key or set of keys

**Figure 9.5**     User-centric trust model.

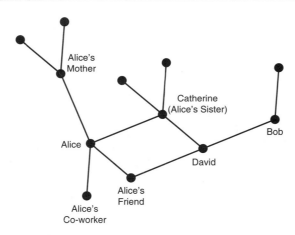

on an organization-wide basis. Such organizational trust policies cannot be implemented in any kind of automatic and enforceable way with the user-centric model.

# Cross-Certification

*Cross-certification* is a useful mechanism for binding together previously unrelated CAs so that secure communications between their respective subject communities can be enabled. The actual mechanics of cross-certification (for example, the specific protocol messages exchanged) may be identical to certification (see Chapter 6 for a discussion of certification), except that both the subject and the issuer of the resulting cross-certificate are CAs (rather than the subject being an end entity). When the distinction is important, the following terminology from RFC2510 can be used:

- If the two CAs belong to the same domain (for example, within an organization's CA hierarchy, where a CA at one level is certifying a CA at the next level below), the process is referred to as *intradomain cross-certification*.

- If the two CAs belong to different domains (for example, when a CA in one company is certifying a CA in another company), the process is referred to as *interdomain cross-certification*.

Cross-certification can occur in one or two directions. That is, $CA_1$ can cross-certify (that is, sign the identity and public key of) $CA_2$ without $CA_2$ cross-certifying $CA_1$; such *unilateral cross-certification* results in a single cross-certificate and would be the typical practice in the CA hierarchy mentioned earlier. Alternatively, $CA_1$ and $CA_2$ can cross-certify each other; such *mutual cross-certification* results in two distinct cross-certificates and can be a more common occurrence, for example, between companies wanting to enable secure communications between their respective employees.

According to the terminology given in the 1997 version of X.509 [X509–97], from the perspective of $CA_1$, a cross-certificate issued for it (that is, with $CA_1$ as the subject and some other CA as the issuer) is called a *forward cross-certificate;* one issued by it is called a *reverse cross-certificate*. The *forward* and *reverse* nomenclature proved to be confusing to many (even experts sometimes got them backward), so these terms were renamed in the 2000 version of X.509 [X509–00]. Specifically, *forward* has been changed to "issued to this CA" and *reverse* has been changed to "issued by this CA."

If an X.500 Directory is used as the certificate repository (see Chapter 11 for repository options), the appropriate "issued to this CA" and "issued by this CA" cross-certificates may be stored in a cross-certificate pair structure in the directory entry of each relevant CA. This structure can be helpful in facilitating certificate path construction. (See Figure 9.6.)

**Figure 9.6**    Example of mutual cross-certification between $CA_1$ and $CA_2$.

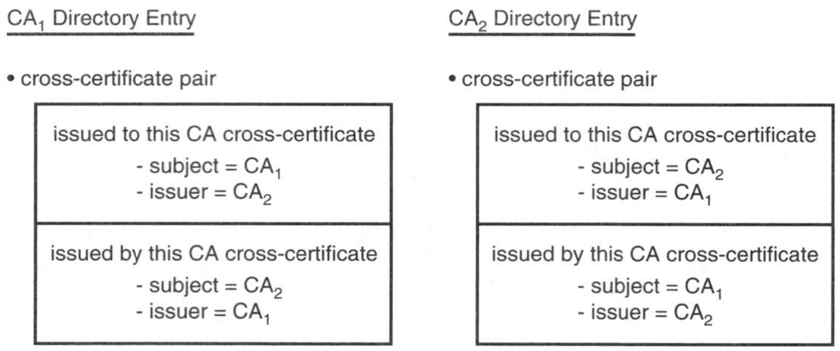

CA$_1$ Directory Entry                        CA$_2$ Directory Entry

• cross-certificate pair                    • cross-certificate pair

| issued to this CA cross-certificate<br>- subject = $CA_1$<br>- issuer = $CA_2$ | issued to this CA cross-certificate<br>- subject = $CA_2$<br>- issuer = $CA_1$ |
| --- | --- |
| issued by this CA cross-certificate<br>- subject = $CA_2$<br>- issuer = $CA_1$ | issued by this CA cross-certificate<br>- subject = $CA_1$<br>- issuer = $CA_2$ |

The mechanism of cross-certification can be used to extend trust between (or among) distinct relying party communities. In particular, cross-certification between two CAs is one way that a given CA can recognize that another CA is authorized to issue certificates in (typically a specified part of) a name space. (This is the fundamental trust extension mechanism for the distributed trust architecture but is equally applicable to the Web model. It can be used to characterize trust extension in the user-centric model as well, because in that model each user effectively acts as its own CA.) Thus, cross-certification allows otherwise disparate PKI domains to easily establish an interoperability path. An (undesirable) alternative would be to exchange root CA keys and to populate every end entity's software or hardware tokens with the root CA key of the external domain.

For example, assume that Alice has been certified by $CA_1$ and holds a trusted copy of $CA_1$'s public key and that Bob has been certified by $CA_2$ and holds a trusted copy of $CA_2$'s public key. Initially, Alice may trust only entities whose certificates have been signed by $CA_1$ because these are the certificates she can verify. She cannot verify Bob's certificate (because she does not hold a trusted copy of $CA_2$'s public key); similarly, Bob cannot verify Alice's certificate. After $CA_1$ and $CA_2$ have cross-certified, however, Alice's trust can be extended to the subject community of $CA_2$—including Bob—because she can verify $CA_2$'s certificate, using her trusted copy of $CA_1$'s public key, and then verify Bob's certificate, using her now-trusted copy of $CA_2$'s public key.

However, the distinct advantage that cross-certification brings to the concept of trust extension is *control*, using one or more of the standard extensions defined for cross-certificates, such as name constraints, policy constraints, and path-length constraints.

$CA_1$ may cross-certify $CA_2$ but limit in some desired way the subject community of $CA_2$ that the relying party community under $CA_1$ will trust. Trust can be extended, on an organization-wide basis within the domain of $CA_1$, only to certain individuals, only to certain groups, only for specific purposes, and so on, in the domain of $CA_2$. This kind of organizational control over trust extension, centrally determined by the CA$_1$ administrator, is difficult or impossible to achieve with the Web model or with the user-centric trust model. It also is irrelevant in a strict CA hierarchy model (because there is only one domain; there is no other domain to which trust can be extended).

In particular, through the *name constraints* certificate extension, CA$_1$ may stipulate that only certificates issued by CA$_2$ to subjects within a specified portion of the name space will be accepted as valid by the relying party community under CA$_1$. This portion of the name space may be constrained as required for the business purpose, encompassing a single user, a group, a department, the entire organization, or whatever naming restriction is relevant. Thus, for example, one company may use this mechanism to ensure that only certificates from the other company's purchasing department will be accepted as valid.

The *policy constraints* certificate extension provides a means to limit the purposes for which a certificate can be used. For example, the name constraints may indicate that all certificates from a particular company are "acceptable," but the policy constraints may limit the acceptable uses to e-mail (so that an arbitrary user certificate from that other company cannot be used to verify a signature on a legal contract).

*Path-length constraints* (part of the basic constraints certificate extension) can be used to limit the number of cross-certificates that can appear in a valid certificate path. For example, CA$_1$ may explicitly decide that end-entity certificates issued by CA$_2$ are acceptable but prohibit certificates issued by any other CA with which CA$_2$ has cross-certified.

See RFC3280 for further discussion on name, policy, and path-length constraints.

## Entity Naming

A certificate is a signed data structure binding a key pair (explicitly the public key, but implicitly the private key as well) to an identity. But what is an *identity*? Ultimately, it must be something uniquely associated with a particular PKI entity, and it must be meaningful within a context of use. Otherwise, secure communication cannot be achieved: Alice uses a certificate for the purpose of encrypting data for Bob or for the purpose of verifying Bob's signature, but if the certificate is actually (unknown to Alice) associated with some other entity, security is effectively compromised.

Depending on the size of the domain, identity uniqueness may be simple or very difficult to achieve. In a small, closed environment, uniqueness may essentially come "for free"; even first names may be sufficient to distinguish between all entities. However, as environments get bigger, uniqueness gets harder to ensure; at the size of the Internet, some argue that globally unique names are a practical impossibility.

Considered in a theoretical light, global uniqueness of entity names is entirely achievable through the X.500 Distinguished Name (DN) mechanism. (See Chapter 6 for a discussion of DNs.) This is a hierarchical naming structure with a root at the top and a naming authority at every node (whose only purpose is to ensure the uniqueness of the nodes immediately below it). The DN mechanism guarantees uniqueness if every entity that will be named in this way officially registers with the appropriate naming authority and accepts the name it is assigned, which is precisely what happens today with Internet Protocol (IP) addresses and e-mail names; this is the basis for addressing and routing in modern electronic communications.

However, the DN mechanism has been less than entirely successful for at least two reasons:

1. The utility of a DN has never really struck a chord with the general public (due, at least in part, to the limited attraction of the X.500 Directory concept and the popularity and widespread use of the e-mail name as an alternative method to identify an entity).

2. In many instances, a body that is authoritative for DNs does not exist: The naming authorities in the hierarchy are not a fundamental requirement for name assignment (that is, two entities can assign the same name to themselves entirely independent of any naming authority). Thus, global uniqueness is guaranteed only if everyone plays by the rules, but there is no way to ensure that such fair play will occur.

This situation has led some to seriously question the usefulness of entity names in certificates. (See, for example, SDSI, SPKI, and related work.) In other contexts, the placeholder for a DN is retained in an X.509 certificate (because this is required by the standard syntax). However, provision is also made for "alternative" names of the subject, such as an IP address or an e-mail name (see the *subjectAltName* extension in the X.509 Recommendation [X509–00] and in RFC3280) to guarantee uniqueness of the total entity name and to provide a link to these other identity mechanisms.

Finally, it is worth noting that even if global uniqueness is difficult (perhaps impossible) to achieve, entity names almost always have local significance; that is, they are meaningful in a local environment. Therefore, it can be very useful for a certificate to bind a key pair to some form of name for a specific entity. In general, a useful practice is to rely on existing infrastructures where "identities" are already in place and authoritative naming registrars have already been established.

# Certificate Path Processing

As alluded to earlier, the purpose of certificate path processing is to find an unbroken path (or chain) of certificates between a given target certificate and a trusted key (a "trust anchor") and to check the validity of each certificate in this path. Ultimately, the final goal is for Alice to determine whether she can trust the public key in Bob's certificate (with respect to the purpose for which she would like to use it). The target certificate (and, consequently, the corresponding public key) is trusted only if every certificate (and the corresponding public key) in the path is found to be trustworthy.

In general, there are two primary phases to certification path processing:

1. *Path construction* involves aggregating all the certificates necessary to form a complete path.

2. *Path validation* involves examining each certificate in the path in turn, determining whether or not the key it contains can be trusted.

The general process surrounding these operations is discussed briefly in the sections that follow. For more complete details regarding path processing operations and algorithms, see X509–00[4] and RFC3280.

## *Path Construction*

Path construction can be a very complicated and time-intensive operation, especially if a large number of cross-certificates are involved. This is because of the difficulties involved in locating the certificate of the entity that has signed a given certificate when that entity is outside the local environment. For example, assume that Alice is attempting to construct a path for Bob's certificate. Furthermore, assume that Bob was certified by $CA_3$, that $CA_3$ is cross-certified with $CA_2$ (among others), that $CA_2$ is cross-certified with $CA_1$ (among others), and that Alice holds a trusted copy of $CA_1$'s public key. (See Figure 9.7.)

Because Alice holds Bob's certificate, she knows that $CA_3$ has certified Bob. Because $CA_3$ has cross-certified with several CAs (three in this example), Alice needs to determine which cross-certificate will add another link to her desired path. $CA_1$ has not signed any of $CA_3$'s cross-certificates (that is, $CA_E$, $CA_F$, and $CA_2$ have signed them), so she needs to do some trial-and-error processing. She examines each of the cross-certificates associated with $CA_E$, $CA_F$, and $CA_2$ to see if $CA_1$ has signed any of these. In this example, $CA_2$ has a cross-certificate signed by $CA_1$, and so her path construction work is complete. Clearly, this task gets significantly more onerous if $CA_3$ and $CA_2$ have cross-certified with many other CAs and/or if the path between $CA_1$ and $CA_3$ involves many more intermediate CAs. In such cases, path construction may involve the use of graph-theoretic pathfinding algorithms, including depth-first (not

---

[4]The certification path validation procedure documented in the 1997 version of X.509 is incomplete. We strongly recommend that you consult the 2000 version of X.509 since it includes a much more detailed and complete certification path validation algorithm.

**Figure 9.7**   Path construction example.

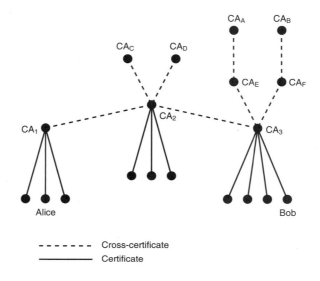

        - - - - - - -  Cross-certificate
        ——————————  Certificate

generally recommended, due to significant extra computation in the general case), breadth-first, or heuristic search techniques.

The underlying assumption in path construction is that Alice can retrieve (or otherwise acquire) all the certificates she needs in order to examine them and assemble the path. (Chapter 11 covers certificate dissemination, storage, and retrieval.)

### Path Validation

Having constructed the certificate path, Alice now needs to determine if it is valid. As discussed in Chapter 6, this involves doing the mathematical computation to see if each digital signature verifies. It also involves examining the validity period of each certificate (to ensure that the certificate has not expired); checking each revocation status (to ensure that the certificate has not been revoked); and looking at any applicable policies, key usage restrictions, name constraints, and so on.

Path validation is typically less onerous than path construction, but keeping track of name, policy, and path-length constraints can get somewhat complicated, particularly if the path is relatively long.

### Trust Anchor Considerations

The trust model in use determines Alice's trust anchor. In particular, with the *strict hierarchy of CAs*, Alice's trust anchor is the CA that is logically farthest from her (the CA at the root of the hierarchy). With the *distributed trust architecture,* Alice's trust anchor is a CA that is logically closer to her (the root of the hierarchy covering her segment of the total PKI community, which may—for example, in the fully peered architecture—even be the closest CA that actually certified her). In the *Web model,* Alice's trust anchor is really a set of anchors (the CA root keys that have come preinstalled in her browser). Finally, in the *user-centric trust model,* Alice's anchor is one or more CAs of her own choosing (which may be fine for her personal environment but less acceptable in a corporate environment).

The choice of trust model therefore plays an important role in determining the overall trust that can eventually be placed in the public key of the target certificate.

## Summary

The trust model is an integral part of PKI architecture and operation. This chapter has given a brief introduction to a number of different trust models, highlighting their similarities and differences.

Choosing the correct trust model (and its corresponding level of security) for the environment to be protected is of critical importance and is one of the early and fundamental decisions to be made when deploying a PKI.

Topics that form an important supplement to this material include understanding the environment under consideration for the PKI deployment. This discussion is presented in the chapters comprising Part III of this book.

# CHAPTER 10

# Multiple Certificates per Entity

In this chapter, we discuss the situation in which a single PKI entity holds multiple valid certificates, and we give a number of reasons why such a situation might not only be possible but also desirable. The concept of different uses for key pairs is presented; some attention is also given to the relationship between key pairs and certificates.

## Multiple Key Pairs

As time goes on and PKI deployments grow in number and in function, a PKI entity will typically have a number of key pairs even if all key pairs, on the surface, appear to be used for the same purpose (such as signing data). This is because a strong correspondence can exist between a key pair and a "role"—that is, between a key pair and one of the many "hats" an entity might wear through the day, including both work and off-work hours. For example, an entity might use one key to sign a $100,000 purchase order for his or her department at work, but another key to electronically sign the rental form for a movie at the video store, and yet another key to sign personal e-mail to a friend.

Such a situation is common to many nonelectronic circumstances of the present. As one simple example, many businesspeople use one credit card while on company travel and another credit card for all other purposes. The business credit card may have been issued to the employee by the company, rather than applied for privately, and may have certain privileges associated with it (such as high spending limits or accident insurance) that the personal credit card does not.

The same model holds for key pairs: The company might generate and issue one key, instead of it being generated locally at the PKI entity's workstation. Furthermore, it might be endowed with particular privileges or restrictions by the issuer (such as signing limits or guarantees of compliance to certain governmental or corporate regulations regarding generation, storage, and backup procedures).

The concept of multiple key pairs per entity is perfectly reasonable for many environments, and such a practice should not seem surprising. By contrast, in many cases it would be surprising if a single key pair could meet all the varied needs of a PKI entity in all the roles that will be played throughout the day, week, month, and year.

# Key Pair Uses

As discussed in the previous section, key pairs might be associated with different entity roles or actions (much as, in today's world, one card is used for gas purchases, another for bank transactions, and another for borrowing a book from the library). Aside from this, however, it is also the case that different key pairs can have intrinsically different uses. In particular, a key pair for the *Digital Signature Algorithm (DSA)* cannot be used for encryption and decryption when implemented according to the specifications. Similarly, a *Diffie–Hellman (DH)* key pair cannot be used for signing data and verifying the signatures. Furthermore, even a key pair for the *Rivest–Shamir–Adleman (RSA)* algorithm—though it can be *arithmetically* used for authentication, integrity, confidentiality, or key exchange—may be constrained by policy, decree, or implementation choice to be used for only a single purpose.

A key pair, then, may be available for only one use, either because this is determined by the cryptographic algorithm with which it is associated or because such a constraint has been externally imposed on it and the relevant key-processing PKI implementation is built to honor this constraint.

However, the field of use of a key pair may be even narrower than this. Consider a digital signature key pair as one example. In many environments, it is important to be able to distinguish between a PKI entity signing some data (1) for the purpose of entity authentication in an on-line challenge–response protocol and (2) with the explicit intent of committing to the document contents. Thus, a key pair may be limited to *particular uses of its signature capability,* rather than all uses.

Even this may not be the finest granularity of use in some environments. For example, a key pair may be designated to authorize purchase transactions and nothing else (that is, it may be used to sign a purchase transaction but may not be used to sign any other type of document or data). However, it may be usable only for purchases up to a predetermined limit (such as $100,000); purchase transactions of a higher value signed by this key will be rejected. Thus, a key pair may be associated with a specific policy that constrains it to

- A particular quality or quantity of use (for example, purchase transactions up to a given value), *within*

- A particular type of use (for example, authorizing purchase transactions), *within*

- A particular category of use (for example, data content commitment), *within*

- A particular service of use (for example, authentication)

Another kind of specificity might constrain key pair use to a particular application or protocol exchange rather than to a particular granularity of its cryptographic capability. For example, a key pair might be usable for entity authentication within the Internet Protocol Security (IPsec) protocol but not for entity authentication within the Secure Sockets Layer (SSL) protocol.

Just as the concept of multiple key pairs per entity is reasonable for some environments because of the different roles that the entity may play, it appears also to be reasonable because of the narrow field of use to which a key pair might be constrained. To accomplish all the tasks that may be associated with even a single role (such as a purchasing agent for a corporation), a PKI entity may be required to hold multiple key pairs. (See Figure 10.1.)

## Relationship between Key Pairs and Certificates

If a PKI entity has multiple key pairs, it is likely to have multiple certificates because the format of a certificate does not naturally allow it to hold more than a single public key (and the X.509 standard does not explicitly support the ability to put multiple keys into the SubjectPublic-KeyInfo field). However, this does not preclude the possibility of a particular public key appearing in several certificates that are simultaneously valid. Thus, it is worth exploring briefly the relationship between key pairs and certificates.

**Figure 10.1**    Multiple keys per user.

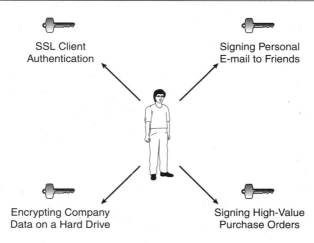

SSL Client
Authentication

Signing Personal
E-mail to Friends

Encrypting Company
Data on a Hard Drive

Signing High-Value
Purchase Orders

By far, the most commonly cited benefit of a given public key appearing in multiple valid certificates is the perceived simplicity of *rollover* (referred to, in this case, as *certificate renewal*). If a key pair (1) has not been compromised (that is, if the private key has not been discovered by an unscrupulous party) and (2) is still "cryptographically sound" (that is, if it is of sufficient length that it is not in imminent danger of cryptanalytic attack), then simplicity arguments might suggest that as the certificate nears its expiration date, the public key might be placed in a new certificate with a new validity period.[1] This extends the life of the key pair and does not force relying parties to update their knowledge of the subject's public key. Furthermore, the subject itself is not forced to change the key it uses and is thus freed from the burden of having to maintain a key history over time.

It turns out that the simplicity argument is relatively weak for many environments. In typical PKI implementations, relying parties do not hold "bare" public keys; rather, they retrieve a *copy* of the appropriate certificate when needed and use whatever public key is contained therein. Thus, the relying party will not notice whether the rolled-over certificate has the same old public key or a brand new public key.

Similarly, the certificate subject typically retrieves whatever private key is labeled as "current" in its local storage and uses that to sign, decrypt, or perform the appropriate cryptographic function. Again, whether this is the same private key as a week ago or a new private key will not be noticed by the subject. Finally, although it is true that maintaining a key history adds some complexity to local subject operation, it should be clear that a key history is required in any case because key compromise or cryptanalytic advances will mandate that a single key pair cannot live indefinitely.

There is a more compelling reason not to put a single public key in multiple certificates, however: It is too easy to "slip up" and not hold all other important aspects of these multiple certificates constant. For example, in one certificate, the key may be associated with a policy restricting use to authentication of e-mail; in another certificate, the policy may allow purchase transactions up to $100,000. In one certificate, the *key usage extension* (see Chapter 6) may specify digital signatures only; in another certificate, the extension may set the non-repudiation bit to TRUE. Such situations may allow an attacker (or even an underhanded certificate subject) to substitute one certificate for another so that what was once merely a signed piece of data

---

[1] Although standards-track specifications exist that advocate the use of public-key technology without the use of certificates (for example, [X9.59]), it should be noted that such proposals are rather limited in their scope because they are targeted for a very specific class of applications that rely on centralized account authorities as the (only) relying party. As such, these proposals are not well suited for distributed applications such as secure e-mail between individual users or for infrastructural support for multiple using applications (which is the ultimate purpose of PKI).

now takes on an entirely new meaning. Mandating that different certificates always contain different public keys is a simple way to entirely preclude the risk of such substitution attacks.[2]

## Real-World Difficulties

The price to pay for having multiple active certificates associated with different policies and key usages is that, for any given activity, the "correct" private key must be selected. For example, signing a particular purchase order may necessitate the use of the "more than $100,000" key rather than the "up to $100,000" key. Cases will inevitably arise in which the user must be consulted. ("Do you agree to be contractually bound by the terms and conditions contained in this document?" If the answer is yes, the non-repudiation key is used.) However, for many situations, this key selection will occur automatically and transparently. (If an SSL session is being established, the client software may search the user's certificates for the one with a key usage extension appropriate for SSL and then use the corresponding private key for user authentication.) As time goes on and PKI software becomes more sophisticated, the vast majority of key selections will likely be transparent.

Another difficulty that may arise is the limitations of current smart cards. In particular, the relatively small amount of available memory may preclude the storage of several private keys (especially if the corresponding certificates also need to be stored). Again, however, in the future this difficulty will diminish as smart cards get greater capacity.

## Independent Certificate Management

One other advantage to having distinct public keys in distinct certificates is the relative ease of independent certificate management in the case of certificate revocation. (See Chapter 8, Certificate Revocation, for a discussion of revocation.) If a single public key is contained in multiple certificates and the private key is compromised (or other circumstances occur that require revocation), it must be "remembered" (or discovered) which certificates contain this key so that they may *all* be revoked. Failure to revoke any of these certificates can constitute a serious security risk. By contrast, such a risk is greatly decreased if a public key appears in one and only one certificate because the administrative burden of finding and revoking that single certificate is relatively light.

---

[2]The fact that a PKI entity has multiple certificates does *not* mean that the entity must remember multiple passwords/PINs to access these key pairs. In typical PKI implementations, a single password/PIN will unlock a file (or storage device, such as a smart card) that contains all the keys associated with that entity.

Furthermore, distinct certificates associated with distinct key pairs are independent constructs: They may have independent validity periods, as well as independent policies, usage, and management procedures. One may expire or be revoked without affecting any of the others. Having the same public key in multiple certificates can complicate the administrative processes involved in certificate management.

## Support for Non-repudiation

If the PKI-enabled service of non-repudiation (see Chapter 5) is to be supported in an organization, the ability to maintain multiple key pairs—and, consequently, multiple certificates—per entity is a fundamental requirement. To have true support for non-repudiation, a necessary condition is that the private key involved in the intended non-repudiable action (such as signing a receipt for proof of delivery) must never be known to another party. Otherwise, the entity involved can simply claim that the other party may have performed the non-repudiable action. Regardless of whether such a claim can be proved (or even whether such a claim is plausible), the mere fact that another party has knowledge of the key may be sufficient to make repudiation a possibility in the opinion of an unbiased external judge. The service of non-repudiation may therefore be precluded.

Thus, the private key that corresponds to a certificate whose purpose is to support non-repudiation must never be exposed to another entity (including trusted entities, such as CAs). In some environments, such a key may be required to be generated on and to never leave a tamper-resistant hardware token. Keys not involved in non-repudiable actions may, by contrast, be required to be backed up by a trusted entity or may be permitted to be stored in software.

For example, in typical corporate environments, operational policy will dictate that private decryption keys must be backed up by a trusted entity. This is because the company simply cannot afford to lose access forever to all stored data encrypted for an employee if that employee happens to forget his or her password or becomes incapacitated in some way. Such data loss would be inconvenient for the company in most cases and may cripple continued operation in others. *Decryption keys must therefore be recoverable* if a corporation is expected to avoid potentially serious loss due to the inability to recover critical stored data. *Signing keys,* on the other hand (especially those that are to be used in non-repudiable actions), *must not be backed up;* they must be attributable—in as concrete a sense as possible—*only* to the entity named in the corresponding public-key certificate.

Such a conflicting pair of requirements necessitates at least two distinct key pairs (and associated certificates) per corporate PKI entity. This has been recognized in a number of prominent PKI requirements and profile documents, including [USDoD] and [RFC3280]. Some environments (Secured Electronic Information in Society [SEIS], for example) go further and mandate at least three distinct key pairs:

- Decryption/encryption

- General-purpose signing/verification

- Non-repudiable signing/verification

In any case, however, it appears that environments employing a single key pair per PKI entity will be much more the exception than the rule as time moves on and experience with PKI grows.

## Summary

This chapter has presented the concept of multiple key pairs and multiple certificates per PKI entity. Separate user "roles," separate key usage, independently managed certificates, and support for non-repudiation all lend weight to the claim that multiple keys/certificates per entity will be a common occurrence in real PKI deployments. The relationship between key pairs and certificates was also explored; that discussion suggested that putting a single public key in several certificates may lead to security risks and unnecessary administrative complexity.

To gain a fuller understanding of this topic, it may be useful to consider two related areas:

- Mechanisms for maintaining an identity across the multiple "roles" that an entity may play (perhaps using a Distinguished Name or a SubjectAltName; see Chapter 6)

- Mechanisms for automatically distinguishing between key types/uses (such as key usage extensions and policy OIDs; see Chapter 6)

# CHAPTER 11

# PKI Information Dissemination: Repositories and Other Techniques

As discussed in Chapter 6, certificates provide a convenient (and typically necessary) structure for protecting the integrity of public keys. Ultimately, certificates need to be acquired by others to be useful (for example, so one end entity can encrypt for or verify signatures of another end entity). In addition, as discussed in Chapter 8, there is the need to disseminate certificate revocation information, including the use of *Certificate Revocation Lists (CRLs)* and/or CRL-based techniques.

The dissemination of certificate and certificate revocation information can occur in a number of ways. The purpose of this chapter is to discuss some of the methods for distributing this information. Most of the focus will be on general repository options, with special emphasis on interdomain information-sharing issues and options. We will also discuss other alternatives, such as out-of-band and in-band information dissemination.[1]

## Private Dissemination

Perhaps the most basic of distribution mechanisms (other than no distribution mechanism) can be referred to as *private dissemination*. In this case, individual users convey certificates directly to one another. This can be accomplished via out-of-band mechanisms such as the following: (1) "hand delivery" via disk or some other storage medium and (2) an attachment to e-mail.

In the private dissemination model, the exchange of revocation information is typically informal and unreliable. Revocation notifications can be conveyed via telephone or through the use

---

[1]Although this chapter concentrates on the use of repositories to store and disseminate certificates and CRLs, repositories can also be used to store and disseminate other PKI-related information, such as cross-certificates and policy-related information.

of e-mail, but there is typically no guarantee that the revocation information will be conveyed reliably to all concerned individuals. Nor is there typically any software in place that can help the end user determine the appropriate course of action when such revocation information is received.

Nonetheless, private dissemination can work reasonably well for small (and presumably friendly) user clusters, in which any two entities either know each other directly or have a relatively small set of mutual acquaintances.

An example of a protocol tailored after this model is *Pretty Good Privacy (PGP)* or, more recently, *OpenPGP*. Note, however, that although e-mail based on PGP enjoys widespread popularity, it is still useful only in relatively small user populations because the trust model is based on personal acquaintances.

Although some environments exist where the private dissemination model is viable, using it in an enterprise domain is inappropriate for at least three critical reasons:

1. Private dissemination of certificates does not scale (that is, only relatively small user communities can reliably be supported).

2. Ad hoc dissemination of revocation information is inherently unreliable. (For example, an informal revocation notification is unlikely to reach all relying parties within a large user community—1,000 users or more—in a timely fashion.)

3. A user-centric trust model (refer to Chapter 9) is inconsistent with the operational model of most enterprise domains in which centralized control over user actions is required.

Therefore, the enterprise must adopt other options, as is discussed in the remainder of this chapter.

# Publication and Repositories

The most common method for the distribution of certificates and certificate revocation information in the enterprise domain is publication. The idea behind publication is that PKI information is posted in a widely known, publicly available, and easily accessible location. Publication is particularly attractive for large communities of users who in general are personally unknown to one another (that is, the PKI information does not have to be distributed directly to each individual).

The idea of publication in the context of public-key cryptography was first introduced in DiHe76. This was the first publicly available paper on public-key cryptography, and it postulated a model whereby public keys could be published and distributed in a form similar to a telephone book.

In today's enterprise, it is common practice to post (or publish) certificates and certificate revocation information (particularly revocation information based on CRLs) to a repository. A *repository* is a generic term used to denote any logically centralized database capable of storing information and disseminating that information when requested to do so.

In the enterprise context, repositories are typically remote servers that are accessed via the *Lightweight Directory Access Protocol (LDAP)* Version 2 [RFC1777] or Version 3 [RFC2251]. (See Box 11.1.)

---

## Box 11.1 LDAPv2 and LDAPv3

Although LDAPv2 [RFC1777] was the mainstay of early enterprise PKI deployments, it is generally considered to be deficient in the following areas:

- The mandatory-to-implement authentication mechanism between a client and the repository is based on a userid and password transmitted in the clear.
- No standard access control scheme exists.
- No standard mechanism for data replication between LDAP data repositories exists (in fact, no support for any server-to-server communications exists).
- Search filters are considered to be inadequate.
- No agreed-on confidentiality mechanism is in place to protect stored data or data in transit.
- No agreed-on signed operations capability exists.

The shortcomings of LDAPv2 are widely recognized, and a number of new features have been introduced with the advent of LDAPv3. The LDAPv3 "core specifications" include RFCs 2251–2256 and 2829–2830. LDAPv3 includes support for stronger authentication mechanisms and includes additional functionality such as support for referrals. LDAPv3 is strongly recommended over LDAPv2.

Note that LDAP continues to evolve. The latest developments surrounding LDAPv3 can be found at

    http://www.ietf.org/html.charters/ldapbis-charter.html

    http://www.ietf.org/html.charters/ldapext-charter.html

Related work also is ongoing under the auspices of the IETF LDAP Duplication/Replication/Update Protocols (LDUP) Working Group. Specifically, the LDUP Working Group is addressing support for replication between LDAP servers. You may retrieve the latest Internet Drafts and RFCs produced by the LDUP Working Group from

    http://www.ietf.org/html.charters/ldup-charter.html

Even when LDAP is the access mechanism to the repository, the repository itself is often based on the information model and protocols as defined in the X.500 Series of Recommendations [X500]. However, the term *repository* can apply to a database or other form of information storage and distribution, such as an on-line revocation status responder. (Refer to the discussion regarding the Online Certificate Status Protocol in Chapter 8.)

Some examples that fall under this definition of repository include the following:

- LDAP servers

- X.500 *Directory System Agents (DSAs)*

- OCSP Responders (although OCSP as described in RFC 2560 is limited to revocation status information only)

- *Domain Name System (DNS)* (with certificate and certificate revocation information supported in accordance with RFC2538)

- Web servers (which may contain certificates and certificate revocation information in accordance with RFC2585, which can be retrieved via the *Hypertext Transfer Protocol,* or *HTTP*)

- *File Transfer Protocol (FTP)*-based servers (which may contain certificates and certificate revocation information in accordance with RFC2585)

- Corporate databases (which may contain certificates and certificate revocation information and which have well-defined management and access practices)

As you can see from this list, client systems can retrieve information from these repositories through a number of different access protocols (although LDAP is the most dominant repository access protocol in the enterprise PKI domain). Ideally, this will enable end entities to retrieve certificates and certificate revocation information on demand, with little to no access control in place (recalling that certificates and CRLs are "self-protected" from an integrity perspective). In fact, anonymous reads are commonly used to retrieve certificates and CRLs within an enterprise domain. However, access control is a concern when it comes to the posting of certificates and CRLs to the repository because unauthorized access may introduce a security risk; for example, one CRL might be swapped for another CRL, or end-user certificates might be substituted for one another.

## Locating Repositories

The location of a given repository (or set of repositories) can be communicated to the client in several ways. For example, a local client configuration file can be initialized with Internet Protocol (IP) addresses or DNS names of primary and optional secondary LDAP servers to be used by that client.

As discussed in Chapter 6, certificate extensions can also be used to "point to" the location where the desired information or service resides. For example, the Authority Information Access (AIA) private extension can be used to point to an OCSP responder associated with the issuer of the certificate, and the Subject Information Access (SIA) private extension can be used to point to a repository associated with the subject CA. Clients can also determine the location of certificate revocation information through the use of the CRL Distribution Point certificate extension. (Refer to Chapter 8 for more information regarding CRL Distribution Points.)

Use of DNS SRV records (see draft-ietf-ldapext-locate-06.txt or its successor) may be an option in the future. Other methods, including out-of-band notifications and/or LDAP Version 3 referrals, can also be used.

## Tradeoffs

The judicious use of one or more repositories certainly has several advantages. One advantage is that many organizations have already deployed an enterprise-wide repository system of some sort, and it is relatively simple to incorporate the additional PKI-related information within the existing enterprise repository infrastructure. And—unlike the private dissemination alternative discussed earlier, in which users exchange certificates with people they know—this method allows complete strangers to establish relationships for subsequent communication. It also provides a central location where this information can be retrieved. This can significantly reduce the number of certificates and CRLs that need to be stored locally when compared to the private disssemination alternative (as discussed previously). The caching of PKI information (to reduce network traffic between the client and the repository) may counterbalance the advantage, however.

Finally, because the certificates and CRLs are "self-protected" (that is, the digital signature on these data structures guarantees integrity of the contents), the storage mechanism itself (that is, the repository) need not be secure from a data-integrity perspective.[2] This lack of need for trusted repositories is viewed as a major advantage in the deployment of PKI. However, as stated earlier, actual publication of the information to the repository may require some form of access control to prevent unauthorized modification of data. Further, the repository can be protected from a confidentiality perspective whenever privacy concerns dictate.

---

[2]If the repository technology stores or supplies information that is not self-protected, the information must be protected through other means. For example, OCSP responses (which contain "raw" revocation information that is not self-protected) must be digitally signed to ensure the integrity of the response (including source and data integrity). Further, if the repository stores raw public keys and/or raw certificate revocation information, the information stored within the repository's database must be protected against unauthorized modification.

On the other hand, a publicly accessible repository does have several disadvantages. For example, a certain amount of network overhead associated with the posting and subsequent retrieval of the certificates and CRLs is introduced. The deployment of on-line repositories capable of handling the performance demand associated with the community of interest it is meant to serve (which can be on the order of millions of users) is also required. Thus, the number of repositories required may be substantial. Issues may also be associated with the replication of information across multiple repositories (for example, impact on performance, propagation delay, and synchronization issues). (See Box 11.2 for more information regarding performance considerations.) In addition, although the PKI-related information stored in the repository is protected from an integrity perspective (recall that certificates and CRLs are digitally signed by the issuing CA), repositories can be subject to certain security attacks, including denial-of-service attacks.

Publicly accessible repositories can also introduce privacy concerns, especially if sensitive information is contained within the certificates and/or CRLs (which is not recommended). Even if nothing is considered sensitive within each certificate per se, the aggregation of the certificates and CRLs associated with a given enterprise may be sensitive. (For example, it may reveal some or all of the corporate structure of the organization.)

## Box 11.2    Performance Considerations

The amount of overhead in terms of network bandwidth and overall performance will naturally depend on the size of the user community, the frequency of updates and retrievals, the certificate sizes, the CRL sizes, and so on.

In any given deployment, certificate and certificate revocation information retrieval must not be the bottleneck in the PKI operation. Repository access and request-processing times must be as short as possible to offer a timely level of service, and certificate and certificate revocation information sizes must be kept as small as possible to minimize the amount of network bandwidth consumed. As discussed in Chapter 8, CRL Distribution Points, Redirect CRLs, and Delta CRLs can help minimize the amount of bandwidth associated with the posting and retrieval of CRLs (when this is the revocation mechanism used). Certificate sizes may be harder to minimize, although certain things can be done to help in this regard. For example, the use of pointers to information, rather than including the information within the certificate itself, can make a substantial difference in the certificate size. Caching of recently used certificates and CRLs is a common practice to help enhance performance and decrease the impact on network overhead, but this must be tempered with the possibility of missing the "freshest" revocation information. (Refer to Chapter 8 for more details.)

Although privacy issues may not be of substantial concern in an intra-organizational context, they do tend to come to the forefront when information sharing in an interdomain context is considered. Specifically, this problem arises when one enterprise domain wants to interoperate with another enterprise domain, either through the use of cross-certification or by virtue of the fact that the two enterprise domains can communicate under a common root Certification Authority (CA). Naturally, this implies that certificate and certificate revocation information from one domain will need to be conveyed to the other, and vice versa. This is discussed further in the next section.

# Interdomain Repository Issues and Options

In the enterprise PKI, certificates and certificate revocation information is typically posted to a public repository, and the certificate revocation information is usually posted in the form of CRLs and/or CRL Distribution Points. The client software responsible for processing end-user certificates retrieves the certificates and CRLs on demand. In the interdomain context, the method used to convey this information and the frequency with which this information is conveyed are subject to agreement between the two cooperating domains.

There is increasing concern at the enterprise level that uncontrolled dissemination of certificates and certificate revocation information might introduce potential vulnerabilities. In this case, the concept of a publicly accessible database repository is at odds with certain corporate policies in which the information within these repositories is deemed to be sensitive in nature and therefore considered inappropriate for general public consumption. Sensitive information can include information regarding external clients, corporate infrastructure, and employee names and related information such as telephone numbers, or it can simply be the aggregate of one or more of these information categories. This has led to a growing unwillingness among a number of organizations to share their corporate database information without the introduction of specific security control measures. Therefore, methods must be established that will allow the scalable dissemination of the requisite certificate and certificate revocation information without exposing the enterprise to these potential security concerns.

It is sometimes possible to avoid populating certificates and CRLs with sensitive information, and the corporate *Directory Information Tree (DIT)* can be organized in a relatively flat hierarchy to prevent the unwanted exposure of corporate infrastructure information that might otherwise be exposed.

In some cases, it is also possible to populate the Distinguished Name (DN) within a certificate with a (locally) unique identifier that has significance only to some central authority (which in essence is the single relying party). In this case, the DN is meaningless to anyone who might intercept the certificate. In practice, this alternative has been used when the relying party is essentially a central entity; for example, for the case in which a bank—and only the bank—validates the certificates of its customers, the DN can be assigned in a manner that has meaning only to that bank. Specifically, the DN might simply be a (locally) unique integer that maps into a specific bank customer account known only to the bank. Such certificates are sometimes referred to as *anonymous certificates* (although this is just one example of what might be considered to be an anonymous certificate). Even though this may be suitable under certain scenarios, note that the use of this particular mechanism is limited; for example, it is impractical for e-mail that is sent and received between individuals.

As might be expected, implementing these particular safeguards is not always possible. Other methods must be established to allow the scalable dissemination of the requisite certificate and certificate revocation information, and these methods must eliminate the potential security concerns to the maximum extent possible. Some of these options are discussed in the remainder of this section.

Figure 11.1 illustrates a number of possible configurations associated with the deployment of repositories in the interdomain scenario. Option A depicts the use of direct access from external entities to the corporate repository (that is, the corporate repository is accessed through the corporate firewall boundary). Option B illustrates two possible scenarios. The first is the partial replication of the data stored within the corporate repository to a point outside the corporate firewall boundary. The repository that houses the partially replicated information is often referred to as a *border repository*. The second scenario is that the border repository becomes an *intermediate repository*, or *proxy*, and incoming requests are chained to the target repository without any further end-user involvement. Note that options A and B can be used together in some environments. The two derivatives under option B can also be used in concert with each other.

The following sections discuss these and other deployment options. These alternatives are not necessarily mutually exclusive; one or more of these options can be deployed as needs dictate.

## Direct Access

The *direct access* alternative enables the end-user client software in one domain to directly access the repository in the other domain, and vice versa; or it enables an external repository to chain directly to the internal corporate repository. This may be appropriate when the trust relationship between the two domains is reciprocal and/or when the repository itself is secure and protected against unauthorized access. This orientation is one embodiment of option A in Figure 11.1.

Besides access control, a confidentiality mechanism may be required to prevent unauthorized disclosure of the information as it is transmitted from one enterprise domain to another. This can be accomplished in a number of ways (for example, through the use of security protocols such as *Transport Layer Security,* or *TLS;* the Encapsulating Security Payload from IPsec; or the use of certain application-layer protocols such as the X.500 *Directory Access Protocol,* or *DAP*).

## Border Repository

Perhaps one of the more popular interdomain deployment alternatives is the use of a border repository. A *border repository* is a separate repository typically maintained outside the corporate firewall boundary or perhaps within a demilitarized zone (DMZ) where multiple firewalls are used. The border repository can be deployed on behalf of an entire PKI domain, or individual departments or organizations within a given PKI can deploy their own.

The applicable certificates and certificate revocation information is posted to the border repository as determined (and controlled) by each enterprise or organization. Alternatively, the border repository can retrieve the information from the internal repository via chaining.

**Figure 11.1**    Interdomain repository deployment options.

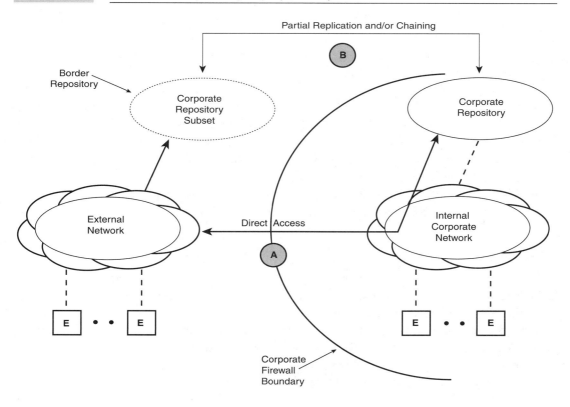

Chaining would require the use of the X.500 Directory System Protocol (DSP), or a proprietary mechanism would be required. Currently, the LDAP specifications do not explicitly support chaining.

External access to the border repository may or may not be controlled, depending on the requirements and sensitivity of the information provided. In any case, remote clients would be able to access the necessary certificates and certificate revocation information without traversing the internal corporate network and, consequently, without directly accessing the potentially sensitive corporate database. Option B in Figure 11.1 illustrates the border repository concept.

The border repository concept was demonstrated as part of the U.S. Federal Bridge CA initiative. This initiative also demonstrated the concept of a bridge repository (or bridge DSA) that can be used to interconnect multiple border repositories. Refer to `http://www.anassoc.com/BCA.html` for additional information.

The border repository option is being utilized in a number of deployments, including the Government of Canada PKI.

### Shared Repository

A *shared repository* permits each PKI domain to post its applicable certificate and certificate revocation information to a common repository so that the other PKI domains can retrieve this information when required. The shared repository can be co-owned and co-operated by two (or more) domains, or a third-party service provider can support the shared repository. The posting and retrieval mechanisms that each domain uses might be different—as long as the structure and frequency of the updates are maintained as mutually agreed upon and as long as the shared repository is capable of supporting multiple protocols for this purpose. Access control to the shared repository can be implemented to prevent unauthorized access to the information stored within the repository, and underlying confidentiality services (for example, TLS) can be used to prevent unauthorized disclosure while the information is in transit.

### Interdomain Replication

Interdomain replication involves copying the applicable certificate and certificate revocation information directly from one domain to the other, and vice versa. However, the capability to automate this process depends on the protocols used. For example, if both domains support Directory Services based on X.500, this can be achieved through existing protocol mechanisms (that is, through the Directory Information Shadowing Protocol, or DISP). On the other hand, if the only common protocol between the two domains is LDAP, an industry-accepted protocol to achieve replication is not yet available. The LDAP Duplication/Replication/Update Protocol

(LDUP) Working Group within the Internet Engineering Task Force (IETF) is currently working on this issue, and so you may see the introduction of an LDAP-based replication protocol in the future. In any case, the underlying session used to copy the information from one enterprise domain to another should be protected. The use of the LDAP Data Interchange Format (LDIF)–based file transfer may offer another short-term alternative.

# In-band Protocol Exchange

Private dissemination and publication are not the only methods that can be used to convey certificates and certificate revocation information. *In-band protocol exchange* of certificates and CRLs can also be supported as part of the communications protocol exchange. For example, this could be achieved with Secure/Multipurpose Internet Mail Extensions (S/MIME) Version 3–based e-mail. Other protocols capable of certificate and CRL exchange include TLS and IPsec (specifically, the Internet Key Exchange, or IKE, protocol). See Chapter 18 for the full set of references for these protocols.

In some environments, in-band protocol exchange of PKI information may be the only way to convey this information to the intended recipients. For example, the Internet relies on this mechanism because no ubiquitous repository system exists that can be used to support the dissemination of certificates and CRLs. However, we are likely to see a shift toward the use of on-line certificate status checking within the Internet for some applications in the near future. Whether a ubiquitous repository system (perhaps based on the DNS) will ever materialize for the Internet remains to be seen.

Note that the use of an in-band protocol exchange of certificate information may supplement the use of a repository rather than completely replace it. For example, the verification certificate (as defined in Chapter 7) of the originator can be sent along with a digitally signed e-mail. This allows the recipient to verify the originator's digital signature without the need to retrieve the verification certificate from a repository. However, the encryption certificate for the intended recipient may be retrieved from a repository on message origination, and the revocation information associated with the originator's certificate may also be retrieved from a repository as part of the digital signature-verification process. This orientation is commonly found in implementation practice today.

# Summary

This chapter presented the various methods used to disseminate certificates and certificate revocation information, with primary focus on the enterprise PKI domain and the use of repositories. We also reviewed a number of deployment alternatives when it comes to sharing public-key–related information between two or more cooperating PKI domains.

As PKI-supported environments scale to tens of thousands, hundreds of thousands, or even millions of users, the timely and robust dissemination of PKI information will be critical. This is one of the most fundamental requirements for the successful deployment of any large-scale PKI. To more fully appreciate the content of this chapter, you should review the following: Certificate revocation techniques, as discussed in Chapter 8, and client-side software necessary to acquire certificates when needed, as discussed in Chapter 12.

CHAPTER

# 12

# *PKI Operational Considerations*

To operate a PKI successfully, you must take into consideration a number of requirements, characteristics, and options. This chapter defines *PKI operational considerations* as those practices, components, or facilities necessary for the PKI to function. (These do not include, for example, explicit PKI operations themselves.) In general, such operational considerations are sufficiently fundamental to the overall architecture that concrete decisions must be made and explicit actions must be taken in advance of PKI deployment.

In this chapter, we discuss a number of these operational considerations, including client-side software, off-line operations, physical security, hardware components, user key compromise, and disaster preparation and recovery.

## Client-Side Software

As discussed in Chapter 3, a PKI is, above all, an infrastructure. By definition, an *infrastructure* is a ubiquitous, "substrate" architecture that is engineered to solve a particular problem and offer a set of services to a wide range of "applications" that may make use of these services. The infrastructure offers consistency and uniformity with respect to these services, across the full range of potential "applications." For the PKI, these "applications" are the client applications, protocol engines, libraries, operating systems, and so on that require security services such as authentication, integrity, confidentiality, notarization, and non-repudiation. (See Chapters 4 and 5.) This security infrastructure must therefore necessarily exist outside (that is, be distinct from) all these "applications."

A client-side PKI component is essential today due to limitations in current software applications (for example, with respect to revocation checking, key life-cycle management, or Certificate Policy enforcement during validation). However, don't conclude from this that a decreased need for client-side PKI software will occur over time as off-the-shelf applications (for example, Web browsers) incorporate greater security awareness and functionality. Such reasoning ignores the fact that regardless of how powerful or how important a client application (such as a Web browser) may be, it is still only one of many applications that Alice will access or run on her platform. For consistent, uniform security *across applications,* the security functionality must be located outside (but callable from) any single application. This is the scalable, manageable architecture that is the true reflection of the definition of a PKI. Note that embedding this security functionality in the operating system is still not sufficiently general because this can hinder multiplatform security uniformity.[1] The client-side PKI component must be an independent library (module, toolkit, applet, or whatever form it takes), callable even by the operating system itself.

In some circumstances, it can be desirable to push particularly complex, computationally expensive, or memory-intensive functionality off the local client. Devices such as Personal Digital Assistants (PDAs), cellular telephones, pagers, and so on may not have the capacity or processing power to incorporate such functionality locally. PKI operations may be one good example of this. The users of these devices may want to enjoy the benefits of authentication, integrity, and confidentiality in their communications, but the devices themselves may be physically unable to implement complete PKI operations (for example, full certificate path validation and key life-cycle management). One possible solution (other than to wait until these devices become sufficiently powerful) is to off-load functionality.[2] The device, instead of doing certificate path processing itself, for example, sends the certificate to some trusted server and says, "You do the path construction and validation for me, and then let me know if it's okay to trust this certificate."

Such an architecture appears to argue in favor of no client-side PKI component because a central server can perform all PKI operations, whereas the local platform simply makes requests

---

[1] Unless every operating system (OS) and software application uses the same client-side PKI component, multiplatform uniformity will not be achieved. Some may argue that PKI support functions in user/ application space are more vulnerable to attack and modification than functions embedded in the OS (accessible through standardized interfaces such as CDSA [CDSA] and CAPI [CAPI]). However, it is not certain that the OS is always less vulnerable. (It depends on the characteristics of the OS and the client-side component.) Also, different OSs will yield different levels of assurance and different PKI functionality for the foreseeable future. Uniformity through a client-side component seems more likely to be achievable, at least in the short term.

[2] It is not universally agreed upon that off-loading PKI functionality is a good architectural decision. Some argue that security and performance implications can render such a model unattractive for some environments. However, this model is being considered in a number of circles as a way of bringing PKI services within reach of the very constrained devices.

for these operations and waits for the responses. However, it can still be argued that some form of client-side module is fundamentally the right architecture, even for these devices. This architecture protects the devices (their operating systems, local applications, and so on) from the need to understand and process security correctly (specifically, the security associated with the request/response protocol with the PKI server). Furthermore, this architecture can ease administration. For example, if a security flaw is found in the request–response protocol itself, it may be much easier to update one client-side module than to modify the (potentially numerous) client applications that have implemented this protocol directly.

Client-side PKI software is an operational consideration. The client-side component may be large or small, long-lived or temporary (see Chapter 3), but its presence is critical to the definition and operation of a PKI. Administrators need to be aware of and take into account this architectural model when planning a PKI deployment across an organization's potentially wide range of platforms and devices.

## Off-line Operations

An architectural decision that must be made with respect to PKI deployment concerns the on-line and off-line requirements of PKI operation: Must users of the PKI be on-line to function, or is off-line operation permissible? This decision is important because some members of the user population will be disconnected from the network on occasion (for example, while traveling). Are these users then simultaneously disconnected from all PKI services, or is some (perhaps limited) functionality still available to them?

Note that this is largely a function of the applications being employed in the environment. Some applications require real-time connectivity (and so users must be on-line); others are designed to operate off-line or in a staged delivery fashion (so that off-line PKI support will also be required).

One example of desirable off-line operation is e-mail composition on a laptop computer. If off-line PKI operation is possible, composed e-mail may be digitally signed and also encrypted for its intended recipients by using certificates, revocation information, and other relevant data that are cached on the local machine. On the other hand, if off-line operation is prohibited (for example, by disallowing local caching of PKI-relevant data), e-mail can be composed but cannot be encrypted for the intended recipients. This means that it must be stored "in the clear" on the local machine until the user is able to reconnect to the network, encrypt the message, and transmit it.

With respect to off-line operation, certain security implications must be taken into consideration. For example, although revocation information (such as a CRL—see Chapter 8,

Certificate Revocation) can be cached locally, such information can be slightly "stale" by the time that the off-line user is ready to consult it. That is, the off-line user, by virtue of being disconnected from the network, may not have access to the most current revocation information (for example, if this has become available subsequent to the time at which the user was last connected to the network). The user, therefore, may accept a certificate that has recently been revoked (that is, declared invalid) as valid. Relying on this certificate is a security risk. In particular, for cases in which the revocation reason is "key compromise," accepting the certificate may cause the user to be the unwitting victim of an impersonation attack.

As well, the possibility of off-line operation necessarily implies that some on-line–only PKI-enabled services will be inaccessible. A time-stamping server, for example, will be unavailable to the off-line user, as will any form of notarization or non-repudiation service. Furthermore, access to certificates and revocation information that have not been cached locally will be unavailable, along with any key life-cycle management functionality (such as key rollover or key recovery). Depending on the policies of the environment, the inability to access such services may have security implications and may limit the PKI-relevant work that the user is trying to accomplish.

Enabling or disabling off-line operation is an operational consideration: Enterprise policy will need to explicitly dictate whether off-line PKI operation would be of value to the user population in a specific environment. This decision may depend to a great extent on the types of applications employed by the users and whether these applications require PKI support for on-line connectivity or off-line operation. In typical environments, many PKI users will require both on-line and off-line operation at different times.

## Physical Security

The most sensitive PKI components should be physically protected in high-security environments to make unintended access, modification, or destruction of these components substantially more difficult. Physical security includes one or more of the following:

- Restricting or eliminating network access

- Locating components in a locked, reinforced room

- Installing proper access control devices (perhaps including biometric devices) to restrict room entry

- Using proper safeguards on tape or CD backups

Furthermore, any data transfer between the network and the physically secured component should use "clean" (for example, demonstrably virus-free) tapes, floppies, or CDs.

It must be recognized, however, that there is always a tradeoff between system security and system ease of use. For example, stringent physical security is likely to introduce manual intervention, operational complexity, and performance delays that may not occur in a system with more relaxed physical security.

The amount of physical security to be incorporated in a given PKI installation is an operational consideration that must be decided prior to deployment. This decision will be based on the system security requirements, a full-risk assessment of the intended environment of operation, and due consideration of the ease-of-use degradation that can be tolerated. In many environments, the "off-line CA" (that is, the Certification Authority removed from the network and located in a locked, windowless room with adequate access control procedures) with an on-line Registration Authority (RA) may be a reasonable and attractive architectural model.

## Hardware Components

A software-only PKI installation (particularly for end-entity operation) is likely to be perfectly suitable for some environments. However, application software (as well as the operating system it runs on) can be vulnerable to penetration from hackers, Trojan horses, viruses, and so on. Even well-intentioned users can cause security breaches by modifying or crashing system software inadvertently.

To help protect against the risks associated with software-only implementations of PKI, selected hardware components can be employed. For example, additional security may be gained through the use of some combination of the following:

- Hardware devices to perform the cryptographic operations

- Smart cards, PCMCIA cards (typically referred to as "PC cards"), or other hardware tokens to store private keys and other sensitive information

- Biometric devices to enable multifactor user identification (and to unlock/enable the client-side PKI functionality)

As with physical security, there is an inevitable tradeoff between system security and ease of use. However, the tradeoff here has greater implications than the tradeoff for physical security (and consequently must be weighed more carefully). With the addition of hardware components, the degradation in ease of use is likely to affect a substantial segment of the PKI user population. The physical security of locked rooms with controlled access, on the other hand, affects only a relatively small number of people (such as CA and RA administrators).

The addition of hardware components is a significant operational consideration because such add-ons can have quite adverse effects on performance (especially smart cards and similar devices due to I/O, memory, or processing limitations), on user appeal or acceptance, and on total PKI-deployment costs.

## User Key Compromise

The topic of *key compromise* (that is, disclosure of a private key to an unauthorized or unintended party) can be considered in two contexts:

- Compromise of an end-entity private key (See Box 12.1.)

- Compromise of a CA private key

Because disclosure of a CA private key is considerably more disastrous than disclosure of an end-entity key, that aspect of key compromise is discussed in the following section; this section focuses on end-entity (or user) key compromise.

### Box 12.1    Knowing or Suspecting Key Compromise

How does Alice come to know or suspect that her key has been compromised? Unfortunately, there are few simple, concrete answers. The difficulty is that this is not equivalent to Eve breaking into Alice's house and stealing the money from her purse. Rather, it is similar to Eve breaking into Alice's house and memorizing the number and expiration date on her credit card but leaving the card in Alice's purse. That is, it may not be immediately obvious to Alice that anything is amiss, but Eve now has the ability to order goods and services over the phone, for example, using Alice's credit card information.

PKI end entities must be trained to watch for anything suspicious in their environments, such as files that have been moved or deleted, directories that have been modified, or objects that have appeared without reason. Just as Alice may check her door locks and windows regularly to see if her house has been broken into, PKI end entities need to be watchful for unsuspected changes in their local environments. Anything unusual should cause a PKI end entity to worry about key compromise and to consider replacing the relevant key pairs. Note that this includes the situation in which the platform itself—a laptop, for example—is lost or stolen.

Of course, Alice may be more certain of key compromise if there is strong evidence that someone else knows her private key. For example, Alice's signature may appear on a document that she is certain she did not sign, or Bob may demonstrate knowledge of the contents of a document that was encrypted only for Alice. In such situations, revocation of the compromised key pair—and generation of a replacement key pair—should be done without delay.

As soon as Alice discovers (or suspects) that her private key has been compromised, she must do the following:

1. Send a revocation request to the appropriate authority so that some kind of notice can be issued to inform all relevant relying parties that they must discontinue use of the corresponding public key.

2. Take steps, if desired, to generate and certify a new key pair so that secure communications with her may continue.

The first action is critically important and must be performed with utmost urgency because delay creates a larger window of opportunity for the entity who now (illegitimately) holds a copy of Alice's key to successfully impersonate Alice. In fact, in an effort to allow Alice to minimize the size of this window, some of the standards specifying techniques for revocation (such as X.509 [X509-00] and PKIX-CMP [RFC2510]) include the concept of an estimated compromise date in both the revocation request and the resulting Certificate Revocation List (CRL). Therefore, Alice may say, in effect, "I discovered this compromise today, but I am just back from a one-week vacation, so the compromise may have occurred any time in the past week. Please revoke this certificate immediately and inform users that my estimated date of compromise is one week ago." This is a very useful mechanism for dealing with uncertainty of the exact date of compromise and for allowing Alice to minimize her resulting risk.

However, this mechanism is also subject to misuse, particularly with respect to the PKI-enabled service of non-repudiation. (See Chapter 5 for a discussion on non-repudiation.) Alice, who wants to repudiate her signature on a contract three days ago, simply needs to send a message to the appropriate authority and claim a suspected compromise four days ago, a week ago, or whatever day suits her purpose. The certificate is revoked, the notification reflects the offered date, and Alice is no longer bound to the contract. Note that there is no way to protect against this sort of misuse by legitimate but dishonest PKI entities. "Estimated compromise date" can therefore be good or bad and should be implemented with caution in a PKI. In particular, if non-repudiation support is to be offered by the PKI, "estimated compromise date" should not be generally available to PKI entities.

The second action, certifying a new key pair, is theoretically optional, but it is typically done in practice so that entities enjoy continued PKI operation. This process of "recertification" may be automated or may require almost as much manual intervention and out-of-band communication as the original initialization process itself. The determining factor is whether the user still has a (noncompromised) signing key and corresponding verification certificate. If so (depending on the flexibility of the protocol in use), a certification request message for the new key pair may be signed with the noncompromised signing key, and the validity of the verification certificate attests to the authenticity of the request. On the other hand, a valid signing key may not be available any longer (for example, if the entity had only one signing key and this is the compromised key). The process of certification of a new key pair could then require an out-of-band exchange with the CA or RA, possibly including a physical meeting or telephone call, to establish the requisite authenticity.

The specific consequences of a key compromise to an end entity, Alice, depend on the key type to a great extent. For example, if a signing key is compromised, Alice must revoke the corresponding certificate immediately but (in an environment that makes proper use of digital time stamping; see Chapter 5) may need to take no further action with respect to previously signed documents. The revocation prevents the perpetrator, Charlie, from impersonating Alice with the (now known) signing key. Time stamps prevent him from signing a new document with a date of three weeks before and claiming that Alice signed it before the compromise. Note, however, that if time stamps are not used, all documents signed by Alice with this key become suspect because it cannot be proved conclusively which ones Alice legitimately signed prior to compromise. Also, even if time stamps are used properly, security concerns may not disappear entirely. For example, Charlie may use his knowledge of Alice's public key and his newfound knowledge of Alice's private key to request a verification certificate for himself, binding that key pair to his name. He may then be able to substitute his certificate for Alice's in the "signer information" of a signed message and successfully impersonate Alice as the signer. This attack will not work if the data originally signed includes a copy of the certificate to be used to verify the signature (a recommended practice whenever possible, by the way), but few enveloping protocols currently include a standardized facility for doing this. (An exception is the "Enhanced Security Services for S/MIME" specification, with its SigningCertificate attribute; see Section 5 of RFC2634 for details.)

If the compromised key is a decryption or key exchange private key, Alice must not only revoke the corresponding certificate immediately but also must find all important documents encrypted with a symmetric key that was protected with this compromised key pair. These documents must then be reprotected. (Otherwise, Charlie may read their contents.) Again, however, no solution is perfect. Copies of Alice's sensitive documents may exist elsewhere without Alice's knowledge. (Charlie may even be in possession of such documents.) Because they were encrypted, Alice may naturally not have been careful about where she stored or backed up these protected documents.

The preceding discussion indicates that key compromise can lead to significant inconvenience and nontrivial security concerns. End entities should be trained to do everything in their power to avoid it at all costs. User key compromise is an operational consideration because an end entity must take explicit action (initiate a revocation request or take steps to acquire a new certificate) in order to keep the PKI operational from his or her point of view.

# Disaster Preparation and Recovery

As noted in the previous section, key compromise may involve an end-entity private key or an authority (for example, CA or RA) private key. Compromise (as well as destruction or any other event resulting in total loss of use) of an authority private key can be disastrous on quite a significant scale. This is because of the trust that a (potentially large) group of PKI entities places in that authority and because of the power it has to enable security in the environment.

In general, authority key compromise is a greater problem than loss of use of a key: Both events require the establishment of trust in a new key, but key compromise also destroys entity trust in existing signed statements from that authority (such as certificates). If Charlie can gain knowledge of the CA's private signing key, Charlie effectively becomes the CA and can issue whatever certificates (with whatever validity periods) he likes within the domain of that CA. He can also create cross-certificates that may cause PKI entities within the domain of the compromised CA to extend trust to an otherwise untrustworthy CA. The security implications of this event are extreme, which is why this topic is typically discussed in the context of PKI disaster scenarios.

## *Relying Party Notification*

One reason why CA key compromise does not have a well-defined and universally agreed-on series of steps for recovery is that, for some environments, simply notifying the relying party community that a disaster has occurred is an unsolved (and unsolvable) problem. For example, in the Web model (see Chapter 9 for a discussion of this trust model), a CA whose public key is embedded in one or more of the popular browsers cannot know precisely who its relying parties are. Browsers have been downloaded or otherwise acquired by tens of millions of Internet users; it is impossible to determine which users have which browsers and who among those users is relying on any particular embedded key. Thus, if the private key of "CA Company, Inc." is compromised, there is no reliable way to inform the relevant PKI entities that this has occurred and to warn them not to accept certificates signed with this key.

For some environments, the problem of relying party notification can be partially addressed by placing the self-signed certificate corresponding to the compromised CA private key on a *Certification Authority Revocation List (CARL.)* (See Chapter 8 for a discussion of CRL and CARL technology.) Although somewhat counterintuitive (it is not immediately obvious why a revocation list signed by a key that it claims was compromised would be trusted by anyone), there is value in doing this. If Charlie has discovered a CA private key, precisely the last thing he wants to do is immediately nullify his newfound power by revoking its corresponding certificate. Even if Charlie wants to do one or two "bad" things and then revoke the certificate to try to cover his tracks in some way, a CARL claiming that the CA's private key was compromised should be taken seriously by the affected PKI entities. Thus, reliance on the corresponding public key should be discontinued.

An alternative mechanism for enabling CARL notification is the one employed in the *Secure Electronic Transaction (SET)* specification [SET]. In this mechanism, a CARL containing the compromised key is issued, signed by the new (that is, replacement) CA private key. Relying parties can validate this signature by retrieving the new CA public key, computing the hash of this key, and comparing the result with the hash value embedded in the old CA certificate. This method works, but it requires that the CA generate its next (replacement) key pair at the time of certification of its current key pair (so that it can include the hash of the next public key in the current certificate). Thus, the current and next key pairs exist simultaneously, increasing the probability that compromise of one may lead to compromise of the other (for example, if they are stored in the same location).

In any case, inclusion in a CARL is only a partial solution, as noted earlier, for at least two reasons. First, a CA public key is not always packaged as a self-signed certificate in the local environment of a given relying party (it may be stored as a "bare" key). In such cases, there is no way to point to this key in a CARL, as currently defined, because CARL syntax points to certificates using issuer name and certificate serial number. Second, and perhaps more important, relying party software may be capable of checking a CRL for an entity certificate, but may not be general enough to also check a CARL (because such revocation lists are typically used only in environments that support cross-certification).

Thus, out-of-band notification of CA key compromise is always useful and always recommended. This may take the form of direct, targeted messaging (whenever members of the relying party community are known to the CA), it may employ mass-market advertising (something a CA may, in some cases, be reluctant to do), or it may use some other means.

## Preparation

Obviously, the best way to prepare for any catastrophe is to try to ensure that the catastrophe never occurs. Therefore, each CA must take every step imaginable to protect its private key(s) so that any form of compromise or loss of use would be highly unlikely. One example of this is the use of high-quality cryptographic hardware for CA private-key protection (for example, FIPS 140-1 Level 3 or 4 devices [FIPS140]).

In the unfortunate event of an actual key compromise, however, a CA can do one or more of the following to help minimize the resultant damage:

- Try, in whatever way possible, to get detailed knowledge of precisely who the relying party community is, so that notifications may be sent to (only) this set of entities if a compromise occurs. This is difficult or impossible in the Web model as currently defined, but it can be achieved in some of the other PKI trust models. Targeted notifications can help minimize the embarrassment of a mass-market advertisement.

- Store the trusted public key as a certificate in the local domain of the relying parties, support the publication of a periodic CARL, and encourage relying party (PKI-relevant) software to do CARL checking. This can help minimize damage because trust in the compromised key can be canceled in an automated way, without end-entity intervention. This mechanism is most suited to environments that check certificate status via revocation lists, but it may also be appropriate for environments in which status is checked via other authorized servers (using, for example, OCSP [RFC2560] or similar protocols; see Chapter 8).

- Have a validity period on the signing key pair that is of reasonable duration. A key that is compromised after ten years of use typically results in much more damage to the relying party community than a key that is compromised after one year of use; shorter validity periods can therefore help minimize damage. There is, however, a tradeoff between trying to reduce the damage that would be caused by key compromise and trying to reduce the disruption that can occur from frequent CA key update.

- Implement a controlled and automated CA key rollover mechanism. Such a mechanism (for example, see the one described in PKIX-CMP [RFC2510]) can help minimize the damage associated with CA key compromise in two ways. First, the fact that this can be completely automated and transparent to the relying party in some environments means that shorter validity periods for self-signed CA certificates can be acceptable. (See the preceding bullet point.) Second, this approach allows a phased rollover of the relying party community to the next CA key so that at any given time the number of entities affected by a CA key compromise will be smaller than the entire relying party community.

It is recommended that CA administrators spend time (prior to PKI deployment!) understanding and preparing for compromise of a CA private key.

## Recovery

*If a CA's private key has been compromised, there is no shortcut to the recovery process.* Nothing ever signed by that key can be trusted, including certificates, CRLs, and CARLs (except, as noted earlier, the statement in a CARL that its own signing key has been revoked may be taken as valid).[3] If that signing key has also been used for other purposes, such as authenticating

---

[3]The fact that everything ever signed by the compromised key is now suspect highlights the desirability of using *key usage* bits (see Chapter 6) to distribute distinct signing functions among multiple CA keys. Each of these keys may then be used in a restricted context (for example, certificate signing, CRL signing, OCSP response signing, Certification Policy signing, Certification Practice Statement signing, and so on), and compromise of one key does not invalidate any of the other signatures.

protocol messages or policy or practice statements (which is not generally recommended usage), these also can no longer be trusted.

The only road to recovery in the case of a compromised CA private key is the long one: The PKI must be reinitialized, essentially from scratch, for the entire affected relying party community. That is, a new CA-signing key pair must be generated, and some trusted, out-of-band process must be used to install a copy of the public key in the local environment of every relevant PKI entity. No other mechanism involving the use of the old (compromised) key can be trusted to shorten, simplify, or circumvent this process. For this set of entities, the PKI must be rebuilt as if it had never existed.

### *Additional Observations*

The compromise of a CA private key brings with it serious security consequences. To those who directly hold a copy of the corresponding public key as a trust anchor, it is an operational disaster. To those who have indirectly been made members of the relying party community through cross-certification, the damage is at some level less extensive. This is because the revocation of the cross-certificate by the directly trusted CA immediately and automatically cancels all further trust in the compromised CA and, by extension, in the certificates of its subject community. For both sets of entities (that is, the direct and the indirect relying party communities), everything signed by the compromised key is immediately invalid unless extensive use has been made of secure time stamps. In that case, it must be proved to an objective third party precisely which signatures were created prior to the time of compromise. The rarity of this practice, combined with the upheaval for entities when it is not done, underscores the importance of careful disaster preparation by CA administrators prior to PKI deployment.

## Summary

This chapter looked at the significance of operational considerations with respect to the deployment of a PKI. It discussed the importance of designing or choosing the appropriate architectural model for the environment to be protected. It also gave a brief overview of a number of topics, including client-side software, off-line operations, physical security, hardware components, end-entity key compromise, and disaster preparation and recovery.

Supplementary material that can lead to a deeper understanding of this area includes the following topics:

- A good understanding of the legal framework for PKI operation (This subject, although itself a PKI operational consideration as defined at the beginning of this chapter, is discussed separately in Chapter 13.)

- A good understanding of the environment under consideration for PKI deployment (This is the focus of the chapters in Part III.)

CHAPTER **13**

# Electronic Signature Legislation and Considerations

Our purpose in this chapter is to discuss some recent legislation and directives that pertain to electronic signatures, to clarify some terminology associated with various forms of electronic signatures, and to place digital signatures into context. We will also highlight some of the requirements and obligations that may apply to Certification Authorities (CAs), subscribers, and relying parties. Before proceeding with this chapter, we would like to point out that we are not attorneys and we are in no way attempting to offer legal advice in this chapter.

## Electronic Signature Legislation

Some rather interesting developments have occurred in the area of electronic signature legislation in the past few years. In many respects, it all started in 1995 with the publication of the American Bar Association (ABA) *Digital Signature Guidelines* [ABA] and the enactment of the Utah Digital Signature Act. Since then, almost every U.S. state has adopted some form of "electronic signature" or "digital signature" legislation. More than 20 countries have also developed legislation or guidelines in this area.[1]

### E-Sign

The U.S. Electronic Signatures in Global and National Commerce Act, or "E-Sign legislation," was signed by President Bill Clinton on June 30, 2000, and became effective on October 1,

---

[1]The law firm of McBride, Baker and Coles maintains an excellent Web site where you can find summaries and pointers to various U.S. state, U.S. federal, and international legislation. See http://www.mbc.com/ecommerce/ecom_overview.asp.

2000. The E-Sign legislation applies to "any transaction in or affecting interstate or foreign commerce" (although there are exceptions such as wills, codicils, matters of family law, and so on, which are listed in Section 103 of the legislation).

The U.S. E-Sign legislation states that

1. A signature, contract, or other record relating to such transaction may not be denied legal effect, validity, or enforceability solely because it is in electronic form; and

2. A contract relating to such transaction may not be denied legal effect, validity, or enforceability solely because an electronic signature or electronic record was used in its formation.

The E-Sign legislation defines an *electronic signature* as

an electronic sound, symbol, or process, attached to or logically associated with a contract or other record and executed or adopted by a person with the intent to sign the record.

As this definition reflects, the E-Sign legislation is technology neutral, and an electronic signature could be instantiated in a number of forms, including

- E-mail signature blocks

- Digitized handwritten signatures

- Digitized voice

- Digital signatures

Thus, the E-Sign legislation lends legal credibility to the use of electronic signatures, but it does not dictate what constitutes an acceptable electronic signature. In fact, the E-Sign legislation suggests that it is up to the parties engaged in the electronic transactions to decide what, if anything, constitutes an agreed-on form of electronic signature.

However, we need to exercise caution here. Not all forms of electronic signature are "created equal," and some will be more secure or reliable than others. For example, in many environments, it is ridiculously easy to forge e-mail signature blocks. It would therefore be unreasonable to assume that something like an e-mail signature block is just as secure or reliable as a digital signature.

## Digital Signatures in Context

Before the E-Sign legislation was enacted, most states had already passed legislation related to the use of electronic signatures. A significant number of national initiatives had been enacted as well. Unfortunately, the terms *electronic signature* and *digital signature* are not treated consistently, and the proliferation of this inconsistent legislation has created some confusion in this area. We would therefore like to take this opportunity to clarify the use of these terms.

As discussed above, an electronic signature is anything in electronic form that can be used to express intent by the signatory. Thus, the term *electronic signature* represents a generic "catch-all" that can be instantiated in a variety of forms. A digital signature is one possible form of an electronic signature that is specifically based on public-key techniques.

More specifically, the ABA *Digital Signature Guidelines* define a digital signature as

> A transformation of a message using an asymmetric cryptosystem and a hash function such that a person having the initial message and the signer's public key can accurately determine (1) whether the transformation was created using the private key that corresponds to the signer's public key, and (2) whether the initial message has been altered since the transformation was made.

Although the term *digital signature* is not explicitly defined in X.509 [X509–00], it implies that a digital signature is specifically based on asymmetric cryptography coupled with a one-way hash function. This is reflected in the example and associated text provided in Clause 6.1 of X.509 [X509–00], which illustrates the steps involved in creating a digital signature using an asymmetric algorithm such as RSA with a one-way hash function such as MD5.

Figure 13.1 illustrates an algorithm-specific example of a digital signature that is consistent with the example provided in X.509 and the definition provided in the ABA *Digital Signature Guidelines.*[2]

For most purposes, a digital signature is arguably the most secure and reliable form of electronic signature. However, we recognize that other forms of electronic signatures may be adequate in some cases. The determination as to which form of electronic signature is the most appropriate should be based on a combination of risk assessment and cost–benefit tradeoff analysis.

---

[2]Note that the example illustrated in Figure 13.1 is slightly different than the one provided in Chapter 2. (See Figure 2.3, which also depicts a digital signature process.) The example provided here is algorithm specific whereas the example provided in Chapter 2 is algorithm independent. Further, if we had illustrated a digital signature using the Digital Signature Algorithm (DSA) rather than RSA, Figure 13.1 would be different. DSA is *not* a reversible algorithm (that is, it cannot be used to encrypt data), so the treatment of the one-way hash function would be different. Thus, Figure 2.3 applies equally to any algorithm for digital signatures, but Figure 13.1 does not. (See MvOV97 if you are interested in additional algorithm-specific details.)

**Figure 13.1**   Digital signature example using RSA/MD5.

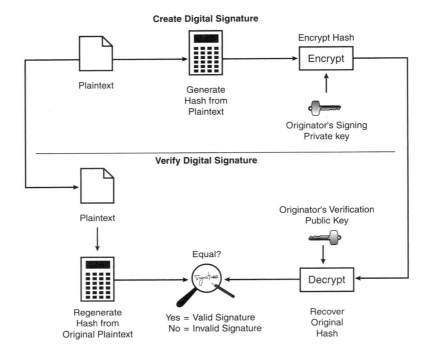

## EU Electronic Signature Directive

The European Union (EU) has also produced an Electronic Signature Directive [EU] for the purpose of promoting uniformity across EU member nations. The EU Electronic Signature Directive defines three forms of signatures:

- Electronic Signature

- Advanced Electronic Signature

- Advanced Electronic Signature using qualified certificates [RFC3039] and a secure signature-creation device

The EU Directive defines an electronic signature as

data in electronic form which are attached to or logically associated with other electronic data and which serve as a method of authentication.

This is consistent with the treatment of an electronic signature as defined in the U.S. E-Sign legislation. Further, the EU Directive states that

Member States shall ensure that an electronic signature is not denied legal effectiveness and admissibility as evidence in legal proceedings solely on the grounds that it is:

- in electronic form, or
- not based upon a qualified certificate, or
- not based upon a qualified certificate issued by an accredited certification-service-provider, or
- not created by a secure signature-creation device.

Thus, we see that the EU Directive is also lending credibility to generic electronic signatures in much the same way as the U.S. E-Sign legislation. However, the EU Directive goes a step further by defining an Advanced Electronic Signature. An Advanced Electronic Signature reflects the definition of an electronic signature as adopted by some U.S. states as well as several European nations. Specifically, an Advanced Electronic Signature exhibits the following properties:

- It is uniquely linked to the signatory.
- It is capable of identifying the signatory.
- It is created using means that the signatory can maintain under his or her sole control.
- It is linked to the data to which it relates in such a manner that any subsequent change of the data is detectable.

In addition, the EU Directive also includes an Advanced Electronic Signature using "qualified certificates" and a "secure signature creation device." For the requirements associated with qualified certificates, refer to Annexes I and II of the EU Directive, and for the requirements associated with secure signature creation devices, refer to Annex III.

## The Significance of Electronic Signature Initiatives

On the surface, one might think that all these electronic signature initiatives will help promote global electronic commerce. In the end, this is certainly one of the goals. However, in the case of the E-Sign legislation, there are still questions surrounding what constitutes a legitimate or valid electronic signature; leaving this to the discretion of the parties involved in the electronic transactions has created a certain amount of confusion.

Further, there are also questions regarding technology-specific state legislation that appears to be in conflict with the more recently passed federal E-Sign legislation. In fact, it would appear that the E-Sign legislation forces U.S. states to adopt and conform to the Uniform Electronic Transactions Act (UETA) or to adopt other technology-neutral legislation that essentially conforms to the E-Sign legislation.

It is unclear what impact the E-Sign legislation will have in the cases where the adopted state-level legislation would appear to be in conflict. In any event, we should not lose sight of the fact that digital signatures are a legitimate form of electronic signature, and nothing should prevent a local, state, or national government from adopting digital signature techniques in response to legitimate business needs.

# Legal Considerations for PKIs

The purpose of this section is to discuss some of the legal issues and considerations associated with CA-licensing requirements and the roles and responsibilities associated with CAs, subscribers, and relying parties. A brief discussion on the way these issues might apply in the context of a private enterprise PKI is also provided.

## CA Requirements

Besides the legal issues associated with electronic signatures, some of the technology-dependent legislation (both state and international) also discusses CA requirements. For example, the EU Directive identifies requirements associated with CAs that issue qualified certificates. As specified in Annex II of the EU Directive, a CA that issues qualified certificates must

(a) demonstrate the reliability necessary for providing certification services;

(b) ensure the operation of a prompt and secure directory and a secure and immediate revocation service;

(c) ensure that the date and time when a certificate is issued or revoked can be determined precisely;

(d) verify, by appropriate means in accordance with national law, the identity and, if applicable, any specific attributes of the person to which a qualified certificate is issued;

(e) employ personnel who possess the expert knowledge, experience, and qualifications necessary for the services provided, in particular competence at managerial level, expertise in electronic signature technology and familiarity with proper security procedures; they must also apply administrative and management procedures which are adequate and correspond to recognized standards;

(f) use trustworthy systems and products which are protected against modification and ensure the technical and cryptographic security of the process supported by them;

(g) take measures against forgery of certificates, and, in cases where the certification-service-provider generates signature-creation data, guarantee confidentiality during the process of generating such data;

(h) maintain sufficient financial resources to operate in conformity with the requirements laid down in the Directive, in particular to bear the risk of liability for damages, for example, by obtaining appropriate insurance;

(i) record all relevant information concerning a qualified certificate for an appropriate period of time, in particular for the purpose of providing evidence of certification for the purposes of legal proceedings. Such recording may be done electronically;

(j) not store or copy signature-creation data of the person to whom the certification-service-provider provided key management services;

(k) before entering into a contractual relationship with a person seeking a certificate to support his electronic signature inform that person by a durable means of communication of the precise terms and conditions regarding the use of the certificate, including any limitations on its use, the existence of a voluntary accreditation scheme and procedures for complaints and dispute settlement. Such information, which may be transmitted electronically, must be in writing and in readily understandable language. Relevant parts of this information must also be made available on request to third-parties relying on the certificate;

(l) use trustworthy systems to store certificates in a verifiable form so that:

- only authorized persons can make entries and changes,

- information can be checked for authenticity,

- certificates are publicly available for retrieval in only those cases for which the certificate-holder's consent has been obtained, and

- any technical changes compromising these security requirements are apparent to the operator.

Some of the technology-specific U.S. state legislation (for example, the State of Illinois Electronic Commerce Security Act) also levy certain requirements and restrictions on CAs.

Granted, some of the requirements listed here are not exactly unambiguous (for example, what constitutes a "trustworthy system"?), but this type of legislation clearly levies certain restrictions on CAs that operate under the jurisdiction of the applicable legislation.

## Roles and Responsibilities

The various components of a PKI, and even the consumers of a PKI, have certain responsibilities that must be honored if the services facilitated by the PKI are to be maintained at an acceptably secure level. Not surprisingly, some technology-dependent electronic signature legislation addresses the responsibilities associated with subscribers as well as CAs. The responsibilities of a relying party must also be addressed (although this appears to be a bit more nebulous when compared to subscribers and CAs).

Figure 13.2 illustrates the three primary roles typically encountered in an electronic-commerce scenario based on PKI technology. The responsibilities associated with each of these entities are described further in the sections that follow.

### Subscriber Responsibilities

As reflected in some of the technology-specific legislation and as discussed in MWC (p. 30), an end user that acquires a certificate for subsequent use (usually called the *subscriber*) is obligated to

- Make truthful representations in applying for a certificate
- Review and accept a certificate before using it
- Make certain representations upon acceptance of the certificate
- Control and keep confidential the corresponding private key
- Promptly revoke the certificate upon compromise of the corresponding private key

**Figure 13.2**    Roles—The usual suspects.

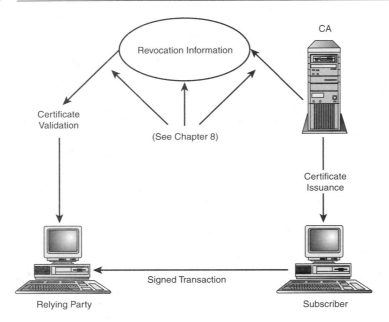

Note that the last two obligations require a substantial amount of understanding on the part of the subscriber. For example, the subscriber needs to be educated on how to "keep his or her private key private." In certain cases, this responsibility may be assisted by technology-specific means (for example, through the use of a smart card or hardware token). In any event, certain guidelines need to be conveyed to the subscriber that will, in certain cases, be technology dependent.

The obligations surrounding "suspected key compromise" are even harder to convey to individual subscribers. For example, what constitutes compromise? Under which circumstances should individuals suspect (or know) that their private keys have been compromised? The events that might constitute a serious breach of security must be conveyed to individual subscribers so that they more fully understand their obligations in this regard. Even the reporting procedures and amount of delay between suspecting a compromise and reporting the suspicion (which might vary from state to state and country to country) have to be understood by subscribers.

### CA Responsibilities

As reflected in some of the technology-specific legislation and as discussed in MWC (p. 30), a CA may be obligated to

- Use a trustworthy system
- Disclose its practices and procedures
- Properly identify a prospective applicant for a certificate
- Publish issued certificates in a repository
- Suspend and/or revoke certificates
- Make warranties to the certificate applicant upon issuance of the certificate
- Make warranties to persons using the certificate to verify digitally signed messages

To summarize in PKI vernacular, the CA is obligated to implement adequate end-entity registration procedures and to develop a Certification Practice Statement, or CPS (see Chapter 6), or equivalent in support of the disclosure requirement (and also in support of independent audits). There is also the obligation to generate and post certificates and certificate revocation information and to make express warranties to both the subscribers and the relying parties using the certificates issued by that CA.

### Relying Party Responsibilities

The responsibilities of a relying party appear to be a bit more obscure than those specified for the subscriber and the CA, at least from a legislative perspective. However, the relying party is likely to be responsible for at least four things:

1. Verification of digital signatures from originating subscribers (including certificate path validation, as discussed in Chapter 9)

2. Knowledge of the rules associated with digital signature acceptance (for example, is a relying party obligated to accept a legitimate digital signature, or is there a choice?)

3. Record keeping to help resolve any disputes that may arise in the future

4. Understanding what to do when things go wrong and/or when an occurrence requires the intervention or action of the relying party

Of course, no one expects the relying party to use a calculator to verify the digital signature. It is tacitly assumed that the relying party will be aided with software that is designed to verify digital signatures (including certification path validation, as discussed in Chapter 9).

The same can be said for record keeping: either software that is local to the relying party helps record relevant transactions or a trusted third party should be available to support this service. At a minimum, important transactions should be stored in their digitally signed form. Time-stamping and/or notarization requirements are likely to be associated with this service in the future as well.

Item 4 in the preceding list deals with things that might require the direct intervention of the relying party. For example, what happens when the necessary revocation information is unavailable? What is the relying party allowed/expected to do or not do in this case? What happens when the relying party receives an indication that a certificate has been suspended? Assistance may be supplied to the relying party; for example, the relying party may be instructed to telephone an authority that can supply additional instructions to the relying party. (See Section 5.3.2 of RFC3280.) However, this may not always be the case.

As in the case of the subscriber, it really comes down to properly educating the individuals involved in these transactions so that they can more fully understand and execute their specific responsibilities.

## Private Enterprise PKIs

So, what do all of these legal considerations mean in the context of a private enterprise PKI? It is unclear if, how, and when some of this legislation might apply in the context of an enterprise PKI, in which confidentiality and/or digital signature services are offered solely to the employees of that organization (that is, the enterprise does not offer services to external sources). One could argue that this should be subject to normal terms and agreements between the organization and the individual employees. However, this may not always be the case.

To illustrate the potential problem, consider the case in which an employee's personnel file is exposed to unauthorized personnel, due to negligence on the part of the company. The negligence could be due to one or more factors. For example, key sizes mandated by the company were known to be inadequate within the industry, and an adversary was able to recover the decryption keys used to protect the employee's personnel record through a brute force attack; this attack could have been prevented had industry-standard key lengths been used. As another example, an adversary might successfully circumvent inadequate security precautions and deceive the corporate key recovery facility into releasing the decryption private key of someone in the personnel department (and thereby gain access to the confidential employee records). What recourse is available to an individual whose sensitive employee records have been compromised and potentially exploited? Alternatively, if that same individual carelessly gave away his or her credentials that are then used to unlock highly sensitive corporate data, what recourse does the organization have? Compliance with applicable legislation may help in some situations.

In addition, if the private enterprise happens to be a state or national governmental agency, it is reasonable to assume that the agency will ask that the PKI vendor comply with the applicable legislation. Even in the case of a private sector enterprise, compliance with certain legislation might be required, either by mandate within the jurisdiction that applies to private-sector enterprise or because the legislation is viewed as a sensible criterion for vendor selection, much like other criteria the enterprise uses to determine which vendor offers the best possible solution in response to their requirements. (See Chapter 24 for more information.)

While the debate over the specificity of legislation continues, it seems prudent to perform the necessary due diligence, even in a private enterprise context. Legislation might help an organization to better understand the level of due diligence required. However, given the inconsistencies between various state and national legislation, note that broad-brush statements such as "The CA/PKI vendor must comply with all applicable legislation and guidelines" may be more harmful than good, especially if there are multiple jurisdictions involved.

## Other Contractual-Based Frameworks

As discussed in Chapters 6 and 9, a number of frameworks can be used to establish contractual relationships between two or more PKI domains. For example, bilateral cross-certification agreements can be used to establish trust relationships between organizations based on certificate policies, CPSs, or both. The bridge CA concept may also be used to establish certification relationships between multiple organizations based on certain policies and rules of conduct, such that each individual organization does not have to analyze the Certificate Policy and/or CPS of another organization. It is unclear how some of the legislation discussed within this chapter applies under these circumstances.

# Confidentiality

The legislation and related issues we have been discussing throughout this chapter have been restricted to the use of electronic signatures. However, there may be legal issues associated with confidentiality requirements as well. It remains to be seen if confidentiality requirements will ever be addressed by legislation in a similar manner to electronic signatures.

Although this reference may be somewhat dated, Baker and Hurst [LOT, pp. 1–39] provide an interesting overview of the political landscape surrounding the cryptographic issues associated with confidentiality services, including export, import, and the domestic use of cryptography. They also include a summary of international initiatives related to cryptography [LOT, pp. 41–78] and a country-by-country guide related to encryption regulations [LOT, pp. 79–241].

# Summary

We have provided highlights from the U.S. E-Sign legislation and the European Union Electronic Signature Directive, clarified the definitions for electronic signatures and digital signatures, and highlighted some of the responsibilities associated with the various entities involved in electronic transactions. Although it is not always clear whether legislation pertains to a given enterprise domain, ultimately the important issue for any enterprise is to mitigate risk to the maximum extent possible. And although the CA-licensing requirements levied by some states or nations may be optional, there are legitimate reasons for an organization to insist that the CA or PKI technology vendor adhere to those requirements, quite possibly demanding that conformance be evaluated by a third-party auditor.

We would also like to point out that a lack of legislative uniformity across domestic and international borders can create serious consequences for both CA service providers and technology vendors. Specifically, how would a given technology vendor be able to offer a set of products that can conform to every variation in legislation that might be encountered? Unless there is significant overlap among all these rules, regulations, and evaluation/audit criteria, this is problematic at best. One can therefore argue that conflicting legislation will do nothing but undermine the very success of global electronic commerce. Fortunately, efforts such as the European Union Electronic Signature Directive should help rectify this undesirable situation.

To better understand the significance of legal framework for PKI operation, a good understanding of PKI concepts is required. (See Chapters 6–12.) In addition, the various deployment issues and alternatives should be reviewed. (See Part III.)

CHAPTER

# 14

# *PKI in Practice*

I (Carlisle) had a conversation a while ago that wandered into the topic of PKI. Specifically, my acquaintance and I began to debate whether PKI had any real value (and, consequently, any real viability). My acquaintance would probably be among the last to describe himself as a PKI expert or a PKI fan (although he's very knowledgeable in security), but I didn't get the impression that he hates PKI either; in fact, by comparison to many, he's probably relatively neutral on the whole technology. He does have, however, enough close connections to Wall Street in New York that he seems to understand in some detail the current operations and future needs of the financial community.

My acquaintance's claim was that of the banks with which he was familiar, all had purchased some form of PKI or another but virtually none had deployed anything more than a pilot. Why? Because the operational model of PKI is incompatible with the bank's existing practice, he said.

The financial procedures in place today don't need PKI; they're based upon a series of peer-to-peer relationships that form a chain, and only the final entity—the purchaser's bank—needs to know a name. (It only needs this as a means to get to the account number.) Thus, strong authentication of the purchaser's name is meaningless to all the intermediate players: They don't care about the name since all they need to know is a credit card number, a credit rating, loan affiliation, or some similar piece of information, in order to approve their step in the transaction. These intermediate players don't need to verify a name, and even if they did, peer-to-peer bilateral relationships don't require PKI.

These are the sorts of conversations that motivate a chapter called PKI in Practice. It is important to clarify what PKI does and does not do, when and to whom it is useful, and how it fits in with both related and complementary technologies that together provide security for an environment. Misunderstandings with respect to the role of PKI are common. Unfortunately, these misunderstandings—people expecting too much or too little—often bring about insufficiently justified purchases or small and tentative pilot activities that don't lead to subsequent environment-wide deployment and use. In such situations, the function of PKI within the overall landscape of security technology is not appreciated, and so the value of PKI is not seen and cannot be utilized. People can come to the "PKI can't help us in this environment" conclusion for cases in which the benefits may in fact be significant.

## What PKI Does

PKI is an authentication technology, a technical means for identifying entities in an environment. Public-key cryptography is used in conjunction with the following to create a technology for identifying entities:

- A mechanism for establishing trust according to a defined trust model

- A mechanism for naming entities such that each entity is uniquely identifiable within the environment of interest

- A mechanism for distributing information regarding the validity of the binding between a particular key pair and a particular name to other interested entities within the environment (such information must be ultimately traceable to an authority trusted by the verifier of the information)

PKI provides authentication—no more, no less. Knowing who someone *is* doesn't necessarily mean that you know *what* he or she can do; it doesn't necessarily mean that you automatically trust that person; it doesn't necessarily mean that you have all the information you need to properly perform your step in a given transaction. Many transaction steps require authorization/entitlement/privilege data about some entity; PKI does not offer assistance here, except perhaps in protecting the integrity, authenticity, or confidentiality of such information (which is originated and used elsewhere). PKI reliably provides a name; in its purest form, it guarantees no more.

## What PKI Does Not Do

First, as noted above, PKI does not typically address authorization issues. Although it is possible to carry such data in the PKI (for example, within the certificate), this is not common practice, nor is it generally recommended. (See Chapter 5 for further details on the need for a separate Privilege Management Infrastructure, or PMI.) This means that if a particular step in a multistep transaction requires only privilege data to carry out its function (like some of the intermediate nodes in the multistep financial transaction mentioned earlier), a PKI will be of little direct use to it (though some indirect benefits may still be attractive).

Second, a PKI does not bring about trust in other end entities. PKI begins with a trust establishment mechanism, whose sole purpose is to enable each entity—through out-of-band means—to *trust* a *Certification Authority (CA)*. From that point onward, PKI operation (in particular, certificate path validation) allows an entity to *trust another key* in the sense that the entity believes that this key validly belongs to an entity with the given name. Recall these two definitions of *trust* presented at the beginning of Chapter 9 (that is, trusting an entity and trusting a key). The distinction is important, but unfortunately in many PKI discussions it is often blurred or ignored, leading to unnecessary misunderstandings. If Alice can come to trust that a particular key pair really belongs to Bob, this can give her some reassurance, but this is quite different from trusting Bob himself. Alice must use other information (possibly preestablished through additional mechanisms or through long-term association) to make this decision. PKI does not enable Alice to trust Bob; she begins by trusting only her chosen CA and then uses PKI to come to believe that a given key pair is held by an entity named "Bob."

Third, PKI does not create unique names for entities; it does not attempt to solve the entity-naming problem. This is quite a common misunderstanding. The job of the CA is not to *create* names but to *bind* key pairs to names (through its signature on a data structure that contains both the public key and the name). The name corresponds to some real-world entity, such as a human user, a machine, or a software object. But—and here is the crux of the discussion—that real-world entity must already be uniquely identifiable within its environment or there would be no point in associating it with an authentication mechanism. The determination that an entity will need to authenticate itself—whether it will use PKI, username/password, retinal scan, or any of dozens of other methods—presupposes that the entity is identifiable, that it has a unique "name" within its environment.

Some have questioned whether name uniqueness is even possible, whether names can ever be globally meaningful. (Perhaps you know only one John Robinson, but how many John Robinsons are in the phone book of a large city? How many John Robinsons are there in the world?) But name uniqueness within any given domain has already been achieved. This is already a solved problem; PKI does not need to solve this. The name "John" may work as an identifier within a single family unit, but if the environment is a classroom, John's last name may be required; if the environment is a phone book, the last name and street address will be needed; for a national database, a city name and province or state will also be included; for the Internet, an entirely different mechanism (a domain name) may be used.

In all environments, though, regardless of size (in particular, even if the environment is global), the pattern is the same: Enough information must be combined together to make the entity uniquely identifiable within the environment. If I write "John Robinson" and a mailing address on an envelope, I can drop it into any mailbox in the world and (barring theft and inadvertent loss) it will get to him. This combination of information—this identifier—is unique and globally meaningful, irrespective of PKI. For any given domain, the identifying information—whatever it happens to be—is what is meant by the "name" of the entity. (See Box 14.1.) Again, PKI does not create this name. It does not need to; the name necessarily preexists. The job of PKI is to bind this name to a key pair.

## Box 14.1 Naming Entities

The terminology around naming is far from universally agreed upon and can therefore be very confusing. The following is suggested as a means of clarifying some of the concepts in this area.

A *name* is a set of information that *distinguishes* an entity from every other within a given environment; that is, it *uniquely identifies,* or makes identifiable, this entity in this environment. The *name* acts as an identifier for this entity. As in the examples in the text, the *name* may just be a given name (such as "John"), may be a given name and family name (such as "John Robinson"), or may include other data (such as street address or whatever). It all depends on the domain: The size and characteristics of the domain determine the amount of information required for uniqueness.

The Privacy section in Chapter 5, points out that the *name,* or "nym," may actually be an *anonym* ("no name"), a *pseudonym* ("false name"), or a *veronym* ("true name"). Commonly, the veronym is what is meant in the security community when discussions refer to the *identity* of an entity. That is, the identity not only *uniquely identifies,* or distinguishes, an entity in a given environment but also represents or readily discloses the real-world given name, family name, or similar information of the entity as well (that is, there is a clear mapping to the human user or real-world object). Because deployments of PKI typically put a veronym in the Subject (or subjectAltName) field of certificates, it is commonly said that PKI binds a key pair to an identity, although conceptually this wording is limiting and using *name* instead (as defined above) is a more technically accurate description.

Confusion in this area arises because words like *identify, identifying information, identifiable,* and *identifier* may be used in two senses: Colloquially, they simply mean to distinguish or single out a given entity from a group of entities; more narrowly, they mean to distinguish specifically by revealing the real-world veronym or *identity* of the entity. Consequently, in some usage, a pseudonym is an acceptable identifier, whereas in other usage only a veronym can be an *identifier.* (This chapter uses the colloquial sense for these words.) Adding to the confusion, the term *identification* is generally used in the security community only in the narrower sense above, so that an *authentication* step reveals a name; if the name happens to be a veronym, however, then this step may equivalently be called *identification.* Finally, many people appear to use *name* only in the narrow sense of a veronym, but this chapter includes *anonym* and *pseudonym* within its definition, as discussed above.

Now, what happens when an entity with "name" A that is unique within a small domain is to be issued a certificate that must be recognizable within a much larger domain (where A may no longer be unique)? The certificate must use for the "name" of the entity the combination of information that is unique within the larger domain: A, B, C, and D. Other entities in the small domain may not know this full combination of information and so may not immediately be able to tell whether this is the A that they know. But this problem is not caused by PKI, it happens all the time in the real world. I may know that my friend John Robinson lives in New York City, but I may not know his street address. The next time I visit the city, I may try to look him up in the phone book, but there may be 15 entries for "J. Robinson." I need to find some way to determine which one is my friend; otherwise, I will give up and won't try to see him on this trip. The same is true in the PKI context: if I can't find a way to tell whether the "name" in a particular certificate corresponds to the A that I know, I simply don't use/trust that certificate. PKI binds a key pair to a name; determining whether the name corresponds to the entity I have in mind is outside the scope of PKI, but something that we do successfully every day in real life. Furthermore, once we have made that connection, PKI ensures that all subsequent certificate-based interactions with that entity will be strongly authenticated.

Some of the confusion with respect to PKI and naming has come about because even though the CA administrator does not create names, the way he or she chooses to encode them into certificates may not be ideally suited to the particular environment. In general, when deploying PKI as an authentication mechanism with a given environment, it will probably be most satisfactory to use the form of identifier already present and familiar in that environment, rather than to force a new name form on all the entities.

In the early days of (X.509-based) PKI, the common thinking was that regardless of existing, workable identifiers in an environment—such as RFC822 (e-mail) names, machine IP addresses, or bank account numbers)—the X.500 Distinguished Name (DN) name form had to be used to encode names in certificates. This led to the false impression that PKI created names and also brought about the questionable practice of putting things like an e-mail address or an account number into the Common Name portion of the DN. Today, the DN name form is not universally mandated; profiles such as PKIX [RFC3280] allow the subject DN in an end-entity certificate to be NULL so that other deployed identifiers in the environment may be utilized instead (specifically, within the subjectAltName field; see Chapter 6).

Fourth, PKI does not make applications, operating systems, or computing platforms "secure." An authentication mechanism cannot in general compensate for bugs (or bad programming practices) in application or operating system software. It cannot prevent the problems resulting from buffer overflows; it cannot remove the threat of Denial of Service (DoS) attacks; it cannot stop viruses, worms, and Trojan horses from causing havoc within a network. (Even a signed applet or attachment may—inadvertently or maliciously—contain nasty code.) PKI does not free a network administrator from all other forms of security awareness and vigilance. Firewalls, intrusion detection systems, installation of security-related software patches, regular backups and off-site storage of critical data, "hot standby" units for critical hardware components, and so on—all may form part of the security landscape in an environment whether or not PKI is used. Strong authentication does not itself make any system secure; it is one of a host of tools that may be used together to enhance security in an environment.

Finally, PKI does not make human users (either end users or administrators) behave more reliably or correctly. An end user will still write his or her password down and leave the note taped to the computer; an administrator will still make a bad configuration decision; a malicious administrator will still be able to compromise security altogether. PKI will not stop people from making mistakes or turn "bad guys" into "good guys." User training with respect to security awareness, acceptable practices, and proper procedures is just as necessary in an environment utilizing PKI for authentication as in an environment utilizing Kerberos, SecureID tokens, or biometrics for authentication.

## The Value of PKI

The previous section has established the following:

- *PKI doesn't provide authorization* (although it may be used to protect authorization information).

- *PKI doesn't create trust in other entities* (although, beginning with a trust model, it can lead to trust that a given key is associated with a given name).

- *PKI doesn't name entities* (even if there was no PKI, I would still need to be able to decide if this e-mail is from a "Fred" I know or a "Fred" I don't know).

- *PKI doesn't make things secure* (even if it may be used as a basis for some aspects of security, all other security-related system/network tools and techniques still need to be utilized).

- *PKI doesn't correct bad human behavior* (people still need to be trained not to do "bad" things; malicious users—especially malicious administrators—can still exist).

So, again, what *does* it do? Why is PKI of any value?

PKI provides strong authentication; it associates a public/private-key pair with a name. On first glance, this may seem a bit meager, but in reality the implications are appealing and in some cases essential. The binding between a key pair and a name means that the key pair can reliably be used for things like digital signatures and confidentiality—not only in real-time communications but also in transactions requiring persistence of the integrity, authentication, or encryption applied to some data. PKI allows for the preservation of a security-related act (such as signing) in a way that would be very difficult to achieve with symmetric-key-based techniques (not least because a different symmetric key must be generated for each Message Authentication Code, or MAC, created for unrelated relying parties, whereas a single signing private key may be used for a year or more to create signatures that all relying parties can verify).

More generally, however, PKI is beneficial in at least four ways. First, the end user finds benefit because single sign-on (or, at a minimum, reduced sign-on) is theoretically achievable. The user may be able to sign in locally using a password and rest assured that strong, public-key–based authentication is used to gain access to a variety of systems and applications, residing both locally and across the network. From the end user's point of view, remembering a small number of passwords is much better than managing many passwords, so the security "obstacle" to getting work done is less obtrusive and more usable. As well, of course, from the organization's point of view, having few passwords per user (instead of many) can substantially reduce the cost and administrative overhead associated with password maintenance and recovery.

Second, the organization deploying PKI finds benefit because the amount of data that must be kept secret in order to maintain systemwide functionality is very small: the private certificate-signing and CRL-signing key(s) of the CA. Entities are responsible for keeping their own private keys from prying eyes, of course, but any compromise here does not destroy the usability of the system as a whole. As well, root keys must be protected in all machines, but only for integrity (not secrecy), which is generally much easier to ensure. (You may be able to tell readily whether data has been changed, but how can you know for certain whether data has been read?)

By contrast, in a technology like Kerberos (as an example), the Key Distribution Center (KDC) must hold and keep secret the symmetric keys it shares with every end user in the environment, as well as those it shares with all the servers for whom it might create tickets. If an untrusted entity is merely able to read any of this potentially large amount of data, the entire system becomes unusable because any ticket may be forged and any communication may be eavesdropped. In PKI the machine holding the critical secret information may be kept off-line, completely disconnected from the network (certificates and Certificate Revocation Lists, or CRLs, may be created off-line and then moved by tape or CD to an on-line server for distribution to the rest of the network); in Kerberos, the KDC must constantly be on-line in order for any entities to communicate.

The benefit of PKI to the organization, then, is this: Because there is so much less information to keep secret (one or two keys as opposed to many) and because it is so much easier to keep that information secret (off-line CA as opposed to on-line key server), the operation and maintenance of the critical components is expected to be more cost effective. In short, because digital data is difficult to protect for secrecy, protecting lots of network-accessible data should be harder—and therefore more costly—than protecting a very small amount of network-inaccessible data.

Third, applications and other system elements requiring authentication find benefit because PKI provides a strong, unforgeable mechanism for authenticating entities. Such applications have protection against impostors and impersonation. It is not perfect, of course: If someone can gain access to Alice's machine and acquire a copy of her password-locked credentials, a trial-and-error attack on her password may be mounted to unlock those credentials and obtain her private key. But such an attack is always possible against technologies that store some authentication secret on the user machine, and it is always possible to significantly reduce the threat by instead storing the credentials on a hardware token that never reveals its secret. Apart from accessing Alice's machine, however, the would-be impostor is stymied: Alice's private key *never* travels over the network as part of an authentication transaction, and its value cannot be guessed or otherwise computed from her public key. Forging her signature is thus essentially impossible, and so no user—including an entity to whom she has authenticated in the past—can successfully impersonate Alice when authenticating to another entity.

Finally, applications and other system elements requiring authorization find benefit because PKI provides a cryptographic link between the privileges and the transaction originator (or between the privileges and a "blob" of data). More specifically, the privileges may be carried in a data structure signed by an attribute authority (for example, a SAML assertion [SAML]) that also carries Alice's public key or her certificate in the Holder/Owner/Subject field. Thus, any entity that can authenticate using the private key corresponding to that public key is the intended owner/holder of those privileges. Alternatively, the signed data structure may hold the privileges and the hash of some data; any data that hashes to the specified value is the intended owner/holder of those privileges.

In either case, PKI (both the signature on the data structure and the inclusion of the relevant public key or hash) ensures that privileges are not associated with the wrong entity or data, which provides the property of *accountability* in transactions. That is, when an entity (or data "blob" such as an applet) initiates a transaction, the application or system element—even if it cares only about authorization—can be confident that the initiator actually possesses the privileges that will be evaluated in order to make the relevant authorization decision. Furthermore, should anything go wrong or should any future situation arise in which decisions must be revisited, the entities involved (the initiator; the attribute authority) can be identified and held accountable for their part in the transaction.

Therefore, although PKI is "merely" an authentication mechanism, it does provide a number of important benefits, including

- Ease of use for the end entity

- Cost-effective operation for the deploying organization

- Protection against impersonation for components that care about authentication

- Accountability for components that care about authorization

- Manageable persistence of signatures and encryption operations

Such benefits can make PKI a much more attractive authentication technology for some environments than any of the alternative mechanisms. Another commonly cited benefit is the smaller number of keys in the environment (compared with symmetric-key–based mechanisms), but this is most relevant to very large environments rather than small, relatively static, peer-to-peer networks of communicating entities and so is not listed here as one of the core benefits.

# When Certificates and People Meet

Ideally, human users in an environment would never see and never even know about public-key certificates. Certificates are not intended for human consumption, although some of the information they contain may be important to display to users. Despite the fact that certificates are integral to the proper functioning of the PKI, they have little intrinsic value to humans, and so their interpretation and handling should not in general be end-user tasks.

Nevertheless, on occasion certificates and people "meet." This occurs perhaps most frequently in secure e-mail deployments. What are the implications for security in such circumstances and what, if anything, can be done?

## *An E-mail Scenario*

Consider an environment in which Secure Multipurpose Internet Mail Extensions (S/MIME) is used to protect e-mail messages. A signed and encrypted message arrives for Alice. Her S/MIME application examines the envelope and extracts the certificate of the signer, "Bob." This certificate is signed by a CA with the name "Certs-R-Us." The S/MIME software looks in its store of trusted end-entity certificates, but this one for Bob is not in that group. It looks in its set of root certificates and doesn't find one for Certs-R-Us. It then looks in its store of trusted CA certificates (ones that have been explicitly imported by Alice in the past) and, again, fails to find one with that name. The software does not directly trust Bob's certificate and has no CA public key with which to validate this certificate.

Consequently, the software will need to see if it can construct a chain of certificates that will lead to the public key of the Certs-R-Us CA. One or more certificates to aid in this task may be included in the "certs" field of the S/MIME envelope. (See RFC2630 for details.) If so, the software can attempt to build the chain, link by link. (I trust *this* key; it was used to sign that certificate, so now I can trust *that* key; that key was used to sign that other certificate, so now I can trust that *other* key, and so on.)

If the "certs" field does not contain any certificates or if it contains anything less than the full chain, then any missing certificates will have to be found, if they exist. Perhaps there is a directory such as X.500 or LDAP that will hold the required cross-certificates; perhaps there is an established Hypertext Transfer Protocol (HTTP) repository; maybe the certificates are held in Domain Name System (DNS) records or in some private storage known to the relevant CAs involved. Perhaps a server employing the XML (eXtensible Markup Language) Key Information Service Specification (X-KISS) portion of the XML Key Management Specification (XKMS) [XKMS] will perform this certificate-finding service on request.

Regardless of how it is done, finding the relevant links in the certificate chain must be attempted. Naturally, for every link found, the certificate must be validated. Is the signature correct? Does the validity period span the current time? Is the referenced policy acceptable? Is the key usage appropriate? Have name constraints been obeyed? And so on, and so on. (See Chapter 9 for further discussion regarding certificate path construction and validation.)

For the sake of this discussion, assume that a complete chain from a trusted CA public key on Alice's machine to the public key of Certs-R-Us could not be found. What does her S/MIME software do? Typically, it will pop up a dialog box on her screen saying, in effect, "I can't find any reason to trust Bob's certificate. Do you want to trust it anyway?" Alice, if she is anything like the vast majority of users in the real world, will simply click OK without giving the situation a second thought, and Bob's certificate will be added to a local store of end-user certificates. (The next time a message arrives signed by "Bob," that is, verifiable using this certificate, she won't even be asked if she wants to trust it because it will already be considered "trusted.") The signature on the e-mail message will be verified with the public key in Bob's certificate; Alice will then decrypt the content with her own private key, and read it.

Worse yet, Alice's S/MIME software may find an explicit reason *not* to trust Bob's certificate (for example, the key usage is inappropriate, or the certificate has been revoked), but Alice is likely to still click OK—she will go ahead and trust the certificate anyway simply because she failed to carefully read or failed to understand the dialog box.

Given the fairly common scenarios just described, it would not be surprising to find system administrators in Information Technology (IT) departments who throw up their hands and conclude that secure e-mail is a sham. If most people continue with whatever they wish to do even in the presence of untrustworthy certificates, what is the point of installing and administering all this sophisticated PKI software to do proper path validation checking? The answer is probably twofold. First, there will always be some specific environments and some segments of the user population in general environments for whom security is very important. In such cases, warnings in pop-up dialog boxes will be read, understood, and heeded. The value of path validation to such users will be high, and the deployment of PKI will probably be greatly appreciated. Second, it must be remembered that PKI, since it is an infrastructure, is expected to serve many more applications than e-mail, and the security it provides as a strong authentication technology can be expected to be highly beneficial to these other applications (especially those that do not rely on the human user to make the final security decisions). Consequently, IT administrators may find great value in deploying PKI regardless of any unfortunate end-user behavior in the specific application of secure e-mail.

With respect to S/MIME dialog boxes, user education will always be helpful. If people are trained to recognize the consequences of these unwitting security decisions (that is, clicking OK without even reading the warning text may cause the certificate to be placed in a "trusted" store, which can open a door for the entry of e-mail-borne worms, viruses, or Trojan horses from this unknown signer in subsequent e-mails), then they may be careful to avoid such snap decisions in the future.

It is clear, though, that secure e-mail is a bit of a special case when it comes to security decisions; it may never be possible to fully automate such decisions because they may depend on the actual content of the message. In particular, Alice's software may have no way of validating Bob's certificate because it cannot form the necessary chain; however, because of some things said in the message, Alice may know that this really must be from the "Bob" that lived down the street from her when she was a teenager. In such situations, it is perfectly reasonable that the trust decision rests with Alice rather than with her software; she is the most appropriate source for the final word about whether Bob's certificate should be added to her local store. To accommodate such situations, however, a simple change to secure e-mail software may prove to be beneficial: The dialog box questioning what to do with Bob's certificate should *appear* after reading the message content, not before. When Alice clicks to close the window containing the body of the e-mail message, she should be asked *at that time* whether to trust this certificate; before she has seen the message, she is probably in no better position to answer that question than is her software.

## A Web Scenario

Certificates and people occasionally also meet in another large deployed infrastructure of public-key certificates: browsers and servers on the Web using the Secure Sockets Layer (SSL) [Resc00] protocol for protected communications. Although the meetings are less frequent here than they are for secure e-mail (typically, only a "lock" icon or similar indicator shows that communications are secure), users do occasionally display the certificate of the Web server with whom they are interacting out of curiosity or to see why a secure session was not established. For this environment, it is not clear that the end user is ever the best judge regarding whether to trust a certificate (Web site content is *not* analogous to e-mail content with respect to giving contextual clues about the true source of the data), and so purely automated decision making for this application seems entirely appropriate. However, the need for user awareness and education in this environment (for example, if the SSL connection could not be established because the server certificate failed to validate, should Alice send her credit card information to the server anyway?) is as great (or greater) here as it is for secure e-mail.

## Summary

Understanding PKI means understanding it in practice, understanding its use in the context of the real world. Ignoring the glossy advertisements, the high-pressure salespeople, the nay-sayers with an axe to grind, and the crowds on the bandwagon of the day, understanding this technology means learning what it can—and cannot—actually do for a given environment. Separating fact from fiction can take some effort. Legends and wrong impressions abound, both in the popular media and in more academic print. See, for example, [ElSc00] for a good example of a collection of mistaken impressions about what PKI is and what it does; several of its misconceptions were dealt with earlier in this chapter, but there are many others.

In this chapter, we have attempted to clarify some of the major issues with respect to using PKI in the real world, describing in concrete terms what PKI is and what its major benefits are. Also discussed was the use of certificates in S/MIME and SSL and the role and responsibilities of the human users in such environments.

A full understanding of the issues with respect to PKI in practice requires familiarity with concepts regarding certificates in general (as discussed in Chapters 3–13) and with the environment in which they will be used (as discussed in Part III).

# CHAPTER 15

# The Future of PKI

Perhaps you have read sequentially through Chapters 1–14 and have simply arrived here as the next step in your progression through this book. More likely, however, you have skipped to this chapter on purpose, enticed by the deliberately provocative title. *The future of PKI? Lots of people are offering opinions; what will these guys say?* Well, keeping in mind the famous quote by Nobel Prize–winning physicist Niels Bohr ("Prediction is very difficult, especially about the future"), let's begin with a bit of a disclaimer: This chapter will not attempt to predict a particular, specific place or time for the flowering of PKI. You won't find statements such as "PKI is absolutely essential for e-commerce" or "HIPAA needs PKI" or "The year 20xx will be the year of PKI." No. The future discussed here is much more general (and much less risky to anyone's reputation!) than that. It is more along the lines of "Will this technology survive at all and, if so, why?"

It has been easy to find articles in the popular press claiming that PKI is critically important and will be ubiquitous "any day now." On the other hand, it has also been getting easier to find articles saying that PKI is finished, that it has missed its day in the sun and will soon be a forgotten fad. In this chapter, we offer our personal opinions as to why PKI has thus far failed to reach its full potential and predict a future for this technology that lies somewhere between the above two extremes.

## What Happened?

Some claim that PKI is dead; others swear that it's only resting; still others feel that it is alive and in fact thriving. But regardless of what camp you're in, there is no dispute that PKI has reached nothing like the heights of popularity and ubiquity that its strongest proponents predicted in its early days. What happened? Why has no year yet been the "year of PKI"?

Undoubtedly, there are many reasons. There can never be a single reason why a particular vision of the future fails to come to pass in exactly the way described by its supporters: Too many variables are in play; too many circumstances in the real world cannot be anticipated. However, we'd like to suggest that two reasons might dominate. First, with PKI there can be a fairly large gap in many situations between what is "sold" and what is "bought." Especially in its early days, the trade media, analysts, and overzealous salespeople often portrayed PKI as a simple install that would solve all security problems. In reality, many administrators found that the technology they acquired was relatively difficult or complicated to install and solved only some of their security problems. This mismatch occasionally resulted in disappointment, followed by disillusionment, followed by anger, followed by (at times loudly voiced) criticism. The conclusion was that PKI was at fault when in fact it was only that the nature and value of this technology—what it is and what it can do—was not properly communicated or understood.

The second reason, however, is at least equally important. Some PKI proponents emphasized the infrastructural aspect of this technology, the fact that it is an underlying substrate for security that many different services can build on and many different applications can plug into. (See Chapter 3 for further discussion.) But in large part, these proponents failed to realize that *sometimes an infrastructure needs an infrastructure*. This is true of PKI. It can be difficult to build and deploy this technology on *nothing* and make it work; some other infrastructure needs to preexist.

An analogy may help illustrate the point. A road system (highways, secondary roadways, and so on) can certainly be regarded as an infrastructure. By definition it is a transportation network for moving goods and people around, much like a communications network such as the Internet is useful for moving data around. But the transportation infrastructure itself needs an infrastructure to make it workable and useful. Specifically, it requires three things.

1. *A recognized authoritative body* This agency—the Department of Transportation, say—is the body responsible for funding and bootstrapping the initial construction of the road system, for maintaining the infrastructure in proper working order, for planning and executing any fundamental changes in its layout and operation, and for resolving legal and other disputes when local authorities are unable to do so. The recognized authoritative body gets and keeps the infrastructure working.

2. *A motivation* There must be some reason to have a road system. In the simplest analysis, the roads facilitate getting from "here" to "there," but more fundamentally, "here" and "there" must exist beforehand or the road infrastructure would have no value. This infrastructure needs a preexisting set of places, or there would be no reason to build it.

3. *Users* What will use the road system? Unless cars, trucks, motorcycles, and so on exist or will exist in the very near future, this infrastructure will turn into an extremely expensive make-work project that will quickly be questioned, ridiculed, abandoned, and forgotten.

When we think about PKI, we discover that it, too, needs an infrastructure around it in order to be viable. In particular, it requires the same three things that the road infrastructure required.

1. *A recognized authoritative body* Who gets and keeps the PKI going? What is the bootstrapping agency? It is fine for Alice to set herself up as a CA in her basement or garage, but who else regards her as a source of authority? Who has any reason to trust the certificates she issues for any purpose? This is less problematic within a company or other closed organization because a particular person or department can be declared to be the authoritative body; all employees will recognize this body because company memos, official statements of company policies or procedures, and so on will give assurance that this authoritative body is legitimate. On the Internet, there is no analogous assurance mechanism to quickly establish legitimacy; consequently, the *recognized authoritative body* is hard to create. Without such an agency, the worldwide Internet PKI is difficult to put in place, whereas organizational PKIs can be bootstrapped relatively easily by comparison.

2. *A motivation* What is the purpose for the PKI? Why is it to be deployed? Without any motivation or with the wrong motivation, the PKI is unlikely to prove to be useful and therefore is unlikely to survive.

3. *Users* Who are the users of the PKI, and how do they use it? Often, descriptions suggest that the users may be humans, but this is only a conceptual model. In reality, it is software that interacts directly with the PKI: applications that make use of the services that PKI offers. What is the interface between these applications and the services? Is this interface convenient and intuitive for these applications and for those who must administer them?

PKI needs a proper infrastructure within which it can thrive. In many cases, however, this infrastructure does not exist in the environments where PKI has been deployed, and in other cases the infrastructure is only partially present or partially understood. The somewhat limited success of PKI has been the result.

So what happened? What was missing in the infrastructural framework for PKI? First, the difficulty of establishing a recognized authoritative body in an open environment (such as the Internet) has already been mentioned. Clearly, the formation of the company Verisign sprang from an early recognition of the need for such a body and an attempt to fill that void. Many years have passed, and it may be said that Verisign now has some level of recognition in this role, but that level still falls short of what can be so easily achieved when there is an independent assurance of legitimacy. Alice can quickly come to believe that a particular department in her company is the authoritative body for PKI, not just because they say so but also because other things in her work environment (office memos, official mailings of policies and procedures, signs and posters in the mailroom or lounge, conversations with coworkers) indicate that this is true. Reproducing that independent assurance in the Internet environment is difficult because there is no such thing as an "official notice" of any news or event.

Second, regardless of the environment for deployment, getting the motivation right has been hard. For a long time, PKI was marketed as a means of achieving Single Sign-On (SSO). Unfortunately, however, even though SSO (or at least reduced sign-on) may be an attractive benefit of PKI, for the vast majority of Web servers on the Internet, it is not a motivation; it is not even in fact relevant. The end user may visit many different secure sites during a single browser session—each requiring a username and password—and would love to have only a single password to remember and manage as he or she surfs around the Web. But, from the perspective of any given Web site, that user has only a single password: the one that this site knows. The site has no concept of SSO with respect to its users, and so SSO can hardly be a motivation for deploying PKI as the authentication mechanism. The user would derive tremendous SSO benefit from PKI, but the user doesn't deploy PKI. A Web site may have the financial and administrative resources to deploy a PKI but will find SSO to be no motivation whatsoever.

The situation within an enterprise may be slightly different. Here, a given employee may need to authenticate to many different networks, servers, and applications within the organization. If the same set of people (administrators, help desk personnel, and so on) are responsible for a number of these different authentication points, then SSO may be a motivating factor for PKI (because the administrative and help desk costs associated with managing multiple passwords per user can be very high). However, administration is not always well coordinated across an organization; in such cases, a different group of people may well be responsible for each administration point, and SSO will not be a strong motivation for PKI even in this environment.

Third, the "user" portion of the infrastructure required for PKI has generally been inadequately understood. How do the using applications interact with the PKI: What is the nature of the data exchanged, and what is the "distance" between them? With respect to the nature of the data, too often the exchange has involved cryptographic algorithms, certificates, or specific security functionality. That is, the data exchange required detailed security knowledge in the application that in many cases was quite unrealistic. Application programmers should be concerned primarily with programming their applications, not understanding the ins and outs of cryptography and PKI. High-level APIs (Application Program Interfaces) certainly made a step in the right direction, but did they go far enough in addressing the sorts of questions that application programmers would most naturally need to ask (especially for specific application environments)? The answer, in many cases, is no.

With respect to the "distance" between the application and the PKI, the concern is whether the PKI intelligence resides locally (that is, on the same machine as the application) or remotely. From the point of view of the application, it probably matters little whether the interaction with the PKI occurs across an API to a toolkit or over a protocol to a server. However, to the administrators of the system, there can be a significant difference. Local toolkits can mean faster execution times during operation but slower rollout times when the PKI software is upgraded. Getting the upgraded toolkit to every user desktop can be a nontrivial task if many desktops are involved. By contrast, upgrading the software on one or two servers can ensure that every using application immediately gets access to the new version when the interaction occurs via a protocol. The characteristics of a given environment need to be taken into account when deciding how to manage the application/PKI interaction.

As a consequence of these shortcomings in the surrounding infrastructure then, PKI—especially the Internet-wide PKI, but to a large extent enterprise-wide PKIs as well—failed to achieve the kind of success so long predicted.

## How the World Is Changing

It may be argued that in all three of the required areas outlined previously, the world is evolving to meet the infrastructural needs of PKI. This is not to suggest that any kind of coordinated, deliberate effort to effect this change is ongoing, far from it. However, the necessary conditions for PKI to thrive are beginning to be established.

### A Recognized Authoritative Body

PKI needs an agency to bootstrap the deployment and use of public-key certificates. This agency must be recognized by all as an authoritative body in this area, the recognition supported by assurance mechanisms of several different kinds. Furthermore, given that trustworthy identity certificates require some kind of out-of-band initialization step (typically a physical meeting), this agency must be one that can establish this sort of procedure successfully. All this may seem hard to achieve, but the answer is not that difficult: Governments the world over are in various stages of planning rollouts of public-key certificates to their citizens. A country's government has exactly the resources and characteristics required to be the recognized authoritative body for PKI. Newspaper articles, magazine advertisements, television commercials, mass mailings, and word of mouth between citizens—all can lend assurance to the government's claim to such a role. Furthermore, people in most (if not all) countries are already accustomed to making a physical visit to a local governmental office to obtain things like passports and driver's licenses; a similar procedure to obtain an "electronic passport"— stored on a diskette, CD, or hardware token, for example—would not seem unusual, surprising, or onerous to anyone.

The government, then, being certain of the identity of the individual because of the procedures involved in the physical visit (as certain of the identity as they are when issuing a passport, for example), can issue a public-key certificate for that citizen, binding the identity (that is, the veronym; see Chapter 14) to a key pair. The certificate, of course, would be signed with the government's private key, and its corresponding public key would be a trusted root in the systems of various relying parties. In particular, these relying parties may simply be root Certification Authorities (CAs) for other PKIs. The advantage to such a scheme is that the government-issued certificates are not used on a daily basis in any particular environment; their primary purpose is to facilitate completely on-line enrollment into other PKIs while maintaining trust in the claimed identity.

In exactly the same way as a driver's license may be used as proof of identity to obtain a membership at a video store (and then never used again in subsequent interactions with the store), the government-issued certificate may be used only to obtain certificates in other PKIs. Furthermore, in exactly the same way that physical passports are recognized by authorities in other countries (for example, at the airport, when entry is attempted into another country), certificates issued by one government may be recognized by CAs residing in any other country, perhaps through a cross-certificate issued by the private key of the authoritative body in the CA's country.

While it is true that current PKI plans in many countries are focusing on government-issued certificates for the purposes of accessing on-line governmental services and information, the preceding discussion is essentially independent of such proposals. Here, the identity certificate—analogous to a physical passport—enables on-line registration into other PKIs (including one for authenticating to on-line governmental services, if it was deemed useful or necessary to keep this a separate PKI).

Specifically, the identity certificate (and corresponding private key) would be used to authenticate the initialization request message in an enrollment protocol to obtain a certificate for that desired PKI. If the channel that carries the enrollment protocol is confidentiality protected, the request could conceivably be for a certificate containing a pseudonym or other information quite different from the identity certificate (depending on the policy of the CA). Thus, the concept of a government-issued identity certificate does not automatically imply that all of Alice's on-line interactions across the Internet will be easily traceable to Alice through simple monitoring of certificate activity.

## A Motivation

It has been mentioned that SSO may not be a strong motivation for PKI in many circumstances. For both organizational and Internet environments, though, the notion of *accountability* may be a more compelling motivation. Whether the user is your employee or someone surfing to your Web site to order something, you may want some strong assurance of who they are so that if anything goes wrong, you will be able to track them down and inform them or, depending on the situation, hold them responsible. In many cases, identity is not required to approve or complete a transaction. However, it will almost certainly be required if something fails or if questions or disputes arise after the fact. Being able to hold the involved parties accountable—or simply ensuring that they can be notified—necessitates some form of identifying information, which is precisely what PKI is designed to reliably deliver.

Not that many years ago, the Web was little more than a library, perhaps only a magazine rack. You could essentially go there and read all day, skimming this article, that report, and the other opinion piece. The data was all there, and it was all free; "protected sites" were those whose addresses were not widely known. There was no reason to have an identity in cyberspace: Anonymous surfing could get you everything you wanted.

After a little while, the Web began to include some advertising. Goods and services were described, along with some contact information (a phone number, or a mailing address) so that you could order the items you saw. The next step was inevitable: ordering and paying online. This certainly awakened a desire for *security* (since credit card information was traveling around on all those unprotected wires!), but it did not bring about a requirement for *identity*. The Secure Sockets Layer (SSL) protocol with server-end authentication created an encrypted, integrity-protected channel to a known site over which it seemed relatively safe to send a credit card number. The server might also ask for some address information if goods needed to be shipped anywhere, but essentially it didn't really matter *who* you were. (Recall the well-known cartoon captioned "On the Internet, nobody knows you're a dog.") Identity was unimportant because as long as the merchant had a credit card number and somewhere to send the goods (even better if the "goods" were electronic and could immediately be sent back over the same SSL channel), the merchant got its money.

These days, the Web is evolving further into a large mall or a major big-city street. There is still plenty of shopping available, but the "service" side is growing tremendously. You can go to the doctor, get your taxes done, and do practically everything at your bank that used to require a personal visit. Identity is becoming increasingly important, not only for accountability but also for access to and manipulation of very personal information about you that resides at some server site.

In the early stages, this need for identification is often handled through SSL: Once the protected channel is established, Alice can send a username and password over the channel to authenticate herself. But the problems with this identification scheme are well known: Passwords are weak, the server must necessarily know the password beforehand, Alice will use the same password at multiple servers, and so on. Much more important, though, is the fact that servers are left with no evidence whatsoever that Alice initiated or completed any particular transaction (because the password or symmetric key used to authenticate all communications is known at the server site). This seems like a risky foundation upon which to build a service business that deals with financial, health-care, or other highly personal customer data.

Much more attractive—and ultimately much more viable—is a foundation that enables digitally signed transaction requests and digitally signed completed forms (that is, meaningful digital receipts) that may be archived for an appropriate length of time. It seems inevitable that the evolution of the Web will see a corresponding increase in demand for the sorts of services that PKI is ideally suited to provide.

## Users

In the past, the application access point to the PKI has primarily been through APIs to toolkits. There are two possible difficulties with this approach. First, the security industry has had little success in trying to standardize APIs for this purpose, meaning that applications would have to be recoded if the PKI provider changed. Although some achievements have been made in interfaces to cryptographic functions (for example, BSAFE, CAPI) and services (for example, GSS-API), APIs to generic PKI services have yet to gain anything like broad acceptance. Second, for very large deployments, software upgrades can carry a significant administrative burden because the new version of the toolkit must be installed on every desktop. For some environments, the toolkit approach may be perfectly acceptable; for other environments, however a different form of interaction with the PKI is likely to be preferable.

Recently, the security industry and the standards community have begun to explore alternatives to the concept of an API to a toolkit on the user's desktop. In an attempt to combat the two difficulties mentioned above, much work is being done in the area of standardizing protocols to a server that interacts with the rest of the PKI. If broad agreement can be reached on the format and details of the protocol, then application developers will be able to code to this protocol without fear that a change in PKI provider will require their applications to be modified. Furthermore, if a server is the primary point of interaction with the PKI, then PKI software upgrades will not necessitate any changes to each user's desktop information; upgrades will affect only the server components of the environment.

Standardization efforts in this direction include Online Certificate Status Protocol (OCSP), delegated path discovery and delegated path validation through Simple Certificate Validation Protocol (SCVP), off-loaded digital signature validation through the Delegated Signature Validation (DSV) protocol in IETF PKIX, and key management services—both key registration (X-KRSS) and key information (X-KISS) services—in W3C XKMS. Many of these efforts appear to have fairly broad-based support from vendors as well as potential users, and so the difficulties experienced in some environments regarding application/PKI interaction may soon be addressed in standards-compliant commercial products.

In short, vendors in the early days of PKI may perhaps be accused of assuming too much of their users, or expecting (unreasonably) that applications would readily "bend" to accommodate the addition of PKI to their environments. Now, more care is taken to understand the needs and desires of application programmers and other important elements of the environment in which PKI will sit, to ensure that PKI can add its security services as effectively—but as painlessly and unobtrusively—as possible.

## Reasons for Cautious Optimism

As with any relatively new technology, PKI may fail to achieve great market success. And, without question, when a technology is as overhyped and overmarketed as PKI has been for the past several years, its chances for success appear to be diminished greatly. Still, there seem to be solid reasons for cautious optimism in this area.

PKI has struggled to "live up to its billing" in some ways because the infrastructure itself requires an infrastructure in order to be successful, and this surrounding infrastructure has largely been absent. In many environments, there was no recognized authoritative body to establish the PKI, the motivation for deployment was missing or misguided, and the using applications were not properly understood or accommodated.

But the world is changing, and the evolution looks very promising for PKI. First, governments worldwide are poised to become recognized authoritative bodies with respect to PKI in their own countries. National identity certificates (with due consideration taken in the architecture to address privacy concerns) coupled with cross-certification or cross-recognition between nations could be the bootstrapping mechanism needed to really set PKI in motion. Second, the emergence not so much of e-commerce but of personalized e-services will provide a strong motivation for identification across the Web. Authorization issues (in particular, access to highly personal data), as well as a greater need for accountability, may foster an increasing appreciation across the industry for the inherent strengths of PKI technology. Third, the creation of standardization activities around protocols to servers that interact with a PKI displays a growing understanding of environments with very large numbers of applications and/or very large user populations. Standards—and compliant products—in this area will help make PKI more attractive to these important environments.

Finally, it must be recognized that PKI technology itself is still evolving. It continues to change to meet real-world business requirements as these environments grow and become better understood. Those claiming that PKI is dead typically have in mind a very narrow definition for PKI and/or have had a "sour" experience with PKI in the past and fail to realize that the field has matured significantly since then. Some features that may not have been possible in older products can be found in selected products today and will be commonplace tomorrow. Furthermore, the integration of PKI with other technologies and infrastructures (such as authorization, electronic forms, or Web Services) to provide more comprehensive solutions to actual business problems is an encouraging trend.

## Summary

Prediction is of course difficult: Will PKI survive or not? We have discussed a number of changes taking place in many areas to establish both the internal mechanisms and the surrounding infrastructure that PKI needs to not only survive but also thrive. Certainty is a luxury of the naïve, but there indeed appears to be significant reason for optimism with respect to the wide-scale deployment and success of PKI.

CHAPTER

# 16

# *Conclusions and Further Reading*

Part I of this book has considered the many aspects of PKI. The treatment has been intention-ally generic, in the sense that every attempt has been made to avoid references to specific ven-dor interpretations or product implementations of any particular topic. Instead, the focus of the discussion has been to introduce concepts, explain terminology, highlight issues, and dis-cuss the benefits of this technology, all as an aid to understanding this subject area.

## Conclusions

PKI is a rich and complex topic, encompassing all the facets required to turn public-key cryp-tography into an infrastructural platform for security services. Put simply,

$$PKI = (PK)^I$$

*PKI* is *public key* raised to the power of an *infrastructure*. Thinking of PKI first and foremost as an infrastructure puts many of its concepts into perspective and helps clarify why things such as user transparency and cross-application/cross-platform consistency are intrinsic to the definition of PKI. This results in such concepts as automated key and certificate life-cycle management and application-independent client software being fundamental to a proper PKI implementation. (Otherwise, the implementation is providing public-key technology and ser-vices, but not an infrastructural solution.)

The PKI, as described by the extended definition in Chapter 3, encompasses functionality to meet a wide range of security needs. A particular PKI implementation for a particular operat-ing environment may not require this full functionality; some subset of the described func-tionality may be sufficient. However, the extended definition is useful because a PKI that meets this description should be able to meet the needs of any environment today, as well as the growing needs of that environment as time moves on.

## Suggestions for Further Reading

One primary reason for writing this book was the relative scarcity of good introductory material on this topic. PKI has received a lot of attention in the trade journals, but very little of this literature aims to explain concepts and terminology to any significant breadth or depth. Moreover, only a small number of sources explain a broad range of PKI topics in sufficient detail so that a beginner may quickly become familiar with this area.

If you're interested in further reading in the areas of public-key cryptography and PKI, you may want to consult the following references.

Austin, T. *PKI: A Wiley Tech Brief.* New York: Wiley, 2000. [Aust00]

Feghhi, J., J. Feghhi, and P. Williams. *Digital Certificates: Applied Internet Security.* Reading, MA: Addison-Wesley, 1999. [FFW99]

Ford, W., and M. Baum. *Secure Electronic Commerce: Building the Infrastructure for Digital Signatures and Encryption* (2nd ed.). Englewood Cliffs, NJ: Prentice Hall, 2000. [FoBa00]

Housley, R., and T. Polk. *Planning for PKI: Best Practices Guide for Deploying Public Key Infrastructure.* New York: Wiley, 2001. [HoPo01]

Menezes, A., P. van Oorschot, and S. Vanstone. *Handbook of Applied Cryptography.* Boca Raton, FL: CRC Press, 1997. [MvOV97]

Nash, A., W. Duane, C. Joseph, and D. Brink. *PKI: Implementing and Managing E-Security.* Berkeley, CA: RSA Press (McGraw-Hill Professional Publishing), 2001. [NDJB01]

Schneier, B. *Applied Cryptography: Protocols, Algorithms, and Source Code in C* (2nd ed.). New York: Wiley, 1996. [Schn96]

# PART

# II

# Standards

17  Introduction. . . . . . . . . . . . . . . . . . . . . . . 221

18  Major Standards Activities . . . . . . . . . . . . . 223

19  Standardization Status and Road Map . . . . . 237

20  Standards: Necessary but Not Sufficient . . . . 243

21  Conclusions and Further Reading. . . . . . . . . 253

CHAPTER 17

# Introduction

In Part II of this book, we take a brief look at the standards and nonstandards activities most relevant to PKI technology. This part is deliberately small because we recognize that such activities are volatile and fluid at best, defying prediction and challenging the wisdom of static preservation in a book. Nevertheless, it is of value to highlight the major groups working in this area, to provide some background in terms of their history and purpose, and to give pointers to the specifications that are stable enough to warrant implementation efforts.

Chapter 18, Major Standards Activities, presents some of the most prominent activities taking place within formal standards bodies. As you will notice, a good number of these activities are have occurred within the Internet Engineering Task Force (IETF) of the Internet Society, although several XML-based projects are gaining prominence as well.

Chapter 19, Standardization Status and Road Map, provides the current and projected near-term standardization status of some of the most significant specifications and includes references to where these documents may be found and where their progress may be tracked.

Chapter 20, Standards: Necessary but Not Sufficient, considers the fact that the existence of a "standard," whether it is the product of a formal standards body or not, is necessary but not sufficient to guarantee that the products of different vendors will interoperate with one another. Some of the reasons for this are given, along with a discussion of the usefulness of profiling activities and interoperability initiatives.

Finally, Chapter 21, Conclusions and Further Reading, contains concluding remarks and some suggestions for further reading on the topic presented in this part of the book.

CHAPTER 18

# Major Standards Activities

In this chapter, we discuss a number of the high-visibility standards activities relevant to PKI concepts or techniques. It is not meant to be exhaustive, but it does include many groups that have captured significant attention in recent times as awareness of security (and especially PKI) has grown.

The groups listed here are interrelated to various degrees. Those defining certificate formats include X.509, SPKI, OpenPGP, EDIFACT, and SSTC; these to a large extent are independent efforts. Those profiling certificates (primarily X.509v3 certificates) for specific environments and uses include PKIX, TC68, S/MIME, IPsec, TLS, WAP, XMLdsig, XMLenc, and SOAP; these efforts overlap to a much greater degree. Certificate and CRL (Certificate Revocation List) repository issues (primarily, again, for X.509 formats) are the topic of the X.500, LDAP, and XKMS efforts.

## X.509

The *X.509* [X509–97, X509–00] portion of the ISO and CCITT/ITU-T X.500 suite of standards is in many ways the single most important factor in the transition of PKI concepts from small, closed-network, trial environments to large, open deployments. As noted in Chapter 6, the concept of a certificate makes public-key technology feasible when the entities are for the most part unknown to one another. Therefore, to bring PKI to large multinational corporations or to millions of Internet users, a useful certificate format was necessary. To allow interoperability among multiple tools and applications, a certificate format needed to be standardized and widely adopted. It is precisely this role that X.509 has played: This specification defined and standardized a general, flexible certificate format. Its widespread adoption is perhaps testimony (in equal measure) to its technical suitability for many environments and its availability as an international standard just at the time when a number of vendors were ready to begin implementing products.

The real utility of X.509 comes from the powerful extension mechanism it has defined for its Version 3 certificates and Version 2 CRLs. This mechanism is perfectly general in that any extension whatsoever may be defined and placed into a certificate or CRL; furthermore, a criticality flag indicates whether or not a verifier must understand and examine this extension as part of its verification process. Thus, certificate and CRL contents can readily be tailored to specific environments with or without restricting their usability in other environments, as desired.

Although it is an international standard, X.509 has continued to evolve in some ways. Any problems found through operational experience have been (and will continue to be) addressed in the standard through a formal defect reporting and resolution process. Amendments to the standard can also be incorporated in some cases to clarify text or to provide additional detail; one example of this is the amendment addressing the definition and use of Attribute Certificates for general privilege management. (See Chapter 5.)

# PKIX

The Internet Engineering Task Force (IETF) is the body primarily responsible for creating, standardizing, and promoting the protocols/functions that make the Internet useful and interesting (examples include TCP/IP, SMTP, FTP, Telnet, and HTTP). This work is carried out by a number of working groups; these are organized into various areas of common interest.

One working group in the IETF Security Area is *Public-Key Infrastructure, X.509,* commonly referred to as *PKIX*. The PKIX Working Group was formed at the end of 1995 with the explicit intention of tailoring the certificate and CRL work done in the X.509 standard (then the 1993 version, but the 1997 version [X509–97] was rapidly being completed) to the Internet environment to specify an Internet PKI (IPKI).

As the vision of the working group was being formalized in the IETF, it was recognized that defining an Internet PKI was more extensive than profiling the X.509 certificate and CRL work. Thus, the PKIX charter was written to encompass four specific areas of activity [PKIX]:

1. The certificate and CRL profile

2. Certificate management protocols

3. Operational protocols

4. Certificate Policy (CP) and Certification Practice Statement (CPS) framework

The first item was the original motivating task—the profile of the X.509 syntax, including detailed specification of the mandatory, optional, critical, and noncritical extensions (see Chapters 6 and 8 for a discussion of extensions) in a "PKIX-compliant" certificate or CRL.

The second item was to specify the protocols for all the management operations required in the IPKI, including initialization/certification of entities and their key pairs, certificate revocation, key backup and recovery, Certification Authority (CA) key rollover, cross-certification, and so on.

The third item, operational protocols, was to specify the protocols for day-to-day IPKI operation, such as certificate/CRL retrieval from a public repository and on-line checking of the revocation status of a certificate.

Finally, the fourth item was to provide guidelines to writers of CP and CPS documents, suggesting topics and formats that may be useful for inclusion in particular environments, and so on.

These four PKIX work items became the subjects of separate documents for two reasons: (1) The work could move ahead independently under independent authors, and (2) no one part would have its progression impeded by unforeseen delays in any of the other parts. In due course, the certificate management protocol and operational protocol work items were also split into multiple documents to accommodate the needs and desires of different PKI environments. The specifications that have stabilized within the PKIX Working Group include RFC2459 (now superseded by RFC3279 and RFC3280), RFC2510, RFC2511, RFC2527, RFC2559, RFC2560, RFC2585, RFC2587, RFC2797, RFC3029, RFC3039, RFC3161, and RFC3281.

PKIX has played an essential and significant role in bringing the concept of a PKI to the Internet. The protocols and functions it has defined make a PKI possible, even in the diverse enclaves of the Internet, because their flexibility and generality can satisfy the requirements of greatly differing environments. The work continues to evolve as well: The PKIX Charter was expanded in 1999 to include new work items on time-stamping protocols, data certification services, and Attribute Certificates.

# X.500

The ISO/ITU-T suite of standards for the directory, commonly known as the *X.500* series of specifications [X500], is the framework within which the X.509 document was originally created. The X.500 Directory is a highly sophisticated repository of arbitrary information and includes such features as client-to-directory access protocols, server-to-server communication protocols, full and partial replication of directory data, chaining of servers to respond to a query, and complex search filtering capabilities. Recognition of the need for access control to the directory, including the requirement for strong authentication in some environments, led to the specification of certificate and CRL formats and other PKI concepts in the X.509 standard.

Of particular importance to PKI, X.500 has defined a *schema*, a standardized method to store certificate and CRL data structures in an entity's directory entry. Thus, regardless of which vendor has supplied the X.500-compliant directory in an environment, the PKI implementation will be able to retrieve the certificates and CRLs it needs to operate correctly. Although the directory has achieved nothing like the worldwide deployment its originators hoped, the standardized schema alone has made it an important part of many PKI deployments. Furthermore, the technical feasibility of linking directory servers together makes it possible for these independently deployed PKIs to be joined together when necessary to permit secure communications between and among separate communities.

## LDAP

The *Lightweight Directory Access Protocol (LDAP)* [HoSm97] was originally conceived as a simple-to-describe, simple-to-implement subset of the capability of the *X.500 Directory Access Protocol (DAP)*. Over time, this "subset" of useful functions and features has expanded to incorporate the needs of the many different environments that have chosen to use LDAP as the access protocol for their repository (X.500-compliant directory or otherwise). This has led some to question whether the "L" in LDAP still applies, just as the "S" in some of the IETF "Simple" protocols occasionally raises eyebrows.

Nevertheless, many vendors worldwide deploy LDAP Version 2 [RFC1777]; LDAPv3 [RFC2251], with its useful extension mechanism for incorporating new capabilities over time in a standardized way, will likely see even greater deployment. The IETF Working Group LDAPext [LDAPext] has been formed to define and standardize particularly useful extensions for LDAPv3, such as an access control mechanism.

As with X.500, a schema [RFC2587] has been specified for LDAP-compliant repositories to provide a standardized method and location for certificate and CRL information storage for PKI entities. This greatly enhances the possibility of interoperability between PKI products from different vendors in an LDAP environment.

## ISO TC68

Working Group 8 of Sub-Committee 2 of Technical Committee 68 in ISO (*ISO TC68/SC2/WG8,* referred to here simply as *TC68*) is concerned with standardizing aspects of public-key technology, primarily for the use and purposes of the financial industry [TC68]. This working group, like PKIX, has profiled the X.509 certificate and CRL structures for the particular needs of its focus environment. To that end, it has specified the optional or mandatory, critical or noncritical status of the X.509-defined extensions. (See Chapters 6 and 8 for further details on the certificate and CRL extension mechanism.) It has also defined new extensions required to meet the unique needs of the financial sector.

# ANSI X9F

The *American National Standards Institute (ANSI)* committee X9 (Financial Services) develops and publishes standards for the financial services industry to facilitate delivery of financial products and services. Subcommittee *X9F* is responsible for standards related to data and information security and includes working groups focused on cryptographic tools (X9F1), protocols (X9F3), and digital signature and Certificate Policy (X9F5), among others. X9F has published a significant number of standards (see, for example, the on-line catalog at `http://www.x9.org`) and is active in submitting some of its more mature draft documents as new work items to the related ISO group TC68.

# S/MIME

In 1995 a consortium of industry vendors led by RSA Data Security, Inc., took the *Multipurpose Internet Mail Extensions (MIME)* specifications in the IETF and decided on the particular mechanisms required to add security—specifically in the form of encryption and digital signatures—to MIME-compliant messages. The *Secure MIME (S/MIME)* specifications, though not the product of any formal standards body, achieved some measure of recognition and consensus in the Internet messaging community. To build on and expand this success, the S/MIME documents (then at Version 2) were brought into the IETF process [RFC2311, RFC2312], and all enhancements to this work were to be carried out within an IETF S/MIME Working Group created for this purpose.

The initial and primary focus of the S/MIME Working Group was to incorporate a number of new security features into the specifications while maintaining compatibility (to the greatest extent possible) with products implemented according to the previous version of the specifications. In particular, the standards-track S/MIMEv3 specifications [RFC2630–RFC2634] include the ability to label messages securely (for example, "secret," "top secret," or "company confidential") and the ability to request and receive a *signed receipt* (that is, proof that the intended recipient actually received a prior message). Also included is the ability to use key management techniques other than RSA (for example, Diffie–Hellman; see Chapter 2 for a discussion of the RSA and DH algorithms).

The S/MIMEv3 specifications include discussion of PKI concepts such as certificate format, certificate processing, and CRLs. These specifications give a profile for X.509 certificates that is compliant with PKIX [RFC2459] but that specifies the extensions relevant to S/MIME. Furthermore, provision is made in the message envelope to carry arbitrary numbers of certificates and CRLs to assist the recipient with the task of path construction and certificate validation.

# IPsec

The upgrade of the Internet Protocol Version 6 (IPv6) included a set of new features and functions, one of which was due consideration, within the standards-track specifications, of the security architecture for this protocol [RFC2401]. A new IETF working group was created to design and standardize the IP Security (IPsec) set of concepts and protocols. An important component of this architecture is a protocol for key exchange between IP nodes for the purpose of authenticity, integrity, and confidentiality. This work is embodied in the *Internet Key Exchange (IKE) protocol* [RFC2409], a combination of a general framework for key management in this environment [RFC2408] and a specific protocol for accomplishing key exchange within this framework [RFC2412].

IKE provides for strong, X.509-certificate-based authentication at the IP layer and, to this extent, can be deployed in a manner that is compatible with the PKIX profile [RFC2459].

# TLS

The *Transport Layer Security (TLS)* specification [RFC2246, Resc00] is the IETF standards-track version of the Secure Sockets Layer Version 3.0 (SSLv3.0) protocol found in millions of client browsers and Web servers around the world. TLS creates a secure channel between source and destination entities at the transport layer, providing certificate-based authentication, information integrity, and data confidentiality.

Like S/MIME, the TLS specification includes discussion of a profile for X.509 certificates that aims for compatibility with the PKIX profile [RFC2459]. While total compatibility is not always possible due to the conflicting requirements of these different user groups, such efforts help illustrate the respect for and influence of the PKIX specifications within many segments of the IETF community. The efforts undergone in the PKIX Working Group to define a PKI for the Internet appear to be meeting the goals of these various groups and serving the IETF community well. Interestingly, other (that is, non-IETF) standards groups and industry sectors also take PKIX compatibility into consideration when finalizing their specifications; this means that the PKIX work is general enough to encompass the needs of communities other than IETF.

# SPKI

The *Simple Public Key Infrastructure (SPKI)* IETF Working Group was created in 1996 as an alternative to the PKIX effort. One fundamental premise of this group was that X.509 is a complicated and bulky certificate format that, by explicitly binding a key pair to an *identity,* rests upon an inherently flawed foundation. The proponents of SPKI argue that the concept of a globally unique identity (that is, an X.500 DistinguishedName, as adopted by X.509) will never be realized. Instead, they advocate the idea of the public key as the identity of relevance. Where necessary and meaningful, a name or other identifying information may be associated with the key (building on the work in [SDSI]), but this is optional and, in any case, intended to have only local significance.

The SPKI specifications [RFC2692, RFC2693] discuss the concepts and philosophy behind this approach to an Internet PKI and provide the detailed certificate format and processing rules required for implementation. (See also [SPKI].) Unlike the initial focus of both X.509 and PKIX, SPKI explicitly encompasses authorization as well as authentication: The sophisticated certificate format makes it possible to express, in a general way, what a key is *allowed to do*. Such capability unfortunately (and perhaps not surprisingly) has done much to diminish the originally intended simplicity of the *Simple* Public Key Infrastructure. This has perhaps cost it some credibility and lost it some enthusiasts in specific environments. Nevertheless, the SPKI specifications have reached a level of maturity and stability within the working group, and its proponents have begun to concentrate their efforts on implementation and interoperability testing.

Although SPKI embodies a number of interesting ideas and research contributions, it has not gained the widespread support of the corporate and governmental environments that X.509 has enjoyed. To date, few vendors have included SPKI certificates in their products, and it now appears likely that the SPKI definition of an Internet PKI will never occupy more than a niche market.

# OpenPGP

Like S/MIME, SSL, and X.509, the popular *Pretty Good Privacy (PGP)* security framework was brought under the auspices of the IETF to formalize the specification within a recognized standards body and to make it more relevant to the wider Internet community. This resulted in the *OpenPGP* Working Group and associated specification [RFC2440].

OpenPGP defines the PGP certificate format (an alternative to both X.509 and SPKI) and specifies the processing rules required to validate such a certificate, predicated on the familiar PGP "Web-of-trust" model. (See Chapter 9.) It also specifies the enveloping protocols required to construct and process PGP-protected e-mail messages.

Despite a loyal installed base of significant size, OpenPGP has not captured a large portion of the corporate or governmental security infrastructures. One reason might be that the inherently user-centric trust model cannot easily be controlled centrally on an organization-wide basis (to ensure, for example, that each individual user will conform to a predefined corporate policy regarding the appropriate trust anchor(s) for certificate path verification). Another reason might be that its key management can become quite complex over time for inexperienced users. However, it seems likely that OpenPGP will continue to be popular with individual Internet users. In an effort to ensure this popularity and to enhance interoperability with other applications and environments, the OpenPGP specification also includes discussion regarding interworking with alternative certificate formats such as X.509.

## EDIFACT

The X.400 Electronic Data Interchange standards effort has produced a certificate format known as *EDIFACT* [EDIFACT]. Although used in selected business environments, this format does not have the momentum behind it that X.509 has; furthermore, it does not seem to have been widely adopted in any noncorporate environments (such as governmental, academic, or individual Internet user environments). EDIFACT will likely phase out over time in favor of alternate certificate formats.

## IEEE

The Standards Association of the Institute of Electrical and Electronics Engineers (IEEE) has a number of activities related to security. The most relevant to PKI is IEEE P1363, "Standard Specifications for Public Key Cryptography," which includes specifications of common public-key cryptographic techniques (including mathematical primitives for key derivation, public-key encryption, and digital signatures) and cryptographic schemes based on those primitives. P1363 has been adopted as an IEEE standard, although work continues on a supporting/companion document called IEEE P1363a, "Standard Specifications for Public Key Cryptography: Additional Techniques." A study group also has been established within the working group to investigate newer schemes and protocols not considered in P1363 and P1363a; such specifications will appear over time as P1363–1, P1363–2, and so on. Further information on these efforts may be found at [IEEE].

## WAP

The Wireless Application Protocol Forum (WAP Forum, now known as the Open Mobile Alliance) has undertaken a number of activities within its WAP Security Group (WSG). In particular, its list of documents include the "Wireless Transport Layer Security Specification," the "WAP Certificate and CRL Profiles Specification," and the "WAP Public Key Infrastructure Definition." The general WPKI model is that server certificates use the WTLS certificate format, whereas client certificates use the X.509 format (in order to interoperate to the maximum extent possible with existing IPKIs). Furthermore, the WTLS specification allows various levels of security, including anonymous key exchange to create an encrypted channel, server-side certificate-based authentication, and mutual (that is, client-side and server-side) certificate-based authentication. These and related WSG documents may be found at [WAP-WSG]. (See also `www.openmobilealliance.org`.)

## XML-Based Activities

Interest in PKI and, more generally, security-related protocols has grown considerably within the XML (eXtensible Markup Language) community in the last few years. Prominent standards bodies actively embracing and developing XML security specifications include the World Wide Web Consortium (W3C) and the Organization for the Advancement of Structured Information Standards (OASIS). Within W3C, work was undertaken on specifications for XML syntax with respect to encryption (XML Encryption) and digital signature (XML Signature), as well as XML protocols for key management (XML Key Management Specification) that allow a client to obtain key information (including values, certificates, management, or trust data) from a Web service. Further details are available from the pages of the relevant working groups, linked under the W3C Web site [W3C].

Within OASIS, the Security Services Technical Committee is developing the Security Assertion Markup Language (SAML), an XML framework for exchanging authentication and authorization information. The underlying authentication mechanism may be PKI-based, but SAML encompasses a number of other authentication technologies as well so that it may be used in as many environments as possible. A number of other OASIS technical committees are likely to make use of SAML, as well as the W3C specifications mentioned above, to add security to various aspects of their work; such committees include Business Transaction Processing (BTP), electronic business XML (ebXML), Provisioning Services Markup Language (PSML), eXtensible Access Control Markup Language (XACML), and Web Services Security (WSS). Information regarding the technical committees and the status of their work can be found by following the relevant links under the OASIS Web site [OASIS].

## Other Activities

A number of activities within various communities are not formal standards activities but their output will specify (or dictate) product implementation at some level of detail for a variety of vendors. Such specifications have the strength of a formal standards document within a particular community of interest. The importance of such activities should not be understated. Although there are numerous examples of formal standards that fell into oblivion because they were never widely adopted, the presence and energy of the activities discussed here suggest that PKI will not ultimately suffer the same fate. A growing number of communities, both large and small, are actively planning or building PKIs to satisfy their own requirements.

In this chapter, we discuss a few of the many such activities, but the examples included are meant to be representative, not comprehensive. Furthermore, similar activities will arise from time to time to address the needs of other particular environments or industry sectors.

## U.S. FPKI

The U.S. *Federal Public-Key Infrastructure (FPKI)* [FPKI] is an initiative by the U.S. government to define a PKI suitable for its own use. One focus is the production of an acceptable profile for X.509 certificates and CRLs (see earlier in this chapter, as well as Chapter 19, for a discussion of X.509), but the ultimate goal is a full PKI specification. This specification encompasses all relevant PKI entities—including end entities, CAs, RAs (Registration Authorities), bridge CAs (to link CAs from different domains), and so on—in terms of their functionality and primary implementation characteristics. It also includes the security-relevant communications protocols between these entities and the operational policies and procedures required for the PKI to be useful.

The U.S. FPKI set of specifications imposes compliance requirements on vendors wanting to sell PKI products to the U.S. government. However, the hope is that the FPKI is sufficiently similar to PKIs for other environments that compliance will not unduly restrict vendors from selling their products, unmodified, to these other communities.

## MISPC

The *Minimum Interoperability Specifications for PKI Components (MISPC)* [MISPCv1] may be seen as one component of the full U.S. FPKI vision, though in some respects it is largely independent of that effort. The goal in MISPC, as implied by its title, is to understand and to specify the minimum functionality required of PKI entities that will still enable them to interoperate usefully with other PKI entities. Thus, for example, the certificate and CRL profile portion of MISPC identifies which of the many optional fields in the X.509 and PKIX specifications really must be implemented for these data structures to be processable by other entities in the PKI.

Interestingly, MISPC is more than a detailed specification; a CD containing a complete reference implementation compliant with the specification is also available. Thus, vendors have a straightforward way of testing whether their products are MISPC compliant.

## GOC PKI

The *Government of Canada Public-Key Infrastructure (GOC PKI)* [GOCPKI], the first large-scale governmental PKI initiative in the world, has a goal similar to the U.S. FPKI initiative: It defines a PKI suitable for Canadian federal government use. It is a full PKI specification, including certificate and CRL profiles, entity functionality and characteristics, communications protocols, and operational policies and procedures.

The GOC PKI will impose compliance requirements on vendors, but it is hoped that this will not preclude these *Commercial Off-the-Shelf (COTS)* products from being suitable for other environments as well.

## SET

The *Secure Electronic Transaction (SET)* specification [SET] defines protocols for certificate issuance and processing rules in the context of credit card payment over the Internet. Initiated in February 1996 by MasterCard and VISA and completed in May 1997 (SET v1.0), this specification was intended to be the backbone for electronic commerce (e-commerce) over the World Wide Web.

SET was created to meet the following business requirements:

* To provide confidentiality of payment information and to enable confidentiality of order information transmitted along with the payment information

* To ensure the integrity of all transmitted data

* To provide authentication that a cardholder is a legitimate user of a branded payment card account

* To provide authentication that a merchant can accept branded payment card transactions through its relationship with an acquiring financial institution

Interoperability testing between SET components implemented by different vendors is an ongoing activity (although of much less importance now than when this effort began). The SETCo Web site documents and maintains the results [SET].

## SEMPER

*Secure Electronic MarketPlace, EuRope (SEMPER)* [SEMPER] is a project designed to facilitate e-commerce, primarily in the European countries but ultimately on a worldwide scale. It specifies the functionality and operational characteristics of the principal entities involved in e-commerce transactions (the purchaser, the purchaser's bank, the merchant, and the merchant's bank), as well as the required secure communications protocols between them.

An aspect of SEMPER that currently seems to be more developed than similar projects elsewhere is the approach to risk management and the legal implications of entity actions. For example, which party or parties incur the cost of various kinds of failure modes in the defined electronic transactions? A detailed and fairly comprehensive risk model within the SEMPER project addresses these and similar questions. Comparable initiatives in other countries might do well to look at the progress made within SEMPER on this important topic.

The SEMPER final report was issued in the summer of 2000, published by Springer-Verlag in its *Lecture Notes in Computer Science* (LNCS) series (Vol. 1854).

## ECOM

The Electronic Commerce Promotion Council of Japan [ECOM] has been in existence since January 1996. Its goal is to facilitate close cooperation across industry (globally) in promoting e-commerce and standardization.

The council expects to be active until at least 2005. It will make rules and recommendations to the Japanese government to achieve secure e-commerce in both business-to-business and business-to-consumer environments; to establish, maintain, and manage international standards based on user needs; and to conduct activities to further promote e-commerce and make international contributions in this field.

## JCP

The Java Community Process (JCP) is an open organization of international Java developers and licensees whose charter is to develop and revise Java technology specifications, reference implementations, and technology compatibility kits. Among the numerous Java Specification Requests (JSRs)—work items for standardization within the community—are several related to PKI. These include JSR 55 (certification path creation, building, and verification), JSR 74 (Public Key Cryptography Standards, or PKCS, #1, #5, #7, #8, #9, #10, and #12), JSR 104 (XML trust services), JSR 105 (XML Digital Signature services), JSR 106 (XML Digital Encryption services), and JSR 155 (Web Services Security Assertions based on the OASIS SAML specification). These and related efforts are eventually expected to be included in future versions of the Java 2 Micro Edition (J2ME), Java 2 Standard Edition (J2SE), and Java 2 Enterprise Edition (J2EE) platforms. Further information can be found at [JCP].

## ICE-CAR

The Interworking Public Key Certification Infrastructure for Commerce, Administration and Research (ICE-CAR) project, a successor to the ICE-TEL project, began in January 1999. Its objective was to provide all technology components that support the secure use of the Internet for commercial and administrative applications in Europe; these applications included e-commerce, intra-organizational communication, health-care applications, and research. An additional goal was to promote the availablity of technically compatible and interconnectable

PKIs in order to guarantee the authenticity and validity of public keys used in these various environments. (The project has produced numerous technical reports that are available for download from the Deliverables section of the main Web site; see [ICE-CAR] for further details.)

Europe continues to be very active in PKI-based standarization and interoperability efforts. Notable examples doing related and complementary work to ICE-CAR include the European Electronic Signature Standardization Initiative [EESSI], Electronic Signature Testsuite for Inter-Operability [ESTIO], and Trust Infrastructure for Europe [TIE].

## Summary

We have looked briefly at a number of standards activities that have particular relevance to PKI for one of the following reasons:

- They define and formalize PKI concepts.

- They specify certificate formats and processing rules.

- They make particular use of certificates to accomplish security functions (such as authenticity, integrity, and confidentiality).

Much of this activity has taken place within the various working groups of the IETF, highlighting its importance in the area of security and PKI. More recently, W3C, OASIS, and similar standards bodies have taken up the challenge to bring security technology (including PKI) to the growing base of XML applications.

The list of nonstandards activities provided in the latter portion of this chapter is not meant to be exhaustive, but it does attempt to highlight some of the most important and most visible work in this area. These activities differ in terms of their approach (how are the problems being solved?), their focus (which aspect(s) of PKI are being addressed?), and their scope (for which user community is this being tailored?). However, what they have in common is that within the community of interest, each activity puts constraints upon vendor implementations in the same way that a formally approved standard specification might.

The primary benefits of these activities typically include decreased time to completion of the specification and increased participation of the members of the eventual user community. This ultimately results in PKI products that are relevant and readily available for use to the communities for which they are targeted.

We will examine the standardization status of some of the more important specifications in this area, in Chapter 19.

# Standardization Status and Road Map

This chapter presents a snapshot of the current status (at the time of this writing) of PKI and PKI-related standardization efforts. The reason for including such a snapshot in this book is to demonstrate that this field has reached at least the first plateau of stability in the various standards arenas. Not every problem has been solved; not every protocol has been defined; not every service has been specified; not every possible piece of syntax has been nailed down. But significant progress has been made, and a solid foundation for PKI implementation, deployment, and interoperation has been laid.

Also included in this chapter is a brief look at the "next wave" of standardization work that is currently ongoing in various groups.

## Current Standardization Status

In this section, we discuss the documents that have reached some level of stability and standardization within PKI-relevant standards groups.

### X.509

*X.509* is an *International Standard* [X509-00]. It has reached the highest level of standardization within ISO/ITU-T and therefore is considered to be a stable document. However, there is a formal defect-reporting system whereby errors, editorial corrections, or clarifications can be incorporated into the standard through an amendment process. Such an amendment is currently underway, but this includes primarily clarifying material and minor editorial modifications to the base text on certificates and CRLs (Certificate Revocation Lists) for PKI and PMI (Privilege Management Infrastructure) operation.

## *PKIX*

The full set of core PKIX documents is at *Proposed Standard* status. Although this is only the first level of standardization within the IETF (standards-track documents in IETF may progress from Proposed Standard to *Draft Standard* and finally to *Standard*), many vendors consider Proposed Standard to be sufficiently stable and suitable for implementation. This set of documents includes

- Certificate and CRL Profile [RFC3279, RFC3280]
- LDAPv2 Profile [RFC2559]
- LDAPv2 Schema [RFC2587]
- FTP/HTTP Operational Protocols [RFC2585]
- Online Certificate Status Protocol (OCSP) [RFC2560]
- Certificate Management Protocol (CMP) [RFC2510]
- Certificate Request Message Format (CRMF) [RFC2511]
- Certificate Policy (CP) and Certification Practice Statement (CPS) Framework [RFC2527]
- Certificate Management messages over CMS (CMC) [RFC2797]
- Qualified Certificates Profile [RFC3039]
- Time Stamp Protocol (TSP) [RFC3161]

It therefore covers all the core functionality needed for PKI initialization and operation.

## *X.500*

*X.500* is an *International Standard* [X.500]. The client-to-server Directory Access Protocol (DAP) and the server-to-server Directory System Protocol (DSP) are considered to be stable.

## *LDAP*

*LDAPv2* and *LDAPv3* are Proposed Standards. Version 2 of the Lightweight Directory Access Protocol [RFC1777] is widely deployed and is considered to be quite stable. Version 3 of LDAP [RFC2251] is also deploying rapidly and appears to be quite stable as well.

## *S/MIME*

The full set of core *S/MIME* documents is at Proposed Standard status. This set includes

- S/MIMEv2 Message Specification [RFC2311]
- S/MIMEv2 Certificate Handling [RFC2312]

- S/MIMEv3 Message Specification [RFC2633]

- S/MIMEv3 Certificate Handling [RFC2632]

- Cryptographic Message Syntax [RFC2630]

- Enhanced Security Services for S/MIME [RFC2634]

- Diffie–Hellman Key Agreement Method [RFC2631]

- Electronic Signature Policies [RFC3125]

- Electronic Signature Formats for long-term electronic signatures [RFC3126]

- Domain Security Services using S/MIME [RFC3183]

Therefore, it covers the core functionality needed for an e-mail system whose security rests on the existence of public-key certificates.

## IPsec

The full set of core *IPsec* documents is at Proposed Standard status. This set includes

- Security Architecture for the Internet Protocol [RFC2401]

- IP Authentication Header [RFC2402]

- IP Encapsulating Security Payload [RFC2406]

- The Internet Key Exchange [RFC2409]

- The ESP DES-CBC Cipher Algorithm with Explicit IV [RFC2405]

- The Use of HMAC-MD5-96 Within ESP and AH [RFC2403]

- The Use of HMAC-SHA-1-96 Within ESP and AH [RFC2404]

- The NULL Encryption Algorithm and Its Use with IPsec [RFC2410]

- The ESP CBC-Mode Cipher Algorithms [RFC2451]

It also includes a number of other specifications; see the IP Security Document Roadmap [RFC2411] for a complete list. Therefore, it covers the core functionality needed for an Internet Protocol communications layer whose security rests on the existence of public-key certificates.

## TLS

*The Transport Layer Security (TLS) version 1.0* protocol is a Proposed Standard [RFC2246]. It covers the functionality needed for unilateral or mutual authentication between a client and server in a Web environment whose security rests on the existence of public-key certificates.

Also provided in TLS is message confidentiality and sequence integrity. Note that TLS version 1.0 is the IETF standards-track variant of the *Secure Sockets Layer (SSL)* version 3.0 protocol found in many Web browsers.

### Toolkit Requirements (APIs and Mechanisms)

The specifications needed for toolkit-based session security are Proposed Standard status. The Generic Security Service Application Program Interface (GSS-API) [RFC2078] and the underlying Simple Public-Key GSS-API Mechanism (SPKM) [RFC2025] together enable a toolkit to be implemented that calling applications or protocol engines can plug into for security services. These services enable peer-to-peer *session* security (including unilateral or mutual authentication, key establishment, secure algorithm negotiation, integrity, and confidentiality) that relies on the existence of public-key certificates. A companion API for *store-and-forward* security services, the Independent Data Unit Protection specification (IDUP-GSS-API) [RFC2479] (although an Informational, rather than a standards-track, specification) is also a stable document. IDUP, with suitable underlying mechanisms (such as ones based on S/MIME or OpenPGP), enables toolkit-based store-and-forward security.

### Others

A variety of other PKI-related documents are also on the standards-track within IETF, including OpenPGP [RFC2440] and Domain Name System Security [RFC2538, RFC2539]. Also, a number of public-key-related specifications exist (for example, public-key encoding formats or key agreement protocols) in other standards groups that have reached stability, including IEEE P1363 (formats and protocols for RSA, DSA, ECDSA, and key agreement), ANSI X9.31 (RSA Signatures) and X9.62 (Elliptic Curve DSA), ISO 11770-3 (Key Agreement) and 13888-3 (Non-Repudiation), and the W3C Recommendations XML Signature and XML Encryption.

Clearly, there is now a significant foundation for PKI implementation within the body of standardized specifications.

## Ongoing Standardization Work

Along with all the specifications that are relatively stable, many of the standards groups have other PKI-related work that is ongoing. The following examples from IETF are representative of the scope of standardization work that is currently underway:

- *Privilege Management Infrastructure (PMI)* (specifically in the area of Attribute Certificates): This was looked at primarily in X.509 (2000) and has been profiled in IETF PKIX

[RFC3281], although other groups are following this work and may adopt it or profile it in their own contexts.

- *Secure time-stamping protocols:* This was standardized in PKIX [RFC3161], although other groups (Secure Network Time Protocol [STIME] and ANSI X9.F.4, for example) are following this work closely and intend to adopt or profile it in their own contexts.

- *Data certification server protocols:* This was published as an Informational specification in PKIX [RFC3029]. (This work is sometimes referred to as *protocols for digital notary services,* although this latter terminology is inappropriate because the word *notary* means different things in different countries of the world.) Interest in the notion of third-party data certification appears to be picking up in a variety of environments.

- *Certificate Policy and Certification Practices framework:* This is currently an Informational (rather than a standards-track) specification [RFC2527] but is undergoing a major revision to reflect operational feedback from environments that have used it to write their Certificate Policy and CPS documents.

- *Protocols to off-load PKI-related processing from a constrained client platform to a trusted server* (for example, certificate path construction and validation): This is being looked at in PKIX, although other groups (such as *Wireless Application Protocol,* or *WAP*) are interested in this topic as well. The requirements specification for this functionality has been published as an Informational Request For Comments in PKIX.

- *Extensions to provide additional functionality to the basic LDAP protocol:* This is being looked at in LDAPext and includes such things as strong authentication for requests and responses (including using the *Simple Authentication and Security Layer, or SASL,* mechanism [RFC2222]) and access control to LDAP information.

- *Security policy languages, protocols, and processing procedures:* This is being looked at in IPSEC and has recently seen significant interest in OASIS among the XML community. [See, for example, the eXtensible Access Control Markup Language (XACML) and Rights Language (RL) technical committees.]

Outside the IETF, significant security-related activity is ongoing in WAP (WPKI), W3C (XKMS), OASIS (SAML, XACML, RL, WSS, and others), IEEE (P1363a), and JCP (JSR155 and others). See Chapter 18 for discussion of these efforts.

It is expected that within the two- to three-year time frame, much of this and other work will be relatively stable and available in the portfolios of a number of PKI product vendors or service providers. This work will enhance the functionality of PKI product or service offerings and significantly add to the richness and usefulness of a PKI.

## Summary

This chapter has provided a brief overview of where the standards are now and the directions in which they are currently going. With respect to PKI and PKI-related standards, an impressive list of work products has already achieved consensus and stability within the formal organizations. All indications point to a widespread adoption across the industry (largely because so many of the major PKI-related companies have had active participation in the creation of these specifications).

To make full use of the standards status given in this chapter, the following topics will be beneficial:

- A good understanding of what each of the standards bodies (and corresponding specifications) covers; this is the subject of Chapter 18.

- A good understanding of the environment under consideration for deployment (so that those in charge of deployment can make the necessary decisions and mandate compliance to the standards appropriate for the environment); this is the subject of Part III.

# CHAPTER 20

# Standards: Necessary but Not Sufficient

Although standards are instrumental in promoting interoperability, many standards do not guarantee it in a multivendor environment. Our purpose in this chapter is to explain the role of standards and to discuss the importance of additional activities such as profiling of standards and multivendor interoperability testing. This is followed by specific examples of industry- and government-sponsored interoperability initiatives.

## The Role of Standards, Profiles, and Interoperability Testing

It has been said that a camel is actually a horse designed by committee. Although this may seem a bit disparaging to some, we invoke this anecdote to illustrate the difficulties typically encountered when attempting to reach agreement on the numerous technical (and sometimes political) issues that arise during the standards process. It should be noted that we are not trying to "bash" standards. In fact, standards play a critical role. We are simply trying to make it clear that standards alone are not *always* sufficient to guarantee multivendor interoperability.

Standards come in a variety of forms, and there are numerous standards bodies that engage in the development of these standards. In general, the purpose of a standard is to provide a common specification of syntax and semantics that can be used as a foundation for implementation.[1] However, some of the semantics are sometimes missing or incompletely defined, which can lead to interoperability difficulties.

---

[1]From a PKI perspective, one of the most important standards is the X.509 Recommendation [X509-00] as discussed in Chapter 18.

A number of issues can influence (1) the success or failure of a given standard and (2) whether a given standard is sufficiently detailed and error free that it leads to multivendor interoperability. Some of these issues include the following:

- Participation in the various standards organizations is typically voluntary in nature; there is really no such thing as a "professional standards guru" (although arguably there are a few individuals who might be deserving of such a title).

- Usually, more than one agenda or set of requirements is involved, which often leads to compromise through the specification of options or through the practice of leaving certain issues general enough to accommodate more than one point of view.

- Sometimes there is very little implementation experience, or worse, there is conflicting implementation experience that might be inappropriately reflected in the standard.

- Not all standards committees or subcommittees are "created equal"; the quality of the various standards can vary dramatically, depending on the participants and on the rules of participation established by the governing standards body.

- Very seldom is a given solution perfect in every way, which tends to promote the specification of multiple solutions that address the same problem. For example, a solution that works well in one environment may not address the specific needs of another environment. Sometimes specifying multiple solutions is essential to meet the needs of multiple target domains.

- Sometimes aspects of a standard are misinterpreted, and/or the standard is simply implemented improperly.

- No matter how good a particular solution may be, it is common practice to include extensibility mechanisms within the standards to support new capabilities when and as required. These extensibility mechanisms, although important, can often be the source of some of the most difficult interoperability issues.

Thus, it is reasonable to conclude that standards alone may not suffice to realize multivendor interoperability.

## Profiles and Interoperability Testing

At least two things need to be done beyond the development of a standard to help reach the desired level of multivendor interoperability.

The first is to profile the standards that apply to a particular environment. The purpose of a *profile* is to clearly identify which features of the more generic standard are mandatory, optional, or prohibited for a given environment. Specific usage rules and implementation guidelines are also typically included. In the specific case of a PKI, it is necessary to profile the PKI protocols used, the schema and protocols associated with the ancillary repository components, and the certificates and CRLs (Certificate Revocation Lists) themselves. In particular, both certificates and CRLs include extensions that must be profiled to eliminate ambiguities and adequately specify particular uses for those extensions within a given target environment. (See Box 20.1 for some examples.)

The second thing that is required to realize the goal of multivendor interoperability is to establish interoperability test scenarios and to conduct interoperability testing.

One possible way to accommodate this requirement is to establish vendor-neutral interoperability test centers that would offer reference implementations that can be used to assess the compliance of a given product against a specific set of criteria (which typically includes a set of established profiles).

An alternative (or perhaps complementary) approach that seems to be rather prevalent in the PKI industry is to participate in industry- and/or government-sponsored interoperability initiatives. Examples of some of these interoperability activities are provided in the following section.

# Interoperability Initiatives

The purpose of this section is to briefly highlight of some of the industry- and/or government-sponsored interoperability initiatives and to provide pointers to additional information where appropriate.

## *Automotive Network eXchange*

The *Automotive Network eXchange (ANX)* is a TCP/IP-based network that uses Virtual Private Network (VPN) technology based on the IPSec and PKIX standards. The ANX is designed to provide a common infrastructure that will facilitate secure communications among automotive manufacturers.

The ANX activity has produced a certificate and CRL profile that is included as an annex to the ANX certificate policy document entitled *Automotive Network eXchange (ANX) Certificate Policy* [ANX]. Additional information regarding ANX can be found at http://www.anxo.com.

## *Bridge CA Demonstration*

Initiated in January 1999 and completed in November 2001, the *bridge CA demonstration* was a U.S.-government–sponsored initiative designed to demonstrate interoperability between two (or more) PKI domains based on different trust models. (Trust models are discussed further in

## Box 20.1   X.509 Certificate and CRL Profile Examples

Let's look at some specific examples to illustrate the necessity of a certificate and CRL profile for the X.509 recommendation [X509-00]. Note that the PKIX certificate and CRL profile [RFC3280] defines such a profile for the Internet environment.

Consider the certificate extension *Subject Directory Attributes*. According to the X.509 standard [X509-00], the Subject Directory Attributes extension may be used to "convey any desired Directory attribute values for the subject of the certificate...." Clearly, this is an extremely broad statement, and there is no guarantee that the implementation of this extension in one domain will have any meaning whatsoever in another. Allowed values and the context of their presence need to be defined before one can expect interoperability between two different implementations.

Interestingly, one common use of this extension is to indicate access control information associated with the subject of the certificate. In particular, it can be used to convey security clearance information (among other things). Both the U.S. Department of Defense and the Canadian Department of National Defense have used the Subject Directory Attributes extension in this manner.

As another example, consider the *Authority Key Identifier* extension that can be used to uniquely identify the key used by a CA (Certification Authority) to sign a given certificate or CRL. This allows a convenient method to distinguish between multiple keys that might be associated with a given CA. The key used to sign the certificate or CRL can be identified by several methods. Specifically, the key can be identified by a unique octet string (such as a hash of the public component), or it can be identified through a combination of the Distinguished Name of the certificate issuer and a unique serial number of that key (in relation to the issuer), or both methods may be used.

Given that one implementer may choose to use one method and another implementer may choose another, it makes sense to agree on the specific use of this extension. As an example, a given profile may dictate that only the unique key identifier is to be used and that the value of the unique identifier will be the 160-bit SHA-1 hash of the public key. In this example, not only does the profile dictate the method used to calculate the unique identifier value, but it also goes so far as to say that the alternative method of using the identifier of the certificate issuer combined with the unique serial number is *not* to be used. Note also that this level of specificity is still in compliance with the X.509 standard [X509-00].

Chapter 9.) Specifically, this demonstration was designed to prove that a single CA could act as a bridge between multiple PKI domains through the use of cross-certification. The driving application for this particular demonstration was based on Secure/Multipurpose Internet Mail Extensions Version 3 (S/MIMEv3) [RFC2632–RFC2634].

Profiling activities included a minimum certificate and CRL profile, a directory schema and interoperability profile, and an S/MIMEv3 interoperability profile. Certificate path discovery and validation processes were also established. Information regarding the two phases of this project, as well as the final report, may be found at `http://www.anassoc.com/BCA.html`.

## Federal PKI

The U.S. federal government initiated the Public Key Infrastructure Technical Working Group (PKI-TWG) in October 1994 to address implementation issues associated with the (U.S.) Federal Public Key Infrastructure (FPKI). The PKI-TWG is chaired by the National Institute of Standards and Technology (NIST) and is composed of participants from federal government agencies and industry.

This working group has developed a fairly comprehensive profile entitled *Federal Public Key Infrastructure Certificate and CRL Extensions Profile* [FPKI]. This document, as well as a number of other useful references, can be retrieved from `http://csrc.nist.gov/pki/twg/welcome.html`.

Additional discussion with respect to the FPKI activity is provided in Chapter 18.

## Minimum Interoperability Specification

Formally initiated in June 1996, the NIST launched an initiative to develop a minimum interoperability specification in cooperation with a number of leading industry technology vendors, including

| | |
|---|---|
| AT&T | IRE |
| BBN | Motorola |
| Certicom | Nortel (Entrust) |
| Cylink | Spyrus |
| DynCorp | VeriSign |

The initial specification entitled "Minimum Interoperability Specification for PKI Components, Version 1" [MISPCv1] was published in June 1997. The MISPC initiative also includes a reference implementation that can be used to test conformance against the minimum interoperability profile. This enables the PKI and CA vendor community to demonstrate MISPC compliance.

The MISPC work continued to evolve to take advantage of emerging standards related to PKI technology. The second version of the MISPC document is entitled "Minimum Interoperability

Specification for PKI Components, Version 2—Second Draft" [MISPCv2], published in August 2001. This version of the document adds support for confidentiality services and incorporates some of the Internet Engineering Task Force (IETF) Public Key Infrastructure X.509 (PKIX) work that was formally published between late 1998 and early 2001 (in particular, "Internet X.509 Public Key Infrastructure: Certificate and CRL Profile" [RFC2459], "Internet X.509 Public Key Infrastructure: Certificate Management Protocols" [RFC2510], and "Internet X.509 Certificate Request Message Format" [RFC2511]).

## National Automated Clearing House Association

The National Automated Clearing House Association (NACHA) sponsored a successful interoperability pilot referred to as the *CA Interoperability Pilot (Phase I)*, completed in October 1998. Participating vendors included

CertCo

Digital Signature Trust (DST)

Entrust

GTE CyberTrust

IBM

VeriSign

As illustrated in Figure 20.1, this pilot activity was based on a four-corner model consisting of a consumer, the consumer's bank, a merchant, and the merchant's bank. The pilot essentially

Figure 20.1    Four-corner model.

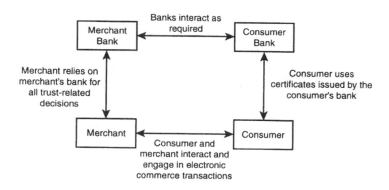

emulated the "Web shopping experience" in which a consumer, using digital signatures to authorize the transactions, would engage in purchasing activities with the merchants. The fundamental operating assumption for this pilot was that participating banks would each act as its own CA and all trust decisions relative to the transactions would emanate from the banks.

From a technology perspective, one primary objective of this pilot activity was to demonstrate that multivendor technologies could be used to support the four-corner model. To that end, the participating banks used different CA products supplied by the participating technology vendors. Further, the participating vendors collaborated to define a certificate and CRL profile, and the interoperability testing was performed against that profile.

The NACHA CA Interoperability Pilot activity was a good example of multivendor (and multibank) cooperation. The valuable lessons learned from this activity have been published in a document entitled "Certification Authority Interoperability: From Concept to Reality—Results of the NACHA Internet Council CA Interoperability Pilot" [NACHA]. NACHA continues to monitor activities in this area, and it is possible that the Phase I pilot activity will lead to the definition and rollout of subsequent initiatives (perhaps including alternative payment models and additional functions supported by the underlying PKI technologies).

Additional information regarding NACHA activities can be found at `http://internet council.nacha.org/`.

## PKI X.509

The IETF PKIX Working Group (which is described further in Chapter 18) is devoted to defining PKI protocols and X.509 certificate and CRL profiles for Internet use. The certificate and CRL profile once known as PKIX Part 1 became a proposed standard RFC in January 1999 [RFC2459] (now superseded by the revised and updated version, RFC3280).

Many view the publication of RFC2459 as a landmark occurrence.[2] Many of the other profiling activities described within this chapter attempt to align with RFC2459 to the maximum extent possible. Although technically this profile was designed for use within the Internet, a significant amount of information can be used to the advantage of the enterprise as well.

---

[2]To help illustrate the importance of RFC2459, the Federal PKI Certificate and CRL Extensions Profile [FPKI] contains an annex that summarizes the degree of compliance with the PKIX-specified profile. Both the NACHA and SIRCA profiles also took the PKIX profile into consideration.

### Securities Industry Root CA Proof of Concept

The *Securities Industry Root CA (SIRCA) proof of concept* was designed to demonstrate the feasibility of an industry root CA in a two-level hierarchy. Somewhat analogous to the bridge CA concept (as discussed in Chapter 9), the purpose of the SIRCA root CA was to facilitate the introduction of trust between two or more PKI domains that would otherwise be required to enter bilateral agreements with every other PKI domain with which they need to conduct business. This significantly reduces the overhead associated with bilateral cross-certification agreements from the order of $N^2$ to $N$, where $N$ is the number of distinct PKI domains.

The SIRCA proof of concept used a relatively simple certificate profile. The driving application for this proof of concept was S/MIMEv2-based e-mail [SMIMEv2, RFC2311, RFC2312]. The S/MIME application was profiled in the sense that it was required that the complete certification path be included with each signed message. Note that CRLs were not profiled because they were not included as part of this activity.

The results of the SIRCA proof of concept were quite encouraging; see `http://www.simc-inc.org/archive9899/Feb16-1999/sirca/Default.htm` for a summary of the project.

### EEMA PKI Challenge

The European Forum for Electronic Business (EEMA), with the funding of the European Commission and the Swiss government, put together a two-year project, called the PKI Challenge, beginning in January 2001. Run by a management consortium of 13 member organizations, the project will work with PKI vendors, users, consultants, academic institutions, Certification Service Providers (CSPs), and other "active participants" to provide a solution to interoperability between PKI-related products and to develop specifications and "best practices" for international standards in this area.

Further information regarding all aspects of PKI Challenge can be found at `http://www.eema.org/pki-challenge`.

# Summary

We have discussed the role of standards as well as the importance of complementary interoperability profiles and interoperability testing to fully realize the benefits of a given set of standards.

A number of interoperability initiatives will help establish useful and interoperable products from multiple PKI and CA vendors, including ANX, bridge CA demonstration, MISPC, NACHA, PKIX, SIRCA, and PKI Challenge.

Pilot activities such as these are instrumental in demonstrating that many PKI vendors are collaborating to offer better levels of service that will respond to the market demand and that these vendors will be able to provide interoperable products in complex and heterogeneous environments.

See the following chapters for additional information regarding standards and other related activities:

- Chapter 18 summarizes numerous standards activities related to PKI.

- Chapter 19 provides a summary of the PKI-related standards, including their status (at the time of this writing) as well as pointers to additional information.

# CHAPTER 21

# Conclusions and Further Reading

The purpose of this chapter is to provide a summary of the significant issues discussed in Part II and to supply suggestions for further reading.

## Conclusions

Part II of this book has concentrated on some of the more significant standards activities related to PKI protocols, services, and information. Part II has explored the role of these standards and has supplied a snapshot of the current state of these standards.

Part II has noted that not all standards are "created equal"; by design, some standards (for example, X.509) require profiling. This part also has emphasized the need for interoperability testing to ensure multivendor interoperability and has introduced a number of industry initiatives related to multivendor interoperability trials. Because this is becoming such an important area, we expect that vendor-neutral, third-party interoperability testing centers may grow in number and significance in the future.

## Suggestions for Further Reading

A number of sources of information are relevant with respect to PKI standards and/or interoperability. These are listed in the following sections.

### Certificate/CRL Syntax and Life-Cycle Management Protocols

Specifications related to certificate and CRL syntax and comprehensive life-cycle management include

Adams, C., and S. Farrell. "Internet X.509 Public Key Infrastructure Certificate Management Protocols." Internet Request for Comments 2510. (March 1999).

Directory Authentication Framework. Joint Recommendation|Standard ITU-T X.509 and ISO/IEC 9594–8 (2000).

Myers, M., C. Adams, D. Solo, and D. Kemp. "Internet X.509 Certificate Request Message Format." Internet Request for Comments 2511. (March 1999).

Myers, M., X. Liu, J. Schaad, and J. Weinstein. "Certificate Management Messages over CMS." Internet Request for Comments 2797. (April 2000).

As discussed throughout this book, the X.509 Recommendation provides the syntax (and semantics) for the Version 3 public-key certificate and the Version 2 Certificate Revocation List (CRL). It also includes the syntax and semantics for Attribute Certificates. RFCs 2510 and 2511 combine to provide comprehensive key/certificate life-cycle management protocol and message exchange formats.

Other important specifications related to PKI protocol and message formats include

- PKCS#7: Cryptographic Message Standard. Version 1.5. RSA Laboratories.
- PKCS#10: Certification Request Syntax Standard. Version 1.5. RSA Laboratories.

Although it is recognized that these Public Key Cryptographic Standards (PKCS) provide the foundation for more than simple PKI-related message exchanges, they are included here because they are commonly used as the basis for certificate request and retrieval over the Internet. They can also be used to facilitate off-line cross-certification. (Chapter 9 discusses cross-certification.)

RFC2797 is a set of protocols for sophisticated certificate management services over the Internet based on PKCS#7 and PKCS#10. This work was done within the Internet Engineering Task Force (IETF) Public Key Infrastructure X.509 (PKIX) Working Group and is currently on the IETF standards track at Proposed Standard status.

## *Certificate/CRL Storage and Retrieval*

Specifications related to the storage and/or exchange of certificate and certificate revocation information between a client and a server include

Boeyen, S., T. Howes, and P. Richard. "Internet X.509 Public Key Infrastructure Operational Protocols—LDAPv2." Internet Request for Comments 2559. (April 1999).

Boeyen, S., T. Howes, and P. Richard. "Internet X.509 Public Key Infrastructure LDAPv2 Schema." Internet Request for Comments 2587. (June 1999).

Housley, R., and P. Hoffman. "Internet X.509 Public Key Infrastructure Operational Protocols: FTP and HTTP." Internet Request for Comments 2585. (May 1999).

All three of these RFCs were developed under the auspices of the IETF PKIX Working Group. RFC2559 specifies the requirements for retrieving certificates and CRLs via Version 2 of the Lightweight Directory Access Protocol (LDAP). RFC2587 is the LDAP Version 2 schema. Work on Version 3 of LDAP has now begun within PKIX. RFC2585 defines the syntax and semantics associated with the retrieval of certificates and CRLs via the File Transfer Protocol (FTP) and the Hypertext Transfer Protocol (HTTP).

Specifications related to the on-line retrieval of revocation information include

Adams, C., P. Sylvester, M. Zolotarev, and R. Zuccherato. "Internet X.509 Public Key Infrastructure Data Validation and Certification Server Protocols." Internet Request for Comments RFC 3029. (February 2001).

Malpani, A., R. Housley, and T. Freeman. "Simple Certificate Validation Protocol (SCVP)." Internet Draft, <draft-ietf-pkix-scvp-09.txt> (subject to update; see www.ietf.org for latest status).

Meyers, M., R. Ankney, A. Malpani, S. Galperin, and C. Adams. "Internet X.509 Public Key Infrastructure Online Certificate Status Protocol—OCSP." Internet Request for Comments 2560. (June 1999).

Pinkas, D., and R. Housley, "Delegated Path Discovery and Delegated Path Validation Protocol Requirements." Internet Draft, <draft-ietf-pkix-dpd-dpv-req-05.txt> (subject to update; see www.ietf.org for latest status).

As discussed in Chapter 8, the On-line Certificate Status Protocol (OCSP) defines a method for returning the revocation status of one or more certificates. The Simple Certificate Validation Protocol (SCVP) is an Internet Draft that provides a method for on-line validation of certificates and certification paths.[1] The Data Validation and Certification Server Protocols (DVCS) is an Internet RFC that replaced the original notion of a "notarization" protocol. Although there is some potential overlap in terms of the functions that these three specifications support, there is sufficient distinction in their services that they can be deployed to meet different requirements (OCSP providing simple revocation status; SCVP providing server-based path construction or validation; and DVCS providing certification or validation of specific data such as a digital signature or an electronic contract).

---

[1]All Internet Drafts are subject to change without notice, and they generally expire six months after issue (although a new issue may replace them). Always consult the IETF Web site (www.ietf.org) for the latest status regarding any Internet Draft.

Some PKI-enabled protocols enable the direct exchange of certificates and, in some cases, certificate revocation information. Examples include the Secure Sockets Layer (SSL)/Transport Layer Security (TLS) protocols, Secure/Multipurpose Internet Mail Extensions (S/MIME), and Internet Protocol Security (IPsec).

## XML-Based Initiatives

Documents related to certificate syntax and life cycle (including storage and retrieval), as well as profiles for specific environments, are also being produced based upon eXtensible Markup Language (XML) constructs and protocol messages. The certificates included in these documents are not always X.509 compatible, but the ultimate goal of these efforts is to bring the benefits of an underlying PKI to XML-based applications. Such initiatives include the following:

- XML Signature (XMLdsig); see `www.w3.org/Signature`

- XML Encryption (XMLenc); see `www.w3.org/Encryption/2001`

- Security Assertion Markup Language (SAML); see `www.oasis-open.org/committees/security`

- eXtensible Access Control Markup Language (XACML); see `www.oasis-open.org/committees/xacml`

- XML Key Management Specification (XKMS); see `www.w3.org/2001/XKMS`

## Interoperability Initiatives

Documents related to PKI interoperability include

Booz-Allen and Hamilton, Inc. "Federal Public Key Infrastructure (PKI) X.509 Certificate and CRL Extensions Profile." (4 January 1999); see this and other documents and presentations at `http://csrc.nist.gov/pki/twg/welcome.html`.

Burr, W., D. Dodson, N. Nazario, and W. T. Polk. "Minimum Interoperability Specification for PKI Components, Version 1." *National Institute of Standards and Technology* (3 September 1997); see `http://csrc.nist.gov/pki/mispc/welcome.html`.

Housley, R., W. Polk, W. Ford, and D. Solo. "Internet X.509 Public Key Infrastructure Certificate and Certificate Revocation List (CRL) Profile." Internet Request for Comments 3280. (April 2002).

Lloyd, S., D. Brink, A. Nash, G. Buhle, and N. Kapidzic Cicovic. "PKI Interoperability Framework." PKI Forum White Paper (March 2001); see `http://www.pkiforum.org/resources.html`.

Lloyd, S., D. Fillingham, R. Lampard, S. Orlowski, and J. Weigelt. "CA-CA Interoperability." PKI Forum White Paper (March 2001); see `http://www.pkiforum.org/resources.html`.

National Institute of Standards and Technology (NIST) Project Team. "Minimum Interoperability Specification for PKI Components, Version 2—Second Draft." (31 August 31 2001 (work in progress).

Prince, N., and J. Foster. "Certification Authority Interoperability: From Concept to Reality—Results of the NACHA Internet Council CA Interoperability Pilot." The National Automated Clearing House Association (1999).

The Federal PKI and RFC3280 documents each define a certificate and CRL profile targeted for use in a specific environment. Both versions of the Minimum Interoperability Specification for PKI Components (also referred to as MISPC) are designed to provide vendors with a minimum set of implementation criteria. The PKI Forum was established in 1999 with the goal of fostering support for standards-based, interoperable PKI as the foundation for secure transactions in e-business applications.

## Standards Bodies' Web Sites

Most of the standards bodies (or other related organizations) provide at least some information on-line. Sometimes you can retrieve the standards (or drafts of the standards) directly via the Internet. Other sites simply provide information on the standards process associated with that particular standards body, along with information on how to order the standards under their control. The pointers to some of these Web sites are as follows:

- International Electrotechnical Commission (IEC); see `www.iec.ch`

- International Standards Organization (ISO); see `www.iso.ch`

- International Telecommunications Union (ITU); see `www.itu.int`

- Internet Engineering Task Force (IETF); see `www.ietf.org`

- World Wide Web Consortium (W3C); see `www.w3.org`

- Organization for the Advancement of Structured Information Standards (OASIS); see `www.oasis-open.org`

## Books

Several books also contain useful material related to standards, including the following:

Austin, Tom. *PKI: A Wiley Tech Brief.* New York: Wiley, 2000.

Ford, Warwick. *Computer Communications Security: Principles, Standard Protocols and Techniques.* Upper Saddle River, NJ: PTR Prentice Hall, 1994.

Housley, Russ, and Tim Polk. *Planning for PKI: Best Practices Guide for Deploying Public Key Infrastructure.* New York: Wiley, 2001.

Menezes, Alfred J., Paul C. van Oorschot, and Scott A. Vanstone. *Handbook of Applied Cryptography.* Boca Raton, FL: CRC Press, 1997, 645–661.

Nash, Andrew, William Duane, Celia Joseph, and Derek Brink. *PKI: Implementing and Managing E-Security* (Berkeley, CA: RSA Press, 2001).

Schneier, Bruce. *Applied Cryptography: Protocols, Algorithms, and Source Code in C* (2nd ed.). New York: Wiley, 1996, 561–595.

Stallings, William. *Cryptography and Network Security: Principles and Practice.* Upper Saddle River, NJ: Prentice Hall, 1995, 1999, 323–473.

PART

# Deployment Considerations

| 22 | Introduction. . . . . . . . . . . . . . . . . . . . . . . . . . 261 |
| 23 | Benefits and Costs of PKI . . . . . . . . . . . . . . 263 |
| 24 | Deployment Issues and Decisions . . . . . . . . 269 |
| 25 | Barriers to Deployment . . . . . . . . . . . . . . . 283 |
| 26 | Typical Business Models. . . . . . . . . . . . . . . 287 |
| 27 | Conclusions and Futher Reading . . . . . . . . 295 |

# CHAPTER 22

# Introduction

The purpose of Part III is to introduce the concepts and issues associated with the deployment of large-scale PKIs. This part of the book is not intended to be a step-by-step deployment handbook. Part III is deliberately small; more specific deployment details could easily be the topic of an entire book. In fact, many PKI vendors offer rather voluminous and comprehensive deployment manuals to their customers, and a number of firms offer consulting services in the area of PKI deployment. The idea behind Part III is simply to familiarize you with the basic issues likely to be encountered when deploying a large-scale PKI in the enterprise domain. Although the focus of this material is directed toward the enterprise, many of these issues also apply to the Internet domain.

Chapter 23, Benefits and Costs of a PKI, discusses the benefits realized through the deployment of a PKI. Cost considerations (from a generic perspective rather than monetary perspective) are also discussed. This chapter identifies sound business reasons for deploying a PKI in the enterprise environment.

Chapter 24, Deployment Issues and Decisions, discusses a number of issues that should be resolved before initial deployment occurs. Essentially, this chapter provides a basic foundation for product selection.

Chapter 25, Barriers to Deployment, addresses some of the more common hurdles to deployment. These are issues one must consider in terms of long-term strategy.

Chapter 26, Typical Business Models, explains some of the more common business models that one may want to implement.

Chapter 27, Conclusions and Further Reading, concludes Part III and offers suggestions for further reading.

# CHAPTER 23

# Benefits and Costs of a PKI

The purpose of this chapter is to consider some of the benefits realized through the deployment of a PKI. It also briefly discusses cost considerations (from a generic rather than monetary perspective).

Ultimately, it should be recognized that a sound and justifiable business case must drive the deployment of any technology. This applies equally to PKI technology. The key is to focus on business drivers, not technology.

It is not the intent of this chapter to provide a boilerplate for the development of a business case, but the chapter does identify many of the factors that should be taken into consideration when developing such a business case.

## Business Case Considerations

As discussed in Chapter 3, a PKI is a comprehensive security infrastructure, not myriad point solutions. A PKI offers a single security infrastructure that can be used across multiple applications in the most heterogeneous of environments. Specifically, a PKI can be used to enable confidentiality, integrity, authentication, and non-repudiation services in numerous contexts, including one or more of the following:

- Secure e-mail

- Secure Electronic Data Interchange (EDI)

- Secure electronic forms

- Secure desktop (for example, encryption of sensitive information on a laptop or PC)

- Secure intranets

- Secure extranets

- End-entity access control

- Secure remote access (for example, in support of mobile users or work-at-home)

- Secure Web applications

- Object signing

- Reduced logon

The benefits realized from offering these services are extensive, albeit in many cases hard to quantify. Benefits that can be realized through the judicious deployment of a PKI include the following:

- **Improvements in workflow efficiency** Significant timesavings can be realized (for example, letters, memos, and contracts can be handled electronically rather than through physical correspondence).

- **Work-force optimization** End users can spend more time on the job at hand rather than spending time dealing with details associated with the security infrastructure itself.

- **Work-force reduction** The deployment and operation of a single, unifying architecture rather than multiple point solutions should require fewer administrative resources.

- **Paper reduction** Savings can be realized in a number of ways, including lower material costs, less storage space, waste reduction, and less environmental intrusion.

- **Less administrative overhead** End users are less likely to require as much ongoing administrative assistance (for example, help desk support).

- **Reduced losses due to electronic theft** Corporate data is protected, which significantly decreases the risk of unauthorized disclosure.

- **Telecommunications cost savings** The ability to create a Virtual Private Network (VPN) over a public network such as the Internet can result in significant cost savings over leasing private lines.

- **Revenue generation** A PKI can be used not only to save money but also, in some cases, as the basis for offering for-fee services (for example, a financial institution may offer transaction validation services based on digital signatures and public-key certificates).

Electronic theft and fraud are clearly on the rise, and we can only assume that this trend will continue. A good source of information that helps illustrate this trend can be found in the Computer Security Institute's 2002 "Computer Crime and Security Survey" [CSI]. The tragic events of September 11, 2001, have also had a side effect of increasing security awareness as a whole, and this heightend awareness seems to be filtering into the technology area.

Statistics aside, the very fact that security is perceived to be a problem makes it something to be addressed.

It is important to recognize that security threats originate from both external and internal sources. Therefore, any comprehensive security solution must be able to secure both internal and external communications and corporate resources.

To help put things into perspective, consider what would happen if the CEO of your company had his or her laptop stolen. Is the sensitive information on that laptop encrypted? If not, try to imagine how much damage would be done if that sensitive corporate data fell into the wrong hands. Recall from Chapters 4 and 5 that a PKI offers the foundation for providing confidentiality services that can be used to protect against threats like this.

Although it is recognized that the CEO's laptop could have been secured without the use of a PKI, these solutions do not offer the comprehensive set of services that a PKI can offer. To illustrate this point, consider the case in which the laptop was not stolen but that the CEO was rendered incapacitated for some reason. How would the encrypted corporate data on that laptop be recovered? Intuitively, the value of a PKI that helps protect *and* recover mission-critical data is extremely high, even if its quantitative benefits can be almost impossible to measure precisely.

## Cost Considerations

Unfortunately, to determine the cost of deploying a PKI, no single formula can be applied to all organizations, and very few sources in the public domain provide a comprehensive, vendor-neutral appraisal.

Many organizations can leverage their existing IT (Information Technology) investments to help offset the cost of deploying the PKI. This applies both to personnel and to facilities. For example, Certification Authorities (CAs) need to be housed in protected facilities so that access by unauthorized personnel can be prevented and accountability can be maintained. Some organizations, especially large organizations, may have these types of facilities already available. Further, existing IT personnel can be utilized to help deploy and operate the components that comprise the PKI. Clearly, the degree of this leverage will tend to vary with each organization.

As discussed in Chapters 3 and 11, a ubiquitous repository service is also an important part of a large-scale enterprise PKI. Exploiting existing directory services is also possible in many organizations. This allows the PKI to consume directory services that are already part of the existing corporate IT infrastructure, thereby reducing procurement costs and distributing operational costs across multiple directory uses.

In any case, a number of considerations must be evaluated to help determine the *Total Cost of Ownership (TCO)* within a given organization, including the following:

- How many hardware components—that is, Registration Authorities (RAs), CAs, directory servers, and so on—are required to meet the demands of the target community? The number of components may depend on a variety of factors including the scale of the target community, geographic considerations, and the amount of autonomy afforded to the various departments or communities of interest.

- What is the cost of the necessary software and support tools? Both initial software procurement and ongoing software maintenance costs should be considered.

- How much of the existing corporate IT infrastructure can be exploited to support the target community? For example, is a separate directory product required, or can an existing corporate directory service be utilized?

- What are the resource requirements associated with the planning, deployment, operation, and ongoing maintenance of the infrastructure?

- What are the resource requirements associated with defining the policies and procedures necessary to support external users and/or external organizations?

- Are the necessary facilities available to house the infrastructure components; if not, what is required, and how much will it cost?

- What are the component availability requirements? Is full redundancy of any of the components (for example, the CAs) necessary?

- What are the training costs? This applies to administrators/operational personnel as well as end users.

- What level of administrative support is required (for example, help desk support, end-entity registration procedures, and so on)?

- Will the deployed PKI interoperate with other PKIs that may be based on technology provided by different vendors? Adopting standards-based technology is essential.

- What is required in terms of law- or policy-related doctrine? Liability protection is essential in many cases, especially when interoperability is required with external users or other PKI domains.

Ultimately, the key to success is to plan ahead; understanding as many of the issues as possible will help lead to the development of a solid business strategy.

# Deployment: Now or Later?

As discussed in Chapters 14 and 15, the perception of PKI has changed dramatically in the past few years. It seems like just yesterday that a number of trade journal articles and conference presentations were suggesting that PKI is still "in its infancy" and caution should be exercised when making a deployment decision. This seemed to stem from a reasonable concern that the technology was still fairly new and that the necessary standards and interoperability testing facilities necessary to guarantee multivendor interoperability were only beginning to mature. However, at the same time, these articles suggested that PKI is inevitably a "must have" technology.

More recently, however, we are hearing a different perspective from some individuals. Some argue that PKI has been overhyped and that it is both too complicated and too expensive to be viable. It is only natural that this might weigh on the minds of the corporate decision makers. However, we are certainly not ready to suggest that PKI is dead. Quite the contrary: we know of no other cost-effective, scalable, and robust technology that can offer the types of services we discuss in Chapters 3–5. We would also argue that PKI is still maturing as a technology, and it continues to evolve in order to meet real-world business requirements. In fact, we are beginning to see a trend where PKI is becoming an essential building block that can be exploited by other security services such as privilege management. We believe that this trend will continue, and we will eventually see products where PKI is simply embedded, or integrated, within the overall security solution, rather than called out as a separate product.

Having said all that, we understand that a degree of uncertainty is still associated with PKI technology. The trend for the past few years has been to launch small-scale PKI pilots, and we would expect this trend to continue. These pilots typically focus on a single application (for example, secure e-mail), and they limit the size of the end-user community (typically no more than a few hundred end users). The main purpose of these pilots is to

- Educate administrators and operations personnel through controlled, hands-on experience

- Establish a small core of educated end users—including key players within the organization—to help promote corporate-level acceptance

- Allow a graceful rollout of new services over time

- Protect the initial PKI investment as new services are offered

- Demonstrate that the PKI technology is viable and that it will offer significant cost savings

- Allow additional time to achieve corporate-level "buy-in" (occasionally, even the most skeptical can be swayed through actual demonstration)

Although no one of course knows what the future will hold, we would expect that most enterprises will continue to proceed with caution. We also believe that it is up to the PKI vendors to work more diligently in the deployment area in order to help these small-scale pilots evolve into a more comprehensive, enterprise-wide security solution. To put it bluntly, there is no substitute for success.

## Summary

In this chapter, we focused on the benefits of a PKI and briefly discussed some of the cost considerations that should be evaluated as part of the business-case-development process. It is clear that the promise of ubiquitous security is seldom a sufficient business driver in itself. Ultimately, the business drivers and associated cost justification should dictate whether a given technology is appropriate.

Besides understanding the benefits and associated costs of a PKI, realizing that corporate-level buy-in is instrumental in achieving a successful deployment is also important. Approval from all major departments will greatly increase the chances that the PKI's deployment will be both graceful and successful. Further, if a given security solution is too intrusive and/or too expensive, it is usually dismissed as nonpractical.

For many environments, a properly deployed PKI offers a nonobtrusive, cost-effective solution that can be used to secure multiple applications across multiple domains.

See Chapters 24 and 25 for additional information related to PKI deployment.

# CHAPTER 24

# Deployment Issues and Decisions

The purpose of this chapter is to briefly discuss many of the issues an organization needs to consider before launching a PKI deployment. Most of these issues will also help an organization determine the best technology vendor (or service organization) available to meet its needs. As with most of Part III, the primary focus is on the enterprise PKI. Some enterprise issues to consider include

- Trust models

- In-sourcing versus out-sourcing

- Build versus buy

- Closed environment versus open environment

- X.509 versus alternative certificate formats

- Targeted applications versus comprehensive solutions

- Standard versus proprietary solutions

- Interoperability considerations

- On-line versus off-line operation

- Peripheral support

- Facility requirements

- Personnel requirements

- Certificate revocation requirements

- End-entity roaming requirements

- Key recovery requirements

- Repository requirements
- Disaster planning and recovery
- Security assurance
- Risk mitigation

# Trust Models: Hierarchical versus Distributed

PKI deployments might be based on any one of the trust models that we discussed in Chapter 9. In practice, some of the more visible large-scale enterprise deployments are based on hierarchies (for example, Identrus), whereas others are based on the distributed trust model (for example, the GOC PKI).

The GOC (Government of Canada) PKI model is an example in which policy enforcement is from the top down, but the relationships between CAs (Certification Authorities) is bilateral rather than unilateral. The "top-level" node in the GOC PKI architecture is a logical root, but a bridge CA actually links the participating governmental departments together via bilateral cross-certification. This "top-level" node is also responsible for establishing cross-certification agreements with other PKIs (for example, the U.S. Federal PKI).

In the enterprise context, it can be argued that the distributed model is more flexible because it allows CAs to come and go with minimal disruption to the other interconnected CA domains. This is true in both an intra- and interorganizational context. In the case of a strict hierarchy, the disruption caused by the failure (for example, due to a compromise of the CA's signing private key) of a particular CA depends on the location (in terms of level) within the hierarchy. The closer to the top of the hierarchy the CA is, the more disruptive the failure of that CA will be to the enterprise as a whole. Of course, it is reasonable to expect that additional safeguards would be implemented for the higher levels—especially at the root level. The additional safeguards might include a longer key size (for example, a 2,048-bit RSA signing key rather than a 1,024-bit RSA signing key), and/or it may include a hardware module where the private-keying material can be stored more securely.

The hierarchical model is currently the rule in the Web environment, and some enterprise domains are also adopting it. A hierarchical model is often perceived to be a good mechanism for maintaining policy-related controls on subordinate CAs.[1] However, this is mainly a perception issue because similar controls can be levied on cross-certified CAs as well (for example, the GOC PKI).

---

[1]Chapter 9 discusses trust models further. We recommend that each organization examine the pros and cons of these trust models in light of their specific requirements.

# In-sourcing versus Out-sourcing

*In-sourcing* is when an enterprise decides to deploy its own internal PKI—utilizing its own resources (including personnel, hardware, and so on) and/or hiring external resources to help with any or all of the PKI's internal operation. The key here is that the PKI is under the control of the enterprise. *Out-sourcing* is when an organization allows an external party to supply and operate some aspects—perhaps even all aspects—of its PKI. In this case, at least some—perhaps all—of the PKI operation is not under the direct control of the enterprise.

Sometimes the decision of whether to in-source or out-source is based purely on economic considerations.[2] However, it is usually much more complicated than that. Not all organizations perceive things the same way, and many factors can affect this decision. For example, some organizations insist on maintaining total control over all aspects of the enterprise, especially anything to do with security and the source of trust associated with offering a particular service. These organizations are usually unwilling to depend on a third-party service provider. On the other hand, some organizations do not consider these factors to be as important with respect to their particular needs. Further, smaller organizations are much more likely to opt for an out-sourcing arrangement due to economic and resource constraints.

Hype and marketing propaganda, rather than the organization's real requirements, can sometimes decide the question of in-sourcing versus out-sourcing. To ensure that the right choice is made, the organization should exercise caution when making this decision. In the end, the basis of this decision should be a cost–benefit tradeoff analysis that takes into consideration as many relevant factors as possible. These factors include the following:

- Total cost of in-sourcing versus out-sourcing (including all related software, hardware, maintenance, personnel, facilities, training, legal fees, and so on)

- Degree of control that the organization feels must be maintained over the operation of the PKI

- The perceived source of trust that will be translated to the consumers of the PKI services (although ensuring that the issued certificates are appropriately branded may help control this)

---

[2]There are various degrees of in-sourcing and out-sourcing. For example, an organization may decide to outsource the services of a *CA* from a third party, but the *Registration Authority (RA)* function would be retained in-house. As another example, an organization may want total control of the PKI, but it requires external resources to help deploy and operate the PKI. Sometimes done as a transitional step, this enables the organization's internal resources to develop—the goal being to take over complete operation of the PKI at some later time.

- Response time associated with PKI-related service requests and information dissemination (for example, for end-entity and CA certificate requests, revocation information dissemination, key recovery requests, and so on)

- Level and availability of help desk support

- Flexibility and scalability considerations

- Ability (and willingness) of the vendor to evolve to meet the future needs of the organization

- Disaster planning and recovery

## Build versus Buy

A *build* option implies that an organization is willing to invest in the development of PKI technology (for example, in CA and/or RA technology). A *buy* option simply means that an organization will purchase PKI products or services, either through in-sourcing or out-sourcing.

Some evidence shows that a few organizations are willing to pursue a build option, but most organizations are not. A number of obstacles make the buy option (whether it be in-source or out-source) more attractive:

1. PKI technology is relatively complex to implement. Most vendors that offer PKI software have invested substantially in the technology, and a return on investment can be realized only through sales to multiple organizations. It is difficult to see how costs would be recovered in an organization that elected to build its own PKI.

2. Given the complexity of the software, it is unlikely that most organizations would have sufficient (and proper) resources in place to even begin such a venture.

3. Existing technology patents might impact the development of such a product. Either royalties would have to be paid or workarounds (which are not always possible) to the patents would be required. A number of patents exist in the areas of revocation technology, time stamping (which is necessary to help support non-repudiation), and privilege management, to name a few. Additional patents related to PKI technology are likely to be introduced in the future.

Given these difficulties, it is fair to say that most organizations do not even consider the option of building their own PKI.

## Closed versus Open Environment

For the purposes of this book, a *closed environment* is an environment where only intradomain communications are of concern. The domain can be a single enterprise, or it can be a collection of enterprises all operating under identical technical and operational procedures and constraints. An *open environment* is an environment where interdomain communications will be required and supported. In this case, multiple technical and operating procedures are likely to be encountered.

Although multivendor interoperability may seem to be a relatively minor concern in a closed environment, multiple sources could conceivably supply technology in such an environment. Therefore, avoiding proprietary solutions that would hinder interoperability is important—especially as the needs of the closed community grow over time.

Multivendor interoperability is clearly a concern in the case of the open environment. The technology selected should be based on industry-accepted standards, and the technology vendor should demonstrate a commitment to achieving multivendor interoperability.

# X.509 versus Alternative Certificate Formats

As discussed in Chapter 6, alternative certificate formats to the X.509 Version 3 public-key certificate exist. Not surprisingly, there are proponents of each format. For example, proponents of the *Simple Public Key Infrastructure (SPKI)* would suggest that the SPKI certificates are attractive because they focus on the notion of roles and authorizations rather than identity. Further, a *Pretty Good Privacy (PGP)* or OpenPGP advocate might claim that PGP certificates are more flexible than X.509 Version 3 public-key certificates and that they are more suitable for establishing trust relationships among individuals.

Although some of these alternative points of view may have merit in certain contexts, much of this debate is moot when it comes to meeting the needs of an enterprise. To date, corporate demand has overwhelmingly been in favor of X.509 Version 3 public-key certificates. If the market evolves in such a way that these environments require support for alternative certificate formats, these requirements will filter back to the technology vendors, and the products will evolve accordingly. At the moment, however, the vast majority PKI vendors support only X.509-based certificates.

In the future, certificate formats based on XML (eXtensive Markup Language)—such as the *assertions* defined by the OASIS Security Services Technical Committee in their Security Assertion Markup Language (SAML) specification—may take on prominence within the XML-based business application developer community. Such formats may replace X.509 certificates at the XML application level but are likely to coexist with X.509 certificates at another level in order to interconnect with other deployed infrastructures. The medium for such interconnection may be based upon the XML Key Management Specification, as defined in the W3C (World Wide Web Consortium), in order to hide the details of the underlying X.509-based PKI from the XML-based application. (See Chapter 18 for further discussion with respect to the SAML and XKMS efforts.)

## Targeted Applications versus Comprehensive Solution

It is possible to implement many of the security services discussed within this book (in particular, Chapters 4 and 5) without the benefit of a PKI. These are typically point solutions, and the specific security features are usually embedded within each application. This may be an option in a limited number of environments, but most mid- to large-scale domains cannot afford to deploy multiple point solutions—especially when a single security infrastructure can meet the needs of multiple applications, thereby leading to a much more cost-effective solution.

However, in small, closed-enterprise domains, point solutions may still turn out to be the most cost-effective way of meeting specific security requirements.

## Standard versus Proprietary Solutions

A solution is said to be based on *standards* when (1) it is based on industry-accepted standards and (2) no unique implementation details pose a threat to interoperability with another technology vendor that is also based on the same standards. A solution is said to be *proprietary* when it is based on unique implementation details that will, by definition, prevent interoperability with other technology vendors.

Given the current interest in and the level of activity with respect to standards and multivendor cooperation, it is difficult to see a business case for adopting proprietary solutions. However, there still may be a small number of environments in which this might be the best choice. Again, this is all part of the cost-benefit tradeoff analysis. However, if interdomain interoperability is even the slightest concern (and in most cases it will be), only standards-based solutions should be considered.

As pointed out earlier, when adopting proprietary solutions—even in an intradomain context—being careful is important because adopting standards-based solutions will help decrease the danger of being locked-in to a single vendor.

## Interoperability Considerations

A number of interoperability issues go beyond the standards themselves. As discussed in Chapter 20, vendors can legitimately claim standards compliance, but multivendor interoperability still might not be possible for a variety of reasons. Understanding these reasons and ensuring that the vendor community cooperates to provide acceptable and interoperable solutions are essential.

### Certificate and CRL Profiles

Even when standards-based techniques are adopted, dictating implementation specifics that can vary from one domain to another is still possible. This is the case with the X.509 certificates and CRLs. Specifically, different certificate and CRL profiles (which are discussed in Chapter 20) are being defined to meet a variety of needs. As a deployment consideration, it is important to select technology vendors that offer flexible certificate and CRL generation so that meeting the requirements associated with multiple certificate and CRL profiles is easy to do.

## Multiple Industry-Accepted Standards

It is not sufficient to simply adopt a technology that is "standards based," especially when multiple standards and protocols are available. For example, end-entity certificates can be initialized through different mechanisms, cross-certification can be facilitated in both on-line and off-line operations, and revocation information can be disseminated in a variety of ways. From a requirement perspective, making sure that the technology meets the needs of the organization is important. The more flexible a vendor product is, the more likely it is that the vendor will be able to meet the needs of the organization—both now and in the future. Thus, vendors should offer multiple solutions based on standards and practices that are in widespread use throughout the industry.

## PKI-Enabled Applications

For a given application to consume the services of a PKI, it must be "PKI enabled." This lets the application invoke the necessary security services and key/certificate life-cycle management functions. Technology vendors should offer standard PKI-enabled applications (for example, secure e-mail via S/MIME) as well as generic toolkits that can be used to integrate other applications into the PKI as necessary.

## Policy/Business Control Issues

As discussed in Chapter 6, Certificate Policies must also be addressed to facilitate interdomain interoperability. Specifically, formal agreements need to be established between enterprise domains that want to communicate under one or more interdomain policies.

From a technology perspective, the established business controls must be enforced by the appropriate PKI components. This means that capabilities to populate the public-key certificates with the appropriate extensions must be supported and the appropriate business control settings must be initialized at the client system. It also means that clients must be capable of understanding and properly processing these business controls during certificate path processing. Chapter 6 provides descriptions of the certificate extensions that can be used to support the necessary business controls, and Chapter 9 briefly presents some cross-certification and certificate path validation issues.

Making sure that the PKI vendor is capable of supporting the organization's requirements in this area can be extremely important, especially in the interdomain context.

# On-line versus Off-line Operations

*On-line operation* is the situation in which end entities are directly connected to the network. Typically, end entities are capable of consuming all PKI-related services. *Off-line operation* enables end entities to consume at least a subset of the PKI services, even though they are not directly connected to the network.

Some techniques (for example, revocation information dissemination using the On-line Certificate Status Protocol) may require end entities to be on-line in order to perform particular PKI-related operations. These techniques are not suitable for off-line operation (for example, verifying signed e-mail on a laptop during circumstances in which access to the organization's PKI is not possible). To facilitate off-line operation, recent revocation information could have been cached that would enable the revocation status to be verified (within a certain window of time). Alternatively, the revocation information could have been supplied along with the e-mail in this example. Off-line operation would also require that the necessary certificates and certification paths are available, which can be facilitated through caching or by including the necessary certificates with the e-mail.

Whether off-line operation should be permitted within a particular environment is a policy decision. After the policy is determined, a technology commensurate with the policy can be selected.

# Peripheral Support

Besides any hardware normally associated with the infrastructure components (for example, CA, RA, repository, and client systems), it should be determined if a cryptographic hardware module is required in association with the operation of the CA. This would enable the CA's keying material to be generated and stored on a hardware crypto-module rather than in software, which provides additional protection of the keying material.

Further, end-user hardware tokens or smart cards may also be required. For example, some environments may require multifactor authentication (see Chapter 12), and they may levy a requirement to store private-keying material on a peripheral module rather than on the end user's personal computer. Biometric devices also may be required—either in lieu of or in addition to the hardware tokens or smart cards.

Not all technology vendors support these peripheral devices to the same degree. However, standard *Application Programming Interfaces (APIs)* have been defined, and vendors should adhere to these if they do offer support for peripheral devices. Once the policy decisions surrounding the requirement for these devices have been made, identifying a technology vendor that meets organizational needs will be easier.

# Facility Requirements

As discussed in Chapter 12, all sensitive PKI components must be adequately protected. Because CAs are the most sensitive component within the PKI, appropriately protected facilities must house them. Appropriate physical and procedural safeguards must also be established. Essentially, unauthorized access must be prevented, and individual accountability should be maintained at all times.

Although the physical and procedural security associated with the RA components is typically not as stringent as that for a CA, it may be necessary to protect these components to some degree as well.

Each organization should determine where these components will be placed and how they will be attended. If the organization does not already have adequate facilities in place, this will clearly have an impact on total cost of ownership, and an organization may determine (along with other factors) that it is more cost effective to use a trusted third-party service provider than to deploy their own PKI.

# Personnel Requirements

As Chapter 23 mentioned and as alluded to earlier in this chapter, qualified personnel are required to maintain and operate the aspects of the PKI that fall under the direct control of the enterprise. The enterprise should determine the number and skill level of the appropriate personnel, which will depend on the scale of the PKI, as well as how much of the PKI is insourced. The types of personnel that may be required include

- *Security officers* responsible for enforcing the security policies dictated by the enterprise

- *Operators* to perform system installs, backups, reboots, and so on

- *Administrators* to perform day-to-day operations such as end-user registration

Also, it may be necessary to enlist the services of skilled consultants and legal counsel to develop and/or analyze Certificate Policies and/or Certification Practice Statements (CPSs).

This too may have a substantial impact on total cost of ownership, and it should be reviewed in conjunction with the other factors discussed within Part III of this book.

# Certificate Revocation

As discussed in Chapter 8, implementing a number of different certificate revocation mechanisms is possible. Variables associated with the dissemination of revocation information include protocols, timeliness, size, performance, scalability, and so on.

It is up to each organization to determine its revocation requirements, and it is up to the technology vendor to meet those requirements. PKI technology vendors will likely offer multiple solutions to maximize the chances of capably meeting the various needs of an extremely diverse market. In any case, ensuring that the technology vendor meets the organization's requirements (both now and in the future) is essential.

## End-Entity Roaming

Many organizations have a requirement to support personnel while traveling on business or personnel who are always moving from one place to another as part of their everyday job (for example, in association with parcel delivery companies). This is sometimes referred to as *roaming*.

The requirements associated with roaming can vary substantially. On the one hand, the roaming user may carry a laptop at all times and therefore have the necessary credentials and client software to engage in PKI-related operations whenever required. In other cases, the roaming user may move from computer to computer, and the software may or may not be the same at each desktop or kiosk. The roaming user may also be unable to personally carry the necessary credentials (for example, a signing private key stored on a hardware token).

If it is determined that roaming is a requirement for a given organization, it is important to ensure that the technology vendor can support this capability in a secure and robust manner.

## Key Recovery

As discussed in Chapter 7, key recovery deals with the secure storage and distribution of encryption keys to recover corporate data that would otherwise be rendered unrecoverable. A given organization must assess the need for this functionality and determine the requirements associated with its implementation if required.[3]

It is possible to implement a key recovery facility as part of a CA or to implement a separate key recovery component. If an organization determines that key recovery is essential to respond to their legitimate business needs, the implementation alternatives should be weighed carefully. Note that some vendors already support this capability, but they may offer only one

---

[3]Legal restrictions or legal mandates associated with key recovery may exist in some countries. Although not devoted solely to the topic of key recovery, "The Limits of Trust: Cryptography, Governments, and Electronic Commerce" [LOT] identifies existing legislation pertaining to confidentiality and digital signatures on a country-by-country basis.

option for achieving key recovery (for example, it may be supported only as a CA function, and a third-party key recovery center may not be available). Although several years old, information related to key recovery requirements (including a draft U.S. Federal Information Processing Standard (FIPS) on "requirements for key recovery products") can be found at `http://csrc.nist.gov/keyrecovery/`.

## Repository Issues

As discussed in Chapter 11, a number of options can be implemented to disseminate end-entity certificates, revocation information, and other PKI-related information such as policy information. A number of technology vendors that support one or more of these services also exist. It is important for each organization to understand these requirements and to select a technology vendor that can best suit the needs as identified.

As in the case of PKI technology vendors, it is also important to ensure that the repository vendor offers flexible functionality and that the vendor is committed to multivendor interoperability. This is important because interrepository communication and information exchange may be required in support of the certificate and revocation information dissemination requirement. (See Chapter 11.)

## Disaster Planning and Recovery

Although careful planning and the implementation of redundant components can minimize the risk associated with many sources of disaster, considering worst-case scenarios and ensuring that the best possible contingency plans are in place is important. This will expedite the recovery of the PKI in the event that a serious disaster does occur.

As discussed in Chapter 12, perhaps one of the most serious disasters that can occur with respect to the PKI is when a CA's key is compromised (or even suspected to have been compromised). An organization should ensure that the appropriate safeguards are in place to minimize the risk of this event and that the technology vendor understands the problem and can provide recommendations and tools to help expedite recovery if such an event were to occur.

## Security Assurance

Security assurance has to do with how much confidence an organization can place in the proper and secure operation of the PKI components. A number of criteria can be used to gauge the level of confidence that should be associated with a given product, and specific certification or accreditation programs can help determine this confidence level in a formal manner. For example, the "Federal Information Processing Standards Publication 140-1" [FIPS140] establishes criteria for evaluating cryptographic modules, and there are independent laboratories approved to perform FIPS 140-1 evaluations. Other criteria and evaluation procedures are available, including government-sponsored endorsement programs that are based on common evaluation criteria. (See `http://www.cse-cst.gc.ca/en/services/common_criteria/documenta-tion.html` for example.) There are also industry-sponsored testing laboratories that certify products against industry-specific criteria—see, for example, the BITS Financial Services Security Lab: `http://www.bitsinfo.org/overview.html`.

PKI products that are known to meet specific criteria may be much more attractive to an enterprise than products that do not. In fact, it is reasonable for an enterprise to specify minimum criteria that must be demonstrably met by a PKI product before that product will be considered.

# Mitigating Risk

In all cases, it is simply in the best interest of an organization to mitigate risk as much as possible. Understanding the organization's needs and requirements, both now and in the future, partially accomplishes this.

When it comes to selecting a specific technology vendor(s), a number of things should be considered to help ensure that the selection is as sound as possible, including

- **Reputation** What do their existing customers have to say about the vendor?

- **Market penetration** How pervasive is the vendor, and what is the estimated market share?

- **Longevity** Is the vendor viable from a long-term perspective?

- **Cooperation** Is the vendor willing and able to cooperate with the customer, especially if the vendor knows in advance that some customization will be required to more fully meet the needs of the organization?

- **Support** What is the level of support (for example, help desk and software upgrades) offered by the vendor?

- **Standards compliance** Is the vendor standards compliant, and does the vendor offer multiple alternatives?

- **Security** Does the vendor offer products that have been formally endorsed by independent evaluation labs with respect to industry-established criteria (for example, FIPS 140–1)?

- **Multivendor interoperability** Is the vendor committed to multivendor interoperability (as demonstrated, for example, through public, formally organized interoperability trials)?

- **Cost** Is the vendor cost effective, and will the organization realize cost savings?

## Summary

This chapter has focused on many of the deployment issues to consider before an organization selects one or more technology vendors and launches its initial PKI deployment. The key is to understand the issues to the maximum extent possible and to make educated decisions based on facts and requirements rather than on marketing hype. If necessary, it is highly recommended that an experienced, vendor-independent consultant be hired to help the organization work through these issues.

See Chapters 23 and 25 for topics related to the deployment issues discussed in this chapter.

# CHAPTER 25

# Barriers to Deployment

The purpose of this chapter is to briefly discuss some of the issues that can impede the successful deployment of a PKI within a given organization. Although solutions are being found to reduce or eliminate some of these potential obstacles, it is important to be aware of some of the difficulties that can be encountered.

## Repository Issues

As discussed in Chapters 8 and 11, many enterprise domains utilize a ubiquitous on-line repository to allow for the timely and robust dissemination of certificates, certificate revocation information (for example, *Certificate Revocation Lists,* or *CRLs*) and any other PKI-related information (for example, policy information). Early PKI deployment experience has demonstrated that this is not without its problems—although these issues are expected to be corrected as the products offered by the vendor community continue to evolve. Our purpose in this section is to discuss some of these issues.

### Lack of Industry-Accepted Standard

One concern with a ubiquitous directory service is that there is no single accepted industry standard for offering these services. Some market segments have adopted the X.500 Directory standards [X500], but numerous (and usually competing) repository-related standards are also already developed or in the process of being developed. For example, the *Lightweight Directory Access Protocol (LDAP),* which was developed under auspices of the *Internet Engineering Task Force (IETF),* defines an access protocol between a client and a remote repository. From a technical perspective, LDAP is in direct competition to the X.500-based *Directory Access Protocol (DAP).*[1]

---

[1]It appears that LDAP has won the battle in terms of an access mechanism between a client and a remote repository. In fact, most X.500 vendors recognize this and now offer LDAP support in addition to DAP.

There are still a number of open issues when it comes to other functions associated with both client-to-server and server-to-server interaction and information exchange. For example, the IETF LDAPext Working Group is developing a number of additional proposed standards, such as access control mechanisms and access control models. Further, the IETF *LDAP Duplication/Replication/Update Protocol (LDUP)* is also under development, which may compete with the X.500 counterpart, the *Directory Information Shadowing Protocol (DISP)*. There are also proprietary solutions, as well as solutions based on standard remote database access. Certificates and CRLs can also be distributed as part of a *Domain Name System (DNS)* function [RFC2538].

Although any one of these solutions may be well suited for a given organization's needs, the breadth of choices can lead to interoperability difficulties when it comes to interorganizational communication. Selecting standards-based solutions may help reduce some of these problems. (Chapters 8 and 11 present certificate and certificate revocation information dissemination in more detail.)

### Multivendor Interoperability

In addition to the standards issue, there is also the issue surrounding multivendor interoperability. Not all directory products are "created equal," and experience has demonstrated that all vendors do not implement some functions; or, if they are implemented, they are not necessarily implemented in a consistent manner from one vendor to another—even if these solutions are based on the same standards. (See Chapter 20 for a discussion of some reasons why standards themselves do not guarantee multivendor interoperability.) However, this is clearly an issue that will improve with experience, and the directory vendors appear eager to eliminate these types of issues by cooperating with their technology partners, customers, and even their competitors.

### Scalability and Performance

Finally, potential scalability and performance issues are associated with the deployment of a ubiquitous repository service. Given the limited number of large-scale PKI deployments, there is little implementation experience with respect to how many repository servers are required to effectively service a given organization. Clearly, this will be a function of the number of end users, but the validity period of the CRLs (assuming caching is allowed) and other implementation variables (for example, whether Delta CRLs are supported, as discussed in Chapter 8) will have an impact as well. Also, the repository is unlikely to be devoted solely to the operation of the PKI; additional load is likely to be introduced by other uses (for example, a generic "white pages" service also may be supported).

# Knowledgeable Personnel

Even though public-key cryptography was introduced over two decades ago [DiHe76], the widespread availability of the technology itself has come to fruition only in recent years. Because this technology is still fairly new from an implementation and deployment perspective, the number of knowledgeable personnel in this particular field is rather limited. Evidence shows that the number of PKI-knowledgeable personnel is growing, but these resources may be difficult to hire and retain.

From a resource perspective, it is important to recognize that personnel requirements are not simply limited to one or two administrative personnel. Not only are PKI-knowledgeable administrators needed, but also fairly senior-level personnel are required to help develop policy-related documents and agreements. For example, Certificate Policies (as discussed in Chapter 6) and interdomain interoperability agreements (for example, cross-certification agreements) may be required in many enterprise environments. Further, the PKI deployment strategy itself needs to be well thought-out and documented appropriately. This also requires fairly knowledgeable senior-level personnel. Of course, it is possible to out-source some or all of these positions, depending on the specific needs of the organization. If internal resources are to be used, we recommend that they be formally trained in their particular area of responsibility.

# PKI-Enabled Applications

For a PKI to be useful, the software operating on behalf of end users, processes, or devices must be able to consume the services that the PKI has enabled. Specifically, encryption/decryption and digital signature generation and verification (as discussed in Chapter 2) must be supported. In addition, the software must be able to access the key/certificate life-cycle management functions (as discussed in Chapter 7).

When the software is able to "tap into the PKI," it is often said to be *PKI enabled* or *PKI aware*. The list of PKI-aware software is growing, and this trend is expected to continue. For example, many of the more popular e-mail and electronic forms packages are now PKI-aware. This trend is also evident in the *Virtual Private Network (VPN)* market where multiple vendors implement public-key techniques (for example, those based on the proposed *Internet Key Exchange (IKE)* standard [RFC2409]).

In addition, Web browser and server technology may be viewed as "partially" PKI enabled. However, even though the Secure Sockets Layer (SSL) or the Transport Layer Security (TLS) [RFC2246] protocols (which base authentication between a client and a server on public-key techniques) are typically supported, the browser/server technology that is currently available clearly requires significant improvements before the Web environment will support full certificate-based services and key/certificate life-cycle management. However, this sitiuation has been improving and will continue to improve in the future.

Numerous applications (for example, legacy applications) will likely remain outside the PKI-enabled list, however. This is due to a variety of factors, including the inability to modify these applications so that they are capable of consuming the services offered by the PKI (because of a lack of available resources and/or the exorbitant cost associated with the necessary software modifications).

## Corporate-Level Acceptance

We cannot overemphasize the need for corporate-level "buy-in." Without the appropriate champions in place to usher in the deployment of the new technology, overcoming many of the hurdles likely to stand in the way of a successful deployment will be extremely difficult. If nothing else, resistance to change is commonly encountered in organizations, regardless of what that change might be. It is therefore necessary to build a solid business case and to "sell" that business case to the critical decision makers within a given organization.

## Summary

This chapter briefly presented some issues that might impede the deployment of a PKI within a given organization. In many cases, however, significant improvements are helping reduce these issues. Eventually, most, if not all, of these issues will be effectively reduced to only minor considerations within many organizations.

The remainder of Part III (but especially the earlier Chapters 23 and 24) provides additional information related to PKI deployment issues.

# CHAPTER 26

# *Typical Business Models*

Part III concentrates on PKI deployment considerations in an enterprise context. In this chapter, we discuss several different business models that might drive the deployment of a PKI. Although this may not be an exhaustive list, we do concentrate on some of today's more prevalent business models, as evidenced by many of the PKI deployments around the globe.

Several initiatives are also designed to offer scalable interdomain trust paths between organizations. Because these initiatives may have an influence on the external communications business model described here, we also give a brief discussion regarding these initiatives.

## Internal Communications Business Model

From a corporate-security perspective, the overall goal in any organization is to provide cost-effective, usable security that is commensurate with the perceived level of risk. If the cost of providing the security is too great or if the deployed security services are too difficult to use or administer, the business case for deploying that solution cannot be justified.

Justifying anything of this nature is extremely difficult without considering the true benefits that will be realized through the judicious deployment of a comprehensive security infrastructure. For example, significant cost savings can be realized by reducing the amount of time that individuals spend logging-in to multiple applications each day. Further, the proper protection of corporate information can help reduce significant financial losses that can result from the theft of unprotected electronic information (either in storage or in transit). Of course, cost considerations are not the only benefits realized from providing comprehensive security services. Improvements in workflow efficiency, reduction in administrative overhead, and even revenue generation are all factors that may contribute to the business case. (These considerations are discussed further in Chapter 23.)

Generally, the business drivers for deploying a particular security solution center on several specific areas, such as the following:

- Enhanced authentication and accountability

- Secure e-mail

- Desktop security (for example, encryption of sensitive files stored on a disk drive)

- Secure remote access

- Secure internal communications (for example, secure intranet)

- Secure external communications (for example, secure extranet)

- Reduced sign-on (see Chapter 3)

- Paper reduction through adoption of secure electronic forms

- Secure (and robust) audit trails

In many cases, a single application is selected to help launch the initial PKI deployment, which is then used as a vehicle to prove the utility and necessity of the PKI itself. As discussed in Chapter 23, launching a small-scale pilot that focuses on a single application enables an ordered and controlled PKI deployment. Over time, additional applications are folded in, which eventually leads to a single infrastructure that is capable of supporting a variety of applications in a number of different contexts.

Thus, the prominent intra-organizational business model is to enhance overall security in a number of areas but in a cost-effective, structured, and user-friendly manner. Ultimately, the benefit of a PKI-based solution is to provide a single infrastructure that can support myriad security services in a complex, heterogeneous, multiapplication, large-scale business environment.[1]

# External Communications Business Models

Our purpose in this section is to briefly discuss some of the business models currently being adopted for external corporate communications. These will be addressed from two perspectives: business-to-business and business-to-consumer.

---

[1]Benefits associated with the deployment of a PKI are discussed further in Chapter 23. Specific deployment considerations (for example, the number and location of CAs, in-source versus outsource, and so on) are addressed in Chapter 24.

## Business-to-Business Communication

The main business driver for business-to-business communications is to provide secure and cost-effective interorganizational communications. Although this may seem to be a rather obvious statement, ubiquitous business-to-business interaction is not guaranteed. Solid business drivers must be in place to motivate corporations (or governments) to interconnect their PKI domains. To many, this falls under the general umbrella of secure electronic commerce (e-commerce).

A given business may want to communicate with a variety of external sources that have deployed or out-sourced their own PKI, including partners, separately incorporated subsidiaries, suppliers, and peers.

Further, a given business may want to communicate with these external sources for a variety of reasons, including

- Purchase-order exchange

- Collaborative research

- Preauthorization of financial transactions

- Payment transfers

- Interorganizational correspondence

- Supply chain management

- Secure document exchange

Not surprisingly, many of the applications listed in the Internal Communications Business Model section of this chapter can be used to accommodate the secure communications between two or more businesses. For example, secure e-mail might be suitable for collaborative research and interorganizational correspondence. On the other hand, some sort of automated payment-transfer protocol would be more appropriate to facilitate payment transfers between financial institutions.

In any case, an agreed-on set of common security capabilities is required to realize effective business-to-business communications.[2] Many view PKI technology as the very foundation to achieve these capabilities.

---

[2]Each organization can run the PKI services independently. In this case, *cross-certification* can be used to establish the necessary trust relationship(s) between the two organizations. Alternatively, a parent organization may offer PKI services to one or more of its subsidiaries, especially if the subsidiary is a relatively small organization that does not have the business need to run an internal PKI. Specific deployment considerations such as these are addressed further in Chapter 25.

### *Business-to-Consumer Communication*

Much of today's business-to-consumer e-commerce would not be possible without the Internet or the World Wide Web (WWW). However, it is important to distinguish between two prevalent business models when it comes to providing business-to-consumer electronic commerce.

The first model is *user centric*. (See Chapter 9.) Individuals obtain their own certificates from a third-party service provider, or they generate their own certificates (as in the case of Open-PGP, as discussed in Chapters 6 and 18). In many cases, the individuals use standard "Web technology" to conduct their business. This is largely an unstructured and uncontrolled model, in which even the most basic certificate/key life-cycle management (see Chapter 7) is simply unavailable (although we have seen recent improvements in this area).

In this model, e-commerce is typically based on the *Secure Sockets Layer (SSL)* protocol or *Transport Layer Security (TLS)* [RFC2246] protocol, which provides a confidentiality pipe between a browser and a server. Server-only or mutual client-server authentication can also be supported. However, the use of SSL/TLS has been criticized because client authentication is generally considered optional and is rarely used in today's Web environment. It has also been criticized due to a lack of "persistent" confidentiality. That is, once the server receives data, it is decrypted. If the server does nothing more to protect that data, it is vulnerable to attack.

In addition, SSL/TLS does not support digital signatures over the data, so there is no way to preserve a persistent digital signature in association with a given transaction, which is a serious limitation in many transaction-based applications. Nonetheless, many of the merchants on the Web rely on SSL/TLS for the protection of the transactions (for example, to protect credit card numbers while in transit between the client and the server).

The second model is more "organization centric." This second model, which has been adopted by a number of organizations, is arguably more controlled and more secure than the first. An example of this model is an organization (a bank, for example) that operates as a Certification Authority (CA); certificates are issued to that organization's constituents for the specific purpose of conducting business between the individual and that organization. This model may also include the use of special-purpose software, typically issued from the organization to the individual, to offer more comprehensive certificate/key life-cycle management and more secure communications than would normally be available. It also enables the organization to more easily control the purpose and scope of the certificates it issues.

## Internal/External Business Model Hybrids

Of course, it is natural for many organizations to offer both internal and external security services based on PKI technology. These two models must *not* be viewed as being mutually exclusive. In fact, many of today's PKI deployments begin with a modest-scale internal pilot (for example, deployment of a single PKI-enabled application with a community of users on the order of tens or hundreds). This is followed by larger-scale initiatives (for example, incorporating additional applications and increasing the number of users), including external business-to-business and business-to-consumer deployments.

## Business Model Influences

Besides internal business requirements, external events sometimes significantly influence the business model. For example, the U.S. health-care industry has witnessed the introduction of legislation that is likely to cast an unprecedented focus on the protection of electronic health-care information. Specifically, the Medical Records Confidentiality Act of 1995 levies severe penalties associated with the unauthorized disclosure of medical information. In addition, the Health Information Portability and Accountability Act of 1996 (HIPAA, also known as the Kennedy–Kassebaum Bill) mandates that the U.S. Congress enact federal laws for the protection of patient information. Clearly, this will have a profound impact on the business model of any health-care organization.

As more and more of the paper-based medical records are replaced with *Electronic Medical Records (EMRs)*, care must be taken to ensure that those records are accessed and updated in accordance with sound business (and ethical) practices *and* all applicable legislation. For example, the technology used to access EMRs can vary significantly, and the individuals that access EMRs also vary. Specifically, access to the EMR can be local or remote (including remote access over the Internet), and personnel accessing the EMR can be a primary care or consulting physician, a nurse, or even the patient him- or herself.

This brief example helps illustrate how secure electronic forms, secure remote access, and individual access control and accountability are required in a business model that must address the proper protection of EMRs.

[NAS] summarizes many of the issues associated with the protection of health-care information.

## Government-Sponsored Initiatives

A number of government-sponsored initiatives—for example, the Government of Canada Public Key Infrastructure (GOC PKI) and the U.S. Federal PKI (FPKI)—can be modeled in the same way as the internal, business-to-business and business-to-consumer models described in the preceding sections. In this case, the internal business model is driven by a need to facilitate interdepartmental communications among civil servants. The business-to-business model represents the need for peer-to-peer communications between governments on a national, regional, or local basis. The business-to-consumer model reflects the need for a government to offer services to its citizens—although the specific applications may vary substantially due to the nature of services traditionally offered by a government (as compared to a private organization).

The deployment strategy of the known governmental deployments also reflects that of an internal/external business model hybrid discussed previously in this chapter. Specifically, the government-based PKIs tend to begin with modest internal deployments (on the order of tens or perhaps hundreds of users), with the plan to expand and extend the reach of the PKI to offer external services to the citizen and to provide for intergovernmental communications.

# Interdomain Trust

Although it is possible for individual businesses to forge their own interorganizational trust relationships on a bilateral basis, a number of initiatives are designed to establish business-to-business trust relationships on behalf of these organizations. The purpose of this section is to briefly discuss a few of these initiatives.

### Identrus

*Identrus* is an organization that is designed to help establish business-to-business trust relationships for the purpose of conducting global e-commerce among financial institutions. Eight major financial institutions founded Identrus, and its membership has grown substantially over the past few years.

The Identrus infrastructure is based on a rooted hierarchy. Thus, each participating financial institution will "fall under" a common root. However, ultimately the basis of trust rests with the participating financial institutions.

Technology to support the Identrus infrastructure can be supplied by multiple vendors, as long as the vendors are capable of offering products that conform to the Identrus infrastructure guidelines.

Additional information regarding Identrus can be found at `www.identrus.com`.

### Bridge CA

We discussed the hub-and-spoke model in Chapter 9, and the U.S. federal bridge CA initiative in Chapter 20. We also see the GOC PKI utilizing the bridge model for both intra- and interdomain cross-certification.

As previously discussed, this bridge capability is extremely powerful because it substantially reduces the number of bilateral cross-certifications and it preserves the autonomy of the individual CA domains (for example, governmental departments that have deployed their own CAs under the umbrella of the larger government-wide PKI domain). This model also allows individual departments to deploy without waiting on external events such as the deployment of a common root CA.

We believe that this model may very well become standard practice in a number of industry segments.

## VeriSign Trust Network

The *VeriSign Trust Network (VTN)* exists because VeriSign has several root keys embedded in the Web browsers, and both individual and server certificates issued by VeriSign "fall under" one of those root keys. Thus, VTN is based on a rooted hierarchy trust model. (See Chapter 9 for further discussion of trust models.) This model can be extended to encompass interorganizational trust, as long as the certificates issued by each organization fall under a common VeriSign root.

## GTE CyberTrust/Baltimore Technologies OmniRoot

In May 1999, GTE CyberTrust announced a new service offering that is referred to as *OmniRoot*. From a "trust network" perspective, the GTE CyberTrust OmniRoot is analogous to the VTN. Specifically, GTE CyberTrust has several root keys embedded within the popular Web browsers available from Microsoft and Netscape. If an organization chooses to operate CAs that are subordinate to the GTE CyberTrust root CA, browsers will recognize certificates issued by those CAs.

Early in 2000, Baltimore Technologies acquired GTE CyberTrust, and the OmniRoot "trust network" is now part of their product portfolio.

## Other Trust Networks

It reasonable to suggest that any organization that issues certificates under the authority of a CA—whose root key is embedded in the browser and/or that issues organizational certificates under a common root—is in a position to claim that it, too, offers a "trust network" (as long as the individuals and the organizations are confident that the CA itself provides a solid foundation to enable those trust relationships). However, it may be important to appropriately constrain these CAs in the future (see Chapter 9 for more information on trust relationships), perhaps through the use of the Name Constraints and/or Policy Constraints certificate extensions. (See Chapter 6 for more about certificate extensions.)

# Summary

This chapter addressed some of the more common business models that may drive PKI deployment. In particular, this chapter presented the following business models:

- Business models related to internal communications requirements
- Business models related to external communications requirements

These models are not mutually exclusive (that is, an organization may implement both business models).

The goal of a PKI is to establish a single infrastructure that is capable of supporting multiple applications across multiple domains. This infrastructure must be cost effective, capable of evolving over time, and based on industry-accepted standards to help ensure interoperability with other domains.

Although the initial PKI deployments may be modest internal efforts, the objective for many organizations (and governments) is to extend the "reach" of interoperability across multiple CA and PKI boundaries. In other words, internal corporate communications is only the first step. Secure communications with external trading partners, subsidiaries, communities of interest (for example, collaborative research among many universities), or even peer organizations within a given industry (for example, the financial sector or the automotive industry) is also a highly desirable goal.

A number of national and regional government initiatives reflect the business models discussed here. For example, the GOC PKI is designed to facilitate secure interdepartmental communications for many of the applications that might be associated with the internal operations of a large corporation. The government of Canada is also working to provide governmental services to Canadian citizens through their Government On-Line (GOL) initiative.

Finally, this chapter briefly discussed a few interdomain trust initiatives.

In addition to the other chapters in Part III of this book, two related topics will help form the foundation for a more complete understanding of the business models and associated business drivers behind PKI deployment. Specifically, you should review the infrastructure concepts provided in Chapter 3 and the concepts associated with trust models provided in Chapter 9.

CHAPTER 27

# *Conclusions and Further Reading*

This chapter provides a summary of the significant issues discussed in Part III and includes a few suggestions for further reading.

## Conclusions

Part III of this book concentrated on the benefits of, and the issues associated with, large-scale PKI deployments in the enterprise domain. The key to achieving a successful deployment of a large-scale enterprise PKI rests in several areas:

- First and foremost, cost justification and the development of a solid business case are essential. Attempting to deploy technology for technology's sake alone is doomed to failure.

- It is important to achieve the maximum amount of corporate-level buy-in. Lack of support within an organization will make deployment extremely difficult, if not impossible.

- It is important to be aware of the various deployment issues before deployment of the PKI actually begins. This can be tempered with the rollout of a small-scale PKI, which may help expose any remaining issues that may not have been obvious initially.

- It is essential to understand the obstacles to deployment and to have a solid deployment strategy.

- Finally, ongoing operational support, including training and help desk support, must be provided.

Addressing each area will aid in the smooth transition from a small-scale, single application rollout to a large-scale, multiapplication deployment.

Part III also discussed some factors that should be taken into consideration before selecting a specific PKI vendor or service provider. As discussed in Chapter 22, some criteria to consider include the following:

- Reputation

- Market penetration

- Longevity

- Standards compliance

- Demonstrated security (for example, through formal endorsement programs such as FIPS 140-1)

- Commitment to multivendor interoperability

- Level of operations support

- Relative cost

Various business models were also discussed, and some of the interdomain trust initiatives were introduced.

## Suggestions for Further Reading

A number of deployment issues and several case studies are covered in *PKI: A Wiley Tech Brief* by Tom Austin [Aust00].

A chapter on Return on Investment (ROI) is available in *PKI: Implementing and Managing E-Security* by Andrew Nash and colleagues [NDJB01].

A number of case studies and reports are available from the PKI vendors themselves. We recognize that some of these may be biased, but hopefully they will give you an appreciation of the things to think about when considering deployment of a PKI. Many of these papers can be found on-line by visiting each vendor's Web site—for example,

    www.baltimore.com

    www.entrust.com

    www.rsasecurity.com

    www.verisign.com

# References

[ABA]     American Bar Association (ABA). "Digital Signature Guidelines: Legal Infra-structure for Certification Authorities and Electronic Commerce" (1995).

[Adam97]     Adams, C. "Constructing Symmetric Ciphers Using the CAST Design Proce-dure." *Designs, Codes and Cryptography 12,* no. 3 (1997): 71–104.

[AES]     National Institute of Standards and Technology. "Advanced Encryption Stan-dard Development Effort." See `http://csrc.nist.gov/encryption/aes`.

[Ande01]     Anderson, R. *Security Engineering: A Guide to Building Dependable Distributed Systems.* New York: Wiley, 2001.

[ANX]     Automotive Industry Action Group. *Automotive Network eXchange (ANX) Certificate Policy.* Southfield, MI: Author, n.d.

[AsVa99]     Ashley, P., and M. Vandenwauver. *Practical Intranet Security: Overview of the State of the Art and Available Technologies.* Boston: Kluwer Academic Publishers, 1999.

[Aust00]     Austin, T. *PKI: A Wiley Tech Brief.* New York: Wiley, 2000.

[Bran00]     Brands, S. *Rethinking Public Key Infrastructures and Digital Certificates: Build-ing in Privacy.* Cambridge, MA: MIT Press, 2000.

[CA-CA]     Lloyd, S., et al. "CA-CA Interoperability." PKI Forum white paper, March 2001; see `http://www.pkiforum.org/pdfs/ca-ca_interop.pdf`.

[CAPI]      Microsoft Corporation. "Cryptographic Application Program Interface (Crypto API)"; see `http://www.microsoft.com/security/default.asp` (in the "Technologies" section) for pointers to documentation and introductory material on this topic.

[CARAT]     "CARAT Guidelines—Guidelines for Constructing Policies Governing the Use of Identity-Based Public Key Certificates." National Automated Clearing House Association (NACHA)—The Internet Council Certification Authority Rating and Trust (CARAT) Task Force, DRAFT Version 1.0 (21 September 1998).

[CDSA]      Intel Corporation. "Common Data Security Architecture"; see `http://developer.intel.com/ial/security` for pointers to documentation, presentations, white papers, articles, and books on this topic.

[Coop98]    Cooper, David A. *A Model of Certificate Revocation*. National Institute of Standards and Technology (17 August 1998).

[CSI]       Computer Security Institute. "Computer Security Issues and Trends: 2002." *CSI/FBI Computer Crime and Security Survey 3*, no. 1, (2002).

[DCE]       The Open Group. *DCE Today*. Upper Saddle River, NJ: Prentice Hall, 1998.

[DiHe76]    Diffie, W., and M. Hellman. "New Directions in Cryptography." *IEEE Transactions on Information Theory 22* (1976): 644–654.

[ECOM]      Electronic Commerce Promotion Council of Japan; see `http://www.ecom.or.jp/ecom_e/`.

[EDIFACT] ISO 9735. EDIFACT specification.

[EESSI]     European Electronic Signature Standardization Initiative; see `http://www.ict.etsi.org/EESSI/EESSI-homepage.htm`.

[ElGa85]    ElGamal, T. "A Public Key Cryptosystem and a Signature Scheme Based on Discrete Logarithms." *IEEE Transactions on Information Theory 31* (1985): 469–472.

[ElSc00]    Ellison, C., and B. Schneier. "Ten Risks of PKI: What You're Not Being Told about Public Key Infrastructure." *Computer Security Journal 16*, no. 1 (2000). See also `www.counterpane.com/pki-risks.html` for an on-line copy of this paper or Chapter 15 of B. Schneier, *Secrets and Lies: Digital Security in a Networked World* (New York: Wiley, 2000) for a somewhat expanded version.

[ESIGN]     Electronic Signatures in Global and National Commerce Act; see `http://frwebgate.access.gpo.gov/cgi-bin/getdoc.cgi?dbname=106_cong_bills&docid=f:s761enr.txt.pdf`.

[ESTIO]    Electronic Signature Testsuite for Inter-Operability; see `http://research.ac.upc.es/ESTIO`.

[EU]    Directive 1999/93/EC of the European Parliament and of the Council of 13 December 1999 on a Community framework for electronic signatures; see `http://europa.eu.int/comm/internal_market/en/media/sign/Dir99-93-ecEN.pdf`.

[FFW99]    Feghhi, J., J. Feghhi, and P. Williams. *Digital Certificates: Applied Internet Security.* Reading, MA: Addison-Wesley, 1999.

[FIPS46]    Federal Information Processing Standards Publication 46. "Data Encryption Standard." Springfield, VA: U.S. Department of Commerce, National Bureau of Standards, National Technical Information Service, 1977.

[FIPS113]    Federal Information Processing Standards Publication 113. "Computer Data Authentication." Springfield, VA: U.S. Department of Commerce, National Bureau of Standards, National Technical Information Service, 1985.

[FIPS140]    Federal Information Processing Standards Publication 140-1. "Security Requirements for Cryptographic Modules." Springfield, VA: U.S. Department of Commerce/NIST, National Technical Information Service, 1994.

[FIPS180]    Federal Information Processing Standards Publication 180-1. "Secure Hash Standard." Springfield, VA: U.S. Department of Commerce, National Bureau of Standards, National Technical Information Service, 1995.

[FIPS186]    Federal Information Processing Standards Publication 186. "Digital Signature Standard." Springfield, VA: U.S. Department of Commerce, National Bureau of Standards, National Technical Information Service, 1994.

[FoBa00]    Ford, W., and M. Baum. *Secure Electronic Commerce: Building the Infrastructure for Digital Signatures and Encryption* (2nd ed.). Englewood Cliffs, NJ: Prentice Hall, 2000.

[FPKI]    United States Federal Public-Key Infrastructure; see `http://csrc.nist.gov/pki/`.

[FPKIpro]    Booz-Allen and Hamilton Inc. "Federal Public Key Infrastructure (PKI) X.509 Certificate and CRL Extensions Profile" (4 January 1999).

[Garf95]    Garfinkel, S. *PGP: Pretty Good Privacy.* Sebastopol, CA: O'Reilly and Associates, 1995.

[GOCCP]    "Digital Signature and Confidentiality Certificate Policies for the Government of Canada Public Key Infrastructure." Treasury Board of Canada Secretariat (April 1999).

[GOCPKI]   Government of Canada Public-Key Infrastructure; see `http://www.cse-cst.gc.ca/`.

[HaSt91]   Haber, S., and W. S. Stornetta. "How To Time-Stamp a Digital Document." *Journal of Cryptology 3*, no. 2 (1991): 99–111.

[HoPo01]   Housley, R., and T. Polk. *Planning for PKI: Best Practices Guide for Deploying Public Key Infrastructure*. New York: Wiley, 2001.

[HoSm97]   Howes, T., and M. Smith. *LDAP: Programming Directory-Enabled Applications with Lightweight Directory Access Protocol*. Indianapolis: Macmillan Technical Publishing, 1997.

[ICE-CAR]  Interworking Public Key Certification Infrastructure for Commerce, Administration and Research; see `http://ice-car.darmstadt.gmd.de`.

[IEEE]     Institute of Electrical and Electronics Engineers Standards Association Working Group P1363; see `http://grouper.ieee.org/groups/1363/index.html`.

[JCP]      The Java Community Process; see `http://www.jcp.org/home/index.en.jsp`.

[KaRo95]   Kaliski, B., and M. Robshaw. "The Secure Use of RSA." *RSA Laboratories' CryptoBytes 1*, no. 3 (1995).

[Kobl87]   Koblitz, N. "Elliptic Curve Cryptosystems." *Mathematics of Computation 48* (1987): 203–209.

[Kohn78]   Kohnfelder, L. "Towards a Practical Public-Key Cryptosystem." MIT S.B. thesis, 1978.

[Lai92]    Lai, X. "On the Design and Security of Block Ciphers." In *ETH Series in Information Processing*. Vol. 1. Edited by J. L. Massey. Zurich: Hartung-Gorre Verlag Konstanz, Technische Hochschule, 1992.

[LDAPext]  The LDAP Extension Working Group charter; see `http://www.ietf.org/html.charters/ldapext-charter.html`.

[Lock94]   Lockhart, H. W. *OSF DCE: Guide to Developing Distributed Applications*. New York: McGraw-Hill, 1994.

[LOT]      Baker, S. A., and P. R. Hurst. *The Limits of Trust: Cryptography, Governments, and Electronic Commerce*. The Hague: Kluwer Law International, 1998.

[MCP]      "Model Certificate Policy." Government Information Technology Services–Federal PKI Steering Committee–Legal/Policy Working Group, Discussion Draft (25 March 1998; revised 8 July 1998).

[Merk78]    Merkle, R. "Secure Communications over Insecure Channels." *Communications of the ACM 21* (1978): 294–299.

[Merk79]    Merkle, R. *Secrecy, Authentication, and Public Key Systems*. Ann Arbor, MI: UMI Research Press, 1979.

[Mill86]    Miller, V. "Use of Elliptic Curves in Cryptography." *Advances in Cryptology, Proceedings of Crypto '85* (LNCS 218) (1986): 417–426.

[MISPCv1]  Burr, W., D. Dodson, N. Nazario, and W. T. Polk. "Minimum Interoperability Specification for PKI Components, Version 1." National Institute of Standards and Technology (NIST) Special Publication 800-15, September 3, 1997; see `http://csrc.nist.gov/pki/mispc/welcome.html`.

[MISPCv2]  National Institute of Standards and Technology (NIST) Project Team. "Minimum Interoperability Specification for PKI Components, Version 2—Second Draft" (2 August 31 2001).

[Mose97]    Moses, Tim. "Limits to the Scale of a Public Key Infrastructure." Proceedings of PKS '97 (27–30 April 1997).

[MvOV97]  Menezes, A., P. van Oorschot, and S. Vanstone. *Handbook of Applied Cryptography*. Boca Raton, FL: CRC Press, 1997. See also `http://cacr.math.uwaterloo.ca/hac`.

[MWC]      Smedinghoff, Thomas J., and Ruth Hill Bro. "Moving with Change: Electronic Signature Legislation as a Vehicle for Advancing E-Commerce." Originally published in the *John Marshall Journal of Computer and Information Law 17*, no. 3 (1999).

[NACHA]    Prince, N., and J. Foster. "Certification Authority Interoperability: From Concept to Reality—Results of the NACHA Internet Council CA Interoperability Pilot." National Automated Clearing House Association. (1999).

[NAS]      Committee on Maintaining Privacy and Security in Health Care Applications of the National Information Infrastructure, Computer Science and Telecommunications Board, Commission on Physical Sciences, Mathematics, and Applications, National Research Council. "For the Record: Protecting Electronic Health Information." U.S. National Academy of Sciences (1997).

[NDJB01]   Nash, A., W. Duane, C. Joseph, and D. Brink. *PKI: Implementing and Managing E-Security*. Berkeley, CA: RSA Press/McGraw-Hill Professional Publishing, 2001.

[OASIS]    Organization for the Advancement of Structured Information Standards; see `http://www.oasis-open.org`.

[PAG]    "PKI Assessment Guidelines, American Bar Association Information Security Committee, Version 0.14" (4 May 2000).

[PGV93]    Preneel, B., R. Govaerts, and J. Vandewalle. "Information Authentication: Hash Functions and Digital Signatures." *Computer Security and Industrial Cryptography: State of the Art and Evolution.* Edited by B. Preneel, R. Govaerts, and J. Vandewalle, 87–131. Berlin: Springer-Verlag (LNCS 741), 1993.

[PKIX]    The PKIX Working Group Charter; see `http://www.ietf.org/html.charters/pkix-charter.html`.

[Pren93]    Preneel, B. "Analysis and Design of Cryptographic Hash Functions." Ph.D. diss., Katholieke Universiteit Leuven, Belgium, 1993.

[Resc00]    Rescorla, E. *SSL and TLS: Designing and Building Secure Systems.* Boston: Addison-Wesley, 2000.

[RFC1305]    Mills, D. "Network Time Protocol (Version 3): Specification, Implementation, and Analysis." Internet Request for Comments 1305 (March 1992).

[RFC1319]    Kaliski, B. "The MD2 Message-Digest Algorithm." Internet Request for Comments 1319 (April 1992).

[RFC1320]    Rivest, R. "The MD4 Message-Digest Algorithm." Internet Request for Comments 1320 (April 1992).

[RFC1321]    Rivest, R. "The MD5 Message-Digest Algorithm." Internet Request for Comments 1321 (April 1992).

[RFC1422]    Kent, S. "Privacy Enhancement for Internet Electronic Mail—Part II: Certificate-Based Key Management." Internet Request for Comments 1422 (February 1993).

[RFC1424]    Kaliski, B. "Privacy Enhancement for Internet Electronic Mail—Part IV: Key Certification and Related Services." Internet Request for Comments 1424 (February 1993).

[RFC1510]    Kohl, J., and C. Neuman. "The Kerberos Network Authentication Service (V5)." Internet Request for Comments 1510 (September 1993).

[RFC1777]    Yeong, W., T. Howes, and S. Kille. "Lightweight Directory Access Protocol." Internet Request for Comments 1777 (March 1995).

[RFC1991]    Atkins, D., W. Stallings, and P. Zimmermann. "PGP Message Exchange Formats." Internet Request for Comments 1991 (August 1996).

[RFC2015]    Elkins, M. "MIME Security with Pretty Good Privacy." Internet Request for Comments 2015 (October 1996).

[RFC2025] Adams, C. "The Simple Public-Key GSS-API Mechanism (SPKM)." Internet Request for Comments 2025 (October 1996).

[RFC2078] Linn, J. "Generic Security Service Application Program Interface, Version 2." Internet Request for Comments 2078 (January 1997).

[RFC2104] Krawczyk, H., M. Bellare, and R. Canetti. "HMAC: Keyed Hashing for Message Authentication." Internet Request for Comments 2104 (February 1997).

[RFC2144] Adams, C. "The CAST-128 Encryption Algorithm." Internet Request for Comments 2144 (May 1997).

[RFC2222] Myers, J. "Simple Authentication and Security Layer (SASL)." Internet Request for Comments 2222 (October 1997).

[RFC2246] Dierks, T., and C. Allen. "The TLS Protocol, Version 1.0." Internet Request for Comments 2246 (January 1999).

[RFC2251] Wahl, M., T. Howes, and S. Kille. "Lightweight Directory Access Protocol (v3)." Internet Request for Comments 2251 (December 1997).

[RFC2252] Wahl, M., A. Coulbeck, T. Howes, and S. Kille. "Lightweight Directory Access Protocol (v3): Attribute Syntax Definitions." Internet Request for Comments 2252 (December 1997).

[RFC2253] Wahl, M., S. Kille, and T. Howes. "Lightweight Directory Access Protocol (v3): UTF-8 String Representation of Distinguished Names." Internet Request for Comments 2253 (December 1997).

[RFC2254] Howes, T. "The String Representation of LDAP Search Filters." Internet Request for Comments 2254 (December 1997).

[RFC2255] Howes, T., and M. Smith. "The LDAP URL Format." Internet Request for Comments 2255 (December 1997).

[RFC2256] Wahl, M. "A Summary of the X.500(96) User Schema for Use with LDAPv3." Internet Request for Comments 2256 (December 1997).

[RFC2311] Dusse, S., P. Hoffman, B. Ramsdell, L. Lundblade, and L. Repka. "S/MIME Version 2 Message Specification." Internet Request for Comments 2311 (March 1998).

[RFC2312] Dusse, S., P. Hoffman, B. Ramsdell, and J. Weinstein. "S/MIME Version 2 Certificate Handling." Internet Request for Comments 2312 (March 1998).

[RFC2314] Kaliski, B. "PKCS #10: Certification Request Syntax Version 1.5." Internet Request for Comments 2314 (March 1998).

[RFC2315] Kaliski, B. "PKCS #7: Cryptographic Message Syntax Version 1.5." Internet Request for Comments 2315 (March 1998).

[RFC2401] Kent, S., and R. Atkinson. "Security Architecture for the Internet Protocol." Internet Request for Comments 2401 (November 1998).

[RFC2402] Kent, S., and R. Atkinson. "IP Authentication Header." Internet Request for Comments 2402 (November 1998).

[RFC2403] Madson, C., and R. Glenn. "The Use of HMAC-MD5–96 within ESP and AH." Internet Request for Comments 2403 (November 1998).

[RFC2404] Madson, C., and R. Glenn. "The Use of HMAC-SHA-1–96 within ESP and AH." Internet Request for Comments 2404 (November 1998).

[RFC2405] Madson, C., and N. Doraswamy. "The ESP DES-CBC Cipher Algorithm with Explicit IV." Internet Request for Comments 2405 (November 1998).

[RFC2406] Kent, S., and R. Atkinson. "IP Encapsulating Security Payload (ESP)." Internet Request for Comments 2406 (November 1998).

[RFC2408] Maughan, D., M. Schertler, M. Schneider, and J. Turner. "Internet Security Association and Key Management Protocol (ISAKMP)." Internet Request for Comments 2408 (November 1998).

[RFC2409] Harkins, D., and D. Carrel. "The Internet Key Exchange (IKE)." Internet Request for Comments 2409 (November 1998).

[RFC2410] Glenn, R., and S. Kent. "The NULL Encryption Algorithm and Its Use with IPsec." Internet Request for Comments 2410 (November 1998).

[RFC2411] Thayer, R., N. Doraswamy, and R. Glenn. "IP Security Document Roadmap." Internet Request for Comments 2411 (November 1998).

[RFC2412] Orman, H. "The OAKLEY Key Determination Protocol." Internet Request for Comments 2412 (November 1998).

[RFC2440] Callas, J., L. Donnerhacke, H. Finney, and R. Thayer. "OpenPGP Message Format." Internet Request for Comments 2440 (November 1998).

[RFC2451] Pereira, R., and R. Adams. "The ESP CBC-Mode Cipher Algorithms." Internet Request for Comments 2451 (November 1998).

[RFC2459] Housley, R., W. Ford, W. Polk, and D. Solo. "Internet X.509 Public Key Infrastructure: Certificate and CRL Profile." Internet Request for Comments 2459 (January 1999). (This specification has been superseded by RFC3280.)

[RFC2479] Adams, C. "Independent Data Unit Protection Generic Security Service Application Program Interface (IDUP-GSS-API)." Internet Request for Comments 2479 (December 1998).

[RFC2510] Adams, C., and S. Farrell. "Internet X.509 Public Key Infrastructure: Certificate Management Protocols." Internet Request for Comments 2510 (March 1999).

[RFC2511] Myers, M., C. Adams, D. Solo, and D. Kemp. "Internet X.509 Certificate Request Message Format." Internet Request for Comments 2511 (March 1999).

[RFC2527] Chokhani, S., and W. Ford. "Internet X.509 Public Key Infrastructure: Certificate Policy and Certification Practices Framework." Internet Request for Comments 2527 (March 1999).

[RFC2538] Eastlake, D., and O. Gudmundsson. "Storing Certificates in the Domain Name System (DNS)." Internet Request for Comments 2538 (March 1999).

[RFC2539] Eastlake, D. "Storage of Diffie-Hellman Keys in the Domain Name System (DNS)." Internet Request for Comments 2539 (March 1999).

[RFC2559] Boeyen, S., T. Howes, and P. Richard. "Internet X.509 Public Key Infrastructure: Operational Protocols—LDAPv2." Internet Request for Comments 2559 (April 1999).

[RFC2560] Myers, M., R. Ankney, A. Malpani, S. Galperin, and C. Adams. "X.509 Internet Public Key Infrastructure: Online Certificate Status Protocol—OCSP." Internet Request for Comments 2560 (June 1999).

[RFC2585] Housley, R. and P. Hoffman. "Internet X.509 Public Key Infrastructure Operational Protocols: FTP and HTTP." Internet Request for Comments 2585 (May 1999).

[RFC2587] Boeyen, S., T. Howes, and P. Richard. "Internet X.509 Public Key Infrastructure: LDAPv2 Schema." Internet Request for Comments 2587 (June 1999).

[RFC2630] Housley, R. "Cryptographic Message Syntax." Internet Request for Comments RFC 2630 (June 1999).

[RFC2631] Rescorla, E. "Diffie-Hellman Key Agreement Method." Internet Request for Comments 2631 (June 1999).

[RFC2632] Ramsdell, B. "S/MIME Version 3 Certificate Handling." Internet Request for Comments 2632 (June 1999).

[RFC2633] Ramsdell, B. "S/MIME Version 3 Message Specification." Internet Request for Comments 2633 (June 1999).

[RFC2634] Hoffman, P. "Enhanced Security Services for S/MIME." Internet Request for Comments 2634 (June 1999).

[RFC2692] Ellison, C. "SPKI Requirements." Internet Request for Comments 2692 (September 1999).

[RFC2693] Ellison, C., B. Frantz, B. Lampson, R. Rivest, B. Thomas, and T. Ylonen. "SPKI Certificate Theory." Internet Request for Comments 2693 (September 1999).

[RFC2797] Myers, M., X. Liu, J. Schaad, and J. Weinstein. "Certificate Management Messages over CMS." Internet Request for Comments 2797 (April 2000).

[RFC2829] Wahl, M., H. Alvestrand, J. Hodges, and R. Morgan. "Authentication Methods for LDAP." Internet Request for Comments 2829 (May 2000).

[RFC2830] Hodges, J., R. Morgan, and M. Wahl. "Lightweight Directory Access Protocol (v3): Extension for Transport Layer Security." Internet Request for Comments 2830 (May 2000).

[RFC3029] Adams, C., P. Sylvester, M. Zolotarev, and R. Zuccherato. "Internet X.509 Public Key Infrastructure Data Validation and Certification Server Protocols." Internet Request for Comments 3029 (February 2001).

[RFC3039] Santesson, S., W. Polk, P. Barzin, and M. Nystrom. "Internet X.509 Public Key Infrastructure Qualified Certificates Profile." Internet Request for Comments 3039 (January 2001).

[RFC3125] Ross, J., D. Pinkas, and N. Pope. "Electronic Signature Policies." Internet Request for Comments 3125 (September 2001).

[RFC3126] Pinkas, D., J. Ross, and N. Pope. "Electronic Signature Formats for Long-Term Electronic Signatures." Internet Request for Comments 3126 (September 2001).

[RFC3161] Adams, C., P. Cain, D. Pinkas, and R. Zuccherato. "Internet X.509 Public Key Infrastructure Time-Stamp Protocol (TSP)." Internet Request for Comments 3161 (August 2001).

[RFC3183] Dean, T., and W. Ottaway. "Domain Security Services using S/MIME." Internet Request for Comments 3183 (October 2001).

[RFC3279] Polk, W., R. Housley, and L. Bassham. "Algorithms and Identifiers for the Internet X.509 Public Key Infrastructure Certificate and Certificate Revocation List (CRL) Profile." Internet Request for Comments 3279 (April 2002).

[RFC3280] Housley, R., W. Polk, W. Ford, and D. Solo. "Internet X.509 Public Key Infrastructure: Certificate and Certificate Revocation List (CRL) Profile." Internet Request for Comments 3280 (April 2002). (This specification supersedes RFC2459.)

[RFC3281] Farrell, S., and R. Housley. "An Internet Attribute Certificate Profile for Authorization." Internet Request for Comments 3281 (April 2002).

[Rive95] Rivest, R. "The RC5 Encryption Algorithm." Proceedings of the Second International Workshop on Fast Software Encryption, Springer-Verlag (LNCS 1008) (1995): 86–96.

[RLTC] OASIS Rights Language Technical Committee. See `http://www.oasis-open.org/committees/rights` for details.

[RSA78] Rivest, R., A. Shamir, and L. Adleman. "A Method for Obtaining Digital Signatures and Public-Key Cryptosystems." *Communications of the ACM 21* (1978): 120–126.

[SAML] OASIS Security Services Technical Committee. "Security Assertion Markup Language." See `http://www.oasis-open.org/committees/security` for details.

[Schn96] Schneier, B. *Applied Cryptography: Protocols, Algorithms, and Source Code in C* (2nd ed.). New York: Wiley, 1996.

[SDSI] Rivest, R., and B. Lampson. "SDSI—A Simple Distributed Security Infrastructure"; see `http://theory.lcs.mit.edu/~cis/sdsi.html`.

[SEIS] Secured Electronic Information in Society, a nonprofit Swedish organization established to promote the development of a framework for IT security. The SEIS specifications have been standardized by the Swedish Standards Institute in documents SS 61 43 30, SS 61 43 31, and SS 61 43 32 (approved September 14, 1998). See `http://www.seis.se` for further information.

[SEMPER] Secure Electronic MarketPlace, Europe; see `http://www.semper.org`.

[SET] MasterCard/VISA. Secure Electronic Transaction; see `http://www.setco.org/`.

[SET1] SET Secure Electronic Transaction Specification. Book 1: Business Description, Visa and MasterCard, Version 1.0 (31 May 1997).

[SET2] SET Secure Electronic Transaction Specification. Book 2: Programmer's Guide, Visa and MasterCard, Version 1.0 (31 May 1997).

[SET3] SET Secure Electronic Transaction Specification. Book 3: Formal Protocol Definition, Visa and MasterCard, Version 1.0 (31 May 1997).

[SHA2]    Draft versions of SHA-256, SHA-384, and SHA-512 currently are available at the following location: `http://csrc.nist.gov/encryption/shs/sha256-384-512.pdf` (to be published in a FIPS publication).

[SPKI]    The Simple Public Key Infrastructure Charter; see `http://www.ietf.org/html.charters/spki-charter.html`.

[Stal99]    Stallings, W. *Cryptography and Network Security: Principles and Practice* (2nd ed.). Upper Saddle River, NJ: Prentice Hall, 1999.

[STIME]    The Secure Network Time Protocol (STIME) Working Group charter; see `http://www.ietf.org/html.charters/stime-charter.html`.

[Stin95]    Stinson, D. *Cryptography: Theory and Practice.* Boca Raton, FL: CRC Press, 1995.

[TC68]    ISO/TC68/SC2. "Banking—Certificate Management Part 1: Public Key Certificates." ISO/CD-15782-1 (20 August 1998); and "Banking—Certificate Management Part 3: Certificate Extensions." ISO/WD-15782-3 (25 February 1998).

[TCPA]    The Trusted Computing Platform Alliance; see `http://www.trustedpc.org/home/home.htm` for details.

[TIE]    Trust Infrastructure for Europe; see `http://www.tie.org.uk`.

[USDoD]    U.S. Department of Defense. "Public Key Infrastructure Roadmap for the Department of Defense." Version 2.0, Revision C (21 April 1999).

[W3C]    World Wide Web Consortium; see `http://www.w3.org`.

[WAP-WSG] Wireless Application Protocol Wireless Security Group; see the Wireless Security section of `http://www.wapforum.org/what/technical.htm`.

[WSS]    OASIS Web Services Security Technical Committee. See `http://www.oasis-open.org/committees/wss` for details.

[X500]    ITU-T Recommendation X.500. "Information Technology—Open Systems Interconnection—The Directory—Overview of concepts, models, and services." International Telecommunication Union. Geneva, Switzerland (2001) (equivalent to ISO/IEC 9594-1:2001; see also related parts 9594-2:2001 through 9594-10:2001).

[X509–97] ITU-T Recommendation X.509. "Information Technology—Open Systems Interconnection—The Directory: Authentication Framework" (June 1997) (equivalent to ISO/IEC9594-8:1997).

[X509–00]   ITU-T Recommendation X.509. "Information Technology—Open Systems Interconnection—The Directory: Public Key and Attribute Certificate Frameworks" (March 2000) (equivalent to ISO/IEC 9594–8:2001).

[X9.59]   ANSI DSTU (Draft Standard for Trial Use) X9.59-199x. "Electronic Commerce for the Financial Services Industry: Account-Based Secure Payment Objects," draft. 19 (August 1999).

[XACML]   OASIS eXtensible Access Control Markup Language Technical Committee. "eXtensible Access Control Markup Language." See `http://www.oasis-open.org/committees/xacml` for details.

[XKMS]   The XML Key Management Specification Working Group of the World Wide Web Consortium (W3C); see `http://www.w3.org/2001/XKMS` for details.

[XrML]   The eXtensible rights Markup Language; see `http://xrml.org` or `http://www.oasis-open.org/committees/rights` for details.

[Zimm95]   Zimmermann, P. *The Official PGP User's Guide* (second printing). Cambridge, MA: MIT Press, 1995.

# Index

*ABA Digital Signature Guidelines,* 185
AC, 59, 60, 82
Access control list (ACL), 59
Accreditation certificate, 137
ACL, 59
Adleman, Len, 17
Administrators, 277
Advanced Encryption Standard (AES), 9
AES, 9
AIA private extension, 78, 163
Algorithms
    CAST-128, 9, 45
    DH, 18
    DSA, 17–18
    ECDH, 18
    ECDSA, 18
    ongoing work, 19
    RSA, 17
    SHA-1, 18–19
Alternative certificate formats, 78–82
Anonymous certificate, 56, 166
Anonyms, 56
ANSI X9F, 227
ANX, 245
Application enabler, 22

*Applied Cryptography: Protocols, Algorithms,*
    *and Source Code in C,* 7
Asymmetric cipher model, 13
Asymmetric ciphers, 12
Attribute certificate (AC), 59, 60, 82
Auditable delegation, 55
Authentication, 37–44
Authentication without identification, 57
Authority Information Access (AIA), 78, 163
Authority Key Identifier, 74, 111, 246
Authorization, 54
Authorization authorities, 54–55
Automatic key update, 30–31
Automotive Network eXchange (ANX), 245

Backup, 97, 98
Backup facility, 97
Barriers to deployment, 283–286
Base Update, 113
Basic Constraints, 76
Bibliography, 297–309
Bilateral cross-certification, 193
Blinded delegation, 55
Book, overview, 3–5
Books. *See* Further reading

Boolean expressions, 59
Border repository, 167–168
Bridge CA, 193, 245–246, 292–293
Bridge repository, 168
BTP, 231
Build vs. buy, 270
Business case considerations, 263–265
Business drivers, 27–28
Business models, 287–294
    external communications models, 288–290
    factors to consider, 291
    government-sponsored initiatives, 291–292
    interdomain trust, 292–293
    internal communications models, 287–288
    internal/external hybrids, 290–291
Business-to-business communication, 289
Business-to-business trust relationship,
        292–293
Business-to-consumer communication, 290
Business Transaction Processing (BTP), 231

CA, 28–29, 85–86
    loose hierarchy, 134–135
    responsibilities, 188–189, 191
    strict hierarchy, 132–134
CA-CA Interoperability, 137
CA certificates, 71
CA Interoperability Pilot (Phase I), 248
CARL, 179–180
CAST-128, 9, 45
Certificate authority, 85
Certificate creation, 94–95
Certificate dissemination, 96. See also PKI
        information dissemination
Certificate expiration, 101
Certificate extension, 74–78
Certificate Issuer, 110
Certificate Management messages over CMS
        (CMC), 254
Certificate path processing, 146–149
Certificate perishability, 76
Certificate policies, 75, 82–85
Certificate policy/certification practices
        framework, 241
Certificate renewal, 101, 102

Certificate repository, 29
Certificate retrieval, 97–98
Certificate revocation, 29–30, 101–102,
        105–129
    CARL, 114–115
    complete CRL, 114
    CRL, 107–113
    CRL distribution points, 115–116
    CRT, 120–122
    Delta CRL, 118–119
    EPRL, 115
    indirect CRL, 119–120
    indirect Delta CRL, 119
    OCSP, 122–125
    on-line query mechanisms, 122
    other options, 126
    overview (table), 128–129
    performance, 127
    periodic publication mechanisms, 107–125
    redirect CRL, 116–118
    scalability, 127
    SCVP, 125
    short-lived certificates, 126
    terminology, 107
    timelines, 127
    updating/posting information, 106
Certificate revocation list. See CRL
Certificate revocation model, 106
Certificate revocation sample scenarios, 102
Certificate revocation tree (CRT),
        120–122, 129
Certificate trust list (CTL), 137
Certificate update, 31, 101, 102
Certificate validation, 98–99
Certificates and certification, 69–87
    AC, 82
    alternative formats, 78–82
    certificate policies, 82–85
    certification authority. See CA
    digital certificate, 71–72
    extensions, 74–78
    perishability, 76
    PGP, 80
    private extensions, 78
    registration authority, 86–87

SET, 81–82
SPKI, 79–80
structure/semantics, 72–78
types of certificates, 70, 78–82
Certification, 85
Certification authority. *See* CA
"Certification Authority Interoperability:
    From Concept to Reality—Results of
    the NACHA Internet Council CA
    Interoperability Pilot," 249
Certification authority revocation list
    (CARL), 114–115, 128, 179–180
Certification practice statement (CPS), 82–84
Certification practice statement (CPS)
    qualifier, 75
Cipher, 8
Ciphertext, 8
Client-side PKI software, 171–173
Client software, 33–35
Closed environment, 272
CMC, 254
CMP, 95
Complete CRLs, 114
Comprehensive PKI, 63
Comprehensive security, 26–27
"Computer Crime and Security Survey," 264
Confidentiality, 43, 45, 194
Core PKI services, 37–48
    authentication, 37–44
    commonality of underlying algorithms, 47
    confidentiality, 43, 45
    entity naming, 47
    integrity, 42–45
    mechanisms, 43–45
    on-line vs. off-line operations, 46–47
    operational considerations, 45–47
    performance, 46
Corporate-level acceptance, 286
Cost considerations, 265–266
CPS, 82–84
CPS qualifier, 75
Criticality flag, 74
CRL, 107–113, 128
    per-CRL extensions, 111–113
    per-entry extensions, 110–111

private extensions, 113
versions, 108–110
CRL Distribution Point, 74–75,
    115–116, 128
CRL Number, 111
CRL profiles, 108
CRL Scope, 112
CRL Stream Identifier, 112
CRMF, 95
Cross-certification, 32, 143–145
Cross-recognition, 137
Cryptographic hash function, 16
*Cryptography: Theory and Practice,* 7
*Cryptography and Network Security:
    Principles and Practices,* 7
CTL, 137

DAP, 167, 283
Data certification server protocols, 241
Data Encryption Standard (DES), 9
Data integrity, 16, 42–45
Data origin identification, 38
Data Validation and Certification Server
    Protocols (DVCS), 255
Decryption, 8
Decryption private key, 93
Delegated path discovery (DPD), 125
Delegated path validation (DPV), 125
Delegation, 55
Delta CRL, 118–119, 128
Delta CRL Indicator, 113
Delta Information, 112
Deployment considerations, 259–296
    barriers to deployment, 283–286
    build vs. buy, 272
    business case considerations, 263–265
    business models, 287–294.
      *See also* Business models
    certificate revocation, 277–278
    closed vs. open environment, 272–273
    cost considerations, 265–266
    disaster planning/recovery, 279
    end-entity roaming, 278
    facility requirements, 277
    factors to consider, 296

further reading, 296
hierarchical vs. distributed models, 270
in-sourcing vs. out-sourcing, 271–272
interoperability considerations, 274–275
key recovery, 278–279
keys to success, 295
mitigating risk, 280
on-line vs. off-line operations, 276
peripheral support, 276
personnel requirements, 277
PKI pilots, 267
repository issues, 279, 283–284
security assurance, 279–280
standard vs. proprietary solutions, 274
targeted applications vs. comprehensive
    solution, 274
vendor selection, 280
X.509 vs. alternative certificate format, 273
DES, 9
Design considerations, 269–281.
    *See also* Deployment considerations
DH, 18
DH communication configurations, 46
DH key pair, 152
Diffie, Whitfield, 11
Diffie-Hellman algorithm, 18
Diffie-Hellman (DH) key pair, 152
Diffie-Hellman paper, 11
Digital certificate, 71–72
Digital signature, 14–16, 44, 71, 185
Digital Signature Algorithm (DSA), 17–18
*Digital Signature Guidelines,* 185
Directory Access Protocol (DAP), 167, 283
Directory Information Shadowing Protocol
    (DISP), 168, 284
Directory information tree (DIT), 165
Disaster preparation/recovery, 179–182
DISP, 168, 284
Dissemination of information. *See* PKI
    information dissemination
Distinguished name (DN), 73, 146, 165
Distributed trust architecture, 135–138
Distributed vs. hierarchical models, 270
DIT, 165
DN, 73, 146, 165

DNS, 284
DNS SRV records, 163
Domain name system (DNS), 284
DPD, 125
DPV, 125
DSA, 17–18
DVCS, 255

E-mail composition (laptop computer), 173
E-Sign legislation, 183–184
ebXML, 231
ECDH, 18
ECDSA, 18
ECOM, 234
EDIFACT, 230
EEMA PKI Challenge, 250
EESSI, 235
Electric power infrastructure, 21
Electronic business XML (ebXML), 231
Electronic Commerce Promotion Council of
    Japan (ECOM), 234
Electronic communications infrastructure, 21
Electronic medical record (EMR), 291
Electronic signature, 185
Electronic Signature Directive, 186–187
Electronic signature legislation, 183–188
Electronic Signature Testsuite for
    Inter-Operability (ESTIO), 235
Electronic Signatures in Global and National
    Commerce Act (E-Sign), 183–184
ElGamal, 18
Elliptic curve DH (ECDH), 18
Elliptic curve DSA (ECDSA), 18
EMR, 291
Encapsulating Security Payload, 167
Encryption, 8, 14
Encryption certificate, 93
End entity, 132
End-entity certificates, 71
End-entity initialization scenario, 91
End-entity public-key certificate revocation
    list (EPRL), 115, 128
End-entity registration, 91–92
End-entity roaming, 278
End-user transparency, 26

End users, 132
Enterprise secure e-mail, 64–66
Entity identification, 37–39
Entity naming, 47, 145–146, 198
Ephemeral-ephemeral DH, 46
Ephemeral-static DH, 46
EPRL, 115, 128
ESTIO, 235
EU Electronic Signature Directive, 186–187
European Electronic Signature
    Standardization Initiative (EESSI), 235
European Forum for Electronic Business
    (EEMA), 250
Extended key usage, 74
eXtensible Access Control Markup Language
    (XACML), 59, 231
Extensions, 74–78
External communications business model,
    288–290
Extranet security, 64, 65

Facility requirements, 277
Federal Information Processing Standard
    (FIPS) 140–1, 94
Federal Public-Key Infrastructure (FPKI),
    232
*Federal Public Key Infrastructure Certificate
    and CRL Extensions Profile,* 247
Fingerprint, 134
FIPS 140–1, 94
Forward cross-certificate, 143
Four-corner trust model, 138–139, 248
FPKI, 232
Freshest CRL, 113
Freshest CRL Pointer, 77–78
Further reading. *See also* Web sites
    bibliography, 297–309
    certificate/CRL storage and retrieval,
        254–256
    certificate/CRL syntax, 253–254
    deployment issues, 296
    interoperability initiatives, 256–257
    life-cycle management protocols, 253–254
    PKI, generally, 218
    standards, 253–258

XML-based initiatives, 256
Future of PKI, 207–216

Generic digital signature process, 15
Generic Security Service Application Program
    Interface (GSS-API), 240
GOC PKI, 232–233, 270
GOL initiative, 294
Government of Canada Public-Key
    Infrastructure (GOC PKI), 232–233
Government On-Line (GOL) initiative, 294
Government-sponsored initiatives, 291–292
GSS-API, 240
GTE CyberTrust/Baltimore Technologies
    OmniRoot, 293

*Handbook of Applied Cryptography,* 7
Handshaking protocols, 47
Hardware components, 175
Hash algorithms, 18–19
Health Information Portability and
    Accountability Act (HIPAA), 291
Hellman, Martin, 11
Hierarchical vs. distributed models, 270
Hierarchy
    loose, 134–135
    policy-based, 135
    strict, 132–134
    trusted-issuer, 134
HIPAA, 291
Hold Instruction Code, 110, 111n
Hub-and-spoke configuration, 138

ICE-CAR, 234–235
Identification, 57, 198
Identifier, 198
Identity, 145
Identity mapping, 62
Identity uniqueness, 145
Identrus, 292
IDUP-GSS-API, 240
IEEE, 230
IEEE P1363, 230
IEEE P1363a, 230
IETF, 224

IETF PKIX Working Group, 224–225, 238, 249, 255
IKE, 228
In-band protocol distribution, 96
In-band protocol exchange, 169
In-sourcing, 271
Independent certificate management, 155–156
Independent Data Unit Protection specification (IDUP-GSS-API), 240
Indexical reference problem, 57
Indirect CRLs, 119–120, 128
Indirect Delta CRLs, 119, 128
Information dissemination.
    See PKI information dissemination
Infrastructure, 171
Inhibit Any Policy, 77
Inhibit Policy Mapping, 77
Institute of Electrical and Electronics Engineers (IEEE), 230
Integrity, 42–45
Inter-enterprise-signed transactions, 66
Interdomain cross-certification, 143
Interdomain replication, 168–169
Interdomain repository deployment options, 167
Interdomain trust, 292–293
Intermediate CAs, 132
Intermediate repository, 166
Internal communications business model, 287–288
Internal/external business model hybrids, 290–291
Internet Engineering Task Force (IETF), 224
Internet Key Exchange (IKE), 228
Internet PKI (IPKI), 64, 224
Internet web sites. See Web sites
Internet X.509 Certificate Request Message Format (CRMF), 95
Internet X.509 Public Key Infrastructure Certificate Management Protocols (CMP), 95
Interoperability considerations, 274–275
Interoperability initiatives, 245–250
Interoperability testing, 244–245

Interworking Public Key Certification Infrastructure for Commerce, Administration and Research (ICE-CAR), 234–235
Intradomain cross-certification, 143
Invalidity Date, 111
IPKI, 64, 224
IPsec, 228, 239
ISO TC68, 226
Issuer, 73, 109
Issuer Alternative Name, 76, 111
Issuer Unique ID, 73
Issuing Distribution Point, 112–113

Java Community Process (JCP), 234
Java Specification Requests (JSRs), 234

KDC, 9
Kennedy-Kassebaum Bill, 291
Kerberos, 59, 60
Key, 8
Key agreement, 17
Key and certificate history, 31
Key archive, 103, 104
Key backup, 97, 98
Key backup and recovery, 30
Key/certificate distribution, 95
Key/certificate life-cycle management, 89–104
    cancellation phase, 100–104
    certificate creation, 94–95
    certificate dissemination, 96. See also PKI information dissemination
    certificate expiration, 101
    certificate retrieval, 97–98
    certificate revocation, 101–102.
        See also Certificate revocation
    certificate validation, 98–99
    end entity registration, 91–92
    initialization phase, 91–97
    issued phase, 97–100
    key archive, 104
    key backup, 97
    key/certificate distribution, 95
    key history, 103

key pair generation, 92–94
key recovery, 99
key update, 100
underlying assumptions, 90
Key compromise, 176–178
Key distribution center (KDC), 9
Key escrow, 98
Key establishments, 16–17
Key exchange, 90n
Key history, 31–32, 103
Key management, 90n
Key pair, 12
Key pair generation, 92–94
Key pair uses, 152–153
Key recovery, 99
Key transfer, 16
Key update, 31, 100
Key usage, 74

Launching a PKI deployment.
    *See* Deployment considerations
LDAP, 226
LDAP data interchange format (LDIF), 169
LDAP Duplication/Replication/Update
    Protocols (LDUP) Working Group, 161,
    169, 284
LDAPext Working Group, 226, 284
LDAPv2, 161, 226, 238
LDAPv3, 161, 226, 238
LDIF, 169
LDUP Working Group, 161, 169, 284
Legal issues, 183–194
    CA responsibilities, 190–191
    confidentiality, 194
    *Digital Signature Guidelines,* 185
    E-Sign, 183–184
    EU Directive, 186–187
    other contractual-based frameworks, 193
    private enterprise PKIs, 192–193
    relying party responsibilities, 191–192
    subscriber responsibilities, 190–191
Life-cycle management. *See* Key/certificate
    life-cycle management
Lightweight Directory Access Protocol
    (LDAP), 226

Lightweight Directory Access Protocol
    (LDAP) Version 2 (LDAPv2), 161,
    226, 238
Lightweight Directory Access Protocol
    (LDAP) Version 3 (LDAPv3), 161,
    226, 238
"Limits to the Scale of a Public Key
    Infrastructure," 127
Local authentication, 38
Local registration authorities (LRAs), 86
Logging-in, 23
Loose hierarchy of certification
    authorities, 134–135
LRAs, 86

MAC, 15, 44
Medical Records Confidentiality Act, 291
Mesh configuration, 137
Message authentication code (MAC),
    15, 44
Minimum interoperability specification,
    247–248
"Minimum Interoperability Specification for
    PKI Components, Version 1," 247
"Minimum Interoperability Specification
    for PKI Components, Version 2—
    Second Draft," 247–248
Minimum Interoperability Specifications
    for PKI Components (MISPC), 232
Minimum-knowledge, 17
MISPC, 232
"Model of Certificate Revocation, A," 127
Multifactor authentication, 39
Multiple certificates per entry, 151–157
    independent certificate management,
        155–156
    key pair uses, 152–155
    multiple key pairs, 151–152
    real-word difficulties, 155
    support for non-repudiation, 156–157
Multiple key pairs, 151–152
Multiple keys per user, 153
Multivendor interoperability, 284
Mutual cross-certification, 143, 144

Name, 198
Name Constraints, 77, 145
Naming entities, 47, 145–146, 198
National Automated Clearing House
     Association (NACHA), 248
Negotiation ("handshaking") protocols, 47
"New Directions in Cryptography"
     (Diffie/Hellman), 11
Next Update, 110
No action, 101
Non-repudiation, 32–33
   complexity, 53
   connection with other services, 52
   defined, 51
   human factor, 53
   secure data archive, 52
   support for, 93, 156–157
   variants, 51
Non-repudiation of origin, 51
Non-repudiation of receipt, 51
Nonblinded delegation, 55
Noncritical extension, 74
Notarization, 50–51

OASIS, 231
Object identifiers (OID), 73n, 83, 85
OCSP component interaction, 123
OCSP request, 123
OCSP responder, 122
Off-line operations, 173–174, 276
Off-line vs. on-line operations, 46–47
Offloading PKI-related processing, 241
OID, 73n, 83, 85
OmniRoot, 293
On-line operation, 276
On-line query mechanisms, 122
On-line vs. off-line operations, 46–47
Ongoing standardization work, 240–241
Online Certificate Status Protocol (OCSP),
     122–125, 128
Open environment, 273
Open Mobile Alliance, 230
OpenPGP, 80, 160, 229–230
Operational considerations. See PKI
     operational considerations

Operators, 277
Ordered List, 112
Organization for the Advancement of
     Structured Information Standards
     (OASIS), 231
Out-of-band distribution, 96
Out-sourcing, 271
Overview of book, 3–5

P1363, 230
Partitioned CRLs, 115
Path construction, 147–148
Path Length Constraints, 76–77, 145
Path validation, 148
PEM, 134n
Performance, 284
Periodic publication mechanisms, 107–125
Peripheral support, 276
Personnel requirements, 277
Pervasive substrate, 21–22
PGP, 80, 142, 160, 229
Physical security, 174–175
Physically secure archive facilities, 62
PKCS 7/10, 95
PKI. See Public-key infrastructure (PKI)
PKI-aware software, 285–286
PKI certificate revocation. See Certificate
     revocation
PKI Challenge, 250
PKI deployment. See Deployment
     considerations
PKI disaster scenarios, 179–182
PKI disclosure statement, 84
PKI-enabled applications, 285–286
PKI-enabled services, 49–67
   comprehensive PKI/current practice,
     63–67
   non-repudiation, 51–53
   notarization, 50–51
   operational considerations, 61–63
   privacy, 56–58
   privilege management, 53–56
   required mechanisms, 58–60
   secure communication, 49
   secure time stamping, 50

PKI information dissemination, 96, 159–170
  in-band protocol exchange, 169
  private dissemination, 159–160
  repository. *See* Repository
PKI interoperability, 245–250
PKI networking, 136
PKI notary, 51
PKI operational considerations, 171–182
  client-side software, 171–173
  disaster preparation/recovery, 179–182
  hardware components, 175
  off-line operations, 173–174
  physical security, 174–175
  user key compromise, 176–178
PKI pilots, 267
PKI-TWG, 247
PKI-usage scenarios, 64–67
PKI X.509, 249
PKIX Working Group, 224–225, 238,
  249, 255
Plaintext, 8
PMI, 59, 240–241
Policy authorities, 85
Policy constraints, 77, 145
Policy decision point (PDP), 59
Policy management authorities, 85
Policy Mappings, 75
Policy qualifiers, 75
Policy server schemes, 60
Power-of-attorney delegation, 55
Pretty Good Privacy (PGP), 80, 142,
  160, 229
Privacy, 56–58
Privacy architecture, 60
Privacy certificates, 62
Privacy Enhanced Mail (PEM), 134n
Private dissemination, 159–160
Private enterprise PKIs, 192–193
Private extensions, 78
Private key, 12n
Private Key Usage Period, 75
Privilege management, 53–56
Privilege management infrastructure (PMI),
  59, 240–241

Privilege management infrastructure
  mechanisms, 59–60
Privilege policy creation mechanism, 58–59
Privilege policy processing engines, 59
Profile, 244
Protocols for digital notary services, 241
Provisioning Services Markup Language
  (PSML), 231
Proxy, 166
Pseudonymous certificate, 56
Pseudonymous privacy, 62
Pseudonyms, 56
PSML, 231
Public-key algorithms. *See* Algorithms
Public-key certificate, 85. *See also* Certificates
  and certification
Public-key cryptography, 12
Public-key infrastructure (PKI), 217
  automatic key update, 30–31
  benefits/costs, 263–268
  certificate authority, 28–29
  certificate repository, 29
  certificate revocation, 29–30
  client software, 33
  cross-certification, 32
  deployment. *See* Deployment
    considerations
  further reading, 218
  future of, 207–216
  key backup and recovery, 30
  key history, 31–32
  non-repudiation, 32–33
  pilots, 267
  real-life scenario, 203–206
  simple definition, 28
  time stamping, 33, 50
  value of, 200–203
  what does PKI do/not do, 196–200
Public Key Infrastructure Technical Working
  Group (PKI-TWG), 247
Publication, 160

RA, 86–87
Real-life scenario, 203–206
Reason Code, 110

Redirect CRLs, 116–118, 128
Reduced sign-on, 25n
References. *See* Further reading, Web sites
Registration authority (RA), 86–87
Relying party responsibilities, 191–192
Remote authentication, 38
Repository
    advantages/disadvantages, 163–165
    border, 167–168
    defined, 161
    deployment issues, 279, 283–284
    direct access, 166–167
    interdomain issues, 165–169
    interdomain replication, 168–169
    locating, 162–163
    performance considerations, 164
    shared, 168
    types, 162
Repudiation, 33
Require Explicit Policy, 77
Reverse cross-certificate, 143
Revocation. *See* Certificate revocation
Revoked Certificates, 110
RFC2459, 72
RFC2559, 255
RFC2585, 255
RFC2587, 255
RFC3280, 72, 108
Rivest, Ron, 17, 19
Roaming, 278
Rollover, 154
Root CA, 132
ROT-13, 9
RSA, 17

S/MIME, 227, 238–239
S/MIMEv3 specifications, 227
SAML, 59, 231
SASI, 241
Scalability, 284
SCVP, 125, 255
Secret key, 12n
Secure communication, 49
Secure e-mail, 49

Secure Electronic MarketPlace, EuRope
    (SEMPER), 233
Secure Electronic Transaction (SET), 81–82,
    180, 233
Secure hash algorithm (SHA-1), 18–19
Secure MIME (S/MIME), 227, 238–239
Secure protocols, 61
Secure sign-on, 23–25
Secure time stamping, 33, 50
Secure time-stamping protocols, 241
Secure VPN, 49
Secure Web server access, 49
Securities Industry Root CA (SIRCA) proof
    of concept, 250
Security Assertion Markup Language
    (SAML), 59, 231
Security assurance, 279–280
Security infrastructure, 21–22
Security officers, 277
SEMPER, 233
Serial Number, 73
Server redundancy, 61
Services of public-key cryptography, 12–17
    core services, 37–48.
        *See also* Core PKI services
    data integrity, 16
    digital signature, 14–16
    encryption, 14
    key establishment, 16–17
    other services, 17
    PKI-enabled services, 49–67.
        *See also* PKI-enabled services
    security between strangers, 12–14
SET, 81–82, 180, 233
SET certificate structure, 81
SHA-1, 18–19
SHA-2, 19
Shamir, Adi, 17
Shared repository, 168
Short-lived certificates, 126
SIA private extension, 78, 163
Signatures, 73, 109
Signing-on, 23
Signing private key, 93

Simple Authentication and Security Layer (SASI), 241
Simple Certificate Validation Protocol (SCVP), 125, 255
Simple Public-Key GSS-API Mechanism (SPKM), 240
Simple Public Key Infrastructure (SPKI), 79–80, 228–229
Simple substitution cipher, 9
Single-factor authentication, 39
Single sign-on (SSO), 24–25
SIRCA proof of concept, 250
SPKI, 79–80, 228–229
SPKM, 240
SSL/TLS, 290
"Standard Specifications for Public Key Cryptography," 230
"Standard Specifications for Public Key Cryptography: Additional Techniques," 230
Standard vs. proprietary solutions, 274
Standards, 219–258
    ANSI X9F, 227
    ECOM, 234
    EDIFACT, 230
    further reading, 253–258
    GOC PKI, 232–233
    ICE-CAR, 234–235
    IEEE, 230
    interoperability initiatives, 245–250
    IPsec, 228, 239
    ISO TC68, 226
    JCP, 234
    LDAP, 226, 238
    MISPC, 232
    ongoing work, 240–241
    OpenPGP, 229–230
    PFKI, 232
    PKIX, 224–225, 238
    role, 243–244
    S/MIME, 227, 238–239
    SEMPER, 233–234
    SET, 233
    SPKI, 228–229
    TLS, 228, 239–240
    toolkit requirements, 240
    WAP, 230–231
    web sites, 257
    X.500, 225–226, 238
    X.509, 223–224, 237
    XML-based activities, 231
Static-static DH, 46
Status Referrals, 112
Strategic decisions, 269–281. See also Deployment considerations
Strict hierarchy of CAs, 132–134
Strict hierarchy of CAs trust model, 133
Subject, 73
Subject Alternative Name, 75
Subject Directory Attributes, 76, 246
Subject Information Access (SIA), 78, 163
Subject key identifier, 74
Subject Public Key Info, 73
Subject Unique ID, 74
Subordinate CAs, 132
Subscriber responsibilities, 190–191
Subsequent authentication, 39
Suggested reading. See Further reading
Symmetric central server architectures, 9
Symmetric ciphers, 8–9

TCO, 266
TC68, 226
This Update, 109
Three-key pairs, 93
TIE, 235
Time Stamp Authority (TSA), 58
Time stamping, 33, 50
TLS, 167, 228, 239–240
Toolkit-based session security, 240
Total cost of ownership (TCO), 266
"Towards a Practical Public-Key Cryptosystem" (Kohnfelder), 70
Transport Layer Security (TLS), 167, 228, 239–240
Trapdoor functions with high computational complexity, 11
Trust, 131–132
Trust anchor, 132, 146
Trust Infrastructure for Europe (TIE), 235

Trust models, 131–149
  certificate path processing, 146–149
  cross-certification, 143–145
  distributed trust architecture, 135–138
  entity naming, 145–146
  four-corner model, 138–139
  loose hierarchy of CAs, 134–135
  policy-based hierarchies, 135
  strict hierarchy of CAs, 132–134
  user-centric trust, 142
  web model, 139–141
Trust networks, 292–293
Trusted-issuer hierarchies, 134
Trusted public key, 132
Trusted time delivery mechanism, 61
Trusted time sources, 58
TSA, 58
Two-key pair model, 93

Unilateral cross-certification, 143
U.S. Federal Bridge CA initiative, 168
U.S. FPKI, 232
User-centric trust, 142
User key compromise, 176–178
User Notice qualifier, 75

Valicert, 120
Validity, 73
Vendor selection, 280
Vendor's web sites, 296
Verification certificate, 93
VeriSign Trust Network (VTN), 293
Veronyms, 56
Version, 73, 109
Version 1 public-key certificate, 71
Version 2 CRLs, 108–110
Version 2 public-key certificate, 71
Version 3 certificate structure, 72

Version 3 public-key certificate, 70, 71
Vignette (real-life scenario), 203–206
VTN, 293

W3C, 231
WAP Forum, 230
WAP Security Group (WSG), 230, 231
Web model, 139–141
Web Services Security (WSS), 231
Web sites. See also Further reading
  standards bodies, 257
  vendors, 296
Wireless Application Protocol Forum
  (WAP Forum), 230
World Wide Web Consortium (W3C), 231
WPKI, 230
WSG, 230, 231
WSS, 231
WTLS, 230

X9F, 227
X9F1, 227
X9F3, 227
X9F5, 227
X.500, 225–226, 238
X.509, 223–224, 237
X.509 public-key certificate, 70
X.509 recommendation certificate/
  CRL profile, 246
XACML, 59, 231
XKMS, 223, 231, 241, 256
XML-based activities, 231
XML Encryption, 231
XML Key Management Specification, 231
XML Signature, 231

Zero-knowledge, 17
Zimmermann, Phil, 80